How Wars End

HOW WARS END

THE UNITED NATIONS AND THE TERMINATION OF ARMED CONFLICT 1946–1964

Volume I

Sydney D. Bailey

Clarendon Press · Oxford
1982

Oxford University Press, Walton Street, Oxford OX2 6DP
London Glasgow New York Toronto
Delhi Bombay Calcutta Madras Karachi
Kuala Lumpur Singapore Hong Kong Tokyo
Nairobi Dar es Salaam Cape Town
Melbourne Auckland
and associate companies in
Beirut Berlin Ibadan Mexico City

Published in the United States by
Oxford University Press, New York

British Library Cataloguing in Publication Data
Bailey, Sydney D.
How wars end: the United Nations and the
termination of armed conflict, 1946-1964
Vol. 1
1. War   2. United Nations
I. Title
355'028   U21.2
ISBN 0-19-827424-6

Library of Congress Cataloguing in Publication Data
Bailey, Sydney Dawson.
How wars end.

Bibliography: p.
Includes index.
1. United Nations—Armed Forces.   2. Pacific settlement of international disputes.   3. War.   4. World
politics—1945-   I. Title.
JX1981.P7B26 Vol. I   341.5'8   82-2080
ISBN 0-19-827424-6   AACR2

Typeset by DMB (Typesetting) Oxford
Printed in Great Britain
at the University Press, Oxford
by Eric Buckley
Printer to the University

By way of explanation

Volume II of this work consists of seven case studies, and volume I is based on them. I have selected for study those cases of armed conflict that came before the Security Council during the period 1946-64, when the Council still had only eleven members. Although some cases had ill-defined beginnings, all had clear endings in the sense that, even if there was no decisive military outcome, hostilities were formally suspended. All were confined within obvious territorial limits, although General MacArthur would have liked to extend the Korean War to China. All the conflicts were conducted without the use of nuclear weapons.

There were, of course, other crucial issues before the Security Council during this period: Iran, the Greek civil war, Czechoslovakia (1948), the Berlin blockade, Guatemala, Hungary, Lebanon and Jordan (1958), Laos, the Congo, Goa, the Cuban missile crisis, civil war in the Yemen, Rhodesia, incidents in the Gulf of Tonkin (1964), Indonesia's 'confrontation' with Malaysia. But none of these was a case of armed conflict that the United Nations was asked to stop, with the exception of one phase in the Congo; and I am satisfied that the cases studied included examples of all the main types of armed conflict to come before the United Nations.

Not all cases of armed conflict are raised at the United Nations. The Stockholm International Peace Research Institute (SIPRI) has collated lists of conflicts from eleven different sources.[1] Of 89 conflicts in one or more lists in the period 1945-64, 40 came before the Security Council and 15 before the General Assembly. Of the remaining 34 conflicts, 16 were instances of civil strife, 8 were within the competence of regional agencies, and 5 concerned China at a time when China was not represented in the United Nations. Vietnam is the most notable of the remaining cases where, until 1964, the United Nations was not directly involved.

[1] *SIPRI Yearbook of the World Armaments and Disarmament 1968/69*, London, Duckworth, 1969, pp. 366-71.

Each case study in volume II is presented in the same general format. An introductory section summarizes the background to the fighting; the second section lists the main actors; and the final section describes the fighting and the efforts to stop it by means of a cease-fire, truce, or armistice. Case 6 (Sinai-Suez 1956-7) is, in part, a continuation of case 3 (Palestine 1947-9). The appendices to each case study give extracts from UN resolutions and other documents relating to the ending of the fighting: some of these documents have not been published previously. Appendix III to case 5 (Korea 1950-3) comprises documents of the International Committee of the Red Cross.

Except in case 5, I usually describe the parties by the terms they themselves prefer, even when the term may have seemed misleading or offensive to the other party. In cases 1 and 4 the Indonesian nationalists are called Republicans, and Federalists are Indonesians who co-operated with the Netherlands until the second 'police action'. In case 3 I refer to the Jewish Agency for Palestine, the Jewish authorities, or the Jews up to 14 May 1948 and the Provisional Government of Israel from 15 May 1948 to 25 January 1949: after the first elections to the Knesset, the Government of Israel ceased to be provisional. Many Israeli leaders, when they use the term 'Israelis', mean the Jewish population of Israel; but there are 400,000 Arabs living in Israel proper and another million now under Israeli rule in the administered or occupied territories. To avoid misunderstanding, I sometimes use the terms 'Jewish Israelis' or 'Israeli Jews' when I expressly do not mean to include the Arab population. Although Israelis insist that the adjectival form of Israel is Israel, I have used Israeli as an adjective, a practice approved by the *Concise Oxford Dictionary*. In 1947-9, the Arab Palestinians were organized as the Arab Higher Committee, and that part of the Arab armed force in Palestine which was not part of a national army was known as the Arab Liberation Army. From the end of September 1948, there was on paper an All-Palestine government, initially based on the Gaza Strip.

Before the Maharajah's accession to India on 26 October 1947, Kashmir means the whole of the Princely State of Jammu and Kashmir. After October 1947, that part of Kashmir lying on the Pakistan side of what in 1949 became the cease-fire line I refer to as Azad Kashmir and the remainder as Indian Kashmir—although the latter term is not always satisfactory. In UN debates about Cyprus in 1964, some speakers referred to Greeks and Turks without making clear whether they meant members of the Greek community in Cyprus or citizens of Greece (or both) and members of the Turkish community in Cyprus or citizens of Turkey (or both). I have tried to avoid this ambiguity, though that has not always been possible.

In case 5 (Korea 1950-3) the claims of brevity have usually had to be paramount, and I often refer to the Republic of Korea as South Korea, the Democratic People's Republic of Korea as North Korea, and after 1949 the Kuomintang régime based on Taiwan as Nationalist China. In dealing with the Korean War after Chinese intervention and during the negotiation and implementation of the armistice, I have sometimes written 'the Communists' or 'the Communist side' rather than 'North Korea and China': the other side should be known as the Unified Command from 7 July 1950, although other formulations were sometimes used, even in official documents.

Another short-cut I have often taken is to write Britain rather than the full and correct formulation, the United Kingdom of Great Britain and Northern Ireland.

In the Korean case, the differences of time and date between Korea and the West are sometimes liable to cause confusion: except when I have indicated to the contrary, I have given the local time and date.

The two general cease-fires in Palestine beginning on 11 June and 18 July 1948 were almost always called truces at the time, and the military observers formed the UN Truce Supervision Organization (UNTSO). Moreover, the UN Mediators and two Chiefs-of-Staff of UNTSO, in writing of their experiences, usually call these periods in which hostilities were suspended 'truces' rather than 'cease-fires'.[2] I describe on pages 29-41 of this volume the usual UN terminology in this regard, and except in quotations I have sought consistency by using the

[2] SC res. 43 (S/714, I), 1 April 1948; 46 (S/723), 17 April 1948; 48 (S/727), 23 April 1948; 49 (S/773), 22 May 1948; 53 (S/875), 7 July 1948; 54 (S/902), 15 July 1948; 56 (S/983), 19 Aug. 1948; 59 (S/1045), 19 Oct. 1948; 66 (S/1169), 29 Dec. 1948; the one example from 1948 of what subsequently became the normal usage of the Security Council was SC res. 50 (S/801), 29 May 1948. Folke Bernadotte, *To Jerusalem*; E. L. M. Burns, *Between Arab and Israeli*; Odd Bull, *War and Peace in the Middle East: The Experiences and Views of a U.N. Observer.*

correct term rather than the one in popular usage in any particular area at the time.

Some of my friends urged me not to prepare the case studies
myself but to delegate the work to research assistants. That
would have increased the number of case studies and provided
a wider basis from which to derive the lessons in volume I, but
on balance it seemed preferable that all the case studies should
be done by one person.

In preparing the case studies, I have been conscious of
Henry Kissinger's comments about the difficulties encountered
by historians in forming reasonable judgements about contemporary history. Kissinger writes that the enormous quantity of
material 'cannot possibly be studied by any one scholar'.
Instructions may simply tell a diplomat what he is to say and
may contain no explanation as to why certain things are being
said or done. Moreover, instructions go out in so many different
channels and under so many different classifications that it is
'next to impossible for somebody who has not been a participant
to determine what was crucial and what was peripheral, what
was written to keep the bureaucracy quiet, what was written
for purposes of later disclosure, and what was written to be
implemented'.[3] If the chief actors always wrote their own
versions of events, it would be easier to discover what really
happened, but there are many reasons why this does not happen.
One can only do one's best.

Dr Johnson told Boswell that the greatest part of a writer's
time is spent in reading: 'a man will turn over half a library to
make one book'.[4] Certainly I have had to read a lot, but the
amount of published material about the cases studied varies in
quantity and salience. Retired Soviet diplomats and politicians
are not in the habit of writing their memoirs; or, if they are, the
memoirs are rarely published. Retired British diplomats and
politicians do sometimes publish memoirs, but usually of
monumental discretion. Retired US diplomats and politicians
are not so inhibited.[5]

---

[3] *The Times*, 19 Dec. 1977, p. 6; see also *White House Years*, Boston, Little, Brown,
1979, p. 483.
[4] 6 April 1775.
[5] e.g., Acheson, Bohlen, Eisenhower, L. B. Johnson, Kennan, Lodge, Murphy,
Truman.

Israeli Jews have written copiously about their war of independence and Sinai-Suez, but there is virtually no comparable material from the Arab side other than polemics. The Indian material about Kashmir is greater in quantity and often better in quality than that from Pakistan and Azad Kashmir, and there is more English-language material about Cyprus from the Greek point of view than from the Turkish. In the case of Korea, the material from the Western standpoint is vast and varied, but there is little of value in English from the standpoint of the Communists.

For the early cases, the documents published as *Foreign Relations of the United States* are of great value: indeed, for some crucial events, they are the only source.

I have included a select bibliography with each case study. Publications cited three or more times are listed in the select bibliography; in the notes they are cited by the author's full name and title the first time, and thereafter by the author's surname only, or by his surname and abbreviated title if there is more than one work by the author in the bibliography.

The maps are intended to help the reader to follow the events described, but the frontiers or *de facto* lines do not necessarily have any official standing.

Acknowledgements

Many people have helped me in preparing this study. I owe a special debt of gratitude to those who have provided me with documents and other publications: Diane Donaghey of the office of the UN Secretary-General; Vivian D. Hewitt, librarian at the Carnegie Endowment for International Peace, New York; Georgia Paine, of the Washington office of the American Friends Service Committee; Sue Geggie, Kirsten Brown, Angela Wootton, and John Montgomery of the library of the Royal Institute of International Affairs; Margaret McAfee, Anne-Marie Paterson, and Prudence Pinsent of the United Nations Information Centre in London; P. Vibert, formerly head of the Documentation Service of the International Committee of the Red Cross; and Joy Fawcett, archivist of the British Red Cross Society.

Others have helped by giving me factual information or access to unpublished documents, or by commenting on drafts of particular sections. To those who occupy official positions and may not be mentioned by name, and to the following, I express my thanks: Samir Ahmed, Professor Nissim Bar-Yaacov, Sir Harold Beeley, Christoph Bertram, Yoav Biran, Lt-Gen. Odd Bull, Major-Gen. E. L. M. Burns, the Hon. Benjamin V. Cohen, Sir Colin Crowe, Martin Eaton, William Epstein, Walter Eytan, James Fawcett, Maria Frankowska, David Fursdon, Lt-Gen. Sir John Glubb, Sheila Harden, Professor Rosalyn Higgins, George Ignatieff, the Hon. Judge Philip C. Jessup, George Kennan, L. L. Kinsolving, Emre Kongar, Robert A. Lovett, J. A. Miles, Sir Anthony Parsons, John Reedman, Major-Gen. Indar Jit Rikhye, Sir Frank Roberts, Shabtai Rosenne, the Hon. Dean Rusk, George L. Sherry, G. V. Shukla, Lt-Gen. Ensio Siilasvuo, Erik Suy, Lord Trevelyan, and Brian E. Urquhart. Needless to say, none of them, named or unnamed, is responsible for errors of fact or faulty judgements, which are mine alone.

Material from my articles, 'Cease-fires, Truces, and Armistices in the Practice of the UN Security Council' and 'Non-military Areas in UN Practice', which appeared in the *American Journal of International Law* in somewhat different form, is reprinted with the permission of the American Society of International Law. I am also grateful for permission to reprint extracts from an article on the problem of beleaguered combatants after a cease-fire, which was published in June 1980 in *The World Today*, the monthly journal of the Royal Institute of International Affairs.

I also thank Mary Bolton, who has deciphered my execrable writing and has typed and retyped the manuscript more times than I can count.

1 May 1980   S.D.B.

Abbreviations and Acronyms

Add.	Addendum (addition of text to main UN documents)
AJIL	*American Journal of International Law*
CEIP	Carnegie Endowment for International Peace
CENTO	Central Treaty Organization; previously the Baghad Pact
Corr.	Corrigendum (to correct errors, revise wording, or reorganize text of UN document, whether for substantive or technical reasons)
ECOSOC	Economic and Social Council
EOKA	National Organization of Cypriot Fighters (Ethnike Organosis Kypriou Agonistou)
Etzel	National Military Organization (Irgun Zvai Leumi)
FRUS	Foreign Relations of the United States
GAOR	General Assembly Official Records
GA res.	General Assembly resolution
GOC	Good Offices Committee on the Indonesian question
ICJ	International Court of Justice
ICRC	International Committee of the Red Cross
Lehi	Fighters for the Freedom of Israel (Lohamei Herut Israel, the Stern Gang)
LNTS	League of Nations Treaty Series
MAC	Mixed Armistice Commission
MDL	Military Demarcation Line
NNRC	Neutral Nations Repatriation Commission
NNSC	Neutral Nations Supervisory Commission
PCC	Palestine Conciliation Commission
POW	Prisoner of War
Rev.	Revision (new text superseding and replacing a previously issued UN document)
RIIA	Royal Institute of International Affairs
SBA	Sovereign Base Area
SCOR	Security Council official records

SC res.	Security Council resolution
TCOR	Trusteeship Council Official Records
TMT	Turkish Defence Organization (Turk Muka-vemet Teskilati)
UNCIO	Documents of the United Nations Conference on International Organization
UNCIP	UN Commission for India and Pakistan
UNCOK	UN Commission on Korea
UNCURK	UN Commission for the Unification and Re-habilitation of Korea
UNFICYP	UN Force in Cyprus
UNKRA	UN Korean Reconstruction Agency
UNRWA	UN Relief and Works Agency for Palestine Refugees in the Near East
UNTCOK	UN Temporary Commission on Korea
UNTS	UN Treaty Series
UNTSO	UN Truce Supervision Organization

Contents

List of Tables

Introduction

I would have liked to call this book 'How to Stop Wars', but that would have been too pretentious a title. To start a war is usually a complex business, but as Fred Iklé has stressed it is almost always easier to start the fighting than to stop it.[1] Many of the factors in a decision to go to war are under the control of the party initiating the use of force, whereas the termination of armed conflict brings in a host of external considerations which it may have been possible (if foolish) to disregard at an earlier stage. In war there is usually, at any particular moment, one party that sees advantages in resorting to an organ of the United Nations, usually the Security Council, so that the achieving of a cessation of fighting is of international concern and not simply a matter between the parties.

The complaint is sometimes made that the United Nations is not brought into the picture until the situation is already grave: 'the time for concerted action [Kurt Waldheim has written] has tended to come only when conflict or disaster is imminent or has already occurred'.[2] That is true but hardly surprising: most patients do not invoke the assistance of a physician until measures of self-help have failed. The Charter expressly assumes that the parties to a dispute will 'first of all' seek to resolve the matter by peaceful means of their own choice.[3] The United Nations is called in when these peaceful means have failed.

Prophylactic diplomacy is no doubt as necessary as prophylactic medicine. If we were more far-sighted, we would seize the opportunity of building the institutions of peace when the patient is well; but in the world of *is* rather than *ought*, many of the most constructive innovations for peace have come under the pressure of dangerous events. Peace-keeping by consent was invented by Lester Pearson and Dag Hammarskjold to

---

[1] Fred Charles Iklé, *Every War Must End*, p. 106.
[2] A/34/1, 11 Sept. 1979 (mimeo), p. 23.
[3] Article 33.

meet the special needs of a particular crisis (see pages 268-271 and Volume II, pages 604-607).

It hardly needs stressing that UN Members, in accepting the obligations of the Charter, have renounced the threat or use of force except in self-defence after an armed attack or in enforcement action under UN auspices,[4] and Richard Baxter has stressed that 'the conclusion of an agreement for the suspension of hostilities reflects not so much a free decision by the parties that they will cease to exercise a right or privilege... as an acceptance by them of the obligations of the Charter not to resort to the use of force'.[5] But whatever the law says, parties *have* resorted to the assize of arms, and are likely to do so in the future. Sometimes war is fought to a finish and ends only with the total victory of one party and the unconditional surrender of the other. More usually, in the contemporary world, armed conflict is brought to an end through some form of external intervention of a non-military kind.

A decision to stop fighting is always closely linked in the minds of the parties to discernible progress towards a political settlement, and it may be taken for granted that one party, and often both, will be reluctant to stop fighting without some assurance that political demands will be met or at least given a fair hearing. Moreover, the parties will complain that an even-handed attitude on the part of the United Nations ignores the distinction between aggressor and victim, that it is not reasonable to call for a cessation of hostilities without some assurance that just political demands will be met.

The United Nations must to some extent ignore complaints of this kind. War is of its nature so destructive of justice that it is always the case that justice cannot be satisfied until the fighting stops, and the main efforts of the intermediary have to be directed to an unconditional cease-fire, with minimal attention to the long-term political goals of the parties. There may be sympathy for one party, but the greater the risk that armed conflict will spread, the more likely is the United Nations to disregard the rights and wrongs of the case and concentrate

---

[4] Articles 2(4), 42, and 51.
[5] R. R. Baxter, 'Armistices and Other Forms of Suspension of Hostilities', p. 384.

its efforts on stopping the fighting. In practice, of course, the United Nations cannot always be single-minded in its search for a cessation of fighting: its task is usually to find a compromise that reconciles its own wish to end the fighting and the wish of one or both parties to link a cease-fire or truce to the basis for a political solution.

The UN role cannot be limited to a call for the fighting to stop, however, for it will be necessary to institute means for monitoring the cessation of hostilities. Indeed, it is in the precarious situation of unsupervised cease-fire that the risks of violation are greatest. In the immediate aftermath of armed conflict, the parties are bound to mistrust the intentions of the other side. One party may take a step that is fully consistent with the obligation to cease hostilities, such as the routine rotation of troops; but the opposing party, suspecting that what is happening is an infringement, may respond with belligerent retaliation. The first party then assumes that the response of the other is a first breach and engages in counter-retaliation. Such risks of violation and breakdown remain high until there is established a system of impartial supervision and if possible a means of direct contact between the parties.

It is sometimes said that it is not always in the international interest to halt armed conflict at the earliest possible moment. 'There is always a humanitarian impulse to stop the fighting', Michael Walzer has written. 'But it isn't always true that such cease-fires serve the purposes of humanity... [T]hey may simply fix the conditions under which the fighting will be resumed, at a later date and with a new intensity.'[6] It may indeed be the case that a cease-fire may prepare the ground for more intense fighting later on, but the impulse to stop the fighting quickly is not only humanitarian, it is also rational. If fighting is resumed, it is not because hostilities were stopped too soon but because the breathing space thus gained was not put to good use. A legitimate criticism of UN peace-keeping is that it has created a false sense of tranquillity, masking the underlying suspicion and anger; but that is not to disparage peace-keeping: it is to suggest that peace-keeping alone is never enough.

[6] Michael Walzer, *Just and Unjust Wars: A Moral Argument with Historical Illustrations*, New York, Basic Books, 1977, p. 123.

All the cases studied initially came before the Security Council, which is the UN organ with primary responsibility for world peace; but in two of the cases (Korea 1950-3, Sinai-Suez 1956-7), the General Assembly also played an important part. The Sinai-Suez case is also noteworthy because those initiating the use of armed force were induced to withdraw after the cease-fire by means of diplomatic pressure exerted largely through the General Assembly, reinforced at times by Soviet military and US political and economic threats and acts.

How shall these seven cases be classified?

Cases 1 and 4, Indonesia   From the Dutch point of view, these were police actions against colonial rebels. For the Indonesian Republicans (and, indeed, a major segment of UN opinion) the Indonesian response to Dutch military action was part of the continuing struggle against colonialism.

Case 2, Kashmir   This started as an invasion of a princely state by foreign volunteers after the lapse of British paramountcy, and India's formal responsibility began when the Maharajah's request to accede was conditionally accepted on 27 October 1947. Pakistan at first gave informal help to the invading tribesmen and to Azad (Free) Kashmir; official but surreptitious intervention by Pakistan's regular military forces began early in May 1948.

Case 3, Palestine   The Palestine War was initially an internal armed conflict in a territory under League of Nations mandate, with some external help to both sides. When the mandate lapsed in May 1948 and the state of Israel was proclaimed in part of the mandated territory, Arab armies intervened to help the indigenous Arabs.

Case 5, Korea   How one describes the war in Korea depends on what view one takes of the legitimacy of the authorities in Seoul and Pyongyang in 1950. Nobody questions that Korea was one nation, and the initial parties were either two internal factions or, more plausibly, two states, each claiming to represent the whole. The United States and other countries that supplied forces to the Unified Command intervened to help South

Korea, and China intervened on the other side in October after forces of the Unified Command had crossed to the north of the 38th parallel.

Case 6, Sinai-Suez This was an ordinary inter-state war, despite the fact that Britain and France purported to be intervening in order to separate the belligerents.

Case 7, Cyprus This began as a conflict between a government and a dissident minority, complicated by the fact that three guaranteeing powers had the right to station forces on the island and to intervene in certain circumstances. It may be questioned whether the Turkish bombing of the Kokkina-Mansoura area in August 1964 was in accordance with the treaty of guarantee, though the provocation was great.

To sum up, the Indonesian cases were complicated by the fact that the Republicans considered themselves to be a government while the Netherlands thought of them as rebels: using modern jargon, these two cases were almost classic examples of military episodes in the course of a struggle for liberation from colonial rule. Sinai-Suez was an ordinary inter-state war. The other cases (Kashmir, Palestine, Korea, Cyprus) had both internal and external elements. Six of the seven cases arose directly or indirectly from the colonial system, and the stance of Britain and France in the seventh (Suez) seemed reminiscent of what Louis Henkin has called the habit of empire.[7]

The cases studied thus included inter-state wars as well as conflicts between a state and organized, disciplined, and uniformed groups within the state, including wars of liberation from colonial rule or in support of self-determination, communal struggles, and civil wars. They were examples of what ordinary people call 'war', even if not formally declared.[8] The term

[7] Louis Henkin, *How Nations Behave: Law and Foreign Policy*, London, Pall Mall, 1968 (for the Council on Foreign Relations), p. 190.

[8] In spite of the legal requirement that war be formally declared, the recent practice has been to start fighting without a formal declaration. The last formal declaration of war of which I am aware was by Argentina against the Axis powers on 27 March 1945, in order to qualify as peace-loving and thus have the right to participate in the San Francisco Conference; see Ruth B. Russell, assisted by Jeanette E. Muther, *A History of the United Nations Charter: The Role of the United States 1940-1945*, Washington, DC, Brookings Institution, 1958, pp. 57, 571.

'war' was used in the Hague Conventions of 1899 and 1907 and other legal instruments until recent times, but in the Geneva Conventions of 1949 and the Additional Protocols of 1977 the term 'armed conflict' was thought to be more all-embracing.

As armed conflict is such a desperate measure, and one that, once launched, so easily threatens to pass out of human control, it might be thought that states and other parties would be reluctant to resort to it and would do so only for clear and compelling political purposes which can be comprehended by their own public and that of the adversary; yet it is surprising how easily people can be induced to fight without knowing the reason why. In the diary of Samuel Pepys, we have a vivid blow-by-blow account of war in the seventeenth century. The Anglo-Dutch war of 1665-7 was fought at sea, and from his post as surveyor-general of victualling, Pepys had inside knowledge of the course of events. He was intensely inquisitive and took great delight in acquiring new information. Every issue regarding the conduct of war found a place in his diary: new taxation, the purchase of supplies, the design of ships and weapons, naval tactics, the health of sailors, morale and discipline, bravery and cowardice, espionage, the distribution of prize money, the demobilization of seamen, the care of prisoners, the part played by the weather, the efficacy of praying for victory, and many other aspects. But the one thing Pepys never once mentions is why the war was being fought. Perhaps, as a good bureaucrat, he got on with the job in hand without asking too many questions, but this would have been uncharacteristic of a man of such probing curiosity and intelligence. He simply has nothing to say about why Britain and the Netherlands found themselves at loggerheads in 1665, or why in 1666 France and Denmark entered the war on the Dutch side or Sweden on the British side. Nor does he seem any more interested in why peace came in 1667. After two years of war, he simply notes that 'all our Court are mightily for a peace', and that the time to end the war was opportune, 'while the King hath money ... [and] may need the help of no more Parliaments'.[9] When peace was concluded six months later, Pepys records that bells were rung but that there were no bonfires, 'partly from the

[9] 14 Feb. 1667.

dearness of firing, but principally with the little content most people have in the peace'.[10]

The fact is that war for Pepys was like the Fire of London or the Plague—something that human beings could not prevent but had to endure with whatever fortitude they could muster. And his friend John Evelyn simply noted of one naval misfortune that it was 'a loss to be universally deplored, none knowing for what reason we first engaged in this ungrateful war'.[11] Not long after this, the Duc de Saint-Simon wrote from the other side of the Channel: 'From the end of summer until the beginning of winter we made several attempts to negotiate a peace, on what grounds I do not know. It served only to swell our enemies' pride... I shall not embark on an account of the treaty. It will doubtless receive the same treatment as those that preceded it.'[12]

We now live in a more ideological age, but, in examining the cases of armed conflict that came before the United Nations between 1946 and 1964, one is struck by a confusion of purpose on the part of those initiating the use of force, as well as by the failure of armed conflict to secure the supposed objectives of the initiators. It is not in every case possible to be sure what the purpose was because, as Fred Iklé has pointed out, war aims tend to change during the course of the fighting. In any case, one has to distinguish between the formal and avowed aim of a belligerent and the subsidiary and perhaps hidden aims of particular groups and factions. Arms manufacturers may want to increase sales, military experts to test new weapons or strategies, politicians and civil servants to enhance their reputations at the expense of rivals, and so on. All these subsidiary aims have some bearing on the process of devising the compromise that becomes the public policy of a belligerent; but the utility of war as a means of pursuing political goals has to be judged by the extent to which the main and avowed war aim has been achieved, not by whether particular groups have gained as a side-effect of the fighting.[13]

[10] 24 Aug. 1667.   [11] 17 June 1666.
[12] *Historical Memoirs of the Duc de Saint-Simon*, ed. and trans. Lucy Norton, London, Hamish Hamilton, 1967, vol. I, pp. 59, 93.
[13] Iklé, *Every War Must End*, pp. 13-16; see also Morton H. Halperin, 'War Termination as a Problem in Civil-Military Relations', in William T. R. Fox (special ed.), *The Annals of the American Academy of Political and Social Science*, pp. 86-95.

Whatever the main goal may be when the fighting starts, it may have to be modified if the cost becomes excessive. This was plain for all to see in the case of the two Dutch 'police actions' in Indonesia, for example, and in the Anglo-French participation in the attack on the Suez Canal in 1956. It is the unsuccessful party that is under the greatest pressure to modify or even abandon the aim it proclaimed when the fighting started. The national reconsideration of war aims while the fighting is in progress is not always easy, especially when it can be argued that critics of the professed goal of the war are helping the enemy.[14]

In the cases studied, it might be charitable to assume that, in Kashmir 1947 and Cyprus 1964, no party expected or wanted war; that armed conflict arose more from a policy of drift or as an unintended consequence of earlier mistakes than from a conscious decision on anyone's part that war was the only rational and honourable option left.[15] But in the other cases, when there was a deliberate resort to armed force, it is surprising how rarely it succeeded in achieving the purposes of the initiators. The two Netherlands 'police actions' in Indonesia (1947 and 1948) did not lead to the elimination of the Indonesian nationalists, but only made more certain the early ending of Dutch rule. The Arab decision to oppose by force the UN partition plan in Palestine in 1947 did not prevent a Zionist state from coming into being. The North Korean attack across the 38th parallel in 1950 did not lead to the collapse of the Syngman Rhee régime. The Anglo-French offensive against Egypt in 1956 did not topple Nasser, and the immediate result was not to assure passage through the Suez canal but its blocking: Israel, it is true, secured access for its shipping through the Strait of Tiran, and Arab guerrilla attacks from the Gaza Strip were ended; but the Gulf of Aqaba was closed by Nasser in 1967, leading to another war, and Palestinian assaults on Zionist targets have continued. If the period 1946-64 is typical, war is not a very effective means of continuing a political struggle.

---

[14] Iklé, *Every War Must End*, pp. 79, 96, 102.

[15] Although Geoffrey Blainey maintains that no wars are unintended or 'accidental'; see Blainey, *The Causes of War*, London, Macmillan, 1973, p. 249; also pp. 127-45.

In the SIPRI list of conflicts already referred to, the 89 conflicts in the period 1945-64 were distributed as follows:[16]

Europe	7
Middle East	22
Far East	30
Africa	13
Latin America	17

According to SIPRI, four of the conflicts did not involve actual hostilities: the Soviet Union and Iran 1945-6, Morocco and France 1952-6, Iraq and Kuwait 1961, Soviet missiles in Cuba 1962.

The small number of conflicts in Europe may be ascribable to three factors: the internal stability of most European countries so that there has been little civil strife sufficiently serious to lead to armed conflict; the acceptance and legitimation of post-war frontiers, so that there are no active border or territorial disputes in Europe other than Gibraltar and northern Cyprus; and the military balance, fragile though it sometimes is, which has virtually eliminated from Europe the advantage of military pre-emption.

Of the 82 conflicts in the Third World, almost 30 per cent were civil conflicts, arising from internal disunity or instability, and 40 per cent were either wars against colonial rule or legacies of the colonial system. Of the remaining conflicts, 5 were related to the internal war in China between the Communists and the Nationalists, 12 were wars to stop infiltration across frontiers or to change borders or acquire territory, and 9 were cases of great power intervention. David Wood has stressed that wars in the Third World have 'normally been on a small scale, when measured in numbers of combatants or of casualties or even duration', except when there has been great power inter-vention.[17]

Since the publication of Quincy Wright's pioneering *Study of War* in 1942, many attempts have been made to devise a taxonomy of armed conflict. Some of this has inevitably focused

---

[16] *SIPRI Yearbook of World Armaments and Disarmament 1968/9*, London, Duckworth, 1969, pp. 366-71.

[17] David Wood, *Conflict in the Twentieth Century*, London, Institute for Strategic Studies, 1968 (Adelphi Paper no. 48), p. 20.

on the external characteristics of conflict: inter-state war, civil wars with or without external intervention, *coups d'état*, armed insurgencies, and so on. Classification of wars by basic causes is more difficult since it is rare for a war to have a single cause.

Until recent times, wars were usually fought mainly for dynastic reasons or to gain access to or control of raw materials or strategic areas.[18] The interesting aspect of armed conflict since 1945, including the seven cases I have studied in detail, is how crucial a factor was the claim that civil and political rights were being denied. This was true of all of the cases in the SIPRI list of armed conflict for liberation from colonial rule, for most of the cases of civil strife, for many of the wars that were colonial legacies or arose from secessionist claims, and for several of those in which there was great power intervention. There were allegations that human rights were being denied in more than half of the 82 conflicts in the Third World between 1945 and 1964. It is for this reason that work to assure basic rights should form part of a multiple strategy for preventing war.

The human rights element in causing war reinforces its ideological character. Lewis Coser, in his study of social conflict, has pointed out that conflicts about ideas are more merciless than those fought for personal reasons.[19] Certainly, one would be unlikely in our ideological age to encounter anything comparable to the near-chivalry of the Napoleonic Wars.

The French and English armies, as they became better acquainted by frequent contact, grew to be very civil to each other...

The advance posts always gave notice to each other when they were in danger. On one occasion, when the French army was advancing suddenly and in force, the French posts suddenly cried out to ours, 'Courez vite, courez vite, on va vous attaquer.'[20]

---

[18] Julian Lider notes that, of all the ways of studying the nature of war, the geopolitical is perhaps the one with the longest tradition, and the one that has had greatest impact on the way statesmen themselves have regarded war; see Lider, *On the Nature of War*, Farnborough, Saxon House, 1978 (under the auspices of the Swedish Institute of International Affairs), p. 13; see also H. A. Calahan, *What Makes a War End?*, pp. 238-9.

[19] Lewis A. Coser, *The Functions of Social Conflict*, pp. 111-19.

[20] Bernard Pool (ed.), *The Croker Papers 1808-1857*, London, Batsford, 1967, pp. 119-20. Even the pitiless Boer War was graced with occasional acts of chivalry between adversaries; see Thomas Pakenham, *The Boer War*, London, Weidenfeld & Nicolson, 1979, pp. 560-1.

The literature dealing directly with war termination is sparse and what little there is is not very satisfactory. When Coleman Phillipson published his pioneering study in 1916, he pointed out that there was at that time no publication in any language that dealt with the subject in a systematic and comprehensive manner.[21] Phillipson examined briefly a number of cases of war termination by surrender or conquest and then, at greater length, war termination by treaties of peace. His study was based on the texts of twenty-six peace treaties and related documents, and he added his own critical observations from the point of view of international law. 'The reader is conducted from the field of battle, where the first pourparlers are exchanged..., to the calmer atmosphere of the council-chamber of plenipotentiaries, who take up the conflict by the less sinister methods of negotiation and diplomacy'. Phillipson expressed the hope that his work would be useful 'when the present Great War comes to an end'.

The next study dealing in part with the termination of armed conflict was also published in time of war. Lt-Cdr H. A. Calahan, an American, in a study published in 1944, reviewed the problem of war termination and the maintenance of peace, based on nine wars since 1781.[22] Calahan commented that, while much was known about how wars begin, historical writers had avoided exploring 'the intricate paths' of war termination; yet the best way to learn how a war will end is to study how in fact past wars have ended. He considered that there are certain common features, even in widely dissimilar wars, so that we may expect the similarities to recur in the future. In reality Calahan paid much greater attention to deterring war than to terminating it. He believed that wars could be prevented only by keeping aggressive nations permanently disarmed. Any nation that threatened world peace should be struck 'early, hard, and without warning'. He pleaded for courage 'to start small wars that we may prevent great ones'.

Lewis Coser, who has made a deep study of social conflict of all kinds, published in 1961 a paper on the termination of conflict, without particular reference to war.[23] Absolute conflict

---

[21] Coleman Phillipson, *Termination of War and Treaties of Peace*.

[22] Calahan, op. cit.

[23] Lewis Coser, 'The Termination of Conflict', *Journal of Conflict Resolution*, vol. 5, no. 4 (1961), pp. 347-53; reproduced in Coser's *Continuities in the Study of Social Conflict*, New York, Free Press, 1967, pp. 40-51.

that ends in total victory and total defeat is the exception: all other conflicts are ended by 'a reciprocal activity' of the parties. No matter how much the victor has brought about the situation in which conflict can be terminated, 'the final decision to end [a] war remains with the potential loser'. To understand when conflict can be terminated requires an understanding of the structure and dynamics of the opposing camp. A leader may have to adjust his aims and strategy so that partial defeat may be presented to his followers as a partial victory. The willingness to 'stop chasing the mirage of victory' and negotiate a compromise depends on a correct assessment of the situation, and one of the key functions of the mediator is to help the two sides to appreciate what the real situation is.

Berenice A. Carroll, in a paper published in Norway at the height of the Vietnam War, examined a number of hypotheses about the duration of wars, the processes that play a part in bringing hostilities to an end, and the forms of war termination.[24] A complicated war termination formula is suggested for heuristic purposes, but the author accepts that to collect the necessary data to apply her formula for even one war would be 'a staggering task'. She concludes that all theories about war termination must remain essentially speculative until more research has been done about how particular wars in the past were terminated.

Carroll also contributed an article to a special issue of *The Annals of the American Academy of Political and Social Science* on problems of war termination, also published during the course of the Vietnam war.[25] Carroll again stresses how few studies there are of war termination. This she ascribes to the prevalence of the notion that 'once war breaks out, its end is inherent in its beginning—simply a mindless, inescapable playing out of forces set in motion at the outset'. She notes that several recent US studies applying conflict theory to problems of war termination reflected political orientations in favour of the status quo. Carroll herself treats war termination as a product of 'many interacting factors', and she expresses the hope that studies of

[24] Berenice A. Carroll, 'How Wars End: An Analysis of Some Current Hypotheses', *Journal of Peace Research* (Oslo), vol. 6, no. 4 (1969), pp. 259-321.
[25] 'War Termination and Conflict Theory: Value, Premises, Theories, and Policies', in Fox, pp. 14-29.

this 'new and undeveloped field' will increase in number, variety, and sophistication.

Professor T. R. Fox, the special editor of the issue of the *Annals*, also noted the paucity of scholarly research. Political scientists have been more concerned to explain how peace is lost than 'how it can be won back again', while strategists have been preoccupied with deterring or winning war. Yet to terminate wars in the future depends on understanding how previous wars have ended.[26] The same point is made by Paul Seabury in an article on the decline of both formal declarations of war and formal treaties of peace.[27]

In spite of the distinction of some of the contributors (e.g., Quincy Wright, Herman Kahn), it must be admitted that this collection of papers is rather disappointing. One reason may be that the articles were written under the impact of a war in which the United States was engaged, so that several contributors were uneasily applying their conclusions to a current case. Moreover, two of the articles deal with thermonuclear war, which is surely *sui generis*.

There are a number of interesting papers concerned with the differing views within a belligerent power and the implications of this for war termination. Morton H. Halperin distinguishes five groups, which nearby always differ but which all claim to represent the national interest.[28] Field commanders tend to believe that the fighting should continue because, if only they are properly supplied and supported, a decisive military victory lies just ahead. Senior military officers in the capital are concerned with 'how the conduct of the war will affect the future definition of the roles and mission of each service', while the general staff is likely to be characterized by 'loyalty to political leaders and sensitivity to their ... interests'. Political leaders will view the national interest largely in the light of 'domestic constraints', and the foreign ministry will consider war termination from the point of view of post-war diplomatic relations.

Fred Iklé has made a notable contribution to the military aspects of war termination. Iklé wrote during the Vietnam

---

[26] 'The Causes of Peace and Conditions of War', in Fox, pp. 1-13.

[27] 'Provisionality and Finality', in Fox, pp. 96-104.

[28] 'War Termination as a Problem in Civil-Military Relations', in Fox, pp. 86-95.

War, but consciously refrained from referring to Vietnam.[29] His main concern was with the way decisions about military operations affect the process of war termination. He notes that the subject of war termination has been neglected, and he suggests that historical examples are needed to flush out the abstract reasoning of strategic analysis. One of his most interesting chapters is entitled 'Ending Wars Before They Start'.

Michael I. Handel is the author of a monograph published in Jerusalem soon after President Sadat's visit.[30] He surveys some of the theories of war termination, with particular reference to three levels of analysis: individual psychology, domestic pressures, and inter-state politics. Handel believes that the level concerned with the impact of personalities and psychological structures on war termination is 'a very important dimension' which has been unjustly neglected, and he calls in aid 'Sadat's so-called initiative in visiting Jerusalem, and Begin's response'. Handel considers that the analysis of domestic forces has also 'not received enough systematic attention or comparative study'. He stresses the importance of non-rational factors and other 'problems, contradictions and difficulties that tend to complicate the study of war termination' at the inter-state level. It is the non-rational elements that undermine and limit the possibility of prediction, so that—as he puts it—the study of war termination 'is not an exact science and never will be'. Handel urges the need for further study so that we may learn 'how to bring wars to an end in the fastest possible way'.

It is notable that virtually all of the studies were written under the impact of particular wars in which the author's nation was engaged. This reinforces the point made by Carroll and others, that the subject has been neglected because of the widespread belief that the end of a war is inherent in its beginning, a belief that is always belied by the actual course of events.

There exists a good deal of literature, even if of variable quality, on the economic and political forces that give rise to conflict, on the domestic interests and pressures that affect national decision-making, on the military strategies that have been devised for deterring war or for winning if deterrence fails, and on ethical and legal constraints on the exercise of

[29] Iklé, *Every War Must End.*
[30] Michael I. Handel, *War Termination—A Critical Survey.*

military coercion. What still needs to be studied is the neglected question of war termination. I hope that my own study will make a modest contribution to the subject and provide some of the data, the need for which has been stressed by Calahan, Carroll, Fox, Seabury, Iklé, and Handel. Only by detailed studies will it be possible to refine theories of war termination and improve the means used by the international community to stop the fighting.

When war breaks out, it is likely that the Security Council will soon be involved. The Council provides a convenient framework for contact and diplomacy, both for the belligerents and for third parties. The belligerents often resent the substantive decisions that the Council takes, but these decisions constitute an authentic manifestation of world opinion, and the Council has a range of procedures for exercising mediation and for expressing disapproval or exerting pressure. The system of collective military security devised at San Francisco, based on an analysis of the failure of the League of Nations to counter aggression, has still not been put into effect, but the Council has available various non-military mechanisms. Peace-keeping by observers or military contingents has been relatively successful, even in the most unpromising circumstances. The Council has also used embargoes and sanctions, but these have not been very effective because of evasions—sometimes in defiance of governmental policy, but sometimes acquiesced in by governments that in public claimed to be respecting UN decisions. Non-military sanctions that are not properly enforced may be useful gestures of disapproval, but they are not effective means of coercion.

It would be foolish to suggest that the problems that were encountered in 1946-64 will all recur. In any case, there is no panacea for bringing armed conflict to an end. My aim, rather, has been threefold: (1) to provide in volume II the raw data that scholars and practitioners may analyse, and in chapter 6 of this volume a check-list of questions that usually arise; (2) to indicate procedures that have in the past been relatively effective; and (3), regarding one or two matters, to suggest new arrangements or institutions that might help the Security Council to fulfil more effectively its responsibilities for maintaining world peace.

CHAPTER 1

Some problems of definition

I have already commented on the paucity of literature dealing expressly with war termination. That does not mean that I have had to coin a new jargon, for the main terms have already been defined in the relevant disciplines, especially law. In this chapter I review some of the salient terms.

1.1 ARMED CONFLICT

Although the Nazi and Fascist leaders were able to persuade some of their followers that war is glorious and evokes the most admirable human qualities, this is not now a fashionable view. Indeed, modern war is so hellish that those who take the sword in our day are likely to make what they are engaged in seem more palatable by using some expression other than war: liberation, police action, separating the belligerents, humanitarian intervention, preventive measures, enforcement action, pacification, peace-keeping, deterrence, and many more.

States and the other entities of which international society is composed are related to each other in a complex way that normally includes both co-operation and competition. When the competitive element becomes overriding and military coercion is used, this is not simply an intensification of hostility but a completely new situation governed by different legal rules,[1] and to some extent by different moral principles too. Acts that were formerly forbidden become licit; attitudes that previously gave rise to shame are now admired; killing is no longer murder. So important is the transition from peace to war that procedures were established to minimize or eliminate uncertainty as to whether two entities were or were not at war. A threat or conditional intention to wage war was called an ultimatum, and active hostilities were supposed not to begin without a prior

[1] Lord McNair *and* A. D. Watts, *The Legal Effects of War*, Cambridge, University Press, 1966.

and formal declaration of war. Moreover, the existence of a state of war was not simply the concern of the belligerents, for it was to be notified without delay to non-participants (neutrals). These practices were codified in Hague Convention III of 18 October 1907.[2] The parties agreed that hostilities between them should 'not commence without a previous and explicit warning', and that neutrals should be notified of the existence of a state of war 'without delay'. The United States and most European powers became parties to this Convention, as did China, Japan, and Siam (Thailand). Although the Convention is still in force, formal declarations of war are now unusual, and the British *Manual of Military Law* states that it is 'possible' that the very issue of an ultimatum, although in accordance with Hague Convention III, would in itself now violate the United Nations Charter.[3]

The United Nations was intended to initiate a new era. The only reference to war in the Charter is the expression of hope that it will be banished for ever. The first of the purposes that 'We the peoples of the United Nations' affirmed when establishing an international organization was 'to save succeeding generations from the scourge of war', and we went on to assert that armed force was not to be used 'save in the common interest'. UN Members have agreed to refrain in their international relations from the threat or use of force, except in self-defence after an armed attack has occurred or in measures of military enforcement under the Security Council.[4] 'The whole object of the Charter', writes Ian Brownlie, 'was to render unilateral use of force, even in self-defence, subject to control by the Organization.'[5]

It is, on the face of it, surprising that war should be governed by legal and moral rules, but sociological studies show that conflict tends to give rise to norms and rules regulating its

---

[2] An English translation is given in the British *Manual of Military Law*, part III, *The Law of War on Land*, pp. 201-2. A revised edition of the Manual is in course of preparation.

[3] Ibid., para. 10, n. 3. The US Manual has a different emphasis on this point: a non-Member of the United Nations or a UN Member that goes to war in violation of the Charter without a declaration of war or conditional ultimatum 'commits a further breach of international law'. *The Law of Land Warfare*, Washington, DC, US Government Printing Office, 1956 (FM 27-10), para. 23.

[4] Preamble and Articles 2(4), 42, and 51 of the Charter.

[5] Ian Brownlie, *International Law and the Use of Force by States*, p. 273.

conduct, and often leads to the establishment of new norms and rules.[6] It is noteworthy that those who violate the laws of war nearly always justify themselves by alleging that the enemy committed a prior breach, thus by implication accepting the relevance of rules prohibiting or limiting the use of force.

We thus have the paradox that a war that is resorted to and conducted in accordance with internationally agreed rules of restraint may be called a just war, whatever the purpose for which it is fought,[7] while all war other than that waged in self-defence or for UN enforcement is contrary to the Charter and in that sense unjust.

In the early days of the United Nations, it was suggested that the International Law Commission should codify the laws of war. This would have been a daunting assignment, even if no attempt had been made to keep pace with burgeoning military technology; but most of the members of the Commission considered that it would be a mistake to embark on this task: 'public opinion might interpret [a decision to launch such a study] as showing lack of confidence in the ... means at the disposal of the United Nations for maintaining peace'.[8]

The International Committee of the Red Cross, no less idealistic than the International Law Commission but perhaps more aware of man's inhumanity to man, had no hesitation about pressing ahead with its own efforts to bring humanitarian law up to date. The four Geneva Conventions of 1949, in Common Article 2, state that the provisions shall apply to all cases of declared war 'or of any other armed conflict', even if the state of war is not recognized by one of the belligerents.[9] Since 1949, there has been a growing tendency to use the term 'armed conflict' rather than 'war' when precision is important. The United Nations has issued studies and reports under the general rubric 'Respect for Human Rights in Armed Conflict'; and the efforts of the International Committee of the Red Cross, which culminated in 1977 in the two Additional Protocols to the Geneva Conventions, were headed 'Reaffirmation and Development of International Humanitarian Law Applicable

---

[6] Coser, pp. 121-8.
[7] See Bailey, *Prohibitions and Restraints in War*, pp. 1-20, 24-36.
[8] GAOR, 4th session, Supplement no. 10, A/925, para. 18.
[9] Geneva Conventions, 12 Aug. 1949.

in Armed Conflicts'.[10] I have used 'Wars' in the title of this study but the more exact 'Armed Conflict' in the sub-title.

1.2 INTERNATIONAL AND INTERNAL WARS

Historically, war has been thought of as a military contest between sovereigns. The UN structure was largely predicated on the assumption that international disputes would be disputes between states, and when the preamble to the UN Charter refers to the scourge of war, it is evident that what the founders had in mind was inter-state war.[11] There has been a great deal of armed conflict since 1945, but little of it has been classical inter-state war; nor has it for long been civil war, as that term is understood by ordinary people,[12] particularly because there has often been external intervention. Such intervention may be the official and formal action of states, as when Pakistan's regular forces entered Kashmir in May 1948 or when Turkish aircraft made bombing raids on Cyprus in August 1964; or it may be intervention by 'volunteers', as when tribesmen invaded Kashmir in 1947, the Chinese intervened in Korea in October 1950, the Indonesians intervened in East Timor in 1975, or the Soviet Union threatened to intervene over Suez in November 1956; or it may be surreptitious intervention, as in some Afro-Asian and Communist assistance to the Indonesian Republicans in 1947-9 or in some of the Jewish and Arab help to those fighting in Palestine in 1947-8. Whatever its precise form, external intervention has the effect of making the conflict a matter of international concern.

A major problem for the United Nations has been that international peace has often been endangered by the aspirations

[10] Additional Protocols, A/32/144, 15 Aug. 1977 (mimeo), annexes.

[11] See Article 35, for example.

[12] The Institute of International Law has defined civil war as an armed conflict not of an international character between an established government and one or more insurgent movements whose aim is to overthrow the government or the political, economic, or social order of the state, or to achieve secession or self-government; or between two or more groups which, in the absence of an established government, contend for the control of the state: but not local disorders or riots, conflicts arising from decolonization, or conflicts between political entities separated by an international demarcation line or which have existed *de facto* as states for a prolonged period, or conflicts between any such entity and a state. See J. H. W. Verzijl, *International Law in Historical Perspective, part IX-A, The Laws of War*, Leiden, Sijthoff and Noordhoff, 1978, p. 513.

and actions of entities other than states, and that the Organization is so constructed that its organs prefer to deal with states
rather than with dissident political organizations, insurgent
groups, liberation movements, communal minorities, and the
like. Nor is it always easy for UN organs to relate to embryonic
governments, such as Azad Kashmir since 1947, the Jewish
Agency for Palestine and the Arab Higher Committee in 1948,
and the Indonesian Republicans before 1950, or to entities
claiming to be governments but which are not widely recognized, such as North Korea and the Turkish Federated State
of Cyprus.

The four Geneva Conventions of 1949 distinguish between
war or armed conflict between parties to the Conventions (inter-
state wars) and 'armed conflict not of an international character'
occurring in the territory of a party (internal wars). Interstate
wars between parties are governed by the detailed provisions
of the Conventions, and internal wars are, 'as a minimum',
subject to certain humanitarian norms which are set out in
Common Article 3 of the Conventions.[13]

In view of the vulnerability of non-combatants in both inter-
state and internal wars, the International Committee of the
Red Cross has been anxious to give them added legal protection,
and two Protocols to the Geneva Conventions were approved
in 1977. Additional Protocol I is stated to apply to war or
armed conflict between parties, including 'armed conflicts in
which peoples are fighting against colonial domination and
alien occupation and against racist régimes in the exercise of
their right of self-determination'. This means that wars of
liberation from colonial or racist rule, which could plausibly
have been regarded as essentially internal, are now considered
to be of an international character, even if there is no intervention by an external power. The authority representing
people struggling against colonial or racist domination or alien
occupation may undertake to apply the Geneva Conventions
and Additional Protocol I by means of a prescribed procedure,
although this is not mandatory.[14]

[13] Geneva Conventions, 1949.
[14] Additional Protocol I, A/32/144, 15 Aug. 1977 (mimeo), Annex I, Articles 1 and
96 (3). The inclusion of 'alien occupation' might be thought to be redundant since the
Geneva Conventions already applied to 'cases of partial or total occupation', of which
'alien' occupation is the usual form.

Additional Protocol II 'develops and supplements' Common Article 3 of the Geneva Conventions relating to armed conflict not of an international character, including conflict between the armed forces of a party and 'dissident armed forces or other organized armed groups which, under responsible command, exercise such control over a part of its territory as to enable them to carry out sustained and concerted military operations and to implement this Protocol'. It does not, however, apply to 'internal disturbances and tensions, such as riots, isolated and sporadic acts of violence and other acts of a similar nature'.[15]

It will be noted that the first Additional Protocol introduces an important new concept into international humanitarian law. It has for long been recognized that persons taking part in armed conflict may owe allegiance to an entity other than a state (resistance movements, for example). What is new in Additional Protocol I is that a national liberation movement may acquire legitimacy not simply from *the fact* of combatancy but from *the purposes* for which the war is being fought (that is to say, if it is a struggle against a colonial or racist régime or alien occupation).

1.3 REGULAR AND IRREGULAR FIGHTERS

For many millenia, war was primarily the business of those who were doing the fighting, and most of the time civilians did their best to keep out of the way. The combatants were those who had chosen the profession of arms and those who had volunteered or been conscripted into service for a particular campaign. A distinction was usually made between enemy fighters, who could defend themselves and retaliate, and who could therefore be attacked, and civilians, who had no means of defence or retaliation, and were therefore supposed to be immune from direct attack. If civilians were harmed, it was as an indirect consequence of an attack on combatants or military objectives, although during sieges civilians were as exposed to harm as were combatants. Grotius considered that innocent people should never be injured, even by accident. There is no right of war against those who are not involved in war, he

---

[15] Additional Protocol II, A/32/144, 15 Aug. 1977 (mimeo), Annex II, Article 1.

wrote: and for Grotius the innocent included children, women, old men, prisoners of war, those performing religious duties, neutrals, farmers, artisans, merchants, and those engaged in literary pursuits.[16]

The concepts of guilt and innocence had a special meaning in this context. Guilt referred not to a share in the general responsibility for causing the outbreak of war or supporting its continuance, but solely to whether a person was directly engaged in combat activities: the guilty were those on the other side who did the fighting; the innocent, those who did not. It was a distinction that was easier for the philosopher or theologian to make in the calm of academe than for a soldier in the heat of battle.

Barrie Paskins gives an interesting explanation of the concept of non-combatant immunity. The combatant sees death in war as 'a fate internally connected with the activity in virtue of which he is a combatant', so that the prospect of death is meaningful. Normally this does not apply to the non-combatant, who 'cannot find in his own life the meaning of his death'.[17]

In order that a distinction could in practice be made between combatants and civilians, combatants wore a distinguishing mark. Uniform clothes were one such distinction, though uniform was also needed for reasons of morale and discipline. A person not wearing uniform or other distinguishing mark was not supposed to fight. If he did so, it was assumed that he was a bandit. If a genuine fighter concealed his identity by wearing civilian clothing and attacked the enemy, this was regarded as treachery and a breach of the rules of war, for a fighter in civilian guise provided the opposing party with a pretext for attacking all those others who seemed to be civilians, thus weakening the concept of non-combatant immunity.

As the rules of war were developed and codified, an attempt was made to specify those who were to be regarded as legitimate fighters, and therefore to expect prisoner of war status if captured, and those who were bandits and operating for private

[16] Hugo Grotius, *The Law of War and Peace*, trans. F. W. Kelsey and others, Washington, DC, CEIP/Oxford, Clarendon Press, 1925, reprinted 1964, pp. 173, 733-40, 756, 790-1 (Book I, chapter 1, section 4, para. 1; Book III, ch. II, secs. VIII-XV; Book III, sec. VIII; Book III, ch. XVII, sec. I; Book III, ch. XVIII, sec. IV, para. 4).

[17] Barrie Paskins and Michael Dockrill, *The Ethics of War*, London, Duckworth, 1979, pp. 223-9.

gain. It was common ground that the laws of war applied to all fighters organized as armies or navies. In the Brussels Declaration of 1874, it was stated that armed forces might comprise both non-combatants (for example, medical units and military chaplains) and combatants; and, second, that the laws of war apply 'not only to armies, but also to militia and volunteer corps' provided that they fulfil four conditions:

That they be commanded by a person responsible for his subordinates;
That they have a fixed distinctive emblem recognizable at a distance;
That they carry arms openly;
That they conduct their operations in accordance with the laws and customs of war.[18]

As international law was progressively codified, these four criteria were repeated. They were incorporated in the Hague Conventions of 1899 and 1907 on the laws and customs of war on land.[19] The Geneva Convention of 1929 on prisoners of war was stated to apply without prejudice to the persons referred to in the Hague Convention of 1907,[20] and the Geneva Conventions of 1949 adopted the same four criteria but added 'organized resistance movements', and also required that the militias, volunteer corps, or resistance movements should belong to a party to the armed conflict.[21]

Ever since the first soldier was surreptitiously infiltrated into the enemy camp, regular warfare has been accompanied by the activities of partisans, insurgents, underground fighters, guerrillas, and similar forms of irregular combat. There has, however, been a great increase in irregular warfare in recent decades, as well as a greater sophistication in the means of conducting and countering it. Guerrilla fighting is the typical response of a dissident group within a state that is militarily weak but believes itself to have widespread support among the population. The short-term aim of guerrillas is not to conduct successful military operations in the conventional sense, but to

[18] *Documents Relating to the Program of the First Hague Peace Conference*, Oxford, Clarendon Press, 1921, p. 34, Articles 9 and 11. The Brussels Declaration never entered into force.
[19] *Hague Conventions of 1899(II) and 1907(IV) Respecting the Laws and Customs of War on Land*, pp. 8-9, Articles 1 and 3 of the Annex.
[20] Geneva Convention relative to the Treatment of Prisoners of War, 1929 (LNTS, vol. 118, no. 343).
[21] Geneva Conventions, 1949, Articles 13/13/4/-.

challenge the authority of the forces of law and order and induce them to over-react in retaliation. Michael Walzer has stressed that irregular fighters blur the distinction between combatants and non-combatants, not primarily because they themselves attack non-combatants (though they often do that) but because they force the opposing party to make such attacks. Irregular fighters, on the one hand, seek to identify themselves with the peaceable common people and, on the other hand, do their best to make it impossible for the established authorities to do so. In effect, they invite the opposing party to attack them in the midst of the surrounding civilians. They then claim that it was the enemy that resorted to indiscriminate warfare, and point out in their propaganda that the security forces are not protecting the innocent but have themselves become oppressors. Their aim is to place the onus of indiscriminate warfare on the opposing army.[22]

The security forces often understand very well if guerrillas have popular support: what they usually fail to appreciate is how difficult it is for ordinary people to put a stop to the terrorism or other underground activity of the militants. The British authorities believed that the Jewish community in Palestine could have put a stop to the terrorist activities of Irgun and the Stern Gang in 1945-8 had it been so minded, and imposed collective punishments to that end, just as Israeli Jews later believed that the Arab states had it in their power to stop Palestinian terrorism against Jewish targets, and took retaliatory military action to that end.

A remarkable insight into the mentality of underground fighters is given in Menachem Begin's account of the Irgun in Palestine. Begin conveys a strong sense of the loyalty and discipline that infused the Jewish underground and of the way moral and political values can be turned upside down in a closed and tightly knit group. What the underground fighter needs most, wrote Begin, 'is the inner consciousness that makes what is "legal" illegal and the "illegal" legal and justified. We had

[22] Walzer, *Just and Unjust Wars: A Moral Argument with Historical Illustrations*, New York, Basic Books, 1977, pp. 179-80; see also Menachem Begin, *The Revolt: Story of Irgun*, pp. 108-9; Richard Clutterbuck, *Guerrillas and Terrorists*, London, Faber, 1977, p. 18; and Paul Wilkinson, *Terrorism and the Liberal State*, London, Macmillan, 1977, p. 60.

this consciousness in supreme measure. We were convinced of the absolute legality of our "illegal" actions...'[23]

'Guerrilla' means little war, but guerrilla forms of fighting have been developed to such an extent in the past half-century that new humanitarian and legal norms were needed, particularly to bring up-to-date the criteria of 1874 on the conditions under which fighters should be entitled to combatant status. The first Additional Protocol to the Geneva Conventions (1977) was the result. Although adopted after the period covered by this study, it is worth mentioning as it to some extent codified general international law, and its provisions will be of considerable importance in the future. As noted above, the Protocol will apply to armed conflicts in which people are fighting against colonial, 'alien', or racist régimes. Armed forces comprise 'all organized armed forces, groups and units which are under a command responsible...for the conduct of its subordinates [and] subject to an internal disciplinary system which, *inter alia*, shall enforce compliance with the rules of international law'. A combatant is still supposed to distinguish himself from the civilian population, but if, 'owing to the nature of the hostilities', an armed combatant cannot do so, he must carry his arms openly while he is engaged in a military deployment preceding the launching of an attack, and during each military engagement.[24]

1.4 COMBATANTS AND CIVILIANS

Three developments of the present century have tended to erode the concept of non-combatant immunity: the highly ideological nature of contemporary war, which tends to involve whole societies rather than just full-time fighters; the development of weapons that cannot easily be used discriminately or proportionately; and the growing sophistication of techniques of insurgency and counter-insurgency. While governments often go out of their way to stress the great difficulty of maintaining the notion that non-combatants shall not be subject to

[23] Begin, pp. 60-1, 73, 108.
[24] Additional Protocol I, 1977, A/32/144, 15 August 1977 (mimeo), Annex I, Articles 1(4), 43(1), 44(3). See Esbjörn Rosenblad, *International Humanitarian Law of Armed Conflict*, pp. 75-102, 148-50.

direct attack, no one has suggested that this is a sufficient reason for abandoning the principle in law or ethics.

Non-combatant immunity had a certain logic when there was an unquestionable distinction between those engaged in the fighting and the rest of the population who, by reason of age, sex, or occupation, took no direct part in combat activities. There could, to be sure, be ambiguous situations, as when civilians found themselves in places under siege or were harmed as an unintended consequence of a legitimate military operation. It could also happen that, as an enemy approached an inhabited area, the civilian population might spontaneously take up arms, using whatever weapons were to hand—the so-called *levée en masse*.[25] Obviously such persons, by their own act, forfeited non-combatant status.

The International Committee of the Red Cross (ICRC), which has more sympathy for the victims of war than for the exigencies of military necessity, has long believed that the trend towards greater vulnerability of civilians can and should be reversed. The attempt to starve the enemy by economic blockade or crop destruction, for example, nearly always hits hardest those least capable of fighting: children, the elderly, those who are sick or disabled, pregnant and nursing women.[26] Terror-bombing of enemy cities has almost invariably proved to be counter-productive, increasing the popular will to continue the war rather than causing the civilian population to exert pressure for surrender—although nobody can say what the effect would be of prolonged nuclear attack.[27] The problem that the ICRC has encountered is not that armed forces or defence ministries are lacking in compassion: it is simply that they dislike renouncing military options for non-military reasons. But human nature being what it is, options that are not formally renounced in time of peace are all too easily resorted to by hot-heads in time of war.

The Fourth Geneva Convention of 1949 affords some legal protection to civilians under occupation, and further progress

[25] *Hague Conventions of 1899(II) and 1907(IV) Respecting the Laws and Customs of War on Land*, p. 8, Article 2 of the Regulations; Geneva Conventions, 1949, Articles 13(6)/ 13(6)/4A(6)/-.

[26] Rosenblad, pp. 103-24, 150-1.

[27] Ibid., pp. 125-43, 151-2.

was made in 1977 with the adoption of the two Additional Protocols to the Geneva Conventions. Combatants are supposed never to direct their military operations against the civilian population or civilian objects. This requires that combatants shall verify that civilian personnel or objects are not in the target area, and shall give advance warning if civilians are likely to be harmed indirectly. Objects that may not be attacked even in reprisal include cultural property, places of worship, objects indispensable to civilian survival, relief societies, civil defence organizations, installations containing dangerous forces, and the natural environment.[28]

In addition to civilians at home, there are often non-combatants accompanying the armed forces: military contractors, labour units, Red Cross staff, members of voluntary societies doing medical work or caring for the welfare of the armed forces, journalists.[29] All non-combatant personnel who might fall into enemy hands should be issued with identity cards: regular members of the armed forces carry different identity cards.[30]

Medical facilities, whether part of the armed forces or not, 'may in no circumstances be attacked', and medical personnel and military chaplains 'shall be respected and protected in all circumstances'. Captured medical personnel and chaplains 'shall not be deemed prisoners of war' and may be retained only if they are needed to attend to the health or spiritual needs of prisoners of war. Wounded, sick, and shipwrecked members of the armed forces are also to be protected and respected. The Red Cross or some other distinctive emblem should be used to

[28] Additional Protocol I, 1977, Articles 48, 51-5, 57, 62, 71 and Additional Protocol II, 1977, Articles 13-18, A/32/144, 15 Aug. 1977 (mimeo), annexes. See also GA res. 2675 (XXV), 9 Dec. 1970.
[29] The General Assembly has passed a number of resolutions on the protection of journalists, see GA res. 2673(XXV), 9 Dec. 1970; res. 2854(XXVI), 20 Dec. 1971; res. 3058(XXVIII), 2 Nov. 1973; res. 3245(XXIX), 29 Nov. 1974; res. 3500(XXX), 15 Dec. 1975.
[30] Geneva Conventions, 1949, Articles 40 and Annex II/42 and Annex/17 and Annex IV.A/-; Hague Convention on the protection of cultural property, 1954 (UNTS, vol. 249, no. 3511), Regulations, Article 21. Additional Protocol I of 1977 provides new guidance regarding identity cards for medical and religious personnel, civil defence workers, and journalists, A/32/144, 15 Aug. 1977 (mimeo), Annex I, Articles 1-2, 14, and Annex II.

identify persons and buildings entitled to protection and respect.[31]

It is obvious that, if religious and medical personnel, vehicles, and establishments are to be immune from direct attack, they have to be kept quite separate from combatant items. If ambulances and armed vehicles are sent in the same convoy, as happened with a Jewish convoy to the Mount Scopus area in Jerusalem on 13 April 1948, it is almost impossible for the adversary to fight in such a way that the medical elements are safe from attack. It is doubtless tempting to locate non-immune and immune items near to each other (anti-aircraft batteries in the grounds of a maternity hospital, for example), but if this is done, it is not reasonable to blame the other side for the indirect effects of legitimate attacks.

The fact that combatants in national liberation struggles have been given added legal protection under Additional Protocol I to the Geneva Conventions went some way to satisfying Third World and Communist sentiments, but the truth is that it is difficult to do this without exposing civilians to new risks from the direct or indirect effects of guerrilla fighting.

1.5 CEASE-FIRE, TRUCE, AND ARMISTICE

There is no question that there has been confusion about the precise meaning of the terms 'cease-fire', 'truce', and 'armistice'. The oldest term is *truce*, which in the Middle Ages usually had a religious connotation as in the phrase 'Truce of God'.[32] Hugo Grotius used 'truce' to mean an agreement by which war-like acts are for a time abstained from, though the state of war continues—'a period of rest in war, not a peace'. If hostilities were resumed after a truce, according to Grotius, there would be no need for a new declaration of war, since the state of war was 'not dead, but sleeping'. In the absence of agreement

[31] Geneva Conventions, 1949, Articles 12, 19-20, 24-6, 28, 30, 35-6, 38-44/12, 22-4, 36-9, 41-51/13-4, 22, 33, 35/16, 18, 20-2; Hague Convention on the protection of cultural property, 1954 (UNTS, vol. 249, no. 3511), Articles 16-7 and Regulations Articles 20-1.

[32] *Recueils de la Société Internationale de Droit pénal militaire et de Droit de la guerre* (Proceedings of the Sixth International Congress held at the Hague, 22-25 May 1973), tome VI, vol. I (hereafter cited as *Cessez-le-feu*), pp. 141 (Belgian Report), 255-6 (French Report); Baxter, p. 358.

to the contrary, it was lawful to rebuild walls or recruit soldiers during a truce, but actual acts of war were forbidden, whether against persons or property: that is to say, 'whatever is done by force against the enemy'. Also forbidden were the bribery of enemy garrisons and the seizure of places held by the enemy. If a truce were violated, the injured party was free to resume hostilities 'even without declaring war'. Private acts did not constitute a violation, however, unless there was public command or approval.[33]

When the codification of international law began in the second half of the nineteenth century, a truce was the procedure by which belligerents entered into parleys, and an armistice was an actual agreement to suspend military operations. According to the Brussels Declaration of 1874, a *parlementaire* was a person who had been authorized by one of the belligerents to enter into communication with the other side. He advanced bearing a white flag, accompanied by a bugler or drummer, sometimes also by a flag-bearer. The enemy commander was not in all cases and under all conditions obliged to receive a *parlementaire*, and he was, in any case, entitled to take all measures necessary for preventing the bearer of the flag of truce from taking advantage of his stay within the radius of the enemy's position to the prejudice of the latter. The *parlementaire* and the accompanying party were inviolable unless they abused their privileged position in order to provoke or commit an act of treason, in which case the enemy commander had the right to detain him temporarily.[34] These provisions were incorporated in the Regulations attached to Hague Conventions II of 1899 and IV of 1907 on the laws and customs of war on land, under the heading 'Flags of Truce', with the addition of a reference to an interpreter accompanying a *parlementaire* and an express provision that the obtaining of information during a truce was an abuse of confidence.[35]

---

[33] Hugo Grotius, *The Law of War and Peace*, trans. F. W. Kelsey and others, Washington, DC, CEIP/Oxford, Clarendon Press, 1925, reprinted 1964, pp. 832-44, 848 (Book III, chapters XXI and XXII, section VIII).

[34] *Documents Relating to the Program of the First Hague Peace Conference*, Oxford, Clarendon Press, 1921, pp. 38-9, Articles 43-5.

[35] *Hague Conventions of 1899 (II) and 1907 (IV) Respecting the Laws and Customs of War on Land*, Washington, DC, CEIP, 1915, pp. 20-1, Articles 32-4.

An armistice, according to the Brussels Declaration, was an actual suspension of military operations by mutual agreement between the belligerents, either general in character and suspending all military operations everywhere, or local and applying only between certain portions of the belligerent armies and within a fixed radius. Once an armistice had been concluded, it was to be notified promptly to the competent authorities and troops, and hostilities were to be suspended at once. An armistice was of undefined duration and the parties could resume military operations at any time so long as the enemy was warned in advance. Violation of an armistice by one of the parties gave the other party the right to denounce it: violation by private persons acting on their own initiative entitled the injured party to demand the punishment of the offenders and, if necessary, compensation for the losses sustained.[36] These provisions were incorporated in the Hague Regulations of 1899 and 1907, with the addition of a statement that in case of urgency hostilities could be resumed at once.[37]

By the end of the Second World War, there was a confusing tendency to regard 'truce' and 'armistice' as synonymous, although 'truce' was increasingly giving way to 'armistice'. 'Les deux expressions ont d'ailleurs le même sens', wrote Rachelle Bernard in 1947.[38] An armistice was now a convention by which the belligerent parties agreed to a formal but sometimes temporary cessation of hostilities. It was normally negotiated directly by the two sides, but occasionally it arose from the initiative of a neutral state or the International Committee of the Red Cross. Its main aim was not to resolve political or economic problems but to suspend hostilities for a time. It constituted an initial contact between the parties, often leading to a peace treaty; but the legal state of war continued: an armistice was not peace. Marcel Sibert, writing between the world wars, considered that while in former times an armistice had been simply an agreement between belligerents to suspend

---

[36] *Documents Relating to the Program of the First Hague Peace Conference*, Oxford, Clarendon Press, 1921, p. 39, Articles 47-52; Coleman Phillipson, *Termination of War and Treaties of Peace*, pp. 56-7.

[37] *Hague Conventions of 1899 (II) and 1907 (IV) Respecting the Laws and Customs of War on Land*, pp. 22-3, Articles 36-41.

[38] Rachelle Bernard, *L'Armistice dans les guerres internationales*, p. 7.

hostilities in order to prepare for peace in more favourable conditions than was possible in time of war, the armistice was becoming a means by which the surrender of the enemy was secured, often including conditions for permanent peace.[39]

There was no clear agreement about acts that were permitted or forbidden during an armistice. A demarcation line would be established and possibly also a demilitarized buffer zone. Each party remained behind the demarcation line, and there was to be no firing or movement across the line by military forces or civilians, although troop movements *behind* the lines were permitted. But beyond these agreed restrictions, there was only uncertainty—about the supply of food to places under siege, for example.[40]

Violations were deterred by the threat of enforcement measures, but the ultimate sanction against a substantial and deliberate breach was the possibility of resuming hostilities. Minor violations of a particular provision of the armistice, committed in good faith, or actions by private persons without the knowledge of the responsible authorities, were not deemed to justify denunciation.[41]

The creation of the United Nations, with its Security Council having the 'primary responsibility for the maintenance of international peace and security', initiated a new era. There was now a distinction between 'truce' and 'armistice': a truce was a consequence of the intervention of an intermediary, usually a subsidiary organ of the Security Council, whereas an armistice resulted from negotiations between the parties. Moreover, a new concept was introduced, the call to *cease fire* or *cease hostilities*. This concept 'est toutefois une notion essentialement pratique...'[42] It arose from an emergency appeal by the Security Council, which was almost always accompanied or quickly followed by a request to a subsidiary organ to try and organize a more durable arrangement—although a cease-fire

---

[39] Marcel Sibert, 'L'Armistice dans le droit des gens', *Revue Generale de Droit Internationale Public*, pp. 657, 658, 662, 663, 666, 700, 714; Bernard, pp. 7-8, 12, 14, 18, 19, 24, 25, 26, 67; Tasker H. Bliss, 'The Armistices', *AJIL*, vol. 16 (October 1922), p. 520; Julius Stone, *Legal Controls of International Conflicts: A Legal Treatise on the Dynamics of Disputes and War-law*, p. 636.

[40] Sibert, pp. 681, 685; Bernard, pp. 68, 69, 71-4, 85.

[41] Sibert, pp. 709, 712; Bernard, pp. 114-16.

[42] Bertrand de Montluc, *Le Cessez-le-feu*, p. 1.

could be proclaimed unilaterally by one of the belligerent parties, as happened in 1949 after the second Dutch 'police action' in Indonesia. There was a tendency to see the terms 'cease-fire', 'truce', and 'armistice' as representing a sequence, 'three stages of progress from war to peace' (Paul Mohn); 'a first link in a chain running from war to peace' (Suzanne Bastid).[43]

The first occasion on which the Security Council acted to put an end to fighting was on 1 August 1947, following the first Dutch 'police action' in Indonesia. The Council called on the armed forces of the Netherlands and the Republic of Indonesia to 'cease hostilities forthwith'.[44] A prolonged wrangle then ensued between the parties in the field as to the precise meaning of the Security Council's resolution.

The members of the Security Council had not, of course, been engaged in writing a textbook on international law: they were eleven states responding to a dangerous situation, but with the usual clashes of ideology and interest. The initiative for convening the Council had been taken by Australia and India. Australia, a member of the Council, submitted a proposal which *inter alia* would have determined that the hostilities constituted a breach of the peace under Chapter VII of the UN Charter. The United States wanted to tone down the Australian draft so as to avoid any reference to Chapter VII, whereas the Soviet Union would have liked to strengthen the Australian text by adding a call for the withdrawal of forces to the positions held before the fighting had begun. France, sympathetic to the Netherlands, thought that the resolution should state that the Council had taken no decision on its own competence in the matter. The Council accepted the US amendment, rejected those of the Soviet Union and France, and then adopted the remaining paragraphs. The three West European members (Belgium, Britain, and France) abstained on all parts, and the Soviet Union (but not Poland) abstained also on the part

[43] Paul Mohn, 'Problems of Truce Supervision', p. 53; *Cessez-le-feu*, pp. 34, 41 (Bastid), p. 152 (French Report). See also the report of the Interim Committee in GAOR, 4th session, Supplement no. 11, A/966, p. 25, paras. 141-3; Leland M. Goodrich and Anne P. Simons, *The United Nations and the Maintenance of International Peace and Security*, Brookings Institution, Washington, DC, 1955, p. 377; and Montluc, pp. 2-5, 20-31, 185-6.

[44] SC res. 27 (S/459), 1 Aug. 1947.

expressing 'concern' about the outbreak of hostilities, as it favoured more vigorous language.[45]

The Netherlands, although not a member of the Security Council, had participated in its deliberations and was cognizant of its decision. The Indonesian Republic was not at that time represented in New York, and it was therefore necessary for Secretary-General Lie to cable the text of the resolution to the Indonesian authorities, a problem complicated by the fact that most of the leading Indonesian nationalists had been detained by the Netherlands authorities two weeks earlier. The UN Secretariat, with the best of intentions, transmitted the text of the resolution to the Indonesians via the Dutch authorities in Batavia (Djakarta). At 14.00 hours on 3 August, Dr A. K. Gani, Deputy Prime Minister and Minister of Economic Affairs in the Indonesian Republic, was released from detention, and later the same day a Dutch official sought to hand to Gani a copy of the Security Council's resolution. Gani refused to accept responsibility for transmitting the cable to the Indonesian leaders in Jogjakarta, so at 00.30 hours on 4 August, the Dutch authorities broadcast the text over the Batavia radio, and later dropped a copy by parachute over Jogjakarta airfield.[46]

In addition to the complication arising from delay in the receipt of the Security Council's resolution by one of the parties to the conflict, the Dutch and the Indonesians interpreted the resolution of the Security Council differently—indeed, it was in their interests to do so. The Netherlands had been pursuing spearhead tactics by advancing along the main lines of communication and seizing strategic points. When the Security Council called for a cessation of hostilities, the Netherlands drew imaginary lines on a map linking their forward positions and regarded these as the *de facto* lines separating the forces of the two sides. The Indonesians, by contrast, had been using guerrilla tactics and thus found many of their active units beleaguered behind the arbitrary Dutch lines.

Both parties acepted that the Security Council's call meant that firing had to stop, but the Netherlands took the view that

[45] SCOR, 2nd year, 173rd mtg (1 Aug. 1947), pp. 1700-10.
[46] Ibid., 174th mtg (4 Aug. 1947), pp. 1716-18, S/465; 178th mtg (7 Aug. 1947), pp. 1841-2, 1850-1, S/469; Special Supplement no. 4, S/586/Rev. 1, p. 72.

it also meant an end to all military operations, while the Indonesians thought that the only other requirement was to stand
fast. The very existence of the by-passed Indonesian forces was
regarded by the Netherlands as a breach of the call to cease
hostilities. The Security Council itself added to the linguistic
confusion by its own inconsistencies of language in later resolutions.[47]

The next attempt by the Security Council to end the fighting
was during the Palestine War of 1948, when the Council used
various terms in calling for the ending of military action: a
cessation of all acts of violence (1 April), a cessation of all
military or para-military activities 'as well as acts of violence,
terrorism and sabotage' (17 April), abstention from hostile
military action (22 May), cessation of all acts of armed force
(29 May), desisting from further military action (15 July). But
whatever the language used in the resolution, the Council almost
invariably referred to the subsequent periods when military
activity was supposedly suspended as 'truces'.[48] In the case of
the second Dutch 'police action' in Indonesia, the Security
Council called for the discontinuance of all military operations
and for the cessation of guerrilla warfare.[49] After 1948, the
Council usually used the expression 'cease fire' or 'cease hostilities' for its initial appeal, reserving the word 'truce' for the
next step, usually arranged by a subsidiary organ.

When the Security Council calls for the fighting to stop, there
is usually a proposal that the Council should also call for the
withdrawal of forces to positions occupied before the outbreak
of fighting, even if the territory thus vacated is not to be reoccupied by the other side: Indonesia in 1947[50] and 1948-9,[51]
Kashmir,[52] Jerusalem,[53] the Negev,[54] and Korea.[55]. A number

---

[47] Ibid., pp. 6-8, 71-2, 90-1, 130-3; 211th mtg (14 Oct. 1947), p. 2570, paras. 2-3
of S/581.

[48] SC res. 43 (S/714, I), 1 April 1948; res. 46 (S/723), 17 April 1948; res. 49 (S/773),
22 May 1948; res. 50 (S/801), 29 May 1948; res. 54 (S/902), 15 July 1948.

[49] SC res. 67 (S/1234), 28 Jan. 1949.

[50] SC res. 30 (S/525, I), 25 Aug. 1947; SC res. 36 (S/597), 1 Nov. 1947.

[51] SC res. 65 (S/1165), 28 Dec. 1948.

[52] SC res. 48 (S/726), 21 April 1948.

[53] SC res. 54 (S/902), 15 July 1948.

[54] SCOR, 3rd year, 367th mtg (19 Oct. 1948), pp. 37-9, S/1044; SC res. 61 (S/1070),
4 Nov. 1948; SC res. 62 (S/1080), 16 Nov. 1948.

[55] SC res. 82 (S/1501), 25 June 1950.

of proposals to call for a withdrawal of forces after the two 'police actions' in Indonesia were defeated (1947[56] and 1948-9[57]). Proposals for withdrawal in the Sinai-Suez case were twice frustrated by the veto;[58] the question was then transferred from the Security Council to the General Assembly; and after repeated calls for withdrawal,[59] the invaders complied, the only instance of total withdrawal after a cease-fire in the cases studied.

A number of writers have commented on the confusion about terminology, and when the International Society for Military Law and Law of War met in the Hague in 1973, almost every participant, including Professor Suzanne Bastid (the general rapporteur), the national reports from Belgium, Britain, France, and the United States, and Colonel G. I. A. D. Draper commented on the semantic problem. Major Fred K. Green, author of the US national report, thought that the term 'cease-fire' 'may eventually supplant the term armistice...'[60] Other scholars and practitioners have caused confusion by using the various terms loosely or inconsistently. The US Army field manual starts its definition of armistice with the words: 'An armistice (or truce as it is sometimes called)...'. The author of the official US history of the armistice negotiations in Korea writes that, for literary reasons, 'the terms "armistice", "truce", and "cease-fire" have been used interchangeably', a

[56] SCOR, 2nd year, 172nd mtg (1 Aug. 1947), p. 1665; 173rd mtg (1 Aug. 1947), pp. 1703-10.
[57] SCOR, 3rd year, 392nd mtg (24 Dec. 1948), pp. 40-1, 52, 55-6; 393rd mtg (27 Dec. 1948), pp. 6, 35; 4th year, Supplement for January 1949, p. 66, S/1233; 406th mtg (28 Jan. 1949), p. 24.
[58] Text in Bailey, *Voting in the Security Council*, pp. 181-2.
[59] GA res. 997 (ES-I), 2 Nov. 1956; GA res. 999 (ES-I), 4 Nov. 1956; GA res. 1002 (ES-I), 7 Nov. 1956; GA res. 1120 (XI), 24 Nov. 1956; GA res. 1123 (XI), 19 Jan. 1957; GA res. 1124 (XI), 2 Feb. 1957; GA res. 1125 (XI), 2 Feb. 1957.
[60] Mohn, p. 52; Baxter, p. 358; Montluc, pp. 1, 20-22, 33-44; Vladimir Dedijer, *On Military Conventions: An Essay on the Evolution of International Law*, p. 123; Shabtai Rosenne, *Israel's Armistice Agreements with the Arab States: A Judicial Interpretation*, pp. 24-5; *Cessez-le-feu*, pp. 31 (Bastid), 143 (Belgian Report), 198-200 (US Report), 253 (French Report), 356 (Monsen), 365 (British Report), 375 (Draper); Stone p. 645; Leland M. Goodrich and Anne P. Simons, *The United Nations and the Maintenance of International Peace and Security*, Washington, DC, Brookings Institution, 1955, p. 337; Morris Greenspan, *The Modern Law of Land Warfare*, p. 386; D. W. Bowett and others, *United Nations Forces: a Legal Study of United Nations Practice*, London, Stevens (under the auspices of the David Davies Memorial Institute), 1964, pp. 73-4.

practice also followed by General Mark Clark.[61] Professor Howard Levie, in an influential article in a distinguished legal journal, used the three terms as though they were synonomous.[62]

There has been a tendency to blame the UN Security Council for the semantic muddle. This was for a time justified, but only during a short period in 1948-9 regarding Palestine. On all other occasions, the Security Council and its subsidiary organs have used a consistent terminology.

The Security Council has seen its task as to call for a halt to the fighting, leading the parties to issue cease-fire orders to their forces. A cease-fire is simply a suspension of acts of violence by military and para-military forces, usually resulting from the intervention of a third party. It is a preliminary and provisional step, providing a breathing space so that a subsidiary organ of the Council can negotiate with the parties a truce of a more detailed and durable kind.[63]

There were three instances in the cases studied of the possible or actual transition from cease-fire to truce:

1. Indonesia, 1948;[64]
2. Kashmir, proposed on several occasions in 1948-9 but never confirmed by the parties;
3. Indonesia, 1949.[65]

In the Kashmir case, the UN Commission for India and Pakistan (UNCIP) adopted a resolution on 13 August 1948 which dealt with both a cease-fire and a truce; in January 1949 the two commanders-in-chief agreed on the terms of a truce but this agreement was never ratified; and the following April UNCIP submitted to the parties two different proposals for a truce, although these were not accepted.[66] In the other cases

[61] *Law of Land Warfare*, Washington, DC, Government Printing Office, 1956 (FM 27-10), para. 479; Walter G. Hermes, *United States Army in the Korean War*, vol. 2, *Truce Tent and Fighting Front*, p. 13, n. 1; Mark W. Clark, *From the Danube to the Yalu*, New York, Harper, 1954.

[62] Howard Levie, 'The Nature and Scope of the Armistice Agreement', pp. 880-906.

[63] Rosenne, p. 25; Mohn, p. 57; Baxter, p. 359; *Cessez-le-feu*, pp. 35 and 36 (Bastid), 152 (Belgian Report), 257 (French Report), 355 (Norwegian Report).

[64] SCOR, 3rd year, Special Supplement no. 1, S/649/Rev. 1, pp. 68-9, 72-5, 77, Appendices IX, XI, and XIV.

[65] Ibid., 4th year, Special Supplement no. 5, S/1373 and Corr. 1, pp. 58-71.

[66] Ibid., 3rd year, Supplement for November 1948, pp. 32-4, para. 75 of S/1100; 4th year, Special Supplement no. 7, pp. 102-5, 111-3, Annexes 17 and 21 of S/1430.

studied there were two instances of only a cease-fire (cases 6 and 7, Suez-Sinai and Cyprus), one instance of an armistice without a prior cease-fire (case 5, Korea), and one instance of a direct transition from numerous general or local cease-fires to armistices (case 3, Palestine).

On the basis of the three instances of transition from cease-fire to truce, I infer that the main elements of a cease-fire were as follows:

1. issuance by the parties of cease-fire orders to all military and para-military forces under their control;
2. parties free to adjust their defensive positions behind the cease-fire lines, but augmentation of military forces or the introduction of additional military potential not permitted;
3. parties to confer regarding local changes in the disposition of military forces with a view to avoiding incidents and facilitating the cease-fire;
4. demarcation of *de facto* lines separating the forces of the two sides, and possibly also demilitarized buffer zones;
5. military observers to be deployed in order to supervise the observance of the cease-fire, deal with local incidents, and report verified violations to the Security Council or a subsidiary organ.

The next stage in the three cases was a truce, which included the following elements:

1. progressive reduction of regular and irregular forces, withdrawal of forces from demilitarized zones, and evacuation of any by-passed military units;
2. arrangements for the civil administration of areas from which military forces would withdraw and provision of civil police to maintain law and order in the demilitarized zones, including temporary use of military personnel under civilian control;
3. restoration of normal transportation, communications, and trade, including free movement for refugees and other non-military personnel;
4. repatriation of prisoners of war and any abducted persons or hostages, and release of political prisoners;
5. measures for guaranteeing human rights and free political activity, prohibition of intimidation and reprisals.

The main elements of an armistice can be found in the four armistice agreements between Israel and its Arab neighbours (1949) and the armistice agreement between the Unified Command in Korea, as one party, and North Korea and China, as the other (1953).

The truces in Indonesia in 1948 and 1949, and the proposed truces in Kashmir in 1948 and 1949, had arisen from initiatives of subsidiary organs of the Security Council (the Good Offices Committee and the Commission for Indonesia in the Indonesian cases, and the UN Commission for India and Pakistan in Kashmir), whereas the five armistice agreements resulted from direct negotiations between the parties. A third party may assist the two sides to agree on the terms of an armistice, as did Ralph Bunche and his colleagues in the Middle East in 1949; negotiations may continue over months or, as in the Korean case, years before agreement is reached. But the main distinguishing mark of an armistice is that it is an agreement negotiated directly between the belligerents: an armistice has never been imposed by the Security Council. An armistice 'defines a situation which the various parties brought about by their own agreement' (Rosenne); 'a consensual contract reached by mutual agreement' (Dedijer). In the absence of agreement to the contrary, an armistice is of unlimited duration.[67]

Armistice agreements concern only military matters. It was widely assumed in the Middle East in 1949 (though possibly not by all the Arabs), and it was expressly laid down in the Korean armistice in 1953, that political negotiations were to follow, and all five armistice agreements were declared to be dictated solely by military considerations.[68] Responsibility for the negotiation of a long-term settlement in the Middle East had been laid on the Palestine Conciliation Commission, one of the functions of which was to promote 'a peaceful adjustment of the future situation of Palestine'.[69] In the Korean case, negotiations on substantive issues were to be at 'a political conference of a higher level'.[70]

[67] Rosenne, pp. 25, 28, 30, 82; Dedijer, p. 67; Levie, pp. 881, 892.

[68] Article IV of the Egypt-Israel armistice agreement and Article II of the Israel-Jordan, Israel-Lebanon, and Israel-Syria armistice agreements; preamble to the Korean armistice agreement.

[69] GA res. 194 (III), 11 Dec. 1948.

[70] Para. 60 of the Korean armistice.

All five armistice agreements provided for the creation of armistice commissions, composed of an equal number of representatives of the two sides, to supervise the implementation of the agreements and to settle complaints of violations.[71]

Several writers, with the Middle East armistices primarily in mind, see an armistice as implying a positive commitment to, or formal acceptance of, an eventual peaceful settlement (Mohn), a step towards the termination of war (Stone), a preliminary step to a peace treaty (Dedijer), a milestone on the way to a peace treaty (Bastid);[72] but there is no dissent from the conclusion that an armistice is not peace and does not end the legal state of war.[73]

The practice of the Security Council has thus coincided with the advice of the so-called Little Assembly (Interim Committee) in July 1949: that the Security Council issues the first appeal or, acting under Chapter VII, can make an order for the cessation of fighting; that subsidiary organs of the Security Council initiate truce arrangements; and that the parties themselves negotiate the armistice.[74] This was the tenor of Ralph Bunche's report to the Security Council in 1949 regarding the four Middle Eastern armistice agreements. These agreements, he wrote, had made the earlier cease-fires 'obsolete' and their restrictive conditions 'unnecessary', but it was open to the Security Council to reinforce the armistices by again calling for the observance of a cease-fire. Bunche submitted a draft resolution, but, on the initiative of France and Canada, his reference to the binding cease-fire of 15 July 1948 as being no longer necessary was changed so that the resolution passed by the Security Council stated that the armistice agreements superseded both the recommended cease-fire of 29 May and the binding cease-

---

[71] Article X of the Egypt-Israel armistice agreement, Article XI of the Israel-Jordan armistice agreement, and Article VIII of the Israel-Lebanon and Israel-Syria armistice agreements; paras. 19-35 of the Korean armistice agreement.

[72] Mohn, pp. 53, 58; Stone, p. 636; Dedijer, p. 130; *Cessez-le-feu*, p. 33.

[73] Phillipson, p. 64; Rosenne, p. 83; Baxter, pp. 359, 372; Montluc, p. 227 n. 1; Alfons Klafkowski, 'Les Formes de cessation de l'état de guerre en droit international', pp. 226-7, 265; L. Oppenheim, *International Law: A Treatise*, 7th edn, ed. H. Lanterpacht, London and New York, 1952, vol. II, pp. 547, 597; Lord McNair and A. D. Watts, *The Legal Effects of War*, Cambridge, University Press, 1966, pp. 13-14; Stone, pp. 638, 643; Levie, p. 884; Dedijer, p. 69; Greenspan, p. 586; *Cessez-le-feu*, pp. 33 (Bastid), 355 (Norwegian Report), 379 (Draper).

[74] GAOR, 4th session, Supplement no. 11, A/966, p. 25, paras. 141-62.

fire of 15 July. Although the armistice agreements included firm pledges against further acts of hostility, the Security Council again affirmed its order, first issued on 15 July, that the parties should observe an unconditional cease-fire.[75]

1.6 RETALIATION AND REPRISALS

The fact that a state is the victim of aggression does not relieve it from the obligation to respect the rules of international law applicable in armed conflict. On the other hand, it would be unreasonable if a belligerent were to be put at a disadvantage because the enemy breaks the law. What, then, are the remedies open to a party against whom illegal acts of warfare have been committed? The British *Manual of Military Law* lists the following means that a party to armed conflict may use to induce the other side to comply with international law:[76]
—complaints lodged with the enemy;
—complaints lodged with neutral states;
—good offices, mediation, and intervention of neutral states;
—compensation;
—punishment of war crimes;
—hostages;
—reprisals.
The difficulty about these remedies is that, on the face of it, all are likely to prove futile or flagitious.

The definition of reprisals in the US army field manual is very clear:

Reprisals are acts of retaliation in the form of conduct which would otherwise be unlawful, resorted to by one belligerent ... for acts of warfare committed by the other belligerent in violation of the law of war, for the purpose of enforcing future compliance with the recognized rules of civilized warfare.[77]

It is a moral paradox of reprisals that illegality is used to stop illegality.

[75] SCOR, 4th year, Supplement for August 1949, p. 6, S/1357; 434th mtg (4 Aug. 1949), p. 35, S/1364; 435th mtg (8 Aug. 1949), pp. 2-3, 5-9, S/1367; SC res. 73 (S/1376, II), 11 Aug. 1949.

[76] *Manual of Military Law*, part III, *The Law of War on Land*, para. 620.

[77] *The Law of Land Warfare*, Washington, DC, US Government Printing Office, 1956 (FM 27-10), para. 497.

The US definition makes clear three essential elements of a reprisal:

—that the opposing party has previously violated the laws and customs of war;

—that a reprisal is an act that in the normal way would itself be a violation;

—that the sole purpose is to prevent further violations by the other party.

Thus, a reprisal is concerned with violations in three tenses: a *past* violation by one party, leading to a *present* violation by the adverse party, in order to prevent a *future* violation by the first party.

Traditionally, reprisals have been subject to certain re-straints. A party alleging that there has been a violation of international law should first propose an impartial inquiry into the facts before resorting to reprisals; the scale of reprisals should be proportionate to the alleged violation and should, to the extent possible, be carried out in the same field as the violation; and if reprisals are unavoidable, they should not contravene the laws of humanity.[78]

It is prohibited to take reprisal action against fighters who are *hors de combat* and thus protected by the Geneva Conventions and Additional Protocol I, as well as against civilians, civilian objects, cultural and religious property, food and other objects indispensable to civilian survival, dangerous installations, and the natural evironment,[79] so that it is probably now the case that the only legitimate form of belligerent reprisal is the use against enemy combatants or military targets of unlawful weapons or means of warfare (e.g. dum-dum bullets, un-anchored contact mines, chemical weapons, biological weapons,

[78] An excellent study of reprisals is in Frits Kalshoven, *Belligerent Reprisals*; see esp. pp. 32-3, 42-3, 340-1, 374. See also Stone, pp. 289-90, 354-5, 366; J. H. W. Verzijl, *International Law in Historical Perspective*, part IX-A, *The Laws of War*, Leiden, Sijthoff and Noordhoff, 1978, pp. 22, 46-8; Greenspan, pp. 408-13; L. Oppenheim, *International Law: A Treatise*, 7th edn, ed. H. Lanterpacht, London and New York, Longmans, 1952, vol. II, pp. 561-5. Richard Falk has proposed twelve limits on the exercise of reprisal action in time of peace. 'The Beirut Raid and the International Law of Retaliation', *AJIL*, vol. 63, no. 3 (July 1969), pp. 415-43.

[79] Geneva Conventions 1949, Articles 46/47/13/33; Hague Convention on the pro-tection of cultural property, 1954 (UNTS, vol. 249, no. 3511), Article 4(4); Additional Protocol I, A/32/144, 15 Aug. 1977, Annex I, Articles 20, 51(6), 52(1), 53(c), 54(4), 55(2), 56(4). See also GA res. 2625(XXV), 24 Oct. 1970, 1st principle, 6th para., and 2675(XXV), 9 Dec. 1970, para. 7.

weapons causing unnecessary suffering).[80] Some would go even further and argue that all reprisals are, as a resolution of the Security Council has put it, 'incompatible with the purposes and principles of the United Nations'.[81] Although the Security Council regards all reprisals as illegal, it does not condemn every resort to reprisal action, for the Council takes account of the extent of provocation and whether the reprisal was proportionate to the original illegality.[82] On the other hand, Secretary-General Dag Hammarskjold pointed out in the Middle East context that even 'acts of retaliation' (which are not necessarily illegal) have been repeatedly condemned by the Security Council.[83]

Leaving aside the often conflicting demands of law and military necessity, it has to be said that some of the most heinous atrocities of all time have been committed in the guise of reprisals.[84] It would be a moral advance if states were to renounce the right of reprisal.

> In the end [writes Frits Kalshoven] a total abolition of belligerent reprisals is the only tenable proposition ... the balance of merits and demerits of belligerent reprisals has now become so entirely negative as no longer to allow of their being regarded as even moderately effective sanctions of the laws of war ... [T]hey have become a complete anachronism.[85]

While abolition must be the goal, this is probably Utopian in the absence of impartial judicial institutions before which individual persons accused of international crimes may be arraigned.

---

[80] Rosenblad, p. 148.

[81] Quincy Wright, 'Legal Aspects of the Viet-Nam Situation', *AJIL*, vol. 60, no. 4 (Oct. 1966), pp. 142-3; SC res. 188 (S/5650), 9 April 1964.

[82] Derek Bowett, 'Reprisals Involving Recourse to Armed Force', *AJIL*, vol. 66, no. 1 (January 1972), pp. 8-14; Robert W. Tucker, 'Reprisals and Self-defense: The Customary Law', *AJIL*, vol. 66, no. 3 (July 1972), p. 595; Nicholas Greenwood Onuf, *Reprisals: Rituals, Rules, Rationales*, Princeton, Center of International Studies, 1974 (Research Monograph no. 42) (litho.), p. 35; Rosalyn Higgins, *The Development of International Law through the Political Organs of the United Nations*, pp. 180-1, 224.

[83] SCOR, 11th year, Supplement for April-June 1956, p. 41, para. 46 of S/3596.

[84] G. I. A. D. Draper, 'Implementation of International Law in Armed Conflicts', *International Affairs*, vol. 48, no. 1 (January, 1972), p. 49.

[85] Kalshoven, pp. 375, 377.

1.7 INQUIRY AND INVESTIGATION

Knowledge of the essential facts is a prerequisite of wise diplomacy, so that the expression 'fact-finding' has been used increasingly in UN circles, especially since 1963, to describe the
process by which objective information is acquired. The Charter, however, envisages the elucidation of the facts as taking
place at two different stages in the development of a situation
or dispute. One of the means of peaceful settlement to which
the parties to a dispute are supposed to resort 'first of all' is
inquiry, which is almost always a bilateral process involving
only the parties.[86] If the parties to a situation or dispute are
unable to resolve the matter at issue, the question may be taken
to the Security Council, which may investigate the matter in
order to determine whether its continuance is likely to endanger
world peace.[87] The Charter does not preclude the Security
Council from conducting investigations in other circumstances
if the Council considers that it needs more information. The
Charter does not specify how an investigation shall be conducted, and the methods used have included the direct hearing of governments, authorities, or individuals (Indonesia,
Hyderabad, Palestine, Korea, Cyprus); establishment of subsidiary organs to investigate (Indonesia, Kashmir, Palestine,
Korea, Cyprus); and requests to the Secretary-General (Palestine, Cyprus).

To avoid confusion, I have avoided the expression 'fact-
finding' wherever possible and have used 'inquiry' for one of the
processes by which the parties seek to resolve their differences
and 'investigation' for the various means used by the Security
Council to inform itself about past or contemporary events.

1.8 PROCEDURE AND SUBSTANCE

The Charter lays down different voting requirements for
'procedural' and 'all other' matters in the Security Council:
in the General Assembly, the distinction is between 'important'
and 'other' questions.[88] The drafters of the Charter seem to

---

[86] Article 33 of the Charter.
[87] Article 34.
[88] Article 27(2) and (3), and 18(2).

have been greatly enamoured of negative concepts (non-governmental organizations, non-permanent members of the Security Council, non-self-governing territories, non-intervention in essentially domestic affairs), but as this negative style is tedious in a book, I have usually used 'substantive' rather than 'non-procedural' for the 'other' matters that may come before the Security Council.

1.9 VETO AND DOUBLE-VETO

Each of the five permanent members of the Security Council (Britain, China, France, Soviet Union, United States) has the right to vote negatively on a substantive proposal in the Security Council and thus to prevent its adoption:[89] the Soviet Union designates this the 'unanimity rule', but others usually call it the 'veto'. There may, of course, be differences of view as to whether a particular proposal is procedural or substantive. If a motion that a proposal is procedural rather than substantive is submitted and put to the vote (as was contemplated at San Francisco),[90] and if one of the permanent members votes negatively on this preliminary question so that the motion is defeated, this has the effect of making the main proposal substantive and thus subject to veto. A successful negative vote on the preliminary question of whether a proposal is procedural or not, followed by a negative vote on the main question, is called the 'double-veto'.

If a proposal fails to secure enough votes for adoption because permanent members have abstained or not participated in the voting rather than voting against it, that is sometimes called the 'hidden veto'.

Although there have been a number of cases where the double-veto has been used, there was no successful use of the double-veto in the cases studied.

---

[89] Article 27(3).
[90] Documents of the UN Conference on International Organization, 1945, vol. XI, pp. 710-14; the text is given in full in Bailey, *Voting in the Security Council*, pp. 105-8.

1.10 OBLIGATORY AND VOLUNTARY ABSTENTIONS[91]

If a party to a dispute is a member of the Security Council and a substantive proposal relating to the peaceful settlement of that dispute is submitted to the Council, the party to the dispute 'shall abstain from voting'.[92] That, in UN jargon, is an 'obligatory abstention'.

The Charter states that decisions of the Security Council on non-procedural matters shall be made by 'an affirmative vote of seven [nine] members including the concurring votes of the permanent members...'[93] The word 'concurring' in this context might seem to be ambiguous. If the founding conference at San Francisco had intended that substantive decisions should require the *affirmative* votes of all of the permanent members, why did the Charter not say so? Does 'concurring' mean something different from 'affirmative'? May it have been the intention that an abstention by a permanent member should be regarded as a form of concurrence?

The matter arose at the San Francisco conference, and the Big Five gave the impression that they did not intend that abstentions should be regarded as concurrence: non-procedural decisions, they stated, would require 'the unanimity of the [five] permanent members plus the concurring votes of at least two of the non-permanent members'.[94] This answer, though apparently clear, did not cover a situation in which one of the permanent members is a party to a dispute and is therefore *obliged* to abstain. Under pressure from some of the medium powers, the Big Five held a closed meeting to review the question of abstentions and accepted the US view that a permanent member could abstain from voting only when it was a party to a dispute, in which event abstention was not voluntary but obligatory.[95] The conference was not told of this understanding among the Five, which in any case was soon to be eroded.

[91] See 'New Light on Abstentions in the UN Security Council', *International Affairs*, vol. 50, no. 4 (October 1974), pp. 554-73.

[92] Articles 27(3) and 52(3).

[93] Article 27(3).

[94] UN Conference on International Organization, vol. XI, pp. 707, 713.

[95] FRUS, 1945, vol. I, 1967, pp. 1258-60; Wellington Koo, Jr, *Voting Procedures in International Political Organizations*, New York, Columbia University Press, 1947, pp. 153-7.

In an attempt to clear up what was obviously an unsatisfactory situation, the United States had second thoughts and drafted a rule of procedure that would have had the effect of revising the San Francisco understanding. Under the proposed new rule, a permanent member would have been given the option of declaring whether its abstention was to be deemed a veto or a form of concurrence. The US text was shown to the other permanent members: while Britain, China, and France were not enthusiastic, they were not opposed to the US proposal, but the Soviet Union objected to having any express rule on the matter.[96]

Before the question could be resolved in general terms, a specific situation arose in the Security Council in which the Soviet Union wished to abstain but not to veto, and the other permanent members raised no objection.[97] During the course of 1947 and 1948, all of the other permanent members followed suit.[98] The practice since then has been that a permanent member of the Council not wishing to vote in favour of a substantive proposal but not wishing to cast a veto has abstained from voting or, in the case of China since 1971, has refrained from participating in the vote. Such an abstention is treated as if it were a form of concurrence and is known as a voluntary abstention. The International Court of Justice has stated that this procedure 'has been generally accepted by the Members' and is evidence of 'a general practice' of the United Nations.[99]

---

[96] FRUS, 1946, vol. I, 1972, pp. 258-9, 262-4, 266, 271-3, 332, 334.

[97] SCOR, 1st year, 1st series, 39th mtg (29 April 1946), p. 243.

[98] Britain abstained on SC res. 30 (Indonesia I), China on res. 51 (Kashmir), France on res. 63 (Indonesia II), and the United States on res. 66 (Palestine).

[99] ICJ Reports, 1971, p. 22.

CHAPTER 2

Preliminaries in the Security Council

2.1 THE PLACE OF THE SECURITY COUNCIL
IN THE UN SYSTEM

Although the Security Council has the primary responsibility for world peace and security, there is continuous interaction with other UN organs, particularly the Secretary-General and the General Assembly. Both the Secretary-General and the General Assembly may submit proposals to the Security Council, and the Security Council may confer responsibilities on the Secretary-General, the General Assembly, or the other UN Councils. In this section I am concerned with the primacy that the Charter ascribes to the Security Council; the relationship of the Security Council to other main UN organs, that is to say, the Secretary-General, the General Assembly, the other two UN Councils (Trusteeship, Economic and Social), and the International Court of Justice; and various subsidiary organs.

THE PRIMACY OF THE SECURITY COUNCIL

UN Members, in accepting the Charter, have conferred on the Security Council 'primary responsibility for the maintenance of international peace and security' and have agreed that in exercising this responsibility the Council 'acts on their behalf'.[1] In two of the cases studied questions have been raised as to whether the Council's primary responsibility was being properly respected. In the Palestine case, the Arabs argued that the General Assembly had exceeded its powers in approving the partition resolution.[2] This charge had interesting implications which seem not to have been publicly explored in UN proceedings at the time. If the partition resolution had been submitted

---

[1] Article 24(1).
[2] SCOR, 3rd year, 254th mtg (24 Feb. 1948), pp. 275-6, 281, 291; 255th mtg (25 Feb. 1948), pp. 296-9; 260th mtg (2 March 1948), pp. 395-6, 398.

to the Security Council as well as to the General Assembly in 1947, and if members of the Security Council had voted in the same way in the Security Council as they did in the General Assembly on 29 November, the resolution would have passed by seven votes in favour (Australia, Belgium, Brazil, France, Poland, Soviet Union, United States), one against (Syria), and three abstentions (Britain, China, Colombia). But if, on the other hand, the resolution had been submitted to the Security Council in 1948, at the time when the Arabs were complaining that the General Assembly had exceeded its powers, then the resolution would have failed by one vote to secure approval. Brazil's term as a non-permanent member of the Council had come to an end and Argentina had been elected to take Brazil's place; and Argentina had abstained on the partition resolution. Thus, throughout 1948, the Arabs acted in the knowledge that the Security Council was trying to implement a plan for Palestine that it might well have failed to approve, had the issue been submitted to it at that time. By then, however, members of the Council (other than Syria) were more interested in stopping the fighting than in re-opening the main political questions arising from the termination of the mandate.

The other case in which questions were raised about the responsibilities of the two policy-making organs concerned with peace and security was interesting for a different reason. When Britain and France cast their vetoes on cease-fire proposals in the Security Council after Israel's invasion of Sinai in 1956, the Soviet Union supported the proposal that the matter should be transferred to the General Assembly, in spite of its firm opposition to the Uniting for Peace procedure under which the Council was acting. When the matter was debated in the General Assembly, no constitutional difficulty arose for the Soviet bloc so long as the proposals for action were confined to condemnation of the guilty parties and demands for them to withdraw; but how were the Soviet Union and its friends to vote on proposals for a UN Emergency Force, which was acceptable to the Arabs but which the Soviet bloc believed could be established only as a result of a decision of the Security Council rather than the General Assembly? The Soviet bloc abstained from voting on the two crucial proposals for the establishment of the UN Force,[3] and their complaints about illegality were at this stage relatively muted.[4] Later, the Soviet Union became more vociferous in asserting that decisions about peace-keeping were within the exclusive competence of the Security Council.

SECURITY COUNCIL AND SECRETARY-GENERAL

The Secretary-General's powers in relation to the Security Council arise in part from his general responsibilities as 'chief administrative officer of the Organization'. Moreover, the Secretary-General is to perform such functions as are expressly entrusted to him by the main UN organs.[5] It was under these provisions that Secretary-General Lie, in response to a request from the UN Mediator in Palestine, transferred fifty guards from UN headquarters to help in supervising the cease-fire and arms embargo.[6]

But these provisions do not exhaust the responsibilities of the Secretary-General, for he also has the right to draw the attention of the Security Council to any matter which in his opinion may threaten international peace and security.[7] This is a significant power with wide implications permanently in reserve. The importance of the Article 99 procedure would diminish if it were used to excess, and it should in any case be stressed that not every reference of a matter to the Security Council by the Secretary-General is an application of Article 99. Trygve Lie made no reference to Article 99 when he transmitted to the Security Council a cable from the UN Commission on Korea on 25 June 1950, and his later claim to have invoked Article 99 on that occasion was almost certainly an after-thought.[8] Hammarskjold gave serious consideration to acting under Article 99 over Suez after the failure of the Menzies mission to Cairo in September 1956, and he would certainly have resorted to Article

[3] GAOR, 1st Emergency Special Session, 565th plenary mtg (5 Nov. 1956), para. 109; 566th mtg (7 Nov. 1956), para. 269.

[4] Ibid., paras. 292-3, 296; 11th session, 589th plenary mtg (22 Nov. 1956), para. 81; 646th plenary mtg (29 Jan. 1957), para. 65; 650th plenary mtg (2 Feb. 1957), para. 30.

[5] Articles 97 and 98.

[6] SCOR, 3rd year, 331st mtg (7 July 1948), p. 34.

[7] Article 99.

[8] SCOR, 5th year, 473rd mtg (25 June 1950), p. 2, S/1496; GAOR, 5th session, 289th plenary mtg (28 Sept. 1950), para. 40.

99 after the Israeli attack on 29 October had not the United States already asked for a meeting of the Council.[9]

Virtually every decision of the Security Council imposes some responsibilities on the Secretary-General, even if it is to do no more than transmit the text to those concerned. Of 199 resolutions in express terms adopted by the Council from 1946 to 1964, seven specifically asked the Secretary-General to undertake particular functions in connection with the cases studied. Two of these decisions related to routine tasks which he would have undertaken even if there had been no request: to convene the Committee of Good Offices on the Indonesian question[10] and to provide the UN Representative for India and Pakistan with the necessary services and facilities.[11] Three resolutions relating to Cyprus asked the Secretary-General to establish a UN force, appoint its commander, appoint also a mediator, and report to the Council on the implementation of the relevant resolutions.[12] But the two resolutions of the Security Council that entrusted almost open-ended responsibilities to the Secretary-General were adopted in 1956 in connection with the Middle East. Dag Hammarskjold was asked by these resolutions to survey 'various aspects of enforcement of and compliance with' the armistice agreements and specified resolutions of the Council, to arrange for measures that would reduce tension, and (at a later stage) to 'continue his good offices ... with a view to full implementation of [the earlier] resolution ... and full compliance with the Armistice Agreements'.[13] These resolutions were unprecedented because they defined aims to be achieved without specifying precisely how the Secretary-General was to pursue them. Hammarskjold increasingly welcomed challenges of this kind.

---

[9] Brian Urquhart, *Hammarskjold*, pp. 161-2; SCOR, 11th year, 751st mtg (31 Oct. 1956), paras. 1-2.

[10] SC res. 35(S/574), 3 Oct. 1947.

[11] SC res. 91(S/2017/Rev. 1), 30 March 1951.

[12] SC res. 186 (S/5575), 4 March 1964; res. 187 (S/5603), 13 March 1964; res. 194 (S/5987), 25 Sept. 1964.

[13] SC res. 113 (S/3575), 4 April 1956; 114 (S/3605), 4 June 1956.

SECURITY COUNCIL AND GENERAL ASSEMBLY

The General Assembly meets if the Security Council so re-quests.[14] There was only one application of this provision in the cases studied, in relation to Palestine in 1948, and this led to the General Assembly's decision to appoint a Mediator.[15]

Those who drafted the UN Charter intended that the Security Council and General Assembly should not deal with the same matter simultaneously, but the Security Council can facilitate the taking up of a matter by the General Assembly by removing an item from the list of matters of which it is seized, a course followed over the Korean question in 1951.[16] In connection with the Indonesian item, the Security Council agreed in 1973 to remove the question from the list of matters with which it was seized, although this was not to facilitate consideration of the matter by the General Assembly but as part of a general process of pruning unnecessary items.[17] Of the other cases studied, the Council remains seized of the India-Pakistan question, the Palestine question, the Suez complaints, and an item on Cyprus.[18]

The most controversial use of the Security Council's power to convoke the General Assembly has been that arising from the Uniting for Peace resolution, adopted by the General Assembly in 1950 in the face of Soviet opposition, which pro-vided for the convening of the General Assembly within twenty-four hours if, because of the veto, the Security Council should be unable to exercise its primary responsibility for world peace.[19] This was resorted to after the second Anglo-French veto at the time of Suez. Peru had hinted earlier that the Security Council might have to use the Uniting for Peace procedure, but it was Yugoslavia that sponsored the proposal in the Council. Britain and France objected (correctly) that the proposal was submitted under the wrong agenda item. They also maintained, first, that the Yugoslav proposal was out of order because the Council had not made a formal determination under Chapter VII of the

[14] Article 20 of the Charter.
[15] SC res. 44 (S/714, II), 1 April 1948; GA res. 186 (S-2), 14 May 1948.
[16] SC res. 90 (S/1995), 31 Jan. 1951.
[17] S/11185, 7 Jan. 1974 (mimeo), p. 1.
[18] S/11593, 7 Jan. 1975 (mimeo), p. 1; S/13737, 11 Jan. 1980 (mimeo).
[19] GA res. 377A(V), 3 Nov. 1950. See Brownlie, pp. 333-4, 345-6.

Charter; second, that the agenda item came within Chapter VI of the Charter rather than Chapter VII; and, third, that the matter to be transferred to the General Assembly was not specified in the Yugoslav proposal. But the Council was in no mood for legal niceties: a British motion that the Yugoslav draft resolution was not in order was defeated, and the Council then approved the Yugoslav proposal by a procedural vote, Britain and France voting against, and Australia and Belgium abstaining.[20]

SECURITY COUNCIL AND THE OTHER TWO UN COUNCILS

There is not normally much direct interaction between the Security Council and the other two UN Councils (Trusteeship, Economic and Social). In the Palestine case, the General Assembly asked the Trusteeship Council to prepare a statute for Jerusalem, but these efforts were of no avail.[21] The general work of the Economic and Social Council (ECOSOC) often impinged on the cases studied regarding humanitarian questions (human rights, refugees and displaced persons, UN aid programmes). The Security Council directed that the record of its discussion of Palestine refugees and Jewish displaced persons should be transmitted to ECOSOC,[22] and after the outbreak of the Korean War the Security Council asked ECOSOC and other UN agencies 'to provide such assistance as the Unified Command may request for the relief and support of the civilian population of Korea...'[23]

SECURITY COUNCIL AND THE INTERNATIONAL COURT OF JUSTICE

Although the International Court of Justice is the principal judicial organ of the United Nations, it played a minimal role in connection with the cases studied. Arising from the assassination of Count Bernadotte in Jerusalem, the General Assembly

---

[20] SCOR, 11th year, 749th mtg (30 Oct. 1956), para. 118; 751st mtg (31 Oct. 1956), paras. 71, 82-6, 88-92, 94, 96-7, 106-7, 125-7, 144, 149-51; SC res. 119 (S/3721), 31 Oct. 1956.

[21] GA res. 181 (II), 29 Nov. 1947; res. 185 (S-2), 26 April 1948; res. 303 (IV), 9 Dec. 1949.

[22] GAOR, 3rd session, 354th mtg (19 Aug. 1948), pp. 55-6.

[23] SC res. 85 (S/1657), 31 July 1950.

obtained from the Court an advisory opinion to the effect that the United Nations had the capacity to bring an international claim with a view to obtaining reparation for injury suffered in the performance of UN duties. As a result, the General Assembly authorized Trygve Lie to present a claim against Israel.[24]

The Court was also involved with the question of paying for the UN peace-keeping operation in Sinai. Secretary-General Hammarskjold at first suggested that those expenses of the UN Emergency Force (UNEF) not borne by contributing states should be allocated on the basis of the regular scale of assessments. When this ran into the opposition of the Soviet bloc, which held that the aggressors should meet the full cost of peace-keeping, Hammarskjold maintained his position of principle but recommended the establishment of a separate account for UNEF.[25] With the passage of time, the accumulated arrears of the states of the Soviet bloc mounted to such an extent that they were in danger of forfeiting their votes in the General Assembly, and the general financial position of the United Nations became extremely precarious. In 1961, the General Assembly asked the International Court of Justice to give an advisory opinion as to whether the expenses of UN peace-keeping constitute 'expenses of the Organization' within the meaning of Article 17 of the UN Charter. The Court advised, by nine votes to five, that peace-keeping expenses in the Middle East (and the Congo) were 'expenses of the Organization', and the General Assembly accepted the advisory opinion.[26] This did not settle the matter, however, for the defaulters continued their refusal to pay. By 1964 seven UN Members from Eastern Europe were two years in arrears, and the nineteenth session of the General Assembly, in order to avoid a crisis that might have culminated in withdrawals from UN Membership, operated without voting. As Soviet opposition to allowing the General Assembly to decide

---

[24] GA res. 258 (III), 3 Dec. 1948; ICJ Reports 1949, pp. 174-88; GA res. 365 (IV), 1 Dec. 1949; Trygve Lie, *In the Cause of Peace*, pp. 193-4.

[25] GAOR, 11th session, Annexes, Agenda item 66, p. 14, para. 6(a) of A/3383; 596th plenary mtg (27 Nov. 1956), para. 227; Fifth Committee, 538th mtg (27 Nov. 1956), paras. 40-5; 541st mtg (3 Dec. 1956), paras. 78-9; GA res. 1122 (XI), 26 Nov. 1956; res. 1089 (XI), 21 Dec. 1956.

[26] GA res. 1731 (XVI), 20 Dec. 1961; ICJ Reports 1962, pp. 151-80; GA res. 1854 (XVII), 19 Dec. 1962.

who should pay for UN peace-keeping was stronger than the US determination to apply the full rigours of Article 19 of the Charter against the seven defaulters (and subsequently to France and others who were later to clock up two years of arrears), the matter was resolved in a rather unsatisfactory way by means of UN borrowing and voluntary governmental contributions.

SUBSIDIARY ORGANS

Organs established in connection with the cases studied are listed in Table 1. All except three (nos. 7, 12, 21) were subsidiary organs of the Security Council itself or of the General Assembly. In examining the composition of these organs, one is at once struck by the dominant role of the United States up to the middle of 1950. Of the first twenty-one organs listed in the table, the United States was a member of nine (nos. 1, 2, 3, 4, 5, 11, 17, 18, 20); three were persons of US nationality (nos. 7, 8b, 12); three more were agencies in which US nationals were employed (nos. 6, 14, 19); and the Unified Command in Korea (no. 21) was under a US commander. Ralph J. Bunche (no. 15) was a member of the UN Secretariat of US nationality. The only cases up to the autumn of 1950 in which the United States was not involved were the UN Mediator for Palestine (no. 13), one of the UN intermediaries on Kashmir (no. 8a), and two bodies concerned with Palestine (nos. 10 and 16).

The corollary of this was the minimal role of the Soviet bloc in the early years. The Soviet Union was a member of a Committee to advise the Acting Mediator in Palestine (no. 17), since it included all the permanent members of the Security Council. The Ukrainian SSR was a member of a drafting subcommittee on Palestine (no. 16). Czechoslovakia was a member of the Commission for India and Pakistan (no. 5) and the Palestine Commission (no. 10), and it was while these bodies were at work that the Communists took over in Prague. The Soviet Union objected to the composition of the two consular commissions for Indonesia and Palestine (nos. 1 and 11) on the ground that this was a deliberate device to exclude Eastern Europe, which was true. The Soviet Union wanted what became the Consular Commission in Indonesia to consist of

Table 1

UN organs in connection with cases studied

No.	Case	Organ	Doc. ref.	Composition
1	Indonesia	Consular Commission	SC res. 30 (S/525, I), 25 Aug. 1947	Australia, Belgium, China, France, United Kingdom, United States
2		Good Offices Committee (GOC)	SC res. 31 (S/525, II), 25 Aug. 1947	Australia, Belgium, United States
3		Sub-committee to prepare a draft resolution	SCOR, 2nd year, 217th mtg (31 Oct. 1947), pp. 2716-17	Australia, Belgium, China, United States
4		Commission for Indonesia	SC res. 67 (S/1234), 28 Jan. 1949	Australia, Belgium, United States
5	Kashmir	Commission for India and Pakistan (UNCIP)	SC res. 39 (S/654), 20 Jan. 1948; SC res. 47 (S/726), 21 April 1948	Argentina, Belgium, Colombia, Czechoslovakia, United States
6		Military Observer Group for India and Pakistan (UNMOGIP)	SC res. 47 (S/726), 21 April 1948	Observers recruited by Chief Military Observer
7		Plebiscite Administrator	Nominated by Secretary-General after specified consultations: see GAOR, 4th session, Supplement no. 1, A/930, p. 24	Admiral Chester W. Nimitz
8		Representative for India and Pakistan	SC res. 80 (S/1469), 14 March 1950; SC res. 91 (S/2017/Rev. 1), 30 March 1951	(a) Sir Owen Dixon, 1950-1; (b) Frank Graham, 1951-
9		President of the Security Council	SC res. 123 (S/3793), 21 Feb. 1957	Gunnar Jarring, Sweden

Table 1 (contd)

No.	Case	Organ	Doc. ref.	Composition
10	Palestine	Palestine Commission	GA res. 181 (II), 29 Nov. 1947	Bolivia, Czechoslovakia, Denmark, Panama, Philippines
11		Consular Truce Commission/Palestine Truce Commission	SC res. 48 (S/727), 23 April 1948	Belgium, France, United States
12		Special Municipal Commissioner for Jerusalem	Appointed by the Mandatory Power in accordance with GA res. 187 (S-2), 6 May 1948	Harold Evans
13		Mediator	GA res. 186 (S-2), 14 May 1948	Count Folke Bernadotte
14		Truce Supervision Organization (UNTSO)	SC res. 50 (S/801), 29 May 1948	Observers initially recruited by Mediator, later by UNTSO Chief of Staff
15		Acting Mediator	SCOR, 3rd year, 358th mtg (18 Sept. 1948), p. 2	Ralph J. Bunche
16		Sub-committee to prepare draft resolution	SC res. 60 (S/1062), 29 Oct. 1948	Belgium, China, France, Ukrainian SSR, United Kingdom
17		Committee to advise Acting Mediator	SC res. 61 (S/1070), 4 Nov. 1948	Belgium (1948), China, Colombia (1948), Cuba (1949), France, Norway (1949), Soviet Union, United Kingdom, United States
18		Palestine Conciliation Commission (PCC)	GA res. 194 (III), 11 Dec. 1948	France, Turkey, United States
19		UN Relief and Works Agency for Palestine Refugees in the Near	GA res. 302 (IV), 8 Dec. 1949; GA res.	—

Table 1 (contd)

No.	Case	Organ	Doc. ref.	Composition
		East (UNRWA)	818 (IX), 4 Dec. 1954; GA res. 1456 (XIV), 9 Dec. 1959; GA res. 1856 (XVII), 20 Dec. 1962	
20		UNRWA Advisory Committee	GA res. 302 (IV), 8 Dec. 1949	France, Turkey, United Kingdom, United States
21	Korea	Unified Command	SC res. 84 (S/1588), 7 July 1950	Commander designated by the United States
22		Commission on the Unification and Rehabilitation of Korea (UNCURK)	GA res. 376 (V), 7 Oct. 1950	Australia, Chile, Netherlands, Pakistan, Philippines, Thailand, Turkey
23		Interim Committee on Korea	GA res. 376 (V), 7 Oct. 1950	As UNCURK (see no. 22)
24		Korean Reconstruction Agency (UNKRA)	GA res. 410 (V), 1 Dec. 1950; GA res. 1020 (XI), 7 Dec. 1957; GA res. 1159 (XII), 26 Nov. 1958; GA res. 1304 (XIII), 10 Dec. 1958	—
25		Advisory Committee on UNKRA	GA res. 410 (V), 1 Dec. 1950	Canada, India, United Kingdom, United States, Uruguay
26		Group on a cease-fire	GA res. 384 (V), 14 Dec. 1950	Nasrollah Entezam (Iran), Lester Pearson (Canada), Sir Benegal Rau (India)
27		Good Offices Committee	GA res. 498 (V), 1 Feb. 1951	Nasrollah Entezam (Iran), Sven Grafström (Sweden), Luis Padilla Nervo (Mexico)

Table 1 (contd)

No.	Case	Organ	Doc. ref.	Composition
28		Additional Measures Committee	GA res. 498 (V), 1 Feb. 1951	Australia, Belgium, Brazil, Burma, Canada, Egypt, France, Mexico, Philippines, Turkey, United Kingdom, United States, Venezuela, Yugoslavia
29		Commission to investigate charges of bacteriological warfare	GA res. 706 (VII), 23 April 1953	Was to have been set up by President of General Assembly, but never established
30	Sinai-Suez	Emergency Force (UNEF)	GA res. 1000 (ES-1), 5 Nov. 1956; GA res. 1001 (ES-1), 7 Nov. 1956	National contingents
31		UNEF Advisory Committee	GA res. 1001 (ES-1), 7 Nov. 1956	Brazil, Canada, Ceylon, Colombia, India, Norway, Pakistan
32	Cyprus	Force in Cyprus (UNFICYP)	SC res. 186 (S/5575), 4 March 1964	National contingents
33		Mediator	SC res. 186 (S/5575), 4 March 1964	(a) Sakari S. Tuomioja; (b) Galo Plaza Lasso

Note: The bodies listed above were subsidiary organs of the Security Council or the General Assembly, except nos. 7, 12, and 21, although the Unified Command in Korea (21) was set up in pursuance of a resolution of the Security Council. Bodies set up as a result of the armistice agreement in Korea were not UN subsidiary organs.

all the members of the Security Council, but a proposal to this effect was vetoed by France when put to the vote the first time and received insufficient votes on the second occasion.[27] When the Security Council was establishing the Commission for

---

[27] SCOR, 2nd year, 193rd mtg (22 Aug. 1947), pp. 2180; 194th mtg (25 Aug. 1947), pp. 2197, 2199-200; 3rd year, 392nd mtg (24 Dec. 1948), pp. 3 (S/1148 and Corr. 1) and 41; Philip C. Jessup, *The Birth of Nations*, p. 46.

India and Pakistan, to consist of nominees of the parties and one independent member (no. 5), Soviet ambassador Gromyko complained that this had been the course followed in establishing the Good Offices Committee in Indonesia (no. 2). 'That Committee has been at work for several months already, but the Security Council does not in point of fact know what it is doing ... The new commission is not a Security Council commission either in form or in fact.' A month later, during the course of a debate on Indonesia, Gromyko repeated his complaint.[28]

In both the Indonesian[29] and Palestine[30] cases, there was confusion because there were subsidiary organs of the Security Council in the field with overlapping functions. Problems may also arise if a subsidiary organ is established by one body but is made answerable to another. The resolution of the General Assembly on the partition of Palestine created a Palestine Commission with 'primary responsibility and full powers in whatever concerns the implementation of the Plan of Partition', but placed the Commission 'under the guidance of the Security Council'. The Palestine Commission was so uncertain of its precise role and powers that it asked the UN Secretariat to prepare a paper on its relations with the Security Council. The Secretariat's paper was clear but hardly illuminating, however: how did it help the Commission to be told that it had 'all power inherent in the functions within the competence expressly assigned to it'? How did it help the Security Council to be told that it 'may, or may not, consider it necessary to issue instructions to the Commission...'?[31] Confusion of the kind that occurred in this case is difficult to avoid when time presses.

Subsidiary organs report, usually to the parent body, whether or not they have been expressly requested to do so. An important weapon at the disposal of a subsidiary organ is the threat to make a report that indicates which party is impeding progress:

[28] SCOR, 3rd year, 230th mtg (20 Jan. 1948), pp. 140, 142; 249th mtg (18 Feb. 1948), pp. 175-6.

[29] SCOR, 2nd year, 217th mtg (31 Oct. 1947), pp. 2701-2; 4th year, Supplement for January 1949, pp. 7-8, 10-14, 17-18, paras. 4, 8, 11 of S/1189, S/1190.

[30] Pablo de Azcárate, *Mission in Palestine, 1948-1952*, pp. 82-4, 169-71; David P. Forsythe, *United Nations Peacemaking*, pp. 40, 44, 73, 78-80, 84-5.

[31] GA res. 181 (II), 29 Nov. 1947; SCOR, 3rd year, Supplement for January-March 1948, pp. 14-24, A/AC.21/13.

this threat was made in the Indonesian case.[32] Or one of the parties, conscious of its own rectitude, may bring pressure to bear on a subsidiary organ to report to its parent body at a time that the party judges to be favourable to its own interests. India made such representations to the UN Commission for India and Pakistan at a critical juncture over Kashmir in 1948.[33] Although subsidiary organs were usually able to reach a common mind about when and what they should report, the Truce Commission in Palestine had to record a US dissent to the view of the other two members that reports should not be sent to the Security Council while the UN Mediator was undertaking delicate negotiations,[34] and the Swedish and Swiss members of the Neutral Nations Repatriation Commission for Korea issued a separate report in 1954.[35]

There are usually informal contacts between a subsidiary organ and the parent body, at both the presiding officer and secretariat levels, but the monthly change in the presidency of the Security Council and periodic changes in the chairmanship of many subsidiary organs inevitably introduces an element of discontinuity. In Indonesia and Palestine, UN organs asked that complaints should be communicated to the organs in the field rather than to the Security Council.[36]

The Security Council may invite a subsidiary organ or its presiding officer, or even all of its members, to participate in its deliberations. In the period 1946-64, the Council invited such participation in connection with the cases studied, as shown in Table 2.

When a subsidiary organ is composed of states, there is often tension between the prevailing mood in the subsidiary organ and the wider diplomatic interests of the states of which the organ is composed. This is apparent from the volumes of documents on US foreign relations up to 1950,[37] and there is every

[32] Organization and Procedure of United Nations Commissions: memoranda submitted by the Secretary-General to the Interim Committee of the General Assembly, no. V, Committee of Good Offices on the Indonesian Question, 1949, para. 56.

[33] SCOR, 3rd year, Supplement for November 1948, p. 40, para. 92 of S/1100; FRUS, 1948, vol. V, part 1, 1975, p. 372.

[34] SCOR, 3rd year, Supplement for June 1948, p. 73, S/808.

[35] GAOR, 8th session, Supplement no. 18, A/2641, pp. 23-9.

[36] SCOR, 3rd year, Supplement for January-March 1948, p. 41, S/703; 320th mtg (15 June 1948), p. 2, S/837.

[37] See FRUS, the volumes concerned with the United Nations, Indonesia, Kashmir, Palestine, and Korea, 1947-1954.

Table 2

Participation of members of subsidiary organs
in the proceedings of the Security Council

Organ no. in Table 1	Organ	No. of times participation invited
2	Good Offices Committee (GOC), Indonesia	7
5	Commission for India and Pakistan (UNCIP)	16
8	Representative for India and Pakistan	5
10	Palestine Commission	1
13	Mediator, Palestine	1
14	Chief of Staff, Truce Supervision Organization (UNTSO)	29
15	Acting Mediator, Palestine	5

reason to believe that the same was and is true for members of UN organs from other countries.

2.2 CONVENING THE SECURITY COUNCIL

The President of the Security Council convenes a meeting in the following circumstances:

1. at the request of any member of the Council;
2. if the General Assembly makes recommendations to the Council or refers a question or situation to it;
3. if the Secretary-General draws the attention of the Council to a matter that in his opinion may threaten the maintenance of international peace and security;
4. if a dispute or situation is brought to the Council's attention by some other means.[38]

Meetings are normally held at UN headquarters, but they may be held elsewhere if this will facilitate the Council's work.[39] During the period covered by this study, meetings were held in London from 17 January to 16 February 1946 and in Paris from 16 September to 29 December 1948 and from 10 November 1951 to 6 February 1952. In the absence of a decision to the

[38] Articles 11(2) and (3), 35, and 99 of the Charter, Rules of Procedure nos. 1-3.
[39] Article 28(3) of the Charter and Rule of Procedure 5.

contrary, the Council meets in public.[40] The President consults the members of the Council informally before calling a meeting, and he is usually able to fix a day and time that is generally acceptable, although sometimes a meeting has been convened without the usual consultations or without the express agreement of all members of the Council.

Of the seven cases within the scope of this study, three were brought to the Council's attention by one or more of the parties (Kashmir, Sinai-Suez, Cyprus), two by non-parties (the two cases on Indonesia), and one by the General Assembly (Palestine). In the Korean case, both the United States and Secretary-General Lie asked for a meeting of the Council, and there was also a report from a subsidiary organ of the Council.

It will be seen from Table 3 that, in three of the seven cases, the Council was able to meet on the same day as the request was received (Korea, Sinai-Suez, Cyprus) and in two other cases on the following day (Indonesia I and II). In all these cases, the time difference between the area of trouble and the place where the Council met helped to create an illusion of alacrity. In the Kashmir case, there was an interval of five days between the request and the first meeting.

Only in the Palestine case does it seem in retrospect that the Council was slow in responding to the gravity of the situation. On 29 November 1947, the General Assembly passed the partition resolution and asked the Security Council to 'take the necessary measures ... for its implementation'. On 7 December, Egypt and Lebanon asked to be allowed to participate in the debate on implementing the partition plan, and the Security Council agreed. On 10 February 1948, the Council took note of a report of the Palestine Commission, an organ that had been established by the General Assembly. It was not until 24 February, three months after the General Assembly had asked the Security Council to implement the partition resolution, that the Council began its substantive debate.[41]

In three of the seven cases, the Security Council issued an appeal for the fighting to stop either on the day of its first

[40] Rule of Procedure 48.
[41] GA res. 181 (III), 29 Nov. 1947; SCOR, 2nd year, Supplement no. 20, p. 172, S/614; 222nd mtg (9 Dec. 1947), pp. 2776-89, S/617, S/618; 3rd year, 243rd mtg (10 Feb. 1948), pp. 56-8; 253rd mtg (24 Feb. 1948), pp. 255-7.

Table 3

Speed of action by the Security Council

Case	Approximate date fighting began	Issue taken to Security Council by	Date submitted	Date of first substantive consideration	Date of first Security Council call to stop fighting
Indonesia I	20 July 1947	Australia and India	30 July 1947	31 July 1947	1 Aug. 1947
Kashmir	19 Oct. 1947	India	1 Jan. 1948	6 Jan. 1948	21 April 1948
Palestine	29 Nov. 1947	General Assembly	GA res. of 29 Nov. 1947 submitted to SC 2 Dec. 1947	24 Feb. 1948	1 April 1948
Indonesia II	19 Dec. 1948	Australia and United States	19 Dec. 1948	20 Dec. 1948	24 Dec. 1948
Korea	25 June 1950	United States and Secretary-General Trygve Lie	25 June 1950	25 June 1950	25 June 1950
Sinai-Suez	29 Oct. 1956	Egypt	30 Oct. 1956	30 Oct. 1956	Anglo-French vetoes on 30 Oct. 1956
Cyprus	8 Aug. 1964	Turkey and Cyprus	8 Aug. 1964	8 Aug. 1964	9 Aug. 1964

meeting or the following day (Indonesia I, Korea, Cyprus), and in another case it would have done so but for Anglo-French vetoes (Sinai-Suez). In the case of Indonesia II, the Council was in difficulties because when the Dutch attack took place the Council had just completed a series of meetings in Paris and was expecting to resume its work in New York after the Christmas break. When the Council met on 20 December, the seats of three members were empty, and it was not until 24 December that there were enough votes to approve a call to cease hostilities.[42]

In the Kashmir case, the delay of fifteen weeks in reaching a substantive decision was caused in part by an adjournment requested by the state that had originally invoked UN action (India) and accepted with considerable reluctance by the Council. A series of Presidents of the Council did their best to produce an agreed formula for a peaceful settlement, but India and to a lesser extent Pakistan were at this stage not very irenic.[43] The delay in the Palestine case of five weeks from the beginning of substantive debate to the first call for the cessation of violence was not due to laziness or filibustering but to the intrinsic complexity of the issues involved, the uncooperative attitude of Britain, and the determination of the Arabs to use all means to prevent the implementation of the partition plan.[44]

Occasionally there have been complaints that the provisional agenda or documents relating to it have not been circulated sufficiently in advance of the meeting. On one occasion, in connection with Palestine, a Syrian complaint to this effect was overruled by a vote of the Council.[45] On another occasion, concerning a report on the Hague round table conference on the future of Indonesia, the agenda was not approved, and almost a month was to elapse before the Council took the matter up again.[46] The Soviet Union, as President of the Council, tried to convene a meeting in August 1948 to consider a request

[42] SCOR, 3rd year, 386th mtg (17 Dec. 1948), p. 37; 387th mtg (20 Dec. 1948), pp. 1-8; 388th and 389th mtgs (22 Dec. 1948), pp. 1-49; 390th and 391st mtgs (23 Dec. 1948), pp. 1-41; 392nd mtg (24 Dec. 1948), pp. 1-38.
[43] Ibid., 244th-246th mtgs (11 and 12 Feb. 1948), pp. 82-135; Supplement for January-March 1948, pp. 26-7, S/668.
[44] Ibid., 253rd mtg (24 Feb. 1948), p. 273.
[45] Ibid., 365th mtg (14 Oct. 1948), pp. 1-4.
[46] Ibid., 4th year, 454th mtg (18 Nov. 1949), pp. 1-4; 455th mtg (12 Dec. 1949).

for military observers in Kashmir and an Israeli communication regarding reprisals, but the provisional agenda was rejected on the grounds that no further authorization was needed for recruiting observers for Kashmir and that it was up to the UN Mediator to interpret the Council's resolutions on Palestine.[47] On one occasion in 1953, the Council itself rather than its President had to resolve a difference of opinion as to whether it should adjourn its consideration of the Palestine question for a week or so, or *sine die*.[48]

2.3 FORMULATING THE AGENDA

The provisional agenda for each meeting of the Security Council is drawn up by the Secretary-General and approved by the President for the month. The first item is always the approval of the agenda, and the remaining item(s) are the matters suggested for the Council's consideration at the meeting in question. Strictly speaking, the substantive agenda usually takes the form of communications to the Secretary-General or President of the Council, but these are almost always placed under a title that indicates the subject matter: the Indonesian question, the Palestine question, etc. If such a blunt formulation is thought likely to cause contention, then a more objective formulation may be used, a practice that has become more common since 1950: 'Complaint of...', 'Question of alleged incident...', etc.

After the outbreak of the Korean War, the provisional agenda had as the title of item 2 'Aggression upon the Republic of Korea', followed by a reference to a letter from the United States. As soon as the Council convened, the President (India) suggested two changes in the agenda: the addition of the words 'Complaint of' before 'Aggression' and a reference also to a cable that had been received from the UN Commission on Korea. With these changes, the agenda was adopted without a vote (and in the absence of the Soviet Union).[49]

Sometimes the wording of the agenda is both lengthy and clumsy. When Britain and France complained in 1956 that

[47] Ibid., 3rd year, 356th mtg (30 Aug. 1948), pp. 1-10.
[48] Ibid., 8th year, 654th mtg (29 Dec. 1953), paras. 4-70.
[49] Ibid., 5th year, 473rd mtg (25 June 1950), pp. 1-2.

Egypt had nationalized the Suez Canal Co., the title of the item was 'Situation created by the unilateral action of the Egyptian Government in bringing to an end the system of international operation of the Suez Canal, which was confirmed and completed by the Suez Canal Convention of 1888'. Egypt's counter-complaint read 'Actions against Egypt by some Powers, particularly France and the United Kingdom, which constitute a danger to international peace and security and are serious violations of the Charter of the United Nations'.[50]

When India complained to the Security Council that Kashmir had been invaded, the item was initially entitled 'Letter dated 1 January 1948...concerning the situation in Jammu and Kashmir', and it was under that item that India addressed the Council. On 15 January 1948, Pakistan replied in writing to the Indian charges, and for three meetings the item was entitled 'Jammu and Kashmir', followed by reference to the letters from India and Pakistan. Pakistan did not confine its reply to events in Kashmir, however, but mentioned also the situation in Junagadh and relations between India and Pakistan in general. On 20 January, Pakistan asked that the Security Council should consider 'the situations [other than the Jammu and Kashmir situation] set out in my letter'. For the President of the Council (Belgium) this raised the question of whether situations other than Kashmir could be properly discussed under the agenda item then being used. To put the matter right, the provisional agenda for the next meeting was changed so as to refer to the 'India-Pakistan question'. Britain proposed that 'Junagadh and other questions' should be listed as a separate item but later withdrew the proposal, not because it was 'inelegant, inappropriate, or wrong' but because it was not going to receive the necessary majority. As there were no other proposals, the agenda was adopted, on the understanding that debate would first be about Kashmir and then about other questions.[51] The Security Council is still seized of the India-Pakistan question; when the Bangladesh War broke out in 1971, a different formu-

---

[50] Ibid., 11th year, 734th mtg (26 Sept. 1956), paras. 6-7.
[51] Ibid., 3rd year, 226th mtg (6 Jan. 1948), p. 1; 227th mtg (15 Jan. 1948), p. 8; 228th mtg (16 Jan. 1948), p. 35; 229th mtg (17 Jan. 1948), p. 89; 230th mtg (20 Jan. 1948), p. 129; 231st mtg (22 Jan. 1948), pp. 143-64.

lation was used: 'The situation in the India/Pakistan sub-continent'.[52]

2.4 IDENTIFYING THE PARTIES

Before the Security Council can act effectively, it must reach an understanding, implicitly if not explicitly, as to who the parties are in the case, as this is not always apparent from the way the issue is formally presented. The question of who the parties are usually presents itself to the Council at an early stage, when requests are received from non-members of the Council to participate in the debate.

The right of participation is specified in the Charter and provisional rules of procedure as follows. A state that is a Member of the United Nations but is not a member of the Security Council *may* be invited to participate in the discussion of a question if the Council considers that the interests of that Member are specially affected, or in the discussion of a situation or dispute that it has brought to the attention of the Security Council; and *shall* be invited to participate in the discussion of a dispute to which it is a party. A state that is not a Member of the United Nations *shall* be invited to participate in the discussion of a dispute to which it is a party and which it has brought to the attention of the Security Council, provided that it has accepted in advance the Charter obligations of pacific settlement. 'Other persons' may be invited to supply the Council with information or give other assistance. States participating in the Security Council may speak and submit motions or proposals, but these motions or proposals are put to the vote only if a member of the Council so requests. When the Council issues an invitation to participate, it is not necessary to specify under which article of the Charter or rule of procedure it is acting. The legal requirements about the participation of non-members of the Security Council are flexible enough to cover almost every contingency. During most of the period covered by this study, the requirements for participation were applied fairly strictly, but the Council acted with increasing indulgence from 1960 onwards.

[52] Ibid., 26th year, 1614th mtg (14/15 Dec. 1971), paras. 3-9.

Only one request by a UN Member to participate in the debate in the seven cases studied was rejected, and that was in connection with Indonesia 1947-8. The Philippines had asked to participate because of its interest in maintaining peace in the area and out of a humanitarian desire to prevent more bloodshed. Belgium and Britain warned that to grant the request would create a precedent that might be awkward in other cases. When the request was put to the vote, the West European and Communist members of the Council abstained, and the motion failed. The following week the Philippines asked that its request be reconsidered, citing in addition to the factors that it had already mentioned its geographical proximity to Indonesia as well as economic and historical ties. When the matter was put to a vote a second time, Belgium, Britain, and France switched from abstention to affirmative votes, and the request was approved, only Poland and the Soviet Union still abstaining.[53] Other requests to participate from UN Members were invariably granted, as were requests to participate by Indonesia in case 1[54] and Jordan in case 3[55] before these two states were admitted to UN Membership.

Requests to participate were also received from individuals, organizations, and entities other than states, and from states that were not Members of the United Nations, and these were dealt with as set out below.

CASE 1: INDONESIA 1947-8

Belgium proposed that East Indonesia and Borneo, two entities established under Dutch auspices, should be invited to participate 'for reasons of equity', as the Republic of Indonesia had already been invited. Discussion centred largely on whether the two territories had the same legal status as the Republic of Indonesia. The Belgian motion was twice put to the vote and failed on both occasions, only the United States and the three

---

[53] Ibid., 2nd year, 178th mtg (7 Aug. 1947), pp. 1837-9, S/458; 181st mtg (12 Aug. 1947), pp. 1914-17, S/485; 184th mtg (14 Aug. 1947), pp. 1979-80.

[54] Ibid., 181st mtg (12 Aug. 1947), p. 1940.

[55] Ibid., 5th year, 511th mtg (16 Oct. 1950), p. 2; 8th year, 635th mtg (9 Nov. 1953), p. 1; 9th year, 670th mtg (4 May 1954), paras. 74, 82.

Council members from Western Europe voting in favour.[56]
The UN Good Offices Committee and Consular Commission
in Indonesia treated the Netherlands and the Indonesian Republicans as 'the parties' referred to in the resolutions of the
Security Council, but individual members of the Good Offices
Committee felt free to meet informally with others outside the
formal scope of the negotiations.[57]

CASE 2: KASHMIR 1947-9

When the Security Council first took up the Kashmir question,
India included in its delegation Sheikh Abdullah, the head of
the interim administration in Indian Kashmir. Sardar Moham-
mad Ibrahim Khan, the President of Azad Kashmir, also went
to New York, but failed to secure a formal hearing. In course
of time allegiances changed, and in 1964 it was Pakistan that
suggested that Sheikh Abdullah should be invited to appear
before the Council, and India that opposed such a 'fantastic
suggestion'. In the event, the Council did not act on the Pakistani suggestion.[58]

The UN Commission for India and Pakistan believed that it
was bound by the Security Council's resolution of 21 April 1948
to regard India and Pakistan as the parties to the dispute, and
it decided to avoid any action that might be interpreted as
recognition of Azad Kashmir. It soon became apparent that
no agreement to stop fighting would be of value unless it were
accepted by Azad Kashmir, and some contact with the movement became unavoidable. The UN Commission insisted,
however, that all meetings with representatives of Azad Kashmir
were to be regarded as informal.[59]

[56] Ibid., 2nd year, 181st mtg (12 Aug. 1947), pp. 1941-3; 184th mtg (14 Aug. 1947),
pp. 1981-92, S/474; 193rd mtg (22 Aug. 1947), pp. 2170-2.
[57] FRUS, 1948, vol. VI, 1974, p. 90; Organization and Procedure of United Nations
Commissions, no. V, Committee of Good Offices on the Indonesian Question,
memorandum submitted by the Secretary-General to the Interim Committee of the
General Assembly, 1949, paras. 3, 28-9.
[58] SCOR, 3rd year, Supplement for November 1948, p. 121, para. 10 of Annex 20
to S/1100; 19th year, 1112th mtg (5 May 1964), para. 90; 1113rd mtg (7 May 1964),
para. 59.
[59] Ibid., Supplement for November 1948, pp. 25-6, 30, 35, 41-2, 47-8, 53, paras.
41, 69, 78.3(1)(b), 96, 97.2-3, 106, 132 of S/1100.

In the related matter of Hyderabad, the Security Council invited the Nawab Moin Nawaz Jung, the representative of Hyderabad, to participate in the debate. After Hyderabad had been occupied by Indian forces, the Nizam (ruler) 'withdrew' his complaint to the Security Council. This led to discussion in the Council about the credentials of the Hyderabad delegation, and it was agreed to invite the Nawab, 'who represented Hyderabad at our last meeting', to speak on the status of his credentials. The Nawab admitted that his accreditation had been withdrawn, but he claimed that the Nizam was no longer a free agent. '[W]e have come to the conclusion that it is our duty to leave to the Security Council the important question as to the status of the [Hyderabad] delegation...'[60]

CASE 3: PALESTINE 1947-9

In the Palestine case, the Security Council agreed to a request to participate from the Jewish Agency for Palestine, and further agreed to the participation of the Arab Higher Committee in the event that a request should be received from that organization. The state of Israel was proclaimed in May 1948, and in July the President of the Security Council invited the representative of the state of Israel to participate. Syria and Egypt objected to this form of invitation, and the President interpreted this as a challenge to his ruling. As there were insufficient votes to overrule the President, his ruling was upheld, whereupon the representative of the Arab High Committee withdrew from the Council chamber.[61] The UN Mediator for Palestine had frequent meetings with the parties, including the Arab League and bodies established by it, and both the Jewish Agency and the Arab League appointed liaison officers to serve with the Consular Truce Commission.[62] Arab rivalries, and especially the distinctive line followed by King Abdullah of Jordan, made many difficulties for UN bodies dealing with Palestine in this period.

[60] Ibid., 357th mtg (16 Sept. 1948), p. 11; 360th mtg (28 Sept. 1948), pp. 13, 15-16.
[61] Ibid., 253rd mtg (24 Feb. 1948), pp. 255-7; 282nd mtg (15 April 1948), p. 2; 330th mtg (7 July 1948), pp. 2-10; Supplement for July 1948, pp. 34-6, S/880.
[62] Ibid., 301st mtg (22 May 1948), pp. 11, 66; 305th mtg (26 May 1948), pp. 43, 46-7; 306th mtg (27 May 1948), p. 2.

CASE 4: INDONESIA 1948-9

The only requests to participate were from the Indonesian Republic (participation agreed in 1947) and UN Members. The UN Commission for Indonesia was asked to 'assist' the Netherlands and the Indonesian Republicans and to 'consult' representatives of other areas in Indonesia. As in the case of the Good Offices Committee, individual members of the UN Commission met informally with individuals and groups outside the formal scope of negotiations.[63]

CASE 5: KOREA 1950-3

The Security Council's handling of Korea and related items was undoubtedly made more difficult by the absence from the United Nations of South and North Korea and (until 1971) the People's Republic of China. On the proposal of the United States, South Korea was invited to participate at the first meeting of the Council on Korea, and South Korea continued to participate until the Soviet Union assumed the presidency of the Council on 1 August 1950. When Britain succeeded to the chair on 1 September, the Council again voted that South Korea should be allowed to participate.[64]

Opposition to the participation of North Korea slowly increased as the gravity of the North Korean attack became apparent. On the first occasion on which the matter was put to the vote, only Yugoslavia was in favour, six members were against, with Egypt, India, and Norway abstaining. Two days later, Norway changed from abstention to 'no', and India also voted 'no' on a subsequent occasion, increasing the negative votes to eight. At a later stage, when the Council was considering allegations about bacteriological warfare in Korea, opposition to a Soviet proposal to invite the participation of North Korea (and China) had grown to ten in a Council differently composed.[65]

[63] SC res. 67 (S/1234), 28 Jan. 1949; Organization and Procedure of United Nations Commissions, no. V, Committee of Good Offices on the Indonesian Question, memorandum submitted by the Secretary-General to the Interim Committee of the General Assembly, 1949, para. 29.

[64] SCOR, 5th year, 473rd mtg (25 June 1950), p. 4; 494th mtg (1 Sept. 1950), p. 8.

[65] Ibid., 473rd mtg (25 June 1950), p. 18; 474th mtg (27 June 1950), p. 17; 494th mtg (1 Sept. 1950), p. 21; 7th year, 585th mtg (1 July 1952), para. 57.

Debate on proposals to invite the participation of the People's Republic of China were singularly confused in 1950. Four proposals to invite China to take part in the debate on Korea were defeated,[66] but an invitation was later issued to China to participate in the debate on its complaint about US aggression against Taiwan; and after China's military intervention in Korea, China was invited to participate in the debate on a report from the Unified Command.[67] As noted above, a Soviet proposal to invite China as well as North Korea to participate in the debate on allegations about US resort to bacteriological warfare in Korea was defeated in 1952. In 1955, after an episode of fighting between Chinese and Kuomintang forces, the Council approved a New Zealand proposal to invite China to participate in the debate, the Soviet Union abstaining because of objections to the formulation of the agenda, and Nationalist China voting against; but China declined the invitation.[68]

CASE 6: SINAI AND SUEZ 1956-7

After the Anglo-French complaint against Egypt had been placed on the agenda, the Council invited Egypt to participate. Requests from Israel and the other Arab states were at first deferred, and later the Council asked them to present their views in writing.[69] After the outbreak of hostilities at the end of October, both Egypt and Israel were invited to participate.[70]

CASE 7: CYPRUS 1964

Little difficulty was encountered in inviting the participation of Greece and Turkey. Cyprus was also invited, but the Turkish Cypriot community insisted that the representative of Cyprus

[66] Ibid., 5th year, 492nd mtg (29 Aug. 1950), p. 21; 496th mtg (6 Sept. 1950), p. 21; 499th mtg (11 Sept. 1950), p. 19; 505th mtg (28 Sept. 1950), p. 21. See also 520th mtg (8 Nov. 1950), p. 5.

[67] SC res. 87 (S/1836), 29 Sept. 1950; SC res. 88 (S/1892), 8 Nov. 1950.

[68] SCOR, 10th year, 690th mtg (31 Jan. 1955), paras. 115-6, 143-6; Supplement for January-March 1955, pp. 29-31, S/3358.

[69] Ibid., 11th year, 734th mtg (26 Sept. 1956), paras. 146-54; 735th mtg (5 Oct. 1956), paras. 7-15; 742nd mtg (13 Oct. 1956), paras. 5-6. See also Supplement for October-December 1956, pp. 21-52, 55-89, S/3673, S/3674, S/3676, S/3680, S/3681, S/3683, S/3684.

[70] Ibid., 748th mtg (30 Oct. 1956), p. 2.

spoke only for the Greek community. Eventually the Council granted a request from Rauf Denktas, the president of the Turkish Communal Chamber, to be allowed to make a statement before the Council.[71]

The UN Mediator later had to decide who were 'the parties' referred to in the Security Council's resolution of 4 March 1964. Having examined the relevant treaties and agreements, the Mediator concluded that the parties were the Greek and Turkish communities in Cyprus, the government of Cyprus, and the governments of Greece, Turkey, and Britain. The Mediator at that time saw his task in two stages: first, to help the two Cypriot communities, 'who bear arms against each other [and] must live under the terms of any settlement', to reach agreement; and, later, to reach an agreement committing the other parties.[72]

SUMMARY

It would seem that the Security Council has without much difficulty secured the participation of the parties to conflicts if they were or were thought likely soon to become UN Members: Indonesia and the Netherlands in cases 1 and 4; India and Pakistan in case 2; the Jewish Agency for Palestine-Israel and the Arab states and (until 7 July 1948) the Arab Higher Committee in case 3; Egypt, Britain, France, and Israel in case 6; Cyprus, Greece, and Turkey in case 7.

There are, however, some significant lacunae. In the light of what we now know, it seems unfortunate that the Security Council was not able to hear a representative of Azad Kashmir in the early months of 1948. On both of its visits to the subcontinent, the UN Commission for India and Pakistan was surprised to discover how much support there was for the Azad Kashmir movement; and the UN Commission commented in 1949 that, if it had fully appreciated the situation in Azad Kashmir the previous year, it would have adopted a different

[71] Ibid., 18th year, Supplement for October-December 1963, pp. 114-15, S/5491; 1085th mtg (27 Dec. 1963), pp. 1-3; 19th year, Supplement for January-March 1964, pp. 72-3, 76-7, S/5551, S/5555, S/5556; 1098th mtg (27 Feb. 1964), paras. 7, 17, 61-2; 1099th mtg (28 Feb. 1964), paras. 3, 41.

[72] Ibid., 20th year, Supplement for Janaury-March 1965, pp. 235-6, paras. 125-7 of S/6253.

line of policy on the withdrawal of forces. It is likely that the Security Council itself would also have acted differently between January and April 1948 if it had been more fully informed.[73]

The Korean conflict was certainly made more difficult for the United Nations by the exclusion of China and the absence of North and South Korea. In 1951, Dean Acheson was able to persuade the new British Foreign Secretary, Herbert Morrison, to adopt a 'moratorium' on Chinese representation in the United Nations, whereby the issue would be deferred year by year. The United States exerted great diplomatic and other pressures for twenty years to prevent UN organs from resolving the issue, and it was not until 1971 that the General Assembly voted to seat China. It is, of course, likely that, without the Korean War, the question of Chinese representation in the United Nations might have been settled sooner. The United States in the 1950s was mesmerized by the idea of a world Communist conspiracy, and Truman and Acheson responded sceptically to British suggestions that all was not well between Moscow and Peking. It has recently been revealed that early in October 1950, before the Chinese had intervened in the Korean War, the Soviet Union made a serious attempt to find a compromise solution to the Korean problem, based on the continued existence of the North Korean régime, the presence of a UN organ in North Korea, and the substitution of uncommitted Asian troops for US forces south of the 38th parallel. With the knowledge of Soviet Foreign Minister Andrei Vyshinsky, a UN official of Soviet nationality, Vassili Kassaniev, approached a Norwegian diplomat in New York, Hans Engen, with a rough outline of the Soviet plan. Engen told US officials what had happened, but the United States could not free itself from the notion that this was simply another Communist plot, and the initiative foundered.[74]

If China had been present in the Security Council in the 1950s and 1960s, it would hardly have been possible to avoid some of the ideological polemics in which Soviet and Chinese representatives have engaged in the Security Council since

[73] Ibid., 3rd year, Supplement for November 1948, p. 52, para. 125 of S/1100; 4th year, Special Supplement no. 7, pp. 39-40, 46, paras. 203, 225 of S/1430.

[74] FRUS, 1950, vol. VII, 1976, pp. 814, 877-80, 897-9, 906-11, 922, 1368, 1397-9; 1951, vol. II, 1979, pp. 246-8, 251-3.

1971. If that had occurred, the world would have had a truer picture of relations between Moscow and Peking. As it was, the Soviet Union was able to have it all ways: on the question of Chinese representation in the United Nations, for example, the Soviet Union proposed that Nationalist China should be expelled and that the People's Republic of China should be *heard*, but at this stage the Soviet Union did not propose that China's UN seat should be transferred from Taipei (Taibei) to Peking (Beijing).

On the Cyprus question, one wonders whether it really helped that, except for a single occasion in February 1964, the Council always heard the Turkish Cypriot point of view from Turkey rather than from a representative of the Turkish community in Cyprus.

When we turn to the participation of UN Members, we find that, in the period 1946-64, requests to participate hardly raised difficult questions of principle: parties to the conflicts, sponsors of items (the Ukraine in connection with Indonesia in 1946 and India in the same connection in 1947), members of subsidiary organs concerned with the matters under debate (Australia and Belgium in connection with Indonesia in 1948 and 1949), and occasionally other countries with a plausible claim to be directly concerned with a matter (UN Members in Asia in connection with case 4, before Indonesia itself had acquired UN Membership). In the Congo crisis beginning in 1960, however, all UN Members in Africa other than South Africa felt themselves to be specially affected and were granted the right of participation. Nowadays the number of requests to participate is often far beyond what is needed for the Council to have a full understanding of what is at stake. If the participation of non-parties threatens to become excessive, their views can be obtained in written form, as was done with the requests of Israel and the Arab states (other than Egypt) on 13 October 1956 on the Suez Canal question.[75]

When there is opposition to the participation of persons or entities other than states, it usually arises from the belief that the granting of a hearing by the Security Council may confer

[75] SCOR, 11th year, 742nd mtg (13 Oct. 1956), para. 5.

a certain legitimacy.[76] That was certainly one reason for Dutch opposition to the participation of the Indonesian Republic in case 1, and it explains the recent US opposition to the participation of the Palestine Liberation Organization in the proceedings of the Security Council.

Apart from the genuine cases of states and other entities wishing to participate, dubious or spurious requests are sometimes submitted to the Council in order to occupy time on marginal matters or to confuse the Security Council about who are the real parties to the case. There was a widespread feeling in case 1 that the Belgian proposal to hear East Indonesia and Borneo, even if sincerely intended, had the effect of creating uncertainty about the claim of the Republicans to represent Indonesian national opinion.

2.5 CREDENTIALS AND REPRESENTATION

The Security Council approved five Rules of Procedure regarding credentials on 9 April 1946, and added one further sentence to the first of these Rules on 28 February 1950. The Rules provide that when a member of the Security Council is represented by the head of government or minister of foreign affairs no credentials are necessary. In other cases, permanent members submit credentials when there is a change of representation, and non-permanent members at the beginning of their two-year term, and the Secretary-General reports on these. During the period covered by this study non-members of the Council submitted credentials, but the Rules of Procedure have been relaxed since 1964, and the Secretary-General now reports on the credentials of non-members only in cases of doubt or difficulty. Nothing is said in the Rules of Procedure about the credentials of a person representing an entity other than a state. Pending the approval of credentials 'of a representative on the Security Council', or if credentials have been objected to, the representative continues to sit 'with the same rights as other representatives'. In 1950 an additional provision was

---

[76] Oscar Schachter, 'The United Nations and Internal Conflict', *Law and Civil War in the Modern World*, ed. John Norton Moore, Baltimore and London, Johns Hopkins University Press, 1974 (under the auspices of the American Society of International Law), p. 427.

made, to the effect that credentials shall be signed by the head of state or government or the minister of foreign affairs.[77] Since 1948, reports of the Secretary-General on credentials have not been included in the provisional agenda of Council meetings but have been circulated in writing to Council members and, in the absence of objection, have been considered approved.

During the debates on the Greek civil war and the Corfu Channel question in 1946-7, East European states that had not then been admitted to UN Membership were invited to participate, and no problems arose regarding credentials. In the Indonesian case, the Republic of Indonesia asked to be allowed to participate and the Security Council agreed, though without determining whether Indonesia was a state or not. The President of the Council indicated initially that credentials from Indonesia had not been submitted, but two days later he reported that credentials had been received and that, in the opinion of the Secretariat, these were in order.[78] In the Hyderabad case the following year, the matter was placed on the agenda and a representative of Hyderabad was invited to participate, though without any question of credentials being formally raised. A week later the Nizam withdrew his complaint to the Council, and this was bound to cast doubt on the validity of the credentials of the representative of Hyderabad. The President of the Council (United Kingdom) placed the facts before the Council, which agreed to invite the representative of Hyderabad to make a statement concerning the validity of his credentials. This he did,[79] but he thereafter took no further part in the Council's consideration of the matter.

As noted above, there is no provision in the Rules of Procedure for the submission or examination of the credentials of representatives of entities other than states, and no problem arose in connection with credentials from the Arab Higher Committee, the Jewish Agency for Palestine, and the Turkish Cypriot community.[80]

[77] Rules, 13-17.

[78] SCOR, 2nd year, 181st mtg (12 Aug. 1947), pp. 1919, 1940; 184th mtg (14 Aug. 1940), p. 1979.

[79] Ibid., 3rd year, 357th mtg (16 Sept. 1948), p. 11; 360th mtg (28 Sept. 1948), pp. 3-13; Supplement for September 1948, p. 7, S/1011.

[80] Ibid., 253rd mtg (24 Feb. 1948), pp. 255-7; 282nd mtg (15 April 1948), pp. 1-2; 19th year, 1098th mtg (27 Feb. 1964), paras. 2-61.

After the victory of the Chinese Communists in 1949, the question to be determined by the Security Council and other UN organs was which of the two authorities claiming to be the government of China—the Communists or the Nationalists— had the right to issue credentials for China. Chou En-lai (Zhou Enlai) sent UN Secretary-General Lie a message to the effect that the Nationalists had no authority to speak for the Chinese people, and the Soviet representative made the same point at several meetings of the Security Council. When the Council failed to expel the representative of Nationalist China, the Soviet Union instituted a boycott of the Security Council, during the course of which the Council took decisions to support South Korea.[81] It was as a result of this episode that the Council approved an Indian proposal to add a sentence to the Rules of Procedure about the issuance of credentials. There was a general wish to establish a uniform procedure for dealing with questions of representation in different UN organs, but it was felt by Council members that this should be left to the General Assembly.[82] The 1950 addition to the Rules did not, in fact, make it easier to resolve questions concerned with rival authorities on the territory of a UN Member.

The Soviet representative returned to the Council on 1 August 1950, when it was his turn to preside, and at once ruled that 'the Kuomintang group' did not represent China. The ruling was challenged, put to the vote, and overruled. The Soviet Union continued to seek ways of placing the issue of Chinese representation before the Council, but it was twenty-one years before the People's Republic of China was seated at the United Nations.[83]

2.6   THE QUESTION OF COMPETENCE

Two questions about the competence of the Security Council may arise: is it within the jurisdiction of the Council *to discuss*

---

[81] A/1123, 21 Nov. 1949 (mimeo); S/1462, 24 Feb. 1950 (mimeo); SCOR, 5th year, 458th mtg (29 Dec. 1950), pp. 1-3; 5th year, 459th mtg (10 Jan. 1950), pp. 1-4; 460th mtg (12 Jan. 1950); 461st mtg (13 Jan. 1950), pp. 1-10.

[82] SCOR, 5th year, 462nd mtg (17 Jan. 1950), pp. 10-13; 468th mtg (28 Feb. 1950), pp. 9-11; Supplement for January-May 1950, pp. 2-3, 16-18, S/1447, S/1457 and Corr. 1.

[83] Ibid., 480th mtg (1 Aug. 1950), pp. 1-12; 10th year, 689th mtg (31 Jan. 1955), paras. 2-27; GA res. 2758 (XXVI), 25 Oct. 1971.

the matter submitted to it? And is the Council competent *to adopt the proposal* before it? It is not always easy in practice to separate the question of the agenda from the question of action that might be taken. Arguments about competence are necessarily presented in legal terms, although considerations of political expediency are virtually always lurking in the background.

In the weeks after the first Dutch 'police action' in Indonesia, there was a good deal of discussion in the Security Council on the question of competence. The Netherlands, supported by its West European friends, put forward two arguments why the Security Council was not competent to deal with the matter. First, as the Indonesian Republic was not a sovereign and independent state, what was happening in Indonesia was necessarily a matter within Dutch jurisdiction: 'the Charter is not applicable to what is now happening in Java and Sumatra'. Second, even if it were assumed for the sake of argument that events in Indonesia were not excluded by the domestic juris- diction clause of the UN Charter, 'is there any danger to inter- national peace or security, let alone breaches of the peace or acts of aggression...?'[84]

The supporters of the Indonesian Republic regarded the fuss about competence as little better than filibustering. 'The object', said Soviet ambassador Gromyko, 'is really to deflect the atten- tion of the Security Council from the substance of the ques- tion...'[85]

France proposed that any decision of the Council to call for an end to the fighting should be without prejudice to the question of the Council's competence, and Belgium proposed referring the question of competence to the International Court of Justice; but both proposals were defeated. At one stage, the President of the Council (Syria) took the line that the Council could take decisions about the fighting and leave the question of compe- tence 'in abeyance'; but he later said that as the Council was seized with the Indonesian question, the Council necessarily

[84] SCOR, 2nd year, 171st mtg (31 July 1947), p. 1645; 173rd mtg (1 Aug. 1947), pp. 1676-8, 1689, 1695-6, 1712-13; 174th mtg (4 Aug. 1947), p. 1716; 178th mtg (7 Aug. 1947), p. 1848; 185th mtg (15 Aug. 1947), pp. 2011-12, 2024-5; 192nd mtg (22 Aug. 1947), pp. 2144-5; 194th mtg (25 Aug. 1947), pp. 2193-4, 2210; 195th mtg (26 Aug. 1947), pp. 2214-15, 2218-19, 2224.
[85] Ibid., 173rd mtg (1 Aug. 1947), pp. 1684, 1692; 194th mtg (25 Aug. 1947), pp. 2210-11; 195th mtg (26 Aug. 1947), pp. 2215-24.

had jurisdiction unless and until a formal motion to delete the item from the agenda were approved.[86]

After the second Dutch 'police action' the question of competence was again raised, and the same arguments were wearisomely deployed.[87]

Before the first cease-fire in Palestine, the Security Council decided to send a questionnaire to the parties. One proposed question would have asked the Arab governments whether they had entered into any agreement among themselves regarding Palestine. Argentina suggested that this would contravene the prohibition on intervention in domestic affairs, and the Council voted to delete the question. Syria proposed adding a question asking the Jewish Agency for Palestine whether any non-Palestinians were serving in its armed force, but the Jewish Agency claimed that this was a matter of domestic jurisdiction, and the Syrian proposal was rejected.[88] Shortly afterwards, a draft resolution was submitted to the Council which asked the parties not to introduce fighting personnel or men of military age into Palestine. Although the Jewish Agency contended that immigration policy was a matter of domestic jurisdiction, the Council agreed to include an appeal along the lines suggested.[89]

The Arabs have always believed that the General Assembly had no right to decide on the partition of Palestine and that the Security Council had therefore no basis for implementing the partition plan. In order to put a definite question before the Security Council, Syria proposed in July 1948 that the Council should request the International Court of Justice to advise on 'the status of Palestine arising from the termination of the Mandate'. This was opposed by the two Communist members of the Council ('a delayed and badly camouflaged attempt to

[86] Ibid., 171st mtg (31 July 1947), p. 1648; 172 mtg (1 Aug. 1947), pp. 1658-9; 173rd mtg (1 Aug. 1947), pp. 1676, 1678, 1701-2; 185th mtg (15 Aug. 1947), pp. 2017, 2024-5; 194th mtg (25 Aug. 1947), p. 2193, S/517; 195th mtg (26 Aug. 1947), pp. 2214, 2221-2, 2224.
[87] Ibid., 3rd year, 388th mtg (22 Dec. 1948), pp. 25-30; 389th mtg (22 Dec. 1948), p. 43; 390th mtg (23 Dec. 1948), pp. 1-3, 6-7; 391st mtg (23 Dec. 1948), pp. 22, 29, 39; 392nd mtg (24 Dec. 1948, pp. 11, 22-3, 25-8; 4th year, 398th mtg (11 Jan. 1949), p. 11; 400th mtg (14 Jan. 1949), p. 8; 402nd mtg (21 Jan. 1949), pp. 2-5, 7; 403rd mtg (25 Jan. 1949), p. 15; 406th mtg (28 Jan. 1949), pp. 9-11; 417th mtg (11 March 1949), p. 3; 420th mtg (21 March 1949), pp. 20, 27-8.
[88] Ibid., 3rd year, 295th mtg (18 May 1948), pp. 27, 35-6, 45.
[89] Ibid., 307th mtg (28 May 1948), pp. 10-11; 310th mtg (29 May 1948), pp. 27, 52; SC res. 50 (S/801), 29 May 1948.

take the whole Palestine question back to its starting point'), the United States, Canada, and Israel, while France thought that the Syrian proposal had come 'too late'. The other Council members supported the Syrian draft, but the number of affirmative votes was one short of the required majority.[90] It is interesting to speculate on what might have happened had there been one more affirmative vote.

When the question of Hyderabad was submitted to the Security Council in September 1948, the Council agreed to place the matter on the agenda, but without prejudging the Council's competence. At a later stage, Pakistan suggested that the question of the Council's competence should be referred to the International Court of Justice for an advisory opinion, but no formal proposal to that effect was placed before the Council.[91]

The Soviet Union argued in the Korean case that the war was a civil war and therefore a matter of domestic jurisdiction, but Britain pointed out that Article 2(7) of the Charter includes the words, 'but this principle [of non-intervention in essentially domestic matters] shall not prejudice the application of enforcement measures...'[92] The Soviet Union also argued that the decisions of the Security Council on Korea were illegal because the Soviet Union had been absent and China's seat had been occupied by the Nationalists, so that the decisions did not have the concurring votes of all of the permanent members.[93] The Western powers replied that the Soviet Union must not be allowed to bring the proceedings of the Security Council to a halt simply by refusing to be present, and that the credentials of Nationalist China had been approved in the normal manner.[94] It was noticeable that several members of the Council

[90] Ibid., 334th mtg (13 July 1948), pp. 52-3, S/894; 335th mtg (14 July 1948), pp. 4-6, 13; 336th mtg (14 July 1948), pp. 24, 26; 337th mtg (15 July 1948), pp. 11-12; 338th mtg (15 July 1948), pp. 30, 67-9; 339th mtg (27 July 1948), pp. 2-17; 340th mtg (27 July 1948), pp. 27-34.

[91] Ibid., 357th mtg (16 Sept. 1948), pp. 4-11; 4th year, 426th mtg (24 May 1949), p. 29.

[92] Ibid., 5th year, 482nd mtg (3 Aug. 1950), pp. 6-8; 486th mtg (11 Aug. 1950), p. 6; 489th mtg (22 Aug. 1950), pp. 3, 20-1.

[93] Ibid., Supplement for June-August 1950, pp. 29-30, S/1517; 480th mtg (1 Aug. 1950), p. 20; 482nd mtg (3 Aug. 1950), p. 8; 486th mtg (11 Aug. 1950), p. 22; 519th mtg (8 Nov. 1950), p. 4; 523rd mtg (16 Nov. 1950), pp. 20-1; 6th year, 531st mtg (31 Jan. 1951), para. 43.

[94] Ibid., 5th year, 475th mtg (30 June 1950), pp. 7-8; 486th mtg (11 Aug. 1950), pp. 6-7; 487th mtg (14 Aug. 1950), pp. 8, 11-12; 526th mtg (28 Nov. 1950), p. 16.

took no part in the debate on the question of competence (India, Egypt, Yugoslavia, Ecuador) but none the less acted thereafter as if the decisions of the Council had been validly taken.

An interesting constitutional question arose after the two Anglo-French vetoes of cease-fire proposals in connection with Sinai-Suez in 1956. Two meetings of the Security Council were held on 30 October to consider a US letter calling for the immediate cessation of military action. After the second veto, the Council took up an Egyptian complaint about the Anglo-French ultimatum. During the debate on this complaint the following day, Yugoslavia proposed that the Council should convene the General Assembly in emergency session under the Uniting for Peace procedure. This procedure had been approved by the General Assembly in 1950, against the opposition of the Soviet bloc. The relevant part of the procedure provides that if, because of lack of unanimity of the permanent members, the Security Council fails to exercise its responsibility 'where there appears to be a threat to the peace, breach of the peace, or act of aggression', the Security Council may, by a procedural (veto-free) vote, call the General Assembly into session within twenty-four hours, in order that the Assembly should make appropriate recommendations. Britain and France argued that neither of the vetoed proposals would have determined that peace had been threatened or breached or that an act of aggression had occurred; moreover, the matter being discussed (the Egyptian complaint) was not the item that had given rise to the vetoes (the US cease-fire letter). At Britain's request, a motion that the Yugoslav draft was out of order was put to the vote but defeated.[95] Technically, Britain and France were probably correct in the second part of their objection, but the Security Council was in no mood to be delayed by technicalities.

There is one aspect of competence that might have given rise to difficulties but did not in practice do so in the cases studied. The Charter was drafted in such a way as to avoid a situation in which the same issue would be dealt with simultaneously in both the General Assembly and the Security Council. If a question relating to peace and security is brought before the General Assembly, the Assembly may discuss it; but if action

[95] Ibid., 11th year, 751st mtg (31 Oct. 1956), paras. 71, 82-4, 96-7, 108, 125-7.

is necessary, the General Assembly should refer the question to the Security Council.[96] It was under this procedure that the General Assembly referred to the Security Council the question of implementing the Palestine partition plan. At a later stage, it was the Security Council that decided that a special session of the General Assembly should be convoked to consider the future of Palestine.[97] In the Sinai-Suez case, the Security Council called an emergency session of the General Assembly when it found itself stymied by the veto.[98] Although Britain and France objected in the Sinai-Suez case on both legal and political grounds, the instances referred to above represented orderly transfers of responsibility from one organ to another. In the Indonesian case, however, the matter was placed on the agenda of the third regular session of the General Assembly in 1949, in spite of the fact that the Security Council was actively seized of the matter. This might have led to difficulties had not care been taken to avoid placing the same or similar proposals for action before the two organs.

Questions about the competence of the Security Council are legitimate and important, but they are raised by states under political pressure: the Netherlands when it became apparent how little international support there was for the two 'police actions' in Indonesia, the Arabs when it became clear that the partition of Palestine was taking shape, the Soviet Union after the Security Council had decided to support South Korea, Britain and France when it was apparent that the world did not accept their claim to be separating the belligerents and protecting the Suez Canal. It is now of little avail to resist placing a matter on the agenda of the Council, because it is the general view that there has to be some preliminary debate before the Council has a basis for deciding on competence. It is still feasible to argue that a particular proposal is *ultra vires*: in particular, that mandatory action requires a prior determination bringing the matter within the scope of Chapter VII of the Charter, or that Chapter VII should not be invoked or its language used in the absence of irrefutable evidence that there is or has been a threat to or breach of the peace or an act of aggression.

[96] Article 11 (2).
[97] GA res. 181 (II), 29 Nov. 1947; SC res. 44 (S/714, II), 1 April 1948.
[98] SC res. 119 (S/3721), 31 Oct. 1956.

2.7 DETERMINATION OF THE NATURE OF THE QUESTION

This rather cumbersome and opaque formulation is used in the official *Repertoire* of the practice of the Security Council to refer to a decision of the Council, explicit or implied, that has consequences beyond what is stated in the material part of the decision because it may affect subsequent proceedings. These consequences may be of two kinds. First, if the Council determines that a question before it is a dispute, three consequences follow:

1. a party to that dispute 'shall' abstain from voting on proposals for peaceful settlement;[99]
2. the Security Council 'shall' invite a non-member of the Council which is a party to the dispute to participate without vote in any discussion relating to the dispute;[100]
3. the Security Council 'shall decide whether to ... recommend ... terms of settlement ...', whereas in other matters it may recommend only 'procedures or methods of adjustment'.[101]

Second, if the Security Council determines under Article 39 that there exists a threat to the peace, breach of the peace, or act of aggression, the Council may make recommendations or decide on measures to maintain or restore international peace and security;[102] in that event, UN Members 'shall' join in affording mutual assistance in carrying out such measures:[103] in other words, and to use everyday parlance, decisions of this sort are binding or mandatory.

DISPUTES (ARTICLES 27(3), 32, AND 37(2) OF THE CHARTER)

If a member of the Security Council abstains from voting, it may not be apparent whether this is an obligatory abstention by a party to a dispute or a voluntary abstention, unless the Security Council has itself already decided that the question is a dispute. Parties to issues before the Council, not wishing to

---

[99] Article 27 (3).
[100] Article 32.
[101] Articles 36 and 37.
[102] Article 39.
[103] Article 49.

deprive themselves of a vote, have hesitated to claim that a dispute existed. Of the cases studied and the related matters, the question whether a dispute existed arose on three occasions: two of the cases had been submitted as disputes, one by a member and one by a non-member.

Indonesia The Indonesian question was submitted to the Security Council in 1947 by India and Australia, India describing the matter as a 'situation' which might lead to friction or give rise to a dispute and Australia claiming that there had been an actual breach of the peace. Australia submitted a proposal that included a determination that hostilities in Indonesia constituted 'a breach of the peace under Article 39 of the Charter' and called on the parties to settle their 'disputes' by peaceful means. The United States proposed that the paragraph containing the formal determination should be deleted, and Australia agreed. The remainder of the text, after further amendment, was then approved. A later resolution of the Council contained a preambular reference to the avoidance of 'disputes and friction', and there were two subsequent references in resolutions to 'their dispute'.[104] The Netherlands was not elected a non-permanent member of the Security Council until after the Indonesian conflict had been resolved: Indonesia became a UN Member in 1950 but was not elected a non-permanent member of the Security Council until 1973: so the question of whether the Netherlands and Indonesia were

---

[104] SCOR, 2nd year, Supplement no. 16, S/447, S/449; 171st mtg (31 July 1947), p. 1626; 173rd mtg (1 Aug. 1947), p. 1703; SC res. 27 (S/459), 1 Aug. 1947; SC res. 31 (S/525, II), 25 Aug. 1947; SC res. 32 (S/525, III), 26 Aug. 1947. It is not clear from the printed official records whether the resolution referred to a dispute or to disputes. The original Australian proposal, printed in the verbatim records and the annual reports of both the Security Council and the General Assembly, called for a settlement of 'their disputes', and the resolution as approved is also printed in the annual report of the Security Council as 'their disputes', (GAOR, 3rd session, Supplement no. 1, A/565, p. 18, and Supplement no. 2, A/620, pp. 28, 30). The Repertoire of Security Council Practice also refers consistently to 'disputes' (pp. 316, 415, 430, 463). The verbatim records of a later meeting of the Council give the text of the resolution in a footnote as 'their disputes' (SCOR, 2nd year, 178th mtg (7 Aug. 1947), p. 1839, n. 1). The text actually put to the vote and approved is given in the verbatim records and the annual *Resolutions and Decisions of the Security Council* as referring to 'their dispute'. Although it is no longer of great moment, I would speculate that the plural form was proposed and approved, and that a single typographical error in the verbatim records was transferred to the *Resolutions and Decisions...* when it was printed in 1964.

parties to a dispute and would have had to abstain from voting never presented itself.

Kashmir   The Kashmir question was submitted to the Security Council by India as a situation whose continuance was likely to endanger the maintenance of international peace and security. Pakistan responded with a counter-complaint about 'disputes which have arisen between India and Pakistan ...'. In its first two resolutions, the Council made no determination, but the third decision dated 21 April 1948 contained a preambular reference to 'the dispute' about Kashmir and went on to use wording derived from Article 33 of the Charter (*'Considering* that the continuation of the dispute is likely to endanger international peace and security ...'). Two previous proposals, sponsored by Canada and China, had also referred to a dispute, but the April text was said to be completely new and not to be based on earlier drafts. It was adopted by the Security Council without a vote. There is nothing in the printed records to show that India or Pakistan took special exception to the idea that a dispute existed. India subsequently objected to the matter being characterized as a dispute, but Pakistan has continued to refer to it as a dispute.[105]

There was for a time a widespread reluctance to elect India or Pakistan to non-permanent membership of the Security Council so long as the Kashmir question was unresolved, but India was keen to serve and eventually the hesitations were overcome.[106] India was a non-permanent member of the Council in 1950-1 and Pakistan in 1952-3. The question arose during that time of whether India and Pakistan could vote on substantive proposals relating to Kashmir. Six decisions on Kashmir were taken in 1950-1, and on all occasions India abstained.[107]

[105] SCOR, 3rd year, Supplement for January-March 1948, pp. 24-5, 38-40, S/667, S/669; Supplement for November 1948, pp. 67-87, 139-44, Annexes 6 and 28 to S/1100; SC res. 47 (S/726), 21 April 1948; FRUS, 1948, vol. V part I, 1975, pp. 272, 334-5; SCOR, 12th year; 762nd mtg (23 Jan. 1957), paras. 8-15, 106, 108, 136; 769th mtg (15 Feb. 1957), paras. 136-7; 774th mtg (21 Feb. 1957), para. 13.
[106] FRUS, 1948, vol. I, 1975, p. 107; 1949, vol. II, 1975, pp. 242-4.
[107] SCOR, 5th year, 470th mtg (14 March 1950), p. 4; 471st mtg (12 April 1950), pp. 5-6, 11; 6th year, 539th mtg (30 March 1951), paras. 62-3; 543rd mtg (30 April 1951), paras. 22, 24; 548th mtg (29 May 1951), para. 99; 566th mtg (10 Nov. 1951), para. 65.

One resolution was adopted in 1952-3, and Pakistan was described as 'Present and not voting'.[108]

Hyderabad In the complaint of Hyderabad in August 1948 about Indian intimidation, reference was made to a 'grave dispute' with India.[109] The Security Council took no substantive decisions on the matter, however, so the question of a formal determination never arose.

THREATS TO PEACE, BREACHES OF THE PEACE,
ACTS OF AGGRESSION (ARTICLE 39)

A tradition has developed in the Security Council that to use the precise language of Article 39, or other parts of Chapter VII of the Charter, has virtually the same effect as actually to cite the Articles in a resolution. Thus, for the Security Council to declare that peace is threatened or breached is thought to bring a matter within the scope of Article 39, whereas to declare that peace is imperilled or endangered is thought not to do so. The result is that much of the negotiation about the wording of resolutions takes the form of a contest between those favouring and those opposing mandatory action. One resolution on Rhodesia contained an almost meaningless but acceptable compromise between the two views, said to have been devised by US ambassador Arthur Goldberg: '*Determines* that the situation ...is extremely grave...and that its continuance in time constitutes a threat to international peace and security'.[110] This was acceptable to those favouring and to those opposing mandatory sanctions, but nobody is sure what the paragraph means.

Indonesia, 1947 Australia complained that the first Dutch 'police action' constituted 'a breach of the peace under Article 39 of the Charter', and submitted a draft resolution containing a determination to that effect. The United States put forward an amended version from which the determination had been eliminated and, after minor amendment, this was approved.[111]

[108] Ibid., 7th year, 611th mtg (23 Dec. 1952), para. 111.
[109] Ibid., 3rd year, Supplement for September 1948, pp. 5-6, S/986.
[110] SC res. 217 (S/6955, as amended), 20 Nov. 1965.
[111] SCOR, 2nd year, Supplement no. 16, pp. 149-50, S/449; 171st mtg (31 July 1947), pp. 1626 (S/454), 1633-4; 172nd mtg (1 Aug. 1947), p. 1658; 173rd mtg (1 Aug. 1947), pp. 1700-3.

Kashmir, 1948   Although the Security Council made no determination under Chapter VII in the Kashmir case, the US State Department took the view that the Council's resolution of 21 April 1948 was one that UN members 'cannot ignore under Article 25 of Charter'. Later in the year, Britain and the United States contemplated asking the Security Council to make a determination that Article 39 of the Charter was applicable, with a view to taking mandatory action, but this was abandoned so that the UN Commission for India and Pakistan (UNCIP) could make another effort to persuade the parties to implement UNCIP's own plan for a truce and plebiscite.[112]

Palestine, 1948   The General Assembly's partition resolution asked that, if there should be any attempt to alter by force the settlement envisaged in the resolution, the Security Council should determine that there had been a threat to peace, breach of the peace, or act of aggression.[113] On 17 May, the United States submitted a proposal that would have determined that the situation in Palestine constituted 'a threat to the peace and a breach of the peace', and would have ordered a cease-fire. The proposed determination under Article 39 was rejected by a vote of the Council, and after *'Orders'* in the cease-fire paragraph had been changed to *'Calls upon'*, the rest of the proposal was approved.[114] The Soviet Union then proposed that the Council should determine that the situation was 'a threat to peace and security', but this was similarly rejected. The Council did, however, warn that, if its cease-fire call should be rejected or subsequently repudiated or violated, the Council would consider acting under Chapter VII of the Charter. After the Israeli offensive in the Negev the following October, the Council made a preambular reference back to its decision of 29 May.[115]

After the expiry of the first cease-fire in July 1948, the United States proposed that the Council should determine that the situation constituted a threat to the peace within the meaning of Article 39, should *order* another cease-fire, and should declare

[112] FRUS, 1948, vol. V part 1, 1975, pp. 339, 426-7, 445-8, 467-8.
[113] GA res. 181 (III), 29 Nov. 1947.
[114] SCOR, 3rd year, 293rd mtg (17 May 1948), p. 2, S/749; 302nd mtg (22 May 1948), p. 54; SC res. 49 (S/773), 22 May 1948.
[115] SCOR, 3rd year, 306th mtg (27 May 1948), pp. 17-18; 310th mtg (29 May 1948), p. 37; SC res. 50 (S/801), 29 May 1948; SC res. 61 (S/1070), 4 Nov. 1948.

that any failure to comply would demonstrate the existence of a breach of the peace. This was approved: it was the first formal determination under Chapter VII of the Charter.[116]

The following November, after the Israeli offensive in the Negev, the Council expressly recalled the July decision that peace was threatened in Palestine,[117] and the July decision was subsequently recalled on a number of occasions.

Korea, 1950   When the Korean war broke out, the UN Commission on Korea reported that the situation was 'serious... and may endanger' peace and security; Secretary-General Lie stated in the Council that the situation represented 'a threat to international peace'; the United States went even further and claimed that there had been 'a breach of the peace and an act of aggression'. Initially the US idea was that the Security Council should find that North Korea was guilty of unprovoked aggression, but other Council members believed that there was insufficient information at that stage for such an extreme determination, so the US draft was toned down so as to find that there had been a breach of the peace, the first formal determination that peace had actually been breached. In two subsequent resolutions, the determination was repeated.[118] As the Soviet Union was boycotting the Security Council over the issue of Chinese representation, there was no veto.

The following year there was considerable pressure from the United States for the General Assembly to find that China had committed aggression in Korea. India and other Afro-Asian states believed that a resolution to this effect would put an end to hopes for an early cease-fire, but the United States was very insistent. After minor amendment, the US draft was approved by 44 votes to 7 (the Soviet bloc): Sweden and Yugoslavia were among the nine abstainers.[119]

[116] SCOR, 3rd year, 334th mtg (13 July 1948), pp. 40-1, S/890; 338th mtg (15 July 1948), p. 66; SC res. 54 (S/902), 15 July 1948.

[117] SC res. 62 (S/1080), 16 Nov. 1948.

[118] SCOR, 5th year, 473rd mtg (25 June 1950), pp. 1-3, S/1495, S/1496; SC res. 82 (S/1501), 25 June 1950; SC res. 83 (S/1508/Rev. 1), 27 June 1950; SC res. 84 (S/1588), 7 July 1950; Lie, p. 329; Dean Acheson, *Present at the Creation*, p. 404.

[119] GA res. 498 (V), 1 Feb. 1951; FRUS, 1950, vol. VII, 1976, pp. 1336-40, 1413-14, 1443, 1600-4, 1610-14, 1617-21, 1626-30; Gladwyn Jebb, *Memoirs*, London, Weidenfeld & Nicolson, 1972, p. 243; Lester Pearson, *Memoirs*, vol. II, *1948-1951, The International Years*, pp. 298-302; K. M. Pannikar, *In Two Chinas: Memoirs of a Diplomat*, pp. 120-1, 124.

Bombing of China, 1950   China complained that its territory had been bombed by 'United States aggression forces', but no proposal was submitted for a formal determination under Article 39.[120]

Armed invasion of Taiwan, 1950   China complained that the presence of US military forces in Taiwan represented 'direct armed aggression on the territory of China', but the only decision of the Council was to invite China to participate in the debate. A Chinese proposal to condemn US aggression, which was put to the vote at the request of the Soviet Union, received only one affirmative vote.[121]

Hostilities off the coast of China, 1955   The Soviet Union complained of US 'acts of aggression' against China, but because China declined to participate, there was no substantive debate.[122]

Lake Tiberias incident, 1955   Following an incident near Lake Tiberias in 1955, three proposals bearing on Article 39 of the Charter were submitted to the Council. Syria proposed that the Council should decide that Israel had committed aggression under Article 39; the Soviet Union proposed that the Council should warn that a future recurrence would require the Council to consider invoking Article 39; while Iran wanted the Council to declare that such acts in the future would constitute a breach of the peace under Article 39. A proposal was submitted by Britain, France, and the United States containing no formal determination but recalling the decision of 15 July 1948 that the situation in Palestine was a threat to the peace. This was adopted unanimously, and none of the other proposals was put to the vote.[123]

---

[120] SCOR, 5th year, Supplement for June-August 1950, pp. 144-5, S/1722.
[121] Ibid., 490th mtg (25 Aug. 1950), pp. 9-10, S/1715; 530th mtg (30 Nov. 1950), p. 22, S/1921; SC res. 87 (S/1836), 29 Sept. 1950.
[122] SCOR, 10th year, Supplement for January-March 1955, p. 27, S/3355.
[123] Ibid., Supplement for October-December 1955, pp. 41-2, S/3519; 11th year, 711th mtg (12 Jan. 1956), para. 53; Supplement for January-March 1956, pp. 1-2, S/3528; SC res. 111 (S/3538), 19 Jan. 1956.

Egyptian complaints, 1956   Egypt complained that British and French military preparations constituted 'a danger to international peace and security' and, later, that the Anglo-French ultimatum was an 'act of aggression'.[124] The Council approved a set of principles for the operation of the Suez Canal, but because of Soviet and Anglo-French vetoes, the Security Council took no other substantive decisions.

Non-compliance with General Assembly resolution, 1956   The Soviet Union held that Britain, France, and Israel were engaged in 'aggressive war' against Egypt and proposed that the Security Council should give Egypt military assistance under Article 42 of the Charter; but the Security Council rejected the provisional agenda containing the Soviet item.[125]

Cyprus, 1963   Cyprus complained in December 1963 of Turkish 'aggression' against Cyprus and intervention in its internal affairs. On 2 March 1964, the Council adopted a proposal submitted by five of the non-permanent members of the Council which included a preambular reference to the situation in Cyprus being 'likely to threaten international peace and security'.[126]

Syrian complaint, 1964   Syria asked the Security Council to consider 'the latest aggression committed by Israel'. A proposal was submitted by Britain and the United States which contained no formal determination (and which was, in any case, vetoed by the Soviet Union).[127]

FORMAL DETERMINATIONS, 1946-64

During the period 1946-64, the Security Council adopted 199

---

[124] SCOR, 11th year, Supplement for July-September 1956, p. 48, S/3656; Supplement for October-December 1956, p. 111, S/3712.

[125] Ibid., pp. 128-30, S/3736; 755th mtg (5 Nov. 1956), para. 27.

[126] Ibid., 18th year, Supplement for October-December 1963, pp. 112-14, S/5488; SC res. 186 (S/5575), 4 March 1964.

[127] SCOR, 19th year, Supplement for October-December 1964, p. 55, S/6044; 1182nd mtg (21 Dec. 1964), para. 41. The text of the vetoed proposal is in Bailey, *Voting in the Security Council*, pp. 196-7.

resolutions, of which three contained express or implied determinations:

Kashmir: 'the dispute';
Palestine: 'a threat to the peace within the meaning of
            Article 39';
Korea: 'a breach of the peace'.

After the determination in the Palestine case, the Security Council ordered rather than called for an indefinite cease-fire in July 1948, and this lasted for several months without critical violations. Ralph Bunche, the Acting Mediator, concluded that a cease-fire could not be maintained indefinitely since it perpetuated conditions that one side or the other found increasingly irksome.[128] The Security Council decided in 1949 that the armistice agreements had superseded the two cease-fires, but at the same time the Council reaffirmed the order in the resolution of July 1948 'to observe an unconditional cease-fire'.[129] Unfortunately, there were many subsequent violations, and even the armistice agreements were increasingly disregarded.

The decisions of the Security Council on Korea between 25 June and 31 July 1950 were taken in unusual circumstances which are unlikely to be repeated. From the Soviet point of view the decisions were illegal because one of the five permanent members (the Soviet Union) was absent and another one (China) was not properly represented. But the other ten members of the Security Council could only take the view that an intentional absence was tantamount to a voluntary abstention: the Council could not allow one permanent member to bring the work of the Security Council to a halt simply by staying away.

It is interesting, though, that the Council's determination that peace had been breached in Korea did not lead to mandatory action. The verbs in the operative paragraphs of the four resolutions that were approved are those that one would expect to find in resolutions outside the scope of Chapter VII of the Charter: 'calls', 'requests', 'recommends', 'welcomes', 'notes', 'authorizes'.

[128] SCOR, 4th year, Supplement for August 1949, p. 4, S/1357.
[129] SC res. 73 (S/1376, II), 11 Aug. 1949.

2.8 INVESTIGATING THE FACTS

Investigation, in the context of Article 34 of the Charter, is concerned with the collection of facts about disputes or situations
that may endanger peace and security, but 'investigation' has
also been used in UN circles to described the process by which
UN observers or peace-keeping personnel seek to establish the
facts following complaints of specific breaches of a cease-fire,
truce, or armistice. Thus, a resolution of the Security Council
on Kashmir asked the UN Commission for India and Pakistan
to 'investigate the facts pursuant to Article 34 of the Charter',
which was the first meaning;[130] while Secretary-General
Hammarskjold, in reporting on the tasks of the first UN Emergency Force in Sinai, indicated that an important function was
the investigation of incidents, which was the second meaning.[131]
Similarly, *observation* has more than one meaning in UN jargon.
It is usually used to describe the continuous work of supervisory
staff or peace-keeping personnel in monitoring the maintenance
of a cease-fire, truce, or armistice, usually along the lines of
demarcation separating the two sides;[132] but it can also refer to
spot-checks by UN personnel to ensure that a military embargo
is being adhered to or that an election is being conducted
freely.[133]

A 1965 report of the Secretary-General on methods of fact-
finding stated that both investigation and observation are
regarded as means of fact-finding.[134] All UN subsidiary organs
are expected to report to their parent bodies unless instructed
to the contrary, and the routine reports of organs in the field
constitute an important source of information which is usually
objective in character.

It is obvious that the United Nations is not short of facts.
The danger, rather, is that it may be smothered by an un-
differentiated flow of facts.

[130] SC res. 39 (S/654), 20 Jan. 1948.

[131] GAOR, 12th session, Annexes, Agenda item 65, p. 5, para. 34 of A/3694.

[132] SC res. 30 (S/525, I), 25 Aug. 1947; 36 (S/597), 1 Nov. 1947; 47 (S/726), 21
April 1948; 73 (S/1376, II), 11 Aug. 1949.

[133] SC res. 50 (S/801), 29 May 1948; 54 (S/902), 15 July 1948; 67 (S/1234), 28 Jan.
1949; GA res. 112 (II), 14 Nov. 1947; 944 (X), 15 Dec. 1955; GAOR, 18th session,
1232nd plenary mtg (7 Oct. 1963), paras. 93-114; 1234th plenary mtg (8 Oct. 1963),
paras. 81-3.

[134] GAOR, 20th session, Annexes, Agenda items 90 and 94, p. 5, para. 5 of A/5694.

Facts, or alleged facts, pour into the United Nations headquarters in a continuous flood—speeches of delegates; conversations, formal and informal, between representatives of governments and UN officials; written communications from other international bodies, governments, would-be governments, non-governmental organisations (some formally recognised, some not), and individuals; reports from UN agencies and officials in the field; information in books, monographs, journals, newspapers, or otherwise in the public domain. The difficulty for the United Nations is not how to accumulate information but how to avoid being suffocated by it; and, secondly, how to distinguish between objective facts and slanted information provided for partisan purposes.[135]

If the Security Council needs information, it may request the Secretary-General or an existing organ to supply it, or it may entrust the task to an organ created specifically for the purpose. In addition to the Charter provisions, the General Assembly has from time to time established new institutions for inquiry or investigation. In 1949 the Assembly asked UN Members to designate 'persons who, by reason of their training, experience, character and standing', might be placed on a panel to be available as members of commissions of inquiry or conciliation.[136] The same year, the General Assembly decided to establish a list of field observers.[137] In 1950 the Assembly created a Peace Observation Commission, as part of the Uniting for Peace arrangements.[138] In 1967, following an initiative by the Netherlands, the Assembly asked the Secretary-General to prepare 'a register of experts…whose services the States parties to a dispute may use…for fact-finding'.[139] The Peace Observation Commission has been used once (in connection with the Balkans in 1951); I know of no instance of either the panel for inquiry and conciliation or the register for fact-finding being used, although the former was referred to when a mediator for Kashmir was being appointed.[140] The panel of field observers has not even been established.

[135] S. D. Bailey 'UN Fact-finding and Human Rights Complaints', *International Affairs,* vol. 48, no. 2 (April 1972), p. 250.

[136] GA res. 268D (III), 28 April 1949.

[137] GA res. 297B (IV), 22 Nov. 1949.

[138] GA res. 377B (V), 3 Nov. 1950.

[139] GA res. 1967 (XVIII), 16 Dec. 1963; res. 2104 (XX), 20 Dec. 1965; res. 2182 (XXI), 12 Dec. 1966; res. 2329 (XXII), 18 Dec. 1967.

[140] SCOR, 6th year, 543rd mtg (30 April 1951), para. 30.

Even if a UN organ in the field has not been expressly entrusted with fact-finding responsibilities, it may yet supply information to the Security Council as an incidental function. The Palestine Commission, for example, was not given fact-finding tasks but it issued five reports on the developing crisis in Palestine in the early months of 1948.

Bodies entrusted with responsibilities of fact-finding in connection with the cases studied are listed in Table 4. The one instance where the Security Council was seriously short of reliable information was in relation to Kashmir. The time-table of events was as follows.

1948

20 January	Security Council decides to establish three-member Commission for India and Pakistan.
10 February	India nominates Czechoslovakia.
21 April	Security Council increases membership of Commission to five.
23 April	Security Council appoints Belgium and Colombia.
30 April	Pakistan nominates Argentina.
7 May	President of the Security Council designates United States.
3 June	Security Council directs Commission to proceed to the areas of dispute 'without delay'.
16 June	First formal meeting of Commission in Geneva is held.
13 July	Commission arrives in India.
22 September	Commission leaves subcontinent.
9 November	Commission issues first interim report.

It will be seen from this time-table that there were delays at every stage.[141] Fifteen weeks were to elapse between the initial decision to create the Commission and the completion of its composition. At every stage India objected to any extension

[141] Taya Zinkin, 'The Kashmir Dispute and the United Nations', London, RIIA, 1966 (Mimeo), p. 4.

Table 4

Organs expressly entrusted with fact-finding responsibilities

Case	Document. ref.	Title of Organ	Mandate
Indonesia I	SC res. 30 (S/525, I)	Consular Commission	'prepare jointly for the information and guidance of the Security Council reports on the situation in the Republic of Indonesia…'
	SC res. 40 (S/689)	Good Offices Committee	'pay particular attention to the political developments in western Java and Madura and to report to the Council…'
	SC res. 41 (S/678)		'keep the Council directly informed about the progress of the political settlement…'
	SCOR, 3rd year, 323rd mtg (17 June 1948), pp. 37-8		Information requested as to the cause, justification, and duration of the suspension of negotiations.
	SCOR, 3rd year, 329th mtg (6 July 1948), p. 30		'an early report on the existing restrictions on the domestic and international trade of Indonesia…'
Kashmir	SC res. 39 (S/654)	Commission for India and Pakistan	'investigate the facts pursuant to Article 34 of the Charter…'
	SC res. 47 (S/726)		'such observers as [the Commission on India and Pakistan] may require…'
	SC res. 51 (S/819)		'study and report to the Security Council…'

Representative for India and Pakistan	SC res. 98 (S/2883)	'keep the Security Council informed of any progress.'
	SC res. 126 (S/3922)	'report to the Security Council on his efforts...'
Palestine	Truce Commission	SC res. 48 (S/727)	'report to the President of the Security Council...regarding its activities and the development of the situation, and subsequently to keep the Security Council currently informed...'
		SC res. 49 (S/773)	'report to the Council on...compliance...'
	Truce Supervision Organization	SC res. 50 (S/801)	'a sufficient number of military observers...'
		SC res. 73 (S/1376, II)	'personnel...as may be required in observing and maintaining the cease-fire...*Requests* the Chief of Staff...to report to the Security Council...'
		SC res. 100 (S/3128)	'the Chief of Staff of the Truce Supervision Organization to inform [the Security Council] regarding the fulfilment of [the] undertaking.'
		SC res. 101 (S/3139/Rev. 2)	'report within three months...'
		SC res. 107 (S/3379)	'keep the Council informed of the progress...'
		SC res. 108 (S/3435)	'report to the Security Council on the action taken...'
		SC res. 111 (S/3538)	'report to the Council as appropriate...'

Table 4 (contd)

Case	Document. ref.	Title of Organ	Mandate
	SC res. 114 (S/3605)		'report to the Security Council whenever any action...requires immediate consideration by the Council.'
	SCOR, 12th year, 782nd mtg (28 May 1957), paras. 201, 214-15.		Request for a supplementary report concerning the situation in the Hula demilitarized zone.
	SCOR, 12th year, 788th mtg (6 Sept. 1957), para. 132		Request to submit reports on the complaints of Israel and Jordan.
	SC res. 127 (S/3942)		'report on the implementation of the present resolution.'
	SC res. 171 (S/5111)		'report as appropriate...'
	SC res. 113 (S/3575)	Secretary-General	'report to the Council in his discretion...'
	SC res. 114 (S/3605)		'report to the Security Council as appropriate.'
	SCOR, 3rd year, 332nd mtg (8 July 1948), pp. 21-3	Mediator	Immediate information requested on the situation in Palestine.
	SC res. 54 (S/902)		'keep the Security Council currently informed concerning the operation of the truce...'
Indonesia II	SC res. 67 (S/1234)	Commission for Indonesia	'observe on behalf of the United Nations the elections to be held throughout Indonesia [and] render periodic reports to the Council...'

Korea	SC res. 82 (S/1501)	Commission on Korea	'keep the Security Council informed on the execution of this resolution...'
	SC res. 84 (S/1588)	Unified Command	'provide the Security Council with reports...'
Sinai-Suez	GAOR, 12th session, Annexes, Agenda item 65, p. 5, para. 34 of A/3694	UN Emergency Force	'investigations of various complaints...'
Cyprus	SCOR, 19th year, Supplement for January-March 1964, p. 22, para. 2 of S/5514	Representative of the Secretary-General	'observe the progress of the peace-keeping operation and to report on it to [the Secretary-General].'
	SC res. 186 (S/5575)	Secretary-General	'the Commander of the Force shall... report to [the Secretary-General]...The mediator shall report periodically to the Secretary-General...'
	SC res. 193 (S/5868)		'Anticipating the submission of the Secretary-General's report...'

of the scope of the responsibilities of the Commission, and this usually had the effect of causing delay.[142] After the full composition of the Commission had been established, another ten weeks elapsed before the Commission reached India. It spent ten weeks on the subcontinent, which in the circumstances was not excessive. Seven more weeks were needed to draft its first interim report, which comprised forty pages of text and eighty pages of documents.

Moreover, the problem was not simply the amount of time taken at each stage. The Commission reported in 1948 that it had not fully appreciated the importance of the Azad Kashmir movement until it had actually left the subcontinent, and a year later the Commission again seemed surprised at the political and military vitality of Azad Kashmir.[143] It would seem that the early decisions on Kashmir were taken on the basis of incomplete information, partly because the issue was initially presented as a dispute between India and Pakistan rather than as a question of self-determination for the Kashmiris.

Two proposed investigations of matters covered by this study were prevented by the veto. The first occurred in 1950, after China had complained of US bombing. The United States proposed that a commission consisting of India and Sweden should 'investigate on the spot and report as soon as possible', but the Soviet Union cast a negative vote, India and Yugoslavia abstained, and Nationalist China did not participate in the vote. The second veto followed allegations that the United States had used bacterial weapons in Korea. The United States proposed that the International Committee of the Red Cross should be asked to investigate, and the Soviet Union again cast the sole negative vote. The United States then proposed that the Security Council should condemn the fabrication of false charges, and this also was vetoed.[144]

---

[142] SCOR, 3rd year, 230th mtg (20 Jan. 1948), pp. 131-2, 135-6; Supplement for June 1948, pp. 78-9, S/825.

[143] SCOR, 3rd year, Supplement for November 1948, p. 52, para. 125 of S/1100; 4th year, Special Supplement no. 7, pp. 40-6, paras. 203-25 of S/1430.

[144] Text of vetoed proposals in Bailey, *Voting in the Security Council*, pp. 173-4 (veto 46) and 175-6 (vetoes 50 and 51).

Neither of these vetoes meant that the Council had to act without information. Indeed, if one surveys all of the proposals for investigation that have been vetoed, including those in connection with matters not covered by this study, it is apparent that proposals for investigation were often made not because information was needed, but to embarrass a party reluctant to expose itself to objective investigation, and that the fact of the veto being used was widely taken as casting doubt on the version of events given by the vetoing state.

CHAPTER 3

The diplomacy of the Security Council

3.1 THE RIGHT OF SELF-DEFENCE

One of the principles of the United Nations, which all Members have agreed to accept and carry out, is that force shall not be threatened or used against the territorial integrity or political independence of any state, except in two eventualities specified in the Charter. First, in the event of an armed attack, Members have the inherent right of individual or collective self-defence until the Security Council has taken the necessary measures. Action taken in exercise of this right 'shall be immediately reported to the Security Council' and does not affect the Council's authority and responsibility for world peace and security. Second, Members may use armed force in collective measures recommended or ordered by the Security Council if the Council considers that non-military measures are not adequate to maintain or restore peace.[1] Most legal scholars take the view that, while the Charter affirms only that UN Members have the right of self-defence, it is a right belonging to all states, whether UN Members or not.[2] Occasionally a UN Member, at a moment convenient to itself, has questioned the efficacy of the United Nations to halt aggression, but Rosalyn Higgins believes that a state that has joined the United Nations has no right to do this.[3]

On a number of occasions Israel has resorted to anticipatory self-defence—reprisals in advance, as it were.[4] While a case for this can sometimes be made, the doctrine requires that the party exercising anticipatory self-defence should know the capabilities and be able to foresee the intentions of others. Professor Higgins would justify the doctrine, 'but always with

---

[1] Articles 2 (4), 42, and 51.
[2] Brownlie, p. 331.
[3] Higgins, *The Development of International Law through the Political Organs of the United Nations*, p. 197.
[4] Yigal Allon, *The Making of Israel's Army,* pp. 73-5.

the proviso that the action in self-defence is proportionate, in nature and degree, to the ... imminent attack'.[5]

While not every use of armed force amounts to aggression, as Britain was at pains to emphasize during the Suez episode,[6] and while there can be aggression without the use of force,[7] it is usually the case that, when a state initiates the use of armed force, the victim is likely to invoke Article 51 of the Charter regarding the right of self-defence; yet it has in practice been rare for Article 51 to be used in the way that the founders intended, and UN diplomats soon learn to treat references by other diplomats to Article 51 or to the right of self-defence with a fair degree of scepticism. Too often Article 51 has been used to justify provocative or aggressive action: Egypt's refusal to allow Israeli cargoes to pass through the Suez Canal,[8] the Anglo-French action over Suez,[9] or military intervention in support of kith and kin (such as Pakistani help to the tribal invaders of Kashmir[10] or the intervention of Arab armies after the lapse of the Mandate in Palestine[11]). When force was used by the Arabs or Israel after 1949 in disregard of the armistice obligations, or used in retaliation, one or both parties were likely to invoke Article 51.[12]

The kith and kin argument is particularly insidious.[13] In one of the early statements about Kashmir, the Prime Minister of Pakistan reminded Nehru of the 'large numbers' of Kashmiris in the Pakistan Army: 'if some of them ... rendered assistance

[5] Higgins, *Development of International Law,* p. 201; see also Brownlie, pp. 257-61, 275-8; and D. W. Bowett, *Self-defence in International Law,* Manchester, University Press, 1958, pp. 187-93.

[6] GAOR, 1st emergency special session, 561st plenary mtg (1 Nov. 1956), para. 100.

[7] Higgins, *Development of International Law,* p. 176.

[8] SCOR, 6th year, 549th mtg (26 July 1951), para. 78; 550th mtg (1 Aug. 1951), paras. 34-42; 553rd mtg (16 Aug. 1951), paras. 56-60; 9th year, 661st mtg (12 March 1954), para. 70.

[9] Selwyn Lloyd, *Suez 1956, A Personal Account,* London, Cape, 1978, pp. 42, 209, 217, 253, 260.

[10] P. L. Lakhanpal, *Essential Documents and Notes on Kashmir Dispute,* 2nd edn, Delhi, International Books, 1965, p. 90.

[11] SCOR, 3rd year, 292nd mtg (15 May 1948), pp. 10, 19-20.

[12] See, for example, SCOR, 6th year, Supplement for April to June 1951, pp. 100-1, S/2121; 19th year, 1162nd mtg (16 Nov. 1954), para. 59; 1164th mtg (27 Nov. 1964), paras. 117, 120.

[13] Richard A Falk, *Legal Order in a Violent World,* Princeton, University Press, 1968, p. 340.

to their kith and kin ... it is scarcely to be wondered at'.[14] Egypt justified the intervention of Arab armies in Palestine in 1948 on the ground that it had 'the unequivocal consent' of their fellow Arabs in Palestine, and Syria pointed out that the majority of Palestinians had asked the Arab states to help.[15] The three states which invaded Egypt in 1956 tried to divert attention from their own misdeeds by stressing the Arab harassment of Jews and of British and French nationals.[16] The kith and kin imperative was used by both Greece and Turkey in the Cyprus case.

The most substantial consideration of the self-defence issue by the Security Council during the period studied took place in 1951, when Israel complained that Egypt was preventing Israeli cargoes from passing through the Suez Canal. Britain and the United States took the view that 'an international tribunal judging the dispute on its legal merits would probably support the Egyptian position', but that, even if Egypt's policy were legal, it was not wise. In 1950, a group of major Western maritime powers (Britain, France, Netherlands, Norway, United States) had made a joint approach to Egypt, suggesting that the restrictions were both unreasonable and impracticable.[17] In order to justify its policy in the Security Council, Egypt claimed that its policy was consistent with the doctrine of self-preservation and that the refusal to allow the passage of enemy cargoes was a normal part of belligerency. Israel argued in response that Egypt could not unilaterally exercise belligerent rights two-and-a-half years after concluding an armistice agreement. Most members of the Security Council rejected the Egyptian case: Britain thought that the concept of self-preservation was 'very vague', and the Netherlands took the line that Article 51 of the Charter could not be applicable, as there had been no armed attack against Egypt. Britain, France, and the United States submitted a proposal to the Security Council finding that

[14] P. L. Lakhanpal, *Essential Documents and Notes on Kashmir Dispute,* 2nd edn, Delhi, International Books, 1965, p. 90 (letter dated 31 Dec. 1947).

[15] SCOR, 3rd year, 292nd mtg (15 May 1948), pp. 10, 17-20.

[16] GAOR, 11th session, Annexes, Agenda item 66, pp. 22-3, 27-8, 30-1, 33, A/3399, A/3400 and Add. 1, A/3444, A/3445, A/3457; 624th mtg (18 Dec. 1956), paras. 139-72; 629th mtg (20 Dec. 1956), paras. 112-40.

[17] FRUS, 1950, vol. V, 1978, pp. 301-2, 315-17.

Egyptian interference with Israeli cargoes 'cannot in the prevailing circumstances be justified on the ground that it is necessary for self-defence', and this was approved by eight votes to none, with three abstentions (Soviet Union, Nationalist China, India). The Soviet Union did not explain its abstention, but Nationalist China argued that an armistice did not end the state of war, and India considered that the Security Council was not the most suitable body for adjudicating complicated legal issues.[18]

The matter came before the Security Council again in 1954, as Egypt had not complied with the 1951 decision. It was then maintained by France and Denmark that Egypt was bound to implement the earlier resolution, because under Article 25 of the Charter all UN Members had agreed 'to accept and carry out the decisions of the Security Council'. The obligation to accept and carry out Security Council decisions, insisted Denmark, 'is not limited to such decisions as you agree with or consider legal. All Member States in ratifying the Charter agreed to a limitation of their sovereignty.' Egypt pointed out, however, that Article 25 concerns 'decisions ... in accordance with the ... Charter', and Egypt believed that the earlier decision did not accord with the spirit of the Charter. A proposal by New Zealand that the Security Council should call on Egypt to comply with the 1951 decision was vetoed by the Soviet Union.[19]

If the debates on the refusal of Egypt to allow cargoes for Israel through the Suez Canal represented the most substantial attention paid by the Security Council to the concept of self-defence, the most far-reaching interpretation of the Charter was contained in Secretary-General Hammarskjold's report in May 1956 on his visit to the Middle East, which he had made at the request of the Security Council in an effort to secure

[18] SCOR, 6th year, 549th mtg (26 July 1951), para. 78; 550th mtg (1 Aug. 1951), paras. 34-42, 93; 551st mtg (1 Aug. 1951), para. 34; 552nd mtg (16 Aug. 1951), para. 58; 553rd mtg (16 Aug. 1951), paras. 15, 40, 56-60, 122, 139; SC res. 95 (S/2322), 1 Sept. 1951. See also Higgins, *Development of International Law,* pp. 177, 200, 205, and D. W. Bowett, *Self-defence in International Law,* Manchester, University Press, 1958, p. 191.

[19] SCOR, 9th year, 663rd mtg (25 March 1954), paras. 12-3, 41; 664th mtg (29 March 1954), paras. 22, 114, 155. The vetoed text is in Bailey, *Voting in the Security Council,* p. 179.

compliance with the armistice agreements. When Hammarsk-jold asked the parties to reaffirm that they would respect the cease-fire, they all agreed but reserved the right to act in self-defence, and this provided Hammarskjold with the opportunity of explaining his stand on the relationship between cease-fire obligations and self-defence. In his view, the reservations about self-defence could not derogate from the cease-fire obligation or permit acts of retaliation in response to a violation by the other side. He maintained that a victim had no right to decide on its own responsibility that the other party was in breach of the cease-fire obligation: in a concrete case of violation, only the Security Council could determine that Article 51 was applicable, since the exercise of self-defence was 'under the sole jurisdiction of the Security Council'.[20] The Council gave prolonged atten-tion to Hammarskjold's report, but the only reference to the self-defence issue during the debate came when Abba Eban of Israel reminded Syria that the only qualification to the cease-fire obligation related to self-defence. Nobody referred to Hammarskjold's far-reaching interpretation of the Charter, and the Council concluded its debate by adopting a British proposal which endorsed certain ideas in the report but noted rather than approved the report as a whole.[21]

In one respect the right of self-defence has been eroded because of the current tendency to legitimize wars of national liberation. One is bound to ask, moreover, whether external help to liberation struggles is compatible with the commitment in Article 2(4) of the Charter not to threaten or use force against the territorial integrity or political independence of any state. Professor Draper goes so far as to argue that the UN Charter has been amended 'in a manner that had no vestige of legality'.[22]

[20] SCOR, 11th year, Supplement for April to June 1956, pp. 16-17, 36, 40-1, 56-61, parts III to VI of S/3584 and paras. 21, 40-2, 44-6 of and Annexes 1-4 to S/3596.
[21] SC res. 114 (S/3605), 4 June 1956.
[22] G. I. A. D. Draper, 'Wars of National Liberation and War Criminality', in *Restraints on War: Studies in the Limitation of Armed Conflict,* ed. Michael Howard, Oxford, University Press, 1979, pp. 145-7, 157-60.

3.2 STOPPING THE FIGHTING

THE TIMING OF THE CALL TO STOP
MILITARY OPERATIONS

As a result of the creation of the United Nations, a new stage can now be interposed in the transition from war to peace. This is the call or order by the Security Council to cease the firing and stop all hostile military actions, issued from wherever the Council is meeting, and perhaps with minimal prior consultation with the parties. The call to stop fighting is usually in the form of a recommendation, but the Security Council does have the power to *order* a mandatory cease-fire if the circumstances warrant such strong action, as happened during the fighting in Palestine in July 1948.[23]

The timing of such a call is crucial; indeed, one experienced diplomat has expressed to me the view that it is the *only* difficult question facing members of the Security Council when armed conflict occurs.[24] If any party to the conflict believes that the outcome is likely to be more favourable if the fighting continues, then a cease-fire call or order by the Security Council may not be sufficient on its own to bring hostilities to an end. At a very early stage in his peace mission in Palestine in 1948, Count Bernadotte was in Cairo and was asked by the secretary-general of the Arab League if the United Nations could guarantee that, if the Arabs suspended military operations, they would not find themselves worse off after the period of suspension. The following day in Haifa, David Ben-Gurion made precisely the same point from the point of view of Israel. 'It was certainly not without interest to note ... how eager they both were to point out that a truce would be of advantage simply and solely to their opponents.'[25] During the discussion of a cease-fire in Korea in 1951, China refused to accept a proposal of the UN General Assembly on the ground that a cease-fire first and negotiations later would help the United States. Later in the year, however, the tables were turned, and the Unified Com-

[23] SC res. 54 (S/902), 15 July 1948.
[24] Conversation with Sir Colin Crowe, 3 May 1974, and letter from Sir Colin, 23 November 1979.
[25] Bernadotte, pp. 34, 38-9.

mand rejected a Communist proposal for an immediate cease-fire simply because it seemed likely to help the other side.[26] The truth is that there is rarely a time during armed conflict when, taking a short and unpacific view, to continue the fighting does not seem likely to benefit someone.

A cease-fire call by the Security Council is not issued in a vacuum, however. When the Council had eleven members, no resolution could be adopted unless seven members voted in favour (nine at present, in the enlarged Council of fifteen), and the permanent members have always had the possibility of veto. If enough members of the Council are determined that the fighting shall stop and are prepared to use diplomatic and other forms of persuasion and pressure to that end, then it is certainly possible eventually to make the Council's decision effective.

This helps to clarify an important aspect of the Council's work when fighting breaks out. What is crucial in the first place in the Security Council is not only the attitudes of the parties but also the policies of the friends and allies of the parties with votes in the Security Council. In 1947, for example, the views of Belgium and Australia had as much influence on the Security Council on the Indonesian question as did those of the Netherlands and the Indonesian Republicans. The Soviet Union has on more than one occasion defended its use of the veto by saying that it has been used to prevent the Security Council from taking decisions that would have been unpalatable to the developing countries,[27] and in recent years the US veto has been used from time to time to protect Israel and South Africa.

It may happen, of course, that members of the Security Council fail to reinforce their votes by resolute diplomacy. The two UN Mediators in Palestine believed that the major powers often failed to back up their votes on Middle Eastern questions with the necessary determination, and most Third World leaders believed that the West could have forced the

---

[26] GAOR, 5th session, Annexes, Agenda item 76, pp. 14-15, A/C 1/653; William H. Vatcher, Jr, *Panmunjom: The Story of the Korean Military Armistice Negotiations,* p. 84.

[27] SCOR, 22nd year, Supplement for April to June 1967, p. 4, S/7841. See also SCOR, 9th year, 656th mtg (22 Jan. 1954), paras. 145-8; 11th year, 743rd mtg (13 Oct. 1956), para. 97; 18th year, 1062nd mtg (30 Aug. 1963), para. 38; 1063rd mtg (3 Sept. 1963), paras. 118-19; 19th year, 1152nd mtg (17 Sept. 1964), para. 62.

Netherlands to adopt a more conciliatory attitude over Indonesia in 1947-9. The US ambassador in India cabled to Dean Acheson a few days after the first Dutch 'police action': 'No one in India or anywhere in Asia will believe that if Governments of United Kingdom and United States of America really desired bring this conflict to end they could not do it immediately without military intervention.'[28]

The interaction between the main parties and their external supporters or patrons is a subtle one, and it is not always obvious to the Security Council who is calling the tune. When Archbishop Makarios issued his Thirteen Points for constitutional reform in Cyprus in 1963, the Turkish community found that the situation was pre-empted before it could devise its own response. '[T]he Makarios proposals were first of all rejected by Turkey and not by the Turkish Cypriots.'[29] Two months later, a reverse situation occurred when Greece (and Turkey) were willing to consider peace-keeping by NATO countries, but this was rejected by Makarios.[30]

CEASE-FIRE AND POLITICAL SETTLEMENT

Whoever takes the lead, whether the parties themselves or their friends, it may be taken as axiomatic that, while the fighting continues, the Security Council will give primary attention to bringing about a cease-fire or truce, whereas the parties will try to make a link between a suspension of military operations and political progress. This was evident in all of the cases studied.

Indonesia   In case 1 (Indonesia 1947-8), the Good Offices Committee (GOC) had been asked to assist in the settlement of the dispute between the Netherlands and Indonesia. As soon as the GOC reached Indonesia, it told the parties how it interpreted its mandate, and indicated that it would 'render all assistance to the parties in reaching a political settlement'. The

[28] FRUS, 1947, vol. VI, 1972, p. 991.
[29] Polyvios G. Polyviou, *Cyprus: the Tragedy and the Challenge,* printed in England by John Swain & Son Ltd, 1975, pp. 39-40; Michael Harbottle, *The Impartial Soldier,* p. 10.
[30] Philip Windsor, *NATO and the Cyprus Crisis,* London, Institute for Strategic Studies, 1964 (Adelphi Paper no. 14), pp. 11-12.

initial response of the Netherlands was that it was 'premature' to take up the question of a political settlement until the cease-fire was being better observed. The GOC realized that the Republican side would not discontinue its guerrilla struggle unless there could be agreement on the framework for political negotiations. The GOC, therefore, issued a series of proposals directed towards a political settlement: eight principles annexed to its Christmas Message in 1947, six Additional Principles drafted by the US member of the GOC (Dr Frank Graham), and two statements of elucidation on the connection between a truce and a political settlement. From the Republican point of view, these GOC documents were decisive in swinging opinion in favour of a truce. When the Security Council received the GOC's report of the *Renville* truce, it expressed satisfaction that the fighting had stopped and that the parties had accepted 'certain principles as an agreed basis for the conclusion of a political settlement'.[31]

After the second Dutch 'police action' (case 4), the Security Council called for the discontinuance of military operations and guerrilla warfare, but it also set out in considerable detail how the political problems should be tackled. The draft resolution had originated with the United States. The original US intention had been not to introduce a new proposal at that particular stage but simply to repeat the criticism of the Dutch action. On 12 January, however, US ambassador Philip Jessup told Washington that 'all delegations are looking to [the United States] for leadership', and he was therefore transmitting a suggested draft, which would have provided that the Republican leaders who had been interned by the Dutch should be allowed to return at once to Jogjakarta so as to be in a position to order their forces to co-operate in the restoration of peace. The Netherlands refused to accept the US draft in its original form and as revised, but Jessup insisted that a strong text was needed, and Dean Rusk (at that time director of the office of UN affairs in the State Department) reluctantly agreed. The US draft was co-sponsored by China, Cuba, and Norway,

---

[31] SCOR, 3rd year, Special Supplement no. 1, pp. 2, 4, 6-7, 17-19, 53, 67-77, paras. 4-5, 8, 14 (3) and (7), 37, 39, 41, and 44 of and Annex 2 to Appendix V and Appendices VIII to XIV of S/649/Rev. 1; SC res. 41 (S/678), 28 Feb. 1948.

amended by Canada, and then approved. It noted that its earlier calls to cease-fire and to release the Indonesian leaders had not been carried out, and it called on the Netherlands government to discontinue military operations and to release 'immediately and unconditionally' all political prisoners arrested since the start of the second 'police action': it also called on the Republicans to cease guerrilla warfare. As the United States considered that the Netherlands had, by implication, rejected the concept of good offices, the GOC was reconstituted as the UN Commission for Indonesia. The new Commission was asked to assist the parties regarding military deployments and the maintenance of law and order, and to observe elections to be held throughout Indonesia. The old Consular Commission was asked to provide the new Commission with military observers and other facilities, but to suspend its other activities. The resolution looked to the resumption of negotiations on the establishment of a federal, independent, and sovereign United States of Indonesia.[32]

It will be seen that the resolution went into considerable detail. The Council had, of course, the advantage of detailed reports and suggestions from the GOC, but the Council would be unlikely nowadays to prescribe the course to be followed in such detail.

Kashmir   In the Kashmir case, the Security Council quickly realized that the only hope of finding a solution lay in making a close link between a cessation of fighting and a procedure by which the people of Kashmir could decide their own future. This was stressed when the President of the Council (Belgium) reported on 22 and 28 January 1948 on his conversations with India and Pakistan. The two states had agreed, he said, that 'in the final analysis the people [of Kashmir] will be free to decide their future by the recognized democratic method of a plebiscite or referendum ...'; it was the view put forward with great cogency when Sheikh Abdullah addressed the Council on 5 February; and it was the basic element that members of the Security Council incorporated in proposals submitted between

[32] FRUS, 1949, vol. VII part 1, 1975, pp. 131-2, 145, 147, 157, 162, 168, 180, 196; SC res. 67 (S/1234), 28 Jan. 1949.

January and April. The same idea was contained in the resolutions of the Security Council of 21 April 1948 and of the UN Commission for India and Pakistan of 13 August 1948. Indeed, the main thrust of UN mediation regarding Kashmir was always to devise acceptable arrangements for an impartial plebiscite, but the United Nations was faced with Nehru's growing conviction that the status of Kashmir had been settled at the time of accession and his steady withdrawal from the commitment to let the question be decided by reference to the people under international auspices. Nehru's intransigence on this point was reinforced once Pakistan had sent its own troops into Kashmir early in May 1948. Pakistan, on the other hand, took the line that there could not be a complete cessation of fighting unless 'conditions for a plebiscite were guaranteed'.[33]

In August and September 1948, the UN Commission for India and Pakistan explored with the two governments the arrangements that might be made regarding a plebiscite. Pakistan continued to give this high priority and held that the Commission's truce proposals were 'so closely interlinked with the final solution of the Kashmir question' that it was 'impossible to separate one from the other', and that, as India and Pakistan would be affected by the result of a plebiscite to an equal degree, they should be in a position of absolute equality and advantage regarding it. India's enthusiasm for a plebiscite had been steadily dwindling, however, with the result that she added some new preconditions: in particular, India maintained that Pakistan 'should have no part in the organization of the plebiscite', and Nehru rejected a pressing appeal from the UN Commission to reconsider some problems connected with a plebiscite, on the ground that there would be no point in discussing a plebiscite while fighting was continuing.[34] The following year, the UN Commission found that there had been a further hardening of the Indian position and an increase in

---

[33] SCOR, 3rd year, 231st mtg (22 Jan. 1948), p. 165; 236th mtg (28 Jan. 1948), pp. 265-6, 268-70; 241st mtg (5 Feb. 1948), pp. 22-5; Supplement for November, pp. 18, 28-9, 31-4, 54, paras. 4, 56-7, 75, 135 of S/1100; SC res. 47 (S/726), 21 April 1948; FRUS, 1948, vol. V part 1, 1975, pp. 271-2, 276, 281, 305, 311, 325-8, 339, 371, 375, 377.

[34] SCOR, 3rd year, Supplement for November 1948, pp. 34, 36, 38, 42-3, 47, 56, 129-30, 134-5, paras. 77, 78, 84, 97, 103, 148-51 of and Annex 26 to S/1100.

preconditions.[35] A succession of UN mediators found India increasingly unwilling to agree on arrangements whereby the problem could be resolved by a plebiscite under UN auspices,[36] so Kashmir continues to be partitioned *de facto*.

Palestine   A distinguishing feature of the Palestine case was that it was the General Assembly's plan for a settlement that sparked off the Arab attempt to defeat partition by armed force. Count Bernadotte always maintained that he was not bound by all the details of the partition resolution,[37] but he clearly could not depart from the framework that Palestine was to be divided into Jewish, Arab, and international sectors. The arguments that he deployed in support of the two general cease-fires were essentially that to continue fighting would not change the underlying realities. He realized that both parties had accepted the first cease-fire 'with important reservations', and that both were actively planning to renew hostilities: both complained that the cease-fires benefited the other side, and both regarded the cease-fires as 'only a phase of hostilities'.[38]

Korea   In Korea there was a clear connection between an end to the fighting and a political settlement, first during the cease-fire discussions in New York and later during the armistice negotiations in Panmunjom. On 14 December 1950, the General Assembly had approved an Afro-Asian proposal for a three-member group to explore the possibilities of a cease-fire. The US view at the stage when the military fortunes of the Unified Command were at a low ebb was that aggression should not be rewarded; a cease-fire would have to come into force before there could be any substantive negotiations. The Chinese delegation in New York was not interested in a cease-fire unless other matters could be dealt with, in particular the withdrawal of foreign troops from Korea, the question of Taiwan, and China's right to be represented in the United Nations. The UN

[35] Ibid., 4th year, Special Supplement no. 7, pp. 36-60, paras. 197-276 of S/1430.
[36] See, for example, SCOR, 13th year, Supplement for January-March 1958, pp. 42-4, paras. 21-33 of S/3984.
[37] Bernadotte, pp. 33, 94, 118, 131, 146, 171; GAOR, 3rd session, Supplement no. 11, A/648, pp. 5, 9, 22, 26.
[38] GAOR, 3rd session, Supplement no. 11, A/648, pp. 3, 31, 36, 44.

Cease-Fire Group was in the awkward position of being an organ of the General Assembly charged with finding a satisfactory basis for stopping the fighting, while another UN organ, the Security Council, had provided an umbrella for military operations.[39]

The Cease-Fire Group consisted of Nasrollah Entezam of Iran, who was president of the General Assembly, Lester Pearson of Canada, and Sir Benegal Rau of India. The titular head of the Chinese delegation in New York was General Wu Hsiu-ch'üan, but UN diplomats had the impression that the real leader was Ch'iao Kuan-hua. Both Wu and Ch'iao were later to be criticized for ideological deviations. The Chinese delegation was unwilling to meet the Cease-Fire Group officially, but it had informal contacts with Sir Benegal Rau who, Pearson noted in his diary, was becoming 'more and more spiritual and ghostlike' as the work proceeded. Rau found the Chinese 'friendly and full of talk of peace', but UN Secretary-General Trygve Lie felt that Rau did not know how to handle Communists. Lie himself alternated between elation and depression, and Pearson noted in his diary on 17 December: 'I do not know whether Lie is influenced more by his desire to spend Christmas in Norway, or to strike another blow for collective security in the United Nations.' Rau was warned from New Delhi not to become too active in the Cease-Fire Group, and Pearson had the impression that Rau was steadily losing 'most of his illusions about negotiating with Communists'. The Chinese delegation left New York on 19 December.[40]

On 15 December, the Cease-Fire Group had drawn up a statement on the cessation of hostilities in all of Korea, to be supervised by a UN commission. Rau sent a copy to K. M. Pannikar, the Indian ambassador in Peking, and the Chinese asked Pannikar whether the proposal had US support. When Pannikar was unable to say unequivocally that the United States would go along with the proposal, China came to the conclusion that what was intended was that one of the parties to the conflict, and one only, should verify the cease-fire. On 2

[39] GA res. 384 (V), 14 Dec. 1950; Leland M. Goodrich, *Korea: A Study of US Policy in the United Nations,* p. 158; Pannikar, p. 121.
[40] Pearson, vol. II, pp. 279-86; FRUS, 1950, vol. VII, 1976, pp. 1299, 1379, 1517, 1546-50, 1554-62.

January the Cease-Fire Group reported that, despite its best efforts, it has been unable to devise an acceptable formula.[41]

In an effort to meet the objection of China and North Korea, the Commonwealth prime ministers, meeting in London in January 1951, devoted a good deal of time to Korea, though Lester Pearson thought that 'much of their discussion was unrealistic'. What Pearson called 'the Bevin plan' seemed to promise support for seating China at the United Nations and for her claim to Taiwan 'if only she will negotiate', but it failed to lay down specifically that a cease-fire would have to come before any political discussions. Pearson was very disconcerted that none of the Commonwealth heads of government seemed to have a copy of the statement of principles that the UN Cease-Fire Group had drafted. 'Nehru certainly had a text', noted Pearson in his diary, 'but did not produce it.' In the end, the prime ministers included in their final declaration a rather anodyne passage about the need to end the fighting in Korea 'around the conference table'.[42]

By now, the Cease-Fire Group in New York had amended its draft proposal. The revision provided for an immediate cease-fire, whether as a result of a formal agreement or of a lull in hostilities, following which the General Assembly would set up an appropriate body, of which China would be a member, to consider Far Eastern problems, including Taiwan and the representation of China.[43]

Pearson presented the supplementary report of the Cease-Fire Group to the political committee of the General Assembly on 11 January. Sir Gladwyn Jebb of Britain had been trying to find a group of middle-of-the-road sponsors for a draft resolution based on this supplementary report, but the Asian states were beginning to have second thoughts and wanted 'to remove the stipulation that a cease-fire must actually take place before any negotiations begin'. Jebb then suggested to Rau 'as a last resort' that perhaps Israel would introduce the draft resolution. Abba Eban, the Israeli ambassador, had previously been peddling a proposal that the United States had regarded as un-

[41] Pannikar, pp. 119-21; GAOR, 5th session, Annexes, Agenda item 76, pp. 6-10, A/C 1/643.

[42] Pearson, vol. II, pp. 287-91; Goodrich, p. 160.

[43] GAOR, 5th session, Annexes, Agenda item 76, p. 13, A/C 1/645.

realistic, and Rau persuaded Eban to introduce a more suitable text. 'This was enough to arouse the ire and opposition of the Arabs, who... recanted their earlier decision of approval, and began to find fault...' Padilla Nervo of Mexico was persuaded over a hurried lunch discussion to raise a rather dubious point of order, after which the chairman of the General Assembly's political committee hurriedly put to the vote the report of the Cease-Fire Group; Norway suggested transmitting the report to Peking; Eban withdrew his draft; and an amended version of the Norwegian proposal was approved by 44 votes to 5 (the Soviet bloc), with 8 abstentions (Nationalist China, the Arab States other than Lebanon, plus the Philippines and El Salvador). Dean Acheson believed that the choice for the United States of whether to support or oppose this plan was 'a murderous one'. In the end, it was decided to support it 'in the fervent hope and belief that the Chinese would reject it' (as they did), and that the allies of the United States would then 'return to comparative sanity' and vote that China was an aggressor (as they did).[44]

On 17 January, Chou En-lai (Zhou Enlai) rejected the revised proposals of the Cease-Fire Group because of the failure to provide a proper link between a cease-fire and political negoti- ations: 'the principle of a cease-fire first and negotiations after- wards would only help the United States to maintain and extend its aggression...' Chou proposed that Far Eastern matters should be dealt with by a conference of Britain, China, France, the Soviet Union, and the United States (as permanent members of the Security Council) together with Egypt and India. For five months, the matter was quiescent.[45]

The famous speech of ambassador Yakov Malik and the informal Soviet soundings, which led to the opening of armistice negotiations, aroused interest at the United Nations precisely because the connection between a cease-fire and a political settlement was so obviously muted.[46] Armistice negotiations opened in July, and the agreed agenda had, as the last item,

[44] Ibid., A/C 1/650; Pearson, vol. II, pp. 291-8; Gladwyn Jebb, *The Memoirs of Lord Gladwyn*, London, Weidenfeld & Nicolson, 1972, pp. 245-6; Acheson, pp. 512-13; FRUS, 1950, vol. VII, 1976, pp. 1499-1503, 1509-10, 1626.

[45] GAOR, 5th session, Annexes, Agenda item 76, pp. 14-15, A/C 1/653.

[46] Allan E. Goodman (ed.), *Negotiating while Fighting, The Diary of Admiral C. Turner Joy at the Korean Armistice Conference*, p. xiii.

'Recommendations to the governments of the countries concerned on both sides'. It was decided in February 1952 that a political conference would convene within three months of the entry into force of the armistice, to consider all aspects of the Korean question and other matters related to peace in the area.[47] The conference met in Geneva in 1954, but no agreement was reached on Korea, which has continued as two separate states.

Sinai-Suez The Sinai-Suez episode was complicated by the differing aims of the intervening powers. The British and French leaders hoped to depose President Nasser, but Britain was also interested in gaining control of the Suez Canal, while France wished to end Egyptian support for the Algerian nationalists. Israel had a two-fold aim, to end guerrilla infiltration from the Gaza Strip and to ensure that Israeli shipping could have access through the Strait of Tiran and in the Gulf of Aqaba.[48] Under the pressure of events, Britain and France had to adjust their goals and claim that their intervention was a temporary and altruistic action until the United Nations could assemble an international force,[49] but Israel temporized for as long as possible. The Gaza Strip, Israel argued, was not Egyptian territory but had been occupied by Arab forces during the attempt to 'overthrow' the General Assembly's partition resolution in 1948. During the eight years of Egyptian rule, according to Israel, no attempt had been made to rehabilitate the refugees or to attend to the welfare of the population. The territory had been used by Arab guerrillas as 'a spring-board for assaults against Israel'. As for the Strait of Tiran, Egypt had used gun positions at Sharm El-Sheikh to prevent ships entering the Gulf of Aqaba and proceeding to the Israeli port of Elath. Inter-

---

[47] Article IV of the Armistice Agreement.

[48] Anthony Eden, *Full Circle,* London, Cassell, 1966, pp. 424-5, 435-6; Selwyn Lloyd, *Suez 1956, A Personal Account,* London, Cape, 1978, pp. 73-5, 82-6; Charles E. Bohlen, *Witness to History, 1929-1969,* New York, Norton, 1973, p. 431; Moshe Dayan, *Diary of the Sinai Campaign,* London, Weidenfeld & Nicolson, 1966, pp. 30-1; Dayan, *Story of my Life,* pp. 163-5.

[49] GAOR, 1st ESS, 561st plenary mtg (1 Nov. 1956), paras. 79, 111; 563rd mtg (3/4 Nov. 1956), paras. 292, 303; 567th plenary mtg (7 Nov. 1956), paras. 99, 124; 591st mtg (23 Nov. 1956), para. 88; Annexes, Agenda item 5, pp. 16-17, A/3293, A/3294.

ference with innocent passage was contrary to international law. Israel should not be expected to withdraw while Egypt claimed belligerent rights. Israel would withdraw only if there were 'simultaneous action to prevent the renewal of hostilities'. Abba Eban went out of his way to remind Secretary-General Hammarskjold that 'one of the central functions' of his high office was 'to serve as a means for the interchange of proposals ...especially when normal methods of inter-State contact are not available'. Israel hoped that Hammarskjold would help to 'elucidate' the problems that had to be solved if Israel were to complete its withdrawal. Hammarskjold, however, adhered firmly to the view that there could be no commitment on political questions of this kind until Israel had complied with the General Assembly's calls for withdrawal, and in this he had the support of the two super-powers and almost the entire Membership of the United Nations. It was not until 1 March that Golda Meir announced that Israel would complete its withdrawal, on the understanding that the initial take-over in the Gaza Strip would be by the UN Emergency Force (UNEF) and that any inter-ference with Israeli shipping through the Strait of Tiran and in the Gulf of Aqaba would entitle Israel to exercise the right of self-defence in accordance with Article 51 of the UN Charter. Meir also noted that any proposal to withdraw the UN Emergency Force would be considered by the UNEF Advisory Committee, so as to give the General Assembly the opportunity of preventing 'precipitate' changes.[50] Although not all of Israel's assumptions and expectations were realized, infiltration from the Gaza Strip and interference with Israeli shipping in the Gulf of Aqaba ceased until shortly before the war of June 1967.

Cyprus   In the Cyprus crisis of 1963-4, a main political question concerned the relevance of the treaties and constitution that had been negotiated in 1959 and 1960. The Greek community had accepted the arrangements with considerable reluctance and

---

[50] GAOR, 11th session, 638th plenary mtg (17 Jan. 1957), paras. 119-71; 642nd plenary mtg (19 Jan. 1957), paras. 91-104; 645th plenary mtg (28 Jan. 1957), paras. 9-12, 60-90; 652nd plenary mtg (2 Feb. 1957), paras. 152-63; 666th plenary mtg (1 March 1957), paras. 2-21; Annexes, Agenda item 66, pp. 45-7, 57-62, 70-1, A/3511, A/3527, A/3563; Abba Eban, *An Autobiography,* New York, Random House, 1977, pp. 238, 246-7.

in the belief that independence could not have been attained without making concessions to the fears and susceptibilities of the Turkish-speaking minority. In practice, in the view of the Greek community, the veto power that each community possessed had made a farce of democratic government. A structure would have to be devised in which the political majority would govern and the political minority would constitute a loyal opposition. History had moved on, and it was neither necessary nor possible to base a future constitution on the principles of bi-communalism.

To the Turkish community, on the other hand, events since 1960 had demonstrated how necessary the communal safeguards had been. If the constitutional guarantees of minority rights were abandoned, there would be blatant discrimination against the Turkish community in all spheres of life, the people of Cyprus would willy-nilly be Hellenized, and in due course Greece would enforce an *anschluss* on Cyprus. The aim of the Turkish Cypriots was to persuade external powers, and in particular the Security Council, to affirm the continuing validity of the 1960 treaties.

The tragedy was that both communities could point to the evidence of history to support their fears. Greek-speaking Cypriots of Orthodox faith had indeed been oppressed during the period of Ottoman rule, and extremist elements on the Greek side now spoke openly of a coming day of reckoning. Each time President Makarios undermined one of the constitutional provisions, Turkey threatened to invade. The danger after 1963 was not *Enosis* (union of Cyprus with Greece) but external intervention, partition, and what came to be called 'Double Enosis' (union of parts of Cyprus with Greece and Turkey). While the Security Council did not pronounce on the treaties during the period leading up to the crisis of August 1964, other than by a preambular reference to the positions that the parties had taken, it was widely assumed in UN circles and later affirmed by the UN Mediator that an agreed settlement could not be based on the treaties, for it was 'the difficulties encountered in applying them that constituted the origin of the crisis'. The very fact that a Mediator had been appointed indicated the conviction of the Security Council that 'some new solution would have to be found'.[51]

Thus, in all cases studied there was a close connection between attempts to end the fighting and the political goals of the parties, and this will nearly always be the case.

FINDING THE RIGHT WORDS

An appeal to stop the fighting needs to be drafted with care. It is necessary to decide whether to address the appeal to 'the parties',[52] or to named states or other entities,[53] or whether to use a more general formulation such as 'the Governments and authorities concerned'.[54] It is also necessary to decide whether the call should be for a cease-fire[55] or whether a more precise or more all-embracing formulation would be more appropriate: cease hostilities,[56] cease fighting,[57] discontinue or abstain or desist from military action,[58] cease acts of armed force[59] or violence,[60] cease all activities of a military or paramilitary nature, as well as acts of violence, terrorism and sabotage,[61] cease guerrilla warfare.[62]

Inconsistent or careless use of language can cause difficulties. After the first Dutch 'police action' in Indonesia, the Security Council called on the parties to cease *hostilities*, but subsequently the Council referred back to its 'cease-*fire* order' and its 'cease-

---

[51] SC res. 186 (S/5575), 4 March 1964; SCOR, 20th year, Supplement for January to March 1965, pp. 237-8, para. 129 of S/6253.

[52] SC res. 27 (S/459), 1 Aug. 1957; 36 (S/597), 1 Nov. 1947; 63 (S/1150), 24 Dec. 1948.

[53] SC res. 32 (S/525, III), 26 Aug. 1947; 43 (S/714, I), 1 April 1948; 46 (S/723), 17 April 1948, 47 (S/726), 21 April 1948; 67 (S/1234), 28 Jan. 1949; SCOR, 19th year, 1143rd mtg (9/11 Aug. 1964), paras. 6-14.

[54] SC res. 49 (S/773), 22 May 1948; 50 (S/801), 29 May 1948; 54 (S/902), 15 July 1948; 66 (S/1169), 29 Dec. 1948; 73 (S/1376, II), 11 Aug. 1949; 92 (S/2130), 8 May 1951; 193 (S/5868), 9 Aug. 1964.

[55] SC res. 32 (S/525, III), 26 Aug. 1947; 36 (S/597), 1 Nov. 1947; SCOR, 3rd year, 367th mtg (19 Oct. 1948), pp. 37-8, S/1044; SC res. 66 (S/1169), 29 Dec. 1948; 73 (S/1376, II), 11 Aug. 1949; 193 (S/5868), 9 Aug. 1964.

[56] SC res. 27 (S/459), 1 Aug. 1947; 63 (S/1150), 24 Dec. 1948; 82 (S/1501), 25 June 1950.

[57] SC res. 47 (S/726), 21 April 1948, 92 (S/2130), 8 May 1951.

[58] SC res. 49 (S/773), 22 May 1948; 54 (S/902), 15 July 1948; 67 (S/1234), 28 Jan. 1949; 193 (S/5868), 9 Aug. 1964.

[59] SC res. 50 (S/801), 29 May 1948.   [60] SC res. 43 (S/714, I), 1 April 1948.

[61] SC res. 46 (S/726), 21 April 1948.   [62] SC res. 67 (S/1234), 28 Jan. 1949.

fire resolution'.[63] The inconsistent language was exacerbated because the Indonesian Republicans considered that the Security Council intended that there should be a stand-fast, while the Netherlands took the view that they were free to conduct military sweeps and mopping-up operations.[64] The Security Council tried to clarify its first resolution by advising the parties that neither of them should use its armed forces in a hostile way so as to extend its control over territory not occupied on 4 August 1947, when the cease-fire had entered into force.[65]

In the India-Pakistan case, the Security Council at one stage asked the UN Commission to 'study and report' on certain Pakistani complaints. India at once expressed surprise that the Security Council should have made such a request and recorded its 'emphatic protest'. India was unwilling to implement the resolution of 21 April 1948 until its objections to the new decision had been 'satisfactorily met'. Naturally the Security Council would not revise its decision just because it was unpalatable to one of the parties, but the President was asked to write to Nehru asking him to 'use his good will with his Government, which is well-known to be ... peace-loving [and] helpful in international relations and in the work of the United Nations.', pointing out that no criticism of India had been intended and that the only wish of the Security Council was to achieve a peaceful settlement.[66]

Another problem arose the same month when Count Bernadotte was uncertain as to the precise meaning of part of the Security Council's first call for a cease-fire in Palestine. Under the resolution of 29 May, the governments and authorities concerned were asked not to introduce fighting personnel into the region, and not to introduce 'men of military age'

[63] SC res. 27 (S/459), 1 Aug. 1947; 32 (S/525, III), 26 Aug. 1947; 36 (S/597), 1 Nov. 1947 (my italics).
[64] SCOR, 2nd year, 205th mtg (29 Sept. 1947), pp. 2427-8, S/573; 207th mtg (3 Oct. 1947), p. 2494, S/568; 211th mtg (14 Oct. 1947), pp. 2570-1, S/581; Special Supplement no. 4, pp. 4-8, 71-4, 77-8, 84, 90-7, 101-4, 109, 134-5, S/586/Rev. 1; 3rd year, Special Supplement no. 1, pp. 62-4, Annex 2 to Appendix VI of S/649/Rev. 1.
[65] SC res. 36 (S/597), 1 Nov. 1947.
[66] SC res. 51 (S/819), 3 June 1948; SCOR, 3rd year, Supplement for June 1948, pp. 78-9, S/825; 315th mtg (8 June 1948), pp. 2-7; Supplement for November 1948, pp. 108-9, Annex 14 to S/1100.

into countries or territories under their control, and not to mobilize them or submit them to military training while the cease-fire was in force. The Israelis objected strongly to any idea that they had to suspend immigration; they maintained that Jewish immigration should continue so long as men of military age were not mobilized and not subjected to military training. Bernadotte cabled New York asking what was the Security Council's 'precise intent'. Syria was the President for the month, and it would have been open to the Syrian representative to have convened the Security Council in order to provide Bernadotte with authoritative guidance. The trouble was that the Council had already decided that it was for Bernadotte to interpret the Council's decisions and that only if his interpretation were challenged should the matter be submitted to the Council for further consideration. In any case, France was strongly opposed to any meeting of the Security Council to interpret a previous decision, and the UN Secretariat believed that further debate might endanger the cease-fire itself. The President of the Council therefore cabled Bernadotte that the Council intended that no military advantage should accrue to either side as a result of the cease-fire, emphasizing that one of the Council's resolutions had stated that the cessation of hostilities would be without predjudice to the rights, claims, or position of the parties. Bernadotte considered that the response from New York was 'more than strange' and Moshe Shertok (Sharett) at first took the line that Israel could not accept a ruling from a national of a country with which Israel was at war. Bernadotte reflected wrily on the role of a person who, not having heard the debates, was expected to interpret the decisions.[67]

[67] SC res. 50 (S/801), 29 May 1948; SCOR, 3rd year, 310th mtg (29 May 1948), pp. 40-52; 311th mtg (2 June 1948), pp. 23-4; 313th mtg (3 June 1948), pp. 27-9; 314th mtg (7 June 1948), p. 2; Supplement for June 1948, p. 77, S/823; Bernadotte, pp. 45, 52-5, 59-60; David Ben-Gurion, *Israel: A Personal History*, pp. 138-40; FRUS, 1948, vol. V part 2, 1976, pp. 1080-7, 1091-2, 1098-9. The text of the Security Council's resolution of 22 May 1948, as printed on p. 19 of *Resolutions and Decisions of the Security Council 1948* has 'rights, claims or positions of the parties', but the Charter has 'position' (in the singular), as have all the other sources: see SCOR, 3rd year, Supplement for May 1948, p. 97, S/773; 302nd mtg (22 May 1948), pp. 58-9; 314th mtg (7 June 1948), p. 2; GAOR, 3rd session, Supplement no. 2, A/620, p. 92; Repertoire of the Practice of the Security Council 1946-1951, p. 329; see n. 286 below for another instance of the same misprint.

Even if the Council is sometimes reluctant to *interpret* a previous decision, it may decide to *elaborate or extend* a resolution as circumstances change. On 15 July 1948, the Council issued a mandatory cease-fire order in Palestine. Five weeks later, acting on the advice of Count Bernadotte, the Council took a five-point decision 'pursuant to' its previous resolution:[68]

1. Each party was responsible for acts by regular or irregular forces operating under its authority or in territory under its control.
2. Each party was under an obligation to prevent violations of the cease-fire by individuals and groups subject to its authority or in territory under its control.
3. Each party had an obligation to bring to trial and to punish those within its jurisdiction involved in any breach of the cease-fire.
4. No party was entitled to violate the cease-fire on the ground that it was engaging in reprisals or retaliation.
5. No party was entitled to gain military or political advantage through violation of the cease-fire.

The nearest the Security Council has come to amending one of its own resolutions occurred the following year in connection with Indonesia. On 28 January 1949, the Council adopted a comprehensive resolution calling for a halt to military operations, the release of all Republican prisoners, and the return of the Republican government to Jogjakarta; and a new Commission for Indonesia was established to help to achieve the transfer of sovereignty to a United States of Indonesia by 1 July 1950. Moreover, the route by which this was to be achieved was prescribed: the establishment of an interim federal government by 15 March 1949, followed by elections to a constituent assembly by 1 October. If it should prove impossible to keep to this time-table, the Commission for Indonesia was to report to the Security Council 'with its recommendations for a solution of the difficulties'.[69]

The UN Commission informed the Security Council in March that it would not be possible to adhere to the time-table

[68] SC res. 54 (S/902), 15 July 1948; 56 (S/983), 19 Aug. 1948.
[69] SC res. 67 (S/1234), 28 Jan. 1949.

because of the Dutch failure to follow the procedures laid down by the Security Council. On the other hand, the Netherlands had proposed holding a round table conference, and the Republicans had agreed to participate. While this was not the process envisaged by the Security Council, the Commission did not wish to interfere with any efforts by the parties to 'arrive freely at agreements'. The Commission wished to know whether it should participate in the round table conference.[70]

The Asian and East Europeans stated that they wanted the Security Council to reaffirm the procedures it had approved in January, but the Western states considered that advantage should be taken of this new possibility of progress. France maintained that the January decision was intended as 'a framework ... a guide to the negotiations [rather than] hard and fast rules'. Britain favoured 'exploratory discussions' and 'no new resolution'. Canada took the same view and thought that the appropriate course for the Security Council would be for the President to report to the UN Commission on the discussion in the Council 'and invite it to take action accordingly'.[71] After considerable discussion, Canada submitted a draft directive to the UN Commission urging it to help the parties to implement the Council's resolution, in particular regarding the cease-fire, the release of Republicans, the restoration of the Republican government to Jogjakarta, and the round table conference. The draft directive made no mention of elections to a constituent assembly, but it stated that it was the sense of the Security Council that a round table conference, with the participation of the UN Commission, 'would be consistent with the purposes and objectives' of the Council's earlier resolution. At the request of the Soviet Union, the draft was put to the vote and approved by eight votes in favour and three abstentions. The Soviet Union and the Ukrainian SSR abstained because they disliked the directive, and France abstained because it believed that the proceedings were *ultra vires*.[72]

---

[70] SCOR, 4th year, Supplement for March 1949, pp. 13-14, 18-19, paras. 14, 25-8 of S/1270; p. 30, Appendix I to S/1270/Add. 1.

[71] Ibid., 417th mtg (11 March 1949), p. 17; 418th mtg (14 March 1949), p. 23; 419th mtg (16 March 1949), p. 6.

[72] Ibid., 421st mtg (23 March 1949), pp. 5, 24-6.

The Security Council was thus able to revise a previous decision by issuing new instructions to a subsidiary organ rather than by adopting a new resolution.

COMMUNICATING THE TEXT TO THE PARTIES

The Security Council directs its cease-fire call to the parties and leaves it to them to translate the call into operational terms. In some cases, the parties have together prepared a cease-fire order that can be used by the two military commands. This course was followed after the two Dutch 'police actions' in Indonesia.[73]

It is obvious that a cease-fire call by the Security Council is effective only if it is respected by all of the parties. It needs only one soldier to ignore or violate a cease-fire for fighting to be resumed. The first step, then, is for all parties whose acquiescence is necessary to be informed of the precise terms of the Security Council's appeal or order. The UN Secretariat transmits the text of the Security Council's decision to all those affected by it, and if the parties are not specified in the text of the decision, a judgement has to be reached as to those parties to whom the decision shall be formally communicated. This is not always straightforward, especially in the case of irregular combatants who may not be under the full control of their own headquarters. When the cease-fire entered into force in Indonesia after the first Dutch 'police action', the Republicans frankly admitted that they did not control all the Indonesian armed groups operating in Netherlands-held territory, especially in Sumatra.[74]

In the early days there was sometimes a lack of certainty as to how the text of a decision of the Security Council was to be communicated to the parties. After the first 'police action' in Indonesia, the Security Council called for the cessation of hostilities. As this was the first time the Council had issued an appeal of this nature, a procedure had to be devised for communicating the text of the Council's resolution to the parties. The resolution was approved at about 20.00 hours

[73] SCOR, 3rd year, Supplement for June 1948, p. 58, S/787; 4th year, Special Supplement no. 5, pp. 58-60, Appendix VIII to S/1373 and Corr. 1.
[74] SCOR, 2nd year, Special Supplement no. 4, p. 77, S/586/Rev. 1.

(New York time) on Friday 1 August. The President of the Council (Syria) then announced:

I instruct the Secretariat to request the Ambassador of the Netherlands in Washington to inform his Government of this resolution.... I also instruct the Secretariat to send a telegram to the Indonesian republic...

The first of the President's instructions caused no difficulty. During the course of the Friday evening, the text was communicated to the Netherlands ambassador in Washington, who immediately telegraphed it to the Hague. The Dutch reply, dated Sunday 3 August, reported that the Netherlands had ordered its forces to cease hostilities at midnight on the Monday. It was more difficult to communicate the text of the resolution to the Indonesian authorities, as the Dutch had detained Dr A. K. Gani, the Republican representative in Batavia (Djakarta). The UN Secretariat sent the resolution by cable on the Friday evening via the Dutch authorities in Batavia, but from that point on there are discrepancies between the Dutch and Indonesian versions of events. According to the Indonesians, the telegram arrived in Batavia at 20.00 hours (local time) on the Saturday, whereas the Netherlands authorities in Indonesia claimed that it did not reach them until late on the Sunday morning. At 14.00 hours on the Sunday afternoon, Dr Gani was released from detention. During the course of the afternoon (Netherlands version) or at 19.30 hours that evening (Indonesian version), the *chef de cabinet* of the Dutch Governor-General (Netherlands version) or the Governor-General himself (Indonesian version) handed the cable to Gani. As all means of communication within Indonesia had been taken over by Netherlands forces, Gani had no means of getting into direct touch with his Republican colleagues in Jogjakarta, so he refused to accept any responsibility in the matter. At 00.30 hours on 4 August, the Netherlands authorities broadcast the text over the radio, and later dropped a copy by parachute over Jogjakarta airfield.[75] In the case of the second 'police action', the Good Offices Committee reported that the Dutch

---

[75] Ibid., 173rd mtg (1 Aug. 1947), p. 1711; 174th mtg (4 Aug. 1947), pp. 1716-18, S/465; 178th mtg (7 Aug. 1947), pp. 1841-2 (para. 2 of S/469), 1850-1; Special Supplement no. 4, pp. 72, 94-5, S/586/Rev. 1.

repudiation of the *Renville* truce agreement never reached the Republican authorities.[76]

In the Palestine case, there were several delays in the receipt of UN communications by the Arabs owing to a misunderstanding in one case, unexplained *force majeure* in another, and no stated reason in a third.[77]

Another problem that is often encountered is a delay in the cease-fire instruction filtering down the chain of command to front-line units.[78] This is sometimes unavoidable, but it explains why the situation immediately after a cease-fire has entered into force is so precarious, since both sides fear that the other will take advantage of the cease-fire for a decisive military action. The sooner UN observers or peace-keeping personnel can be inserted between the two front lines or at other places of tension, the sooner conditions of stability and security will prevail.

REPORTS ON COMPLIANCE

If the Security Council calls for or orders the fighting to stop, it needs to be informed if its decision is being complied with. Until the middle of 1948, it was customary to ask either the parties themselves or a subsidiary organ to report on compliance.[79] In the Kashmir case, the Council asked India and Pakistan to inform the Council immediately of 'any material change in the situation'. Pakistan failed to inform the Security Council that it had sent troops to Kashmir in May 1948, and when this became public knowledge the Security Council changed its practice and thereafter confined its requests for reporting on compliance to one of its own subsidiary organs,

[76] SCOR, 3rd year, Supplement for December 1948, p. 227, para. 6 of S/1129.
[77] Ibid., 299th mtg (21 May 1948), p. 4; 303rd mtg (24 May 1948), pp. 37, 38, 40; Supplement for May 1948, p. 99, S/783; Supplement for July 1948, p. 81, S/907.
[78] FRUS, 1949, vol. VII part 1, 1975, p. 539; SCOR, 5th year, Special Supplement no. 1, p. 1, para. 7 of S/1449; 19th year, Supplement for July-September 1964, p. 175, S/5890.
[79] For requests to the parties, see SC res. 38 (S/651), 17 Jan. 1948; SCOR, 3rd year, 295th mtg (18 May 1948), pp. 33-47; 332nd mtg (8 July 1948), pp. 21-3. For requests to subsidiary organs, see SC res. 39 (S/654), 20 Jan. 1948; res. 41 (S/678), 28 Feb. 1948; res. 47 (S/726), 21 April 1948; res. 48 (S/727), 23 April 1948; res. 49 (S/773), 22 May 1948; res. 50 (S/801), 29 May 1948.

and there was only one subsequent request to the parties to report on compliance during the period 1946-64.[80] In this period, one request to report was addressed to the UN Mediator for Palestine,[81] two to a sub-committee of the Council,[82] thirteen to the Chief of Staff of the UN Truce Supervision Organization in the Middle East,[83] one to the Good Offices Commission in Indonesia,[84] one to the UN Commission for Indonesia,[85] four to the UN Representative for India and Pakistan,[86] and one to the UN Commission on Korea.[87] One was addressed to the Egyptian-Israel Mixed Armistice Commission, which was not a subsidiary organ of the Council but a body created by the armistice agreement of 1949.[88] Occasionally, and in special circumstances, the Council has requested the Secretary-General, or in one case the President of the Council,[89] to report on compliance.[90] In none of the cases studied was a request to report on compliance addressed to a regional agency.

3.3 DEMANDS FOR WITHDRAWAL

If a state resorts to armed force in circumstances other than those specified in the Charter, it is inadmissible that it should thereby gain territory. In 1970 the General Assembly declared that no territorial acquisition resulting from the threat or use of force should be recognized as legal.[91] This strengthened a

[80] SC res. 98 (S/2883), 23 Dec. 1952.
[81] SC res. 54 (S/902), 15 July 1948.
[82] SC res. 61 (S/1070), 4 Nov. 1948; res. 66 (S/1169), 29 Dec. 1948.
[83] SC res. 73 (S/1376, II), 11 Aug. 1949; res. 89 (S/1907), 17 Nov. 1950; res. 93 (S/2157), 18 May 1951; res. 100 (S/3128), 27 Oct. 1953; res. 101 (S/3139/Rev. 2), 24 Nov. 1953; res. 107 (S/3379), 30 March 1955; res. 108 (S/3535), 8 Sept. 1955; res. 111 (S/3538), 19 Jan. 1956; 114 (S/3605), 4 June 1956; SCOR, 12th year, 782nd mtg (28 May 1957), paras. 198-201; 788th mtg (6 Sept. 1957), paras. 97-100; SC res. 127 (S/3942), 22 Jan. 1958; res. 171 (S/5111), 9 April 1962.
[84] SC res. 63 (S/1150), 24 Dec. 1948.
[85] SC res. 67 (S/1234), 28 Jan. 1949.
[86] SC res. 80 (S/1469), 14 March 1950; res. 96 (S/2392), 10 Nov. 1951; res. 98 (S/2883), 23 Dec. 1952; res. 126 (S/3922), 2 Dec. 1957.
[87] SC res. 82 (S/1501), 25 June 1950.
[88] SCOR, 9th year, 685th mtg (11 Nov. 1954), para. 15.
[89] SC res. 123 (S/3793), 21 Feb. 1957.
[90] In connection with Palestine, SC res. 113 (S/3575), 4 April 1956 and res. 114 (S/3605), 4 June 1956; in connection with Cyprus, res. 186 (S/5575), 4 March 1964; res. 193 (S/5868), 9 Aug. 1964; res. 194 (S/5987), 25 Sept. 1964.
[91] GA res. 2625 (XXV), 24 Oct. 1970.

doctrine that had earlier been given specific effect in the pre-amble to the Security Council resolution no. 242 of 1967 on the Middle East.[92]

The acquisition of territory by force is especially objection-able if it follows a breach of a specific cease-fire, truce, or armistice agreement. Ralph Bunche, the Acting UN Mediator for Palestine, stated the rationale for this in 1948.

The fundamental principle under which the truce has been applied [is] that no military advantage should accrue to either side as a result of the truce ... It is unquestionable that any advance of the fighting lines would constitute such an advantage ... At no time ... have [UN observers] permitted any advance by either party to go unchallenged and without an immediate demand for withdrawal.[93]

While it may be generally accepted that territory should not be occupied following a violation of an agreement, it is not always expedient for the Security Council to attach a demand for withdrawal to a resolution primarily designed to stop the fighting. A cease-fire call by the Security Council should be as simple and straightforward as possible, although it is sometimes impossible to secure a cessation of fighting without connecting it in some way to the framework for a long-term political settle-ment.

There may be circumstances in which a call for the with-drawal of forces is included in a cease-fire resolution, not in any expectation that it will be heeded at once, but for other legitimate purposes: as a demonstration of disapproval, as a form of pressure, or simply to place on record what the sponsor regards as normative international behaviour.

In all of the cases studied except the seventh (Cyprus 1964), there were demands for withdrawal of forces. In case 1 (In-donesia 1947-8), the Security Council rejected Soviet and Australian proposals that would have called expressly for with-drawal by both parties,[94] but the Council asked that the Con-sular Commission should report on conditions in areas from which forces might be withdrawn 'by agreement between the

[92] SC res. 242 (S/8247), 22 Nov. 1967.

[93] SCOR, 3rd year, 373rd mtg (26 Oct. 1948), p. 24.

[94] SCOR, 2nd year, 172nd mtg (1 Aug. 1947), p. 1665; 173rd mtg (1 Aug. 1947), pp. 1703-10.

parties'[95] and later envisaged 'some' agreed withdrawals of armed forces.[96] In case 2 (Kashmir), the Security Council recommended that 'tribesmen and Pakistani nationals not normally resident in the State who have entered the State for the purpose of fighting' should withdraw, as well as recommending the progressive withdrawal of Indian forces to the minimum strength needed for maintaining law and order, a call that was later repeated by the UN Commission for India and Pakistan (UNCIP).[97] India came increasingly to regard a withdrawal by Azad Kashmiri and Pakistani forces as a precondition for the implementation of the rest of the programme of the Security Council and UNCIP, and by 1949 India was requiring not only that forces be withdrawn but that they be disbanded and disarmed as well.[98] In case 3 (Palestine), the Security Council ordered the parties to stop all military action and instructed the UN Mediator 'to continue his efforts to bring about the demilitarization of the City of Jerusalem'[99] which, if it had been achieved, would have involved the withdrawal of both Israeli and Arab forces; but the parties made ambiguous or inconsistent responses to Bernadotte's approaches. After the Israeli offensive in the Negev in October 1948, the Security Council called several times for mutual withdrawal of forces from positions occupied after 14 October.[100] In case 4 (Indonesia 1948-9), the Security Council rejected a Syrian proposal which would have asked the UN Committee of Good Offices to report on 'the technical possibility' of withdrawing armed forces to the positions they occupied before the second Dutch 'police action';[101] three times rejected straightforward Soviet proposals for a withdrawal of Dutch forces;[102]

[95] SC res. 30 (S/525, I), 25 Aug. 1947.

[96] SC res. 36 (S/597), 1 Nov. 1947.

[97] SC res. 48 (S/726), 21 April 1948; SCOR, 3rd year, Supplement for November 1948, pp. 32-4, para. 75 of S/1100.

[98] SCOR, 4th year, Special Supplement no. 7, pp. 40-4, 49, 99-100, 108-11, 113-14, 143-7, 173-5, 183-4, paras. 205-6, 209, 211, 214, 219 of and section 2 of memorandum attached to Annex 16, Annexes 20, 22, 36, 48, 50 of S/1430.

[99] SC res. 54 (S/902), 15 July 1948.

[100] SCOR, 3rd year, 367th mtg (19 Oct. 1948), pp. 37-9, S/1044; SC res. 61 (S/1070), 4 Nov. 1948; SC res. 62 (S/1080), 16 Nov. 1948.

[101] SCOR, 3rd year, 392nd mtg (24 Dec. 1948), pp. 52, 55-6.

[102] Ibid., pp. 40-1; 393rd mtg (27 Dec. 1948), pp. 6, 35; 4th year, Supplement for January 1949, p. 66, S/1233; 406th mtg (28 Jan. 1949), p. 24.

and assumed but did not expressly call for the withdrawal of Dutch forces.[103]

Following the invasion of South Korea in 1950 (case 5), the Security Council determined that there had been a breach of the peace and called upon 'the authorities in North Korea' to withdraw to the 38th parallel.[104] China, though not at the time represented in the United Nations, proposed that the Security Council should demand a complete US withdrawal from Taiwan.[105] The withdrawal of all foreign forces from Korea was proposed in the General Assembly by the Soviet bloc, both while the fighting was in progress and after the armistice, and was advocated by North Korea and China during the armistice negotiations; but Yakov Malik's speech in 1951, which led to the opening of armistice negotiations, aroused interest in non-Communist circles precisely because he suggested a *mutual* withdrawal of forces to the 38th parallel rather than a unilateral withdrawal from Korea of all the forces of the Unified Command.

In case 6 (Sinai-Suez), proposals by the United States and the Soviet Union which included calls for withdrawal were vetoed by Britain and France,[106] whereupon the matter was taken up by the General Assembly in emergency special session. Seven resolutions calling for withdrawal were adopted by the General Assembly, and eventually full compliance was achieved.[107] At one stage the Soviet Union proposed that UN Members should provide Egypt with military assistance to expel the invaders, but the United States took the position that the introduction of new forces in this way would be contrary to resolutions of the General Assembly and would thus 'violate the United Nations Charter.'[108]

[103] SC res. 65 (S/1165), 28 Dec. 1948.
[104] SC res. 82 (S/1501), 25 June 1950.
[105] SCOR, 5th year, 528th mtg (30 Nov. 1950), p. 22.
[106] Text in Bailey, *Voting in the Security Council*, pp. 181-2.
[107] GA res. 997 (ES-1), 2 Nov. 1956; GA res. 999 (ES-1), 4 Nov. 1956; GA res. 1002 (ES-1), 7 Nov. 1956; GA res. 1120 (XI), 24 Nov. 1956; GA res. 1123 (XI), 19 Jan. 1957; GA res. 1124 (XI), 2 Feb. 1957; GA res. 1125 (XI), 2 Feb. 1957.
[108] SCOR, 11th year, Supplement for October to December 1956, pp. 128-30, S/3736; Nikita Krushchev, *Krushchev Remembers*, transl. Strobe Talbot, London, Sphere, 1971, pp. 397-9; Dwight D. Eisenhower, *Waging Peace 1956-1961*, London, Heinemann, 1966 New York, Doubleday, 1965, pp. 89-90, 97; Anthony Eden, *Full Circle*, London, Cassell, 1960, pp. 554-6.

In case 7 (Cyprus 1964) the question of withdrawal did not arise, as there had been no Turkish occupation of Cypriot territory.

It is a striking and perhaps surprising conclusion that there was only one case between 1946 and 1964 when there was complete withdrawal, Sinai-Suez 1956-7, and that occurred even though it might have been thought that the Security Council had been rendered impotent because of the two Anglo-French vetoes. While the vetoes made it impossible for the Security Council to take substantive decisions, they did not change the reality of a correspondence or overlap of US, Soviet, and Afro-Asian interests. In the face of this short-lived unity, the three invading states could delay but not avoid withdrawal, which in the course of four months became the *sine qua non* for dealing with issues that had led to the Israeli armed intervention in the first place.

OPERATION TEN PLAGUES

Following the fighting in the Negev in October 1948, the question arose whether withdrawal should precede or follow negotiations between the parties. This case was of such importance that it is worth looking at in some detail.

The July truce in Palestine had left a bizarre situation, in which Israel needed a north-south road to supply the Negev settlements, while Egypt needed a west-east road to supply her units in the Bethlehem area. These two roads intersected at Karatiya, a couple of miles north-west of Faluja, which was within fire of both Israeli and Egyptian positions. The UN Central Truce Supervision Board had worked out an arrangement, which Bernadotte had approved on 14 September, by which the Israelis could cross the junction for six hours in every twenty-four and the Egyptians for a different six hours, in order to transport such supplies and personnel as were permitted under the cease-fire, the arrangements to be 'under the close supervision of the United Nations military observers'.[109]

This scheme never worked properly, though Ralph Bunche (Acting UN Mediator after Bernadotte's assassination) did his

[109] SCOR, 3rd year, Supplement for October 1948, pp. 62-3, Annex to S/1042.

best. Egypt refused to permit Israeli convoys to pass until the supplying of Jewish settlement by air was stopped, while Israel refused to stop the aerial convoys or submit them to UN supervision until Egypt permitted the land convoys through.[110]

On 15 October, the UN Truce Supervision Organization received a communication from the Israeli General Staff complaining that Egyptian intransigence had led to an 'intolerable situation' and stating that an Israeli convoy would pass the Karatiya intersection during the permitted hours that day. When the first Israeli truck reached the crossroads, Egyptian troops opened fire. 'The Egyptians had not failed Israel. The government [of Israel] immediately announced that it was free to act, and the signal was given for Operation Ten Plagues to begin.'[111] Sir John Glubb (Glubb Pasha) has written to the author:

There can be no doubt...that the Israeli attack on the Egyptians was carefully planned. Very large forces had been concentrated by them in advance, in preparation for extensive operations. There was no question of the firing on a caravan suddenly having given rise to the fighting.[112]

Ralph Bunche and other UN officials concerned with the Middle East knew that Israel had provoked the breach of the cease-fire. Both sides were at fault in preparing to resume the fighting: it was Israel that took the fateful decision, but it was Egypt that formally committed the violation.[113] John Reedman, who worked closely with Bunche at this time, has commented that practically all serious breaches, by whomsoever started, and whether engineered or spontaneous, ended up to the advantage of Israel.[114] So it was to prove on this occasion.

Bunche was already in Paris, where the UN General Assembly had convened on 21 September. On the day the fighting

[110] Ibid., pp.55-62, paras. 9-15 of S/1042.
[111] Ibid., pp. 60-1, para. 16 of S/1042; Dan Kurzman, *Genesis 1948: The First Arab-Israeli War*, New York, World Publishing, 1970, p. 576; Azcárate, p. 105; Ben-Gurion, p. 280; Allon, pp. 38-40; Yitzhak Rabin, *The Rabin Memoirs*, Boston, Mass., Little, Brown, 1979, p. 37; John Glubb, *A Soldier with the Arabs*, p. 198; Alec Kirkbride, *From the Wings: Amman Memoirs 1947-1951*, p. 60.
[112] Letter, 5 April 1977.
[113] GAOR, 3rd session, Supplement no. 11, A/648, pp. 3, 31, 36, 44; Azcárate, p. 105.
[114] Letter to the author, 29 May 1977.

had begun, Bunche had told the General Assembly's political committee that the July cease-fire was permanent; a resumption of hostilities would represent defiance of the Security Council and would lead to the application of sanctions. To the Security Council he reported that UN personnel in Palestine were constantly at risk and that their authority was being disregarded by both sides. A campaign of hostility against the United Nations was being deliberately fostered by the Jewish military governor of Jerusalem, Dr Dov Joseph, who, wrote one Jewish observer in his diary, was a 'man of great abilities, tremendous devotion and no charm'. Joseph held a poor opinion of UN representatives, who seemed to him to be 'living symbols of older relationships which the war had made obsolete'. The Jews were no longer 'inferior but aggressive people' or 'religious fanatics'. 'It was going to take time for even men of goodwill to learn to treat us as masters in our own house.'[115]

The response of the Security Council to the new round of fighting was complicated by the fact that the United States had at that time two policies on the Middle East. The State Department, and many if not most senior US diplomats, stood behind the Bernadotte plan, as had been agreed with Britain and which Secretary of State George Marshall had enunciated on 21 September, with Truman's prior approval: Bernadotte's recommendations, Marshall had said, offered 'a generally fair basis for settlement' and the General Assembly should 'accept them in their entirety'.[116]

The other US policy at this time was that of President Truman, subject to intense Zionist pressure, and with less than three weeks to go until the election. The platform of the Democratic Party was to approve the boundaries of the partition plan, modified only to the extent that Israel would agree.[117]

The contradiction between the State Department and the White House led one member of the Policy Planning Staff to

---

[115] GAOR, 3rd session, 1st part, First Committee, 161st mtg (15 Oct. 1948), pp. 162-5; SCOR, 3rd year, 365th mtg (14 Oct. 1948), pp. 18-20, 32-7; Supplement for October 1948, pp. 46-50, S/1022, S/1023; Harry Levin, *Jerusalem Embattled: A Diary of the City under Siege, March 25th, 1948 to July 18th, 1948*, London, Gollancz, 1950, pp. 226-8; Dov Joseph, *The Faithful City: The Siege of Jerusalem, 1948*, pp. 216-17, 271-2.
[116] FRUS, 1948, vol. V part 2, pp. 1351, 1363, 1409-12, 1415-17, 1463-5.
[117] Ibid., pp. 1313, 1381, 1420, 1431, 1438-9, 1445-6, 1450.

lament that the United States had no long-term policy for the Middle East and, in the short-term, only an 'open-ended policy which is set from time to time by White House directives'. General Marshall was meticulous in keeping Truman informed and in getting his approval for US policy, but the pressures on Marshall were different from those on Truman. The tension between the two policies caused great difficulties for the US delegation to the General Assembly, which included such friends of Zionism as Eleanor Roosevelt and Benjamin V. Cohen, as well as the chief Republican adviser on foreign affairs, John Foster Dulles.[118]

Robert Lovett was Acting Secretary of State in Washington while George Marshall was in Europe, and he and Robert McClintock worked valiantly to devise a policy that would be acceptable to the White House but would not undermine Marshall's credibility. Their assumption was that Israel could choose either the partition boundaries or the cease-fire lines, but that it was not reasonable for Israel to claim both the Negev, because most of it had been allocated to the Jewish state under the partition plan, *and* western Galilee, because most of it had been captured during the earlier fighting.[119]

On 29 and 30 September, relations between the White House and the State Department had almost reached breaking point. Truman was campaigning in Oklahoma and was under pressure from Rabbi Abba Hillel Silver and the American Zionist Emergency Council. Clark Clifford, special counsel to the President, phoned Robert Lovett in Washington to say that Truman was about to disavow Marshall's statement of 21 September in support of Bernadotte's proposals. The phone call was interrupted but resumed the next day, with Clifford, established in the freight yards at Tulsa, arguing with Lovett in Washington for an hour and a half, the conversation being 'punctuated by the whistles of on-coming trains'. The conversation was 'strenuous', but eventually Truman was dissuaded

---

[118] Ibid., pp. 1221-2, 1313-15, 1380-1, 1446, 1448-9, 1463, 1470-1. 'Ben Cohen', Eban has written, 'formed a Washington group of informal but perceptive counsellors.' M. W. Weisgal and J. Carmichael (eds), *Chaim Weizmann*, New York, Atheneum, 1963, p. 265.

[119] FRUS, 1948, vol. V part 2, 1976, pp. 1303-6, 1308-10, 1354-7, 1366-9, 1377-8, 1398-1400.

from repudiating Marshall. Robert McClintock, with the interests of posterity in mind, placed a memorandum of record in the files, and he also wrote to Dean Rusk in Paris suggesting that the Americans should now adjust their sights to the extent of giving Israel a salient in the northen Negev which would extend as far as the Gaza-Beersheba road. This gloss on Bernadotte was to be the US position when the fighting broke out in October. On 18 October, Lovett cabled Marshall in Paris to the effect that from now on neither the President nor the State Department would comment on the Bernadotte plan: 'better say nothing than say something wrong'. If it should be necessary to speak or act about Palestine, specific authority and clearance must be obtained from Truman in advance.[120]

During these difficulties, Truman's special representative in Israel, James McDonald, a staunch Zionist, was bombarding Washington with messages urging that Israel should be allowed to have *all* of the Negev. McDonald believed that the State Department had been duped by an Albion that was both perfidious and anti-Semitic.[121] It has never been true that to be critical of Israel's actions is necessarily to be anti-Semitic. James Fawcett, who was legal advisor in the British UN delegation at the time and was later to become president of the European Commission for HumanRights, has written to the author:

I certainly sensed from March 1948 on ... a fairly strong anti-Israel attitude, but I would not characterize it as 'anti-Semitic': it sprang more, I think, from a traditional pro-Arab alignment, anger at the activities of the Stern Gang and the other 'irregular fighters' in Palestine, and a genuine concern that Israel's defiance, however understandable, was weakening the UN.[122]

This was not how most Israelis saw it, however. Walter Eytan, a former director general of the Israeli Foreign Ministry, was appalled by Britain's 'intense hostility' to Israel at that time— 'very real, very vindictive, and very unpleasant'.[123]

[120] Ibid., pp. 1430-1, 1437-9, 1459-60, 1489-90, 1496-7; Harry S. Truman, *Memoirs, vol. II, Years of Trial and Hope*, p. 167.
[121] FRUS, 1948, vol. V part 2, pp. 1375-7, 1384-6, 1392-4, 1408-9, 1414-15, 1428-9, 1450-1.
[122] Letter to the author, 18 April 1977.
[123] Letter to the author, 29 April 1977.

Nor was the United States the only country in which domestic political considerations played a part. George Ignatieff, who was in charge of the UN Department in Ottawa, recalls asking how Canada should vote on one UN proposal. The Hon. Brooke Claxton, who was Acting Secretary of State while Lester Pearson was in Paris, expressed indifference but reminded Ignatieff that, so far as he knew, there were no Arabs in his constituency but quite a number of sympathizers with the Israeli cause.[124]

Throughout this period, the US Policy Planning Staff played virtually no role in the formulation of policy. 'The Policy Planning Staff', George Kennan has written to the author, 'was not involved in operational matters, and was particularly remote from such of them as were conducted, as was our Near Eastern policy of that day, primarily with regard to domestic-political considerations.[125]

This, then, was the background in the United States when the Security Council met on 19 October to consider the new outbreak of fighting. Ralph Bunche said he had called on the parties for a temporary but unconditional cease-fire. This had been accepted by Egypt so long as Israel did the same, but the Israeli reply amounted to a rejection. It was evident from the scale of Israel's military effort, Bunche reported, that the Israeli authorities had anticipated 'serious resistance in their un-supervised effort to push the convoy through'. The Israeli action could have been undertaken only after considerable preparation, 'and could scarcely be explained as simple retaliatory action'.

Having clearly anticipated trouble and having apparently planned well to meet it [wrote Bunche, with less than his usual elegance], it is all the more incomprehensible that United Nations observers should have been obstructed in the area, and should not have been notified of the intent to push the convoy through until it was actually on its way.

The Security Council, basing itself on Bunche's report, decided that 'the indispensable condition' to a restoration of the situation was 'an immediate and effective cease-fire'. After the cease-fire, 'the following conditions might well be considered as the basis

[124] Letter to the author, 21 April 1977.
[125] Letter to the author, 1 April 1977.

for further negotiations': withdrawal by both parties from any positions not occupied at the time of the outbreak of fighting, acceptance of the decision of the Central Truce Supervision Board on convoys, and agreement to negotiate on outstanding problems in the Negev and the permanent stationing of UN observers throughout the area. The Security Council also reminded Bunche that UN observers should be deployed 'on the territories of both parties', and noted with concern the failure of Israel to report on its investigation into the assassination of Bernadotte, as had been promised.[126]

Bunche's proposal, endorsed by the Security Council, contained several elements of ambiguity, but one point seemed clear. A cease-fire was to come first, to be followed by negotiations to prevent further outbreaks of fighting: one basis of such negotiations 'might well' consist of withdrawal by both parties.

There were some who thought that the decision of the Security Council should have made a closer link between a cease-fire and withdrawal. Pablo de Azcárate, a senior UN official in the field, wrote later that he was puzzled by the 'rapid succession of [UN] decisions, each virtually contradicting or at least ignoring the previous one', and he found it difficult to explain to Arabs why the Security Council had reacted 'with singular mildness and resignation'.

I found myself unable to give a satisfactory answer to the criticisms and the questions which politicians, soldiers and journalists addressed to me. The harshest criticism referred to the contrast between the terms employed by the Security Council when forcing the Arabs to accept the second truce [the previous July], naming them explicitly as the guilty party and threatening them unequivocally with sanctions, with those now employed in the resolution of October 19 to deal with the gravest violation of the same truce.[127]

The Israelis, on the other hand, regarded the idea of withdrawal as 'absurd and unjustified': in no circumstances was Israel willing to withdraw from any place that had been taken

---

[126] SCOR, 3rd year, Supplement for October 1948, pp. 55-62, paras. 17-18 of S/1042; 367th mtg (19 Oct. 1948), pp. 2-6, 14-17 (S/1044), 37-8; SC res. 59 (S/1045), 19 Oct. 1948; Ben-Gurion, p. 281; Azcárate, p. 106.
[127] Azcárate, pp. 105-6.

during the October fighting, and Israel was determined to find a way around any demands for withdrawal. The first step was to detach the United States from the Bernadotte plan. Aubrey (Abba) Eban spent an agonizing week trying to delay the passage of a cease-fire resolution in the hope (vain as it proved) that Israeli forces in the Negev could capture the Arab enclave in the Faluja area. 'Eban' wrote Jon Kimche 'fought a covering action with classical English orations...'[128]

It had been intended that the Security Council's decisions of 19 October should be followed by quiet diplomacy. October happened to be the month for the United States to preside over the Council, but it was also the final phase of the US election campaign. George Marshall and ambassador Warren Austin, following Truman's directive to the letter, ensured that the United States played an entirely silent and passive role. Austin cabled Washington to say that the Security Council might soon be faced with a proposal to take enforcement action under Chapter VII of the Charter, to which Bob Lovett replied for the State Department that the United States must abide by the UN Charter but should avoid the limelight. Marshall asked if he should request a postponement of the Palestine debate in the General Assembly so as to avoid 'partisan political pressure', but Washington replied that, while postponement was desirable, it would be a mistake to be so specific about the reason.[129]

Then, on 22 October, Governor Thomas E. Dewey, the Republican presidential candidate, released the text of a letter that he had sent to the American Palestine Committee, attacking US vacillation over Israel's boundaries and expressing support for the original partition plan. Lovett cabled Marshall, 'I anticipate unhappy weekend.' He did, however, send an urgent message to the US delegation in Paris repeating McClintock's suggestion that 'certain concessions would have to be made to Israel in the northern Negev', perhaps as far as the Gaza-Beersheba road. Marshall replied that it would be a serious mistake to tell other delegations that the United States favoured

---

[128] Abba Eban, *An Autobiography*, London, Weidenfeld & Nicolson, 1978, p. 132; Jon Kimche, *Seven Fallen Pillars: The Middle East, 1948-52*, London, Secker and Warburg, 1953, p. 274; FRUS, 1948, vol. V part 2, pp. 1526-7.
[129] FRUS, 1948, vol. V part 2, pp. 1490 n. 4, 1498, 1502-4.

territorial rectifications in favour of Israel, for this would only stiffen Israel's defiance of the Security Council, to which Lovett agreed.[130]

The next day Truman, without consulting Marshall, issued a statement to the effect that the only modifications of the boundaries laid down in the partition plan should be those acceptable to Israel.[131] While it seemed to some foreign governments that the United States could not make up its own mind about the Middle East, Benjamin V. Cohen, who was then Counsellor in the State Department, insists that the White House was not at fault. 'It was the State Department which made it appear that Truman departed and vacillated from State Department policy only for campaign politics. The reverse is true.'[132] Be that as it may, Truman's statement did not help, and was not intended to help, the Security Council's wish to secure withdrawal of Israeli forces.

Bunche, acting under the Security Council's decisions of 19 October, had informed Egypt and Israel that a new cease-fire would take effect at noon GMT on 22 October. By then, Yigal Allon's forces had seized several important places north and east of Gaza, including Isdud, Majdal, and Beersheba: Lachish and the surrounding area was captured after the cease-fire had supposedly entered into effect, leaving an encircled pocket of Egyptian and Sudanese forces in the Faluja area. UN observers resumed their functions in the Negev on 25 October. In the north, fighting was resumed during the night of 21/22 October. The UN observers at once ordered a new cease-fire, to take effect on 23 October, but Israel resumed fighting ten minutes before the deadline. The chief UN observer told both sides that the military operations along the Lebanese front were 'a grave and inexcusable violation', and asked the Israelis to return to the positions held on 21 October. Fighting continued for another week, however, with UN observers being prevented

---

[130] John Snetsinger, *Truman, the Jewish Vote, and the Creation of Israel*, Stanford, Calif., Hoover Institution, 1974, p. 129; FRUS, 1948, vol. V part 2, pp. 1507-9, 1514-15, 1520.

[131] FRUS, 1948, vol. V part 2, p. 1509; Truman, vol. II, pp. 167-8; Jessup, p. 301; Herbert Feis, *The Birth of Israel: The Tousled Diplomatic Bed*, New York, Norton, 1969, p. 66.

[132] Letter to the author, 3 June 1977.

from reaching front-line areas; but on 31 October (by which time Israeli forces had occupied all of Upper Galilee, crossed the frontier into Lebanon, and advanced as far as the Litani River), a new cease-fire entered into force in the north. The Arab Liberation Army simply evaporated.[133]

Before the Security Council met again, Bunche sent identical communications to Egypt and Israel, once more urging compliance with the decisions of the Security Council. Withdrawal of forces could now begin, under UN supervision, and after all forces had withdrawn from positions not occupied when the fighting had broken out, permanent lines could be demarcated. Bunche reported to the Council on 26 October that, although Israel and Egypt had in theory accepted his proposals for sending convoys to isolated Jewish settlements in the Negev, and although they had in theory agreed that the new cease-fire in the Negev should enter into force on 22 October, fighting was continuing both in the Negev and in the Lebanese sector, and UN observers were still prevented from performing their functions. Several requests had been addressed to Israel asking that UN observers should be allowed to operate and thus bring about an effective cease-fire in both sectors. At one stage it seemed likely that Britain would introduce a proposal in support of Bunche's call for withdrawal, but in the event ambassador Sir Alexander Cadogan merely drew attention to the obstruction of UN observers. Warren Austin, President of the Security Council, summed up the debate with great circumspection by saying that the accusations had been placed on the record. 'In due course, after proper consideration, the Security Council will act.' He then adjourned the discussion for two days.[134]

After the meeting, Marshall cabled Lovett in Washington stressing that failure by either party to comply with the Security Council's order to withdraw would be an affront to the Security Council's prestige: the minimum response should be a threat to impose sanctions against the party failing to comply or, if it should be impossible to identify the guilty party, against both.

[133] SCOR, 3rd year, 373rd mtg (26 Oct. 1948), pp. 2-7 (S/1053, S/1055), 23-5; Supplement for November 1948, pp. 8-11, S/1071; Ben-Gurion, p. 291; Glubb, pp. 63, 66, 96; Kirkbride, p. 63.
[134] SCOR, 3rd year, Supplement for October 1948, pp. 70-2, S/1058; 373rd mtg (26 Oct. 1948), pp. 8-27.

The next day, Sir Alexander Cadogan informed Marshall that China would co-sponsor a British proposal to invoke the mandatory enforcement provisions of Chapter VII of the UN Charter. Lovett told the White House what was happening in Paris and expressed the view that the United States should not co-sponsor the proposal for sanctions but should speak briefly in support and vote in favour.[135]

When the Security Council met on 28 October, Bunche urged the Council to make it unequivocally clear that further resort to force in Palestine would not be tolerated. He went out of his way to point out that the recent fighting in the Negev had not been a minor breakdown of the cease-fire but had involved fighting on a large scale. He seemed, however, less interested in punishing the violator than in moving towards peace. The basis of the Council's cease-fire decisions, he said, had always been that no military advantage should accrue to either side. He admitted that in one respect he had deviated from the customary procedure by deliberately pursuing a policy of delay; UN observers had, in the past, always met breaches of the cease-fire or advances in the fighting lines by prompt orders to withdraw, and, with three minor exceptions, these orders had been complied with. He admitted that there might have been some ambiguity regarding the Council's intention on 19 October on the question of the withdrawal of forces. The wording of the Council's decision had been based on one of his own reports, but Bunche said that it had never been his intention to modify 'the fundamental principle on which the truce rests by submitting the vital question of military advantage to negotiation '. The only matters to be the subject of negotiation were outstanding problems in the Negev and the permanent stationing of UN observers throughout the area.[136]

After Bunche had spoken, there followed a pained debate in the Council in which Eban said that, if the Egyptians had not obstructed the Council and tried to bisect Israel, Egyptian forces would not have found themselves 'defeated, sundered and broken up into incoherent fragments'.[137] Britain and China submitted a proposal recalling that violation of the cease-fire

---

[135] FRUS, 1948, vol. V part 2, pp. 1518-24.
[136] SCOR, 3rd year, 374th mtg (28 Oct. 1948), pp. 2-9, 31-2.
[137] Ibid., pp. 13-21.

might lead to action under Chapter VII of the Charter, endorsing the order to withdraw to the positions occupied on 14 October, and appointing a sub-committee to confer with Bunche about non-military enforcement measures to be applied if either or both parties should refuse to comply. France proposed an amendment to make it clear that, if one party withdrew, the other party should not advance: withdrawal, in other words, would lead to demilitarization. This was accepted by the co-sponsors of the proposal. The Soviet Union then proposed postponing further discussion, and the Council agreed.[138] That night, Truman made 'a combative' speech in Madison Square Garden in New York City, again dissociating himself from the Bernadotte proposals, and adding that Israel must be large and strong.[139]

The Security Council met the next morning, and Canada suggested that all draft resolutions and amendments should be referred to a sub-committee. This was approved, the Soviet Union and the Ukrainian SSR abstaining.[140]

While the Security Council sub-committee was at work, the US election campaign was reaching a climax—the 'silly season', as Lovett described it in a cable to Marshall. Truman sent another message to Paris instructing that he be advised of any action that the US delegation contemplated taking on Palestine; and, in a personal, top secret, and urgent message to Marshall, he pressed that the United States should avoid taking any position on Palestine until after the election. Lovett urged the President to agree that the United States should at least 'continue to support the Security Council's efforts to maintain the cease-fire in the light of the deteriorating situation', but Truman said his position would remain unchanged until the election result was known. Marshall was troubled about strains within the US delegation and especially the strong commitment of Eleanor Roosevelt to Israel. Britain was still pressing that the two countries should stand together in support of the Bernadotte proposals.[141]

[138] Ibid., pp. 12-13, 32-3, 36-40.
[139] Truman, vol. II, p. 168; Herbert Feis, *The Birth of Israel: The Tousled Diplomatic Bed*, New York, Norton, 1969, p. 66.
[140] SCOR, 3rd year, 375th mtg (29 Oct. 1948), pp. 19-20, 22; SC res. 60 (S/1062), 29 Oct. 1948.
[141] FRUS, 1948, vol. V part 2, pp. 1527-8, 1534-7, 1539-41.

In the Security Council's sub-committee (composed of Belgium, Britain, China, France, and the Ukrainian SSR), France proposed a new wording for the crucial paragraph on withdrawal, along the lines of its earlier proposal in the Security Council. Forces were to withdraw to provisional lines to be designated by Bunche, leading to permanent truce lines and 'neutral or demilitarized zones' established through direct negotiations or, failing that, decisions of the Acting Mediator. This had the support of all members of the sub-committee except the Ukrainian SSR.[142]

The Security Council met at 15.00 hours on 4 November to consider this new formula, and the United States proposed adding that withdrawal would be without prejudice to the rights, claims, or position of the parties. At about 18.30 Lester Pearson, who had just arrived in Paris from Canada, asked that the debate be adjourned until the next day, but three weeks had already elapsed since the fighting began. The Council closed the meeting at 19.15 and resumed it at 21.30 the same evening, when it adopted the French formula, as amended by the United States, with the Ukrainian SSR voting against, and the Soviet Union abstaining so as not to veto. Pablo de Azcárate was again puzzled by the Council's action, which, he felt, evaded the question of responsibility for the violation of the cease-fire. But things looked very different to the Israelis, and Ben-Gurion was complaining to the Israeli State Council that the cease-fire that the Security Council was demanding was unjust because it 'equates the aggressors with the aggrieved'. He still proclaimed his faith in the United Nations: if it were to perish, 'It would be the blackest day in man's history, and the most tragic in ours.' But the United Nations had 'failed of their duty'. Israel never had, and never would, accept a one-sided truce.[143]

To the surprise of many observers, Truman was elected, securing 49.5 per cent of the popular vote compared with Dewey's 45.1 per cent. Chaim Weizmann, the Israeli President, lost no time in sending a letter to Truman, partly of congratulations

---

[142] SCOR, 3rd year, Supplement for November 1948, pp. 2-3, para. 5 of S/1064.

[143] Ibid., 376th mtg (4 Nov. 1948), pp. 3, 25, 29, 31, 37; 377th mtg (4 Nov. 1948), pp. 40-1; SC res. 61 (S/1070), 4 Nov. 1948; Azcárate, p. 107; Ben-Gurion, pp. 300-4. See n. 286 below.

but mainly setting forth Israel's policy. The cease-fire, he wrote, was becoming not a forerunner of peace, but an instrument of war. Israel's enemies were trying to undermine the partition plan and deprive Israel of the Negev. These hostile manoeuvres were spearheaded by Britain and the Arabs— 'almost like a pack of hired assassins'. Truman, in reply, reiterated his opposition to any territorial changes in the partition plan to which Israel objected.[144]

In an effort to evolve a coherent US policy, Robert McClintock reviewed its basis: a cable from Marshall to James McDonald in Israel on 1 September and Marshall's own policy statement of 21 September, both of which had been cleared with Truman in advance; Truman's directive of 21 October that the United States must abide by its Charter obligations and support a cease-fire but need not play the role of protagonist or speak first; Truman's message of 2 November to the same effect but expressly authorizing support of the draft resolution recommended by the Security Council sub-committee; and finally Truman's Madison Square Garden speech. In the light of all these, McClintock recommended that the United States should save the face of Israel by agreeing to modify Bernadotte's proposed boundaries in the northern Negev, but that Egypt should not occupy the territory thus evacuated: this was, in fact, precisely what the Security Council sub-committee had proposed, although McClintock went further by suggesting that the demilitarized areas should eventually pass to Israel.[145]

The Council met in closed session on 9 and 10 November, during the course of which Bunche submitted a draft resolution looking to an armistice involving such 'ultimate withdrawal and reduction of forces' as would ensure the restoration of peace in Palestine, and stating that the separation of forces would lead to 'broad demilitarized zones' under UN observation. This text, had it been approved, would not have changed any of the Council's previous decisions, but it would have suggested that withdrawal was an ultimate rather than an im-

---

[144] Truman, vol. II, pp. 168-9; FRUS, 1948, vol. V part 2, pp. 1549-51, 1565-7, 1633-4.
[145] FRUS, 1948, vol. V part 2, pp. 1366-9, 1415-16, 1504, 1540-1, 1551-3.

mediate step. The US delegation was authorized to vote for Bunche's text.[146]

Israeli pressure on members of the Security Council was now intense, particularly in opposing the idea of demilitarizing the areas from which forces might withdraw.[147] Pearson of Canada and Parodi of France were having second thoughts about the Security Council's resolution of 4 November. Moreover, two new factors began to make themselves felt at this point. First, with the US election over, Truman accepted that Israel could not have its cake and eat it: 'if Israel wishes to retain that part of Negev granted it under Nov. 29 [1947] resolution it will have to take the rest of Nov 29 settlement which means giving up western Galilee and Jaffa...' From this point on, Truman never wavered from this position, though it was to lead to many disagreeable exchanges with Israeli leaders. The second new factor in the situation was that Bunche had come round to the view that the main stress should not be on precarious cease-fires or truces but on getting the parties to negotiate armistice agreements—though Sir Orme Sargent, Permanent Under-Secretary in the Foreign Office, commented that this would be 'tantamount to piously holding the ring and telling two con-testants, between whom military equilibrium has been de-stroyed by preponderance Israeli arms, to thrash out their problems in their own way'.[148]

It has been suggested to the author that pressure was brought to bear on Bunche to induce him to disregard the resolutions of the Security Council and to accept as irrevocable Israel's determination to have all of the Negev, pressure that would have breached the Charter ban on attempts to influence UN staff in the discharge of their responsibilities.[149] Dean Rusk insists, however, that the US government was careful to treat Bunche as an international civil servant: 'it will be very difficult

---

[146] Ibid., p. 1556, n. 1; SCOR, 3rd year, 378th mtg (9 Nov. 1948) and 379th mtg (10 Nov. 1948), pp. 62-4, S/1076.

[147] Britain was pressing the idea of demilitarized zones for Kashmir and Indonesia also. See FRUS, 1948, vol. V part 1, 1975, p. 447.

[148] FRUS, 1948, vol. V part 2, pp. 1338-40, 1384-6, 1525-7, 1536, 1538, 1544-5, 1553-4, 1559-60, 1562-3, 1565-7, 1570-80, 1602-3; 1949, vol. VI, 1977, pp. 658-61, 681-2, 741-2, 880-1, 944-7, 1051-3, 1058-63, 1072-5, 1102-7, 1124-30, 1148-53, 1165-6, 1168-77, 1207-8, 1235-7, 1248-52, 1305-8, 1438.

[149] Article 100 (2).

to find any evidence that we tried to give him "instructions" while he was serving at the United Nations'.[150] John Reedman, who worked closely with Bunche, considers that Bunche's tactics were not dictated by US pressure: 'They were a realistic and common-sense response to a situation which was daily becoming more unstable.'[151] Brian Urquhart, for many years a close colleague and friend of Bunche in the UN Secretariat, believes that Bunche acted throughout in the international interest:

Knowing Bunche as I did, I think it is unlikely that he would have flinched from actions which might be opposed, and I can only assume that he accepted the situation on the basis that it was practically impossible to change it, and, in the circumstances, the action he took was the only one which was practically possible.[152]

Judge Philip Jessup, who also knew Bunche well, writes that he doubts that Bunche would 'yield under pressure'. Bunche, writes Jessup, possessed an element of statesmanship that enabled him to balance the factors involved in a political crisis 'in order to marshal supporting elements and thus contribute in the end to an earnestly desired solution'.[153] Benjamin V. Cohen, Councellor of the State Department at the time, has written: 'While I find difficulty following the procedural manoeuvres in the Security Council, I am inclined to believe that Bunche finally concluded, probably persuaded by Pearson, that it was a mistake to consider changes in the Partition Plan before an armistice could become effective.'[154] It was for his work on the Middle East that Bunche was awarded the Nobel Peace Prize.

Bunche, like Count Bernadotte before him, had the dual function of supervising the cease-fire and persuading the parties to negotiate a long-term settlement. John Reedman has commented that all the parties violated the cease-fire at one time or another, and Bunche could not avoid making 'judgements which were likely to arouse hostility', thus endangering his

[150] Letter to the author, 28 April 1977.
[151] Letter to the author, 29 May 1977.
[152] Letter to the author, 14 March 1977.
[153] Letters to the author, 29 January and 2 May 1977.
[154] Letter to the author, 3 June 1977.

mediatory task. Pressure on the parties had to be exerted by states, especially the major powers, but decisive pressure in support of Security Council decisions presupposed some identity of interest among the members. Bunche's main aim was to achieve a clearer definition of the cease-fire lines and to provide machinery through which local disputes could be negotiated and monitored. Faced with the increasing ambiguity of Security Council proceedings and the unclear situation on the ground, Bunche 'necessarily became more pragmatic in his approach'.[155]

It is in the light of his often contradictory responsibilities that we must view Bunche's crucial communication of 13 November to Egypt and Israel indicating the provisional demarcation lines, to take effect on 19 November, in accordance with the Security Council's resolution of 4 November. These provisional lines had been defined in consultation with the parties and the Security Council sub-committee. There was to be 'an orderly observed withdrawal of forces in the Negev' and the creation of 'a wide area' in which military movement was to be precluded. Troops were not to move beyond the provisional lines. Patrolling in the demilitarized area would not be permitted, and movement of armed forces or military supplies would be at the discretion of the UN Truce Supervision Organization. These arrangements would be provisional only and within the framework of the existing cease-fire, and would last until permanent lines had been established by negotiation between the parties. Once the provisional lines had been put into effect, the good offices of Bunche and the supervisory personnel would be at the disposal of the parties, in order to establish 'permanent truce lines and such neutral or demilitarized zones as may appear advantageous'. Israel was to withdraw its forces from the Negev completely, except for 'those [forces] maintained in Israeli settlements...for defence purposes prior to 14 October'. In the west, the provisional line for Israel ran from north of Ashkelon and Majdal, while the Egyptian line started about seven miles north of Gaza and then turned south some two miles beyond the Majdal-Gaza highway, leaving a demilitarized zone which nowhere had a depth of less than seven miles. In the east, the line ran south from Jerusalem for about thirty miles and then

---

[155] Letter to the author, 29 May 1977.

east to the Dead Sea, a little to the east of what in 1949 became the armistice demarcation line.[156] Israeli forces were to withdraw from Beersheba, which was to be a demilitarized Arab town under an Egyptian civil administrator. Egyptian forces that had been in the Bir Asluj area prior to 14 October would be allowed to remain, except in the village of Bir Asluj itself, and Egyptian control of the road running from Bir Asluj north-west to Rafah would be 'recognized and maintained'.[157]

Both the General Assembly and the Security Council were due to meet on the afternoon of Monday 15 November, but the previous Saturday the US ambassador in London was summoned to Chequers to talk with Prime Minister Attlee on a matter 'of grave importance'. Attlee said that if the United Nations were to avoid the unhappy fate of the League of Nations, the Members must abide by the Charter. Britain had treaty obligations to Jordan and Egypt, but had scrupulously observed the UN arms embargo. The Cabinet had decided, however, that if Israel continued to defy the United Nations it might be necessary to reinforce Aqaba. Britain would await Israel's reply to Bunche before taking a final decision.[158]

Moshe Shertok (Sharett) spoke in the General Assembly's political committee on 15 November, expressing surprise at the proposal to 'rob' Israel of the Negev, which would be either 'developed by the Jews or remain a desert forever'. Israel could not even consider Bernadotte's proposals. No part of the

[156] The provisional line for the forward Israeli positions in the south was to run from the Mediterranean coast about five miles north of Ashkelon to Julis, east to Ibdis, Juseir, and Zeita (two to three miles to the north of the line Majdal-Negba-Karatiya-Faluja), and thence to Al Huseimayi: the provisional Egyptian line in the same sector was to start about seven miles north of Gaza where the Hasi watercourse reaches the Mediterranean, then through Deir Siyj and in an easterly direction, turning south about two miles beyond the Majdal-Gaza highway, and continuing parallel to the highway as far as the international frontier. The provisional Arab line in the eastern sector was to start in the Government House neutral zone to the south of Jerusalem, west to Beit Safafa and Sharafat, south to Beit Jala, west to Al Khadr and Husan, south-west to Nahhalin, Surif, Beit Aula, and Tarqumiya, south to Dura and Dhahiriya, then east to Samu and the Dead Sea.

[157] UN press release PAL/381, 13 November 1948. It is, perhaps, surprising that this crucial letter was not issued as a document of the Security Council. Israel's reply (n. 163) was issued in provisional mimeographed form but was not included in the printed version of the official Security Council records.

[158] FRUS, 1948, vol. V part 2, pp. 1446, 1517, 1520, 1524, 1530, 1537, 1572, 1579, 1585-91.

Negev could be given up or bartered away, and Israel could not accept western Galilee as a substitute.[159]

The Security Council also met on 15 November and again the following day. Bunche said that the time had come for the Security Council to 'put the full weight of its authority behind a call for an immediate armistice...to move decisively toward a condition of secure peace in Palestine'. In his opinion, the conflict in Palestine was 'utterly futile'. There was no magic in the word 'armistice' as opposed to 'truce'; the essential requirement was to pass from a situation that was 'universally regarded ...as merely an interruption to hostilities' to 'a new framework which will signal at least the beginning of the definitive end of hostilities'. This should be achieved by whatever procedure the parties found possible—preferably by direct negotiations but, failing that, by negotiations through UN intermediaries. The Council should 'specifically and firmly' provide for a separation, withdrawal, and reduction of forces. A proposal drafted by Bunche, amended by the Soviet Union so as to delete any reference to demilitarized zones, was rejected, and instead the Council adopted a text sponsored by Lester Pearson of Canada, with the support of Belgium and France,which reaffirmed the earlier decision that the situation constituted a threat to peace; decided that steps should be taken to bring about 'permanent peace'; called for negotiations under Article 40 of the UN Charter 'with a view to the immediate establishment of the armistice'; and called for such withdrawal and reduction of forces as would ensure the maintenance of the armistice. Syria voted against, and the Soviet Union and the Ukrainian SSR abstained. Israel promptly agreed to enter into armistice negotiations, but the Arab states still hesitated. But in one respect Bunche's interpretation of the decision was ambiguous: the intention of the Security Council on 16 November was that withdrawal should be 'with a view to' an armistice, whereas Bunche suggested that it was the armistice that would 'in principle...involve...withdrawal'. Nobody challenged Bunche's

---

[159] GAOR, 3rd session, 1st part, First Committee, 200th mtg (15 Nov. 1948), pp. 640-7.

interpretation, however, although Syria asked what would happen if the parties could not agree on an armistice.[160]

On 17 November, Attlee again summoned the US ambassador, because Anglo-American relations had become critical. Surely, said Attlee, Truman had not intended that statements made during an election campaign should give Israel *carte blanche* to take military action in defiance of the United Nations?[161]

Dan Kurzman reports that the same day a 'tense' meeting took place between Bunche and Eban, and he quotes Bunche as saying, 'I think I can suggest an arrangement that we can both agree on.'[162]

At midnight on 18 November, Israel handed over its reply to Bunche's memorandum of 13 November. Israel understood that it was 'not the intention' of the Security Council to require the withdrawal of forces from positions held before the 14 October and noted a statement of Bunche to the effect that 'the withdrawal of military forces north of the defined line' was 'inapplicable' to forces maintained in the Negev settlements 'for defence' prior to the October fighting. Israel had 'uninterruptedly' maintained regular mobile forces in the Negev and these had 'moved freely throughout the area'. Israel was pleased that the Security Council was not now demanding the withdrawal from the Negev of forces maintained there before 14 October, for such a withdrawal would 'invite predatory activities by irregulars'. 'The Government of Israel states that forces which entered the Negeb [*sic*] on and after the 14th October...have since been withdrawn to positions north of the line indicated in the Acting Mediator's memorandum.'[163]

John Reedman writes that the Israeli statement was 'not entirely false' as the facts were verifiable by UN observers. There were settlements and enclaves on both sides of the cease-fire line. Israeli forces guarding the settlements were legitimately there, though UN observers lacked precise information about

[160] SCOR, 3rd year, 380th mtg (15 Nov. 1948), pp. 9-11, 20; 381st mtg (16 Nov. 1948), pp. 15, 25, 40-1, 51-3, 55; SC res. 62 (S/1080), 16 Nov. 1948; Azcárate, p. 108; Ben-Gurion, pp. 306-7; see also GAOR, 3rd session, 1st part, First Committee, 213th mtg (25 Nov. 1948), pp. 768-71.

[161] FRUS, 1948, vol. V part 2, pp. 1610-13.

[162] Dan Kurzman, *Genesis 1948: The First Arab-Israeli War*, New York, World Publishing, 1970, p. 636.

[163] UN doc. S/1081, 19 Nov. 1948 (mimeo).

them. After a military incident, the Israelis were doubtless able to reinforce the settlements and then claim that these elements had been there from the beginning. 'What was not verifiable because not previously known to [the UN] observers was the extent of the so-called defensive forces permissible in the various enclaves.'[164]

Bunche let it be known that he was 'very satisfied' with the Israeli reply. 'Without armies to back him up,' wrote one American journalist, Bunche 'swallowed humble pie.' Reedman takes the view, on the other hand, that there was no capitulation by Bunche. Bunche's response provided 'the only basis on which this very messy situation might be brought under better control'. The US delegation in Paris certainly breathed a sigh of relief. Britain, on the other hand, thought that Bunche 'had tricked both them and the Security Council', and Harold (later Sir Harold) Beeley gave a press conference which was described by Marshall as 'cautious and marked by understatement'. No doubt the Arabs felt even more angry and deceived. On 19 November, Egypt again broke the cease-fire, this time by sending a force from Gaza towards Nirim.[165]

There were several elements in the difficulties faced by the Security Council in the five weeks following the resumption of fighting in mid-October. It was, in the first place, unfortunate that Bunche should have suggested that withdrawal of forces should be the subject of negotiations. He later tried to make amends by saying that it had never been his intention to modify the fundamental principle of the cease-fire 'by submitting the vital question of military advantage to negotiation': the only problems to be negotiated concerned the Negev and the deployment of UN observers in that area. By then, however, the damage had been done, as the Security Council had approved Bunche's recommendation without change. The Security Council tried to rectify the position in its resolution of 4 November, which called for withdrawal and, in a separate paragraph,

---

[164] Letter to the author, 29 May 1977.
[165] Ben-Gurion, pp. 310, 312; FRUS, 1948, vol. V part 1, p. 1616; Burns, p. 26; Jon and David Kimche, *Both Sides of the Hill: Britain and the Palestine War* (published in the United States as *Clash of Destinies*), London, Secker and Warburg, 1960, p. 251; Kenneth W. Bilby, *New Star in the Near East*, New York, Doubleday, 1950, p. 162; letter from John Reedman, 29 May 1977.

negotiations on other issues; but the Council added to the misunderstanding by calling for withdrawal to a provisional line that Bunche was to establish rather than to the positions occupied before the outbreak of fighting.[166]

As far as one can tell from the printed records, Bunche still had the idea that withdrawal would come about as a result of negotiation or not at all. In a draft resolution submitted to a closed meeting of the Security Council on 9 November, Bunche suggested that an armistice should involve such 'ultimate' withdrawal of forces as would ensure peace in Palestine. Although Bunche's text was not approved, it was no doubt at the back of his mind when he issued his directive to the parties on 13 November. The resolution approved by the Security Council on 16 November envisaged withdrawal as arising from an armistice still to be negotiated, but 'ultimate' was dropped.[167] There was thus an important contradiction between the Security Council's resolutions of 4 and 16 November.

Another difficulty was the confusion and inconsistency of US policy in the period running up to the election. Truman was proud of his record as a good friend of Israel and the Jews, and in the final three weeks of the campaign, he was much more aware of pressure from Israel and the US Zionists than of the delicate diplomatic situation in Paris.

The Arabs were badly led and at loggerheads with each other. Israel was determined to consolidate the boundaries of the new state so that it would consist of those parts of Palestine that were to have been Jewish under the partition plan, plus other areas that had been captured during the fighting. On Ben-Gurion's advice, Israel's proclamation of independence had not defined the frontiers of the new state, although the Israeli request for US recognition had stated that Israel had been proclaimed within the frontiers of the partition resolution.[168]

The 'inherent contradiction', as Shabtai Rosenne has described it, between the Security Council's resolutions of 4 and

---

[166] SCOR, 3rd year, Supplement for October 1948, pp. 61-2, para. 18 of S/1042; 367th mtg (19 Oct. 1948), pp. 37-8; 374th mtg (28 Oct. 1948), pp. 4-5; SC res. 61 (S/1070), 4 Nov. 1948; Azcárate, p. 107.

[167] SCOR, 3rd year, 378th mtg (9 Nov. 1948), p. 63; PAL/381, 13 Nov. 1948; SC res. 62 (S/1080), 16 Nov. 1948.

[168] FRUS, 1948, vol. V part 2, 1976, p. 989.

16 November was to cause difficulties during the armistice negotiations in Rhodes the following year. Egypt based itself on the first resolution and the principle that no military or political advantage should accrue from a violation of the cease-fire: the armistice lines should correspond to the cease-fire lines that had existed between July and October. Israel preferred the second resolution and the wish to avoid the instability that had prevailed between July and October: the prospect of further fighting could be eliminated only by confirming the *de facto* lines at the time of the opening of negotiations in January 1949. 'Both these approaches', writes Rosenne, 'were of course essentially correct', but it was the second approach that prevailed.[169]

It was an unedifying episode, and nobody emerges with much credit. It was, however, a time of acute and widespread international tension, and those contemporary records that I have seen convey a sense of perplexity and weariness.

3.4 MEANS OF PEACEFUL SETTLEMENT

To the statement in the UN Charter about the obligation to settle disputes peacefully is attached a partial list of such means: negotiation, inquiry, mediation, conciliation, arbitration, judicial settlement, resort to regional agencies or arrangements, to which is added 'or other peaceful means of their own choice'.[170] These means of settlement are to be used 'first of all' (*avant tout*), so that conflicts are usually in a relatively acute stage when they reach the United Nations. The list of means of settlement does not include good offices, which is related to mediation and conciliation; it may be regarded as one of the 'other' means of settlement.

Negotiation is a bilateral process involving only the parties: inquiry could be bilateral but in practice often involves the assistance of others. All of the other means of peaceful settlement mentioned in the Charter depend on the assistance or intervention of third parties. Thomas Franck has examined the nature of the impartiality that is looked for in third parties

---

[169] Rosenne, p. 39.
[170] Article 33.

when their assistance is invoked. This impartiality he charac-
terizes as 'temperamental detachment', which he contrasts
with the temperamental commitment of the parties. Franck
asks in what vocations this attitude of detachment is commonly
found, and he suggests that it is characteristic of teachers,
actors, diplomats, and stock-market analysts. An attitude of
commitment, Franck suggests, is usually found in chairmen of
companies, generals, politicians, missionaries, and bull fighters.[171] This is vivid language, but it does help to illuminate the
concept of the impartiality.

I examine below the means of peaceful settlement used
during the period 1946-64 in connection with the cases studied.

NEGOTIATION

Although the means of settlement listed in the Charter are not
in order of importance, it is not surprising that negotiation
should come first, since it is *par excellence* the means that is
normally used 'first of all'. Moreover, even when an issue has
become acute enough for it to be submitted to the Security
Council, it is natural for members to ask if all the possibilities
of direct negotiation have been exhausted. If armed conflict has
broken out, the first impulse of the Council is to call for the
fighting to stop, but the second impulse is nearly always to encourage the parties to negotiate. In the cases within the scope
of this study, the Security Council favoured such negotiations,
often offering the assistance of the President of the Council, the
Secretary-General, or a subsidiary organ.[172]

There are four matters of a preliminary nature that may
have to be settled in connection with direct negotiations: the
place of meeting, the status of those negotiators who do not
enjoy diplomatic immunity, the agenda, and what publicity
shall be given to the proceedings.

---

[171] Thomas M. Franck, *The Structure of Impartiality: Examining the Riddle of One Law
in a Fragmented World*, New York, Macmillan, 1968 (under the auspices of the CEIP),
pp. 300-1, 306.
[172] SC res. 36 (S/597), 1 Nov. 1947; 61 (S/1070), 4 Nov. 1948; 62 (S/1080), 16 Nov.
1948; 67 (S/1234), 28 Jan. 1949; 73 (S/1376, II), 11 Aug. 1949; 98 (S/2883), 23 Dec.
1952; SCOR, 3rd year, 367th mtg (19 Oct. 1948), pp. 37-8 (S/1044); 4th year,
421st mtg (23 March 1949), pp. 5, 25-6; 457th mtg (17 Dec. 1949), pp. 5, 8.

Place of meeting[173]   Negotiations usually take place on neutral ground or alternately on the territory of each party. In Indonesia, following the first Dutch 'police action', a US ship (the *Renville*) was used as a meeting place.[174] In the Palestine case, the UN Mediator first established his base in Cairo, but he soon moved to the Greek island of Rhodes, and it was there that armistice negotiations between Egypt and Israel took place. In the Korean case, the Unified Command initially suggested that the parties should meet on a Danish hospital ship off the North Korean coast, but the Communist side preferred to meet on land near the *de facto* line separating the military forces of the parties. The first meetings were in the Kaesong area, and consideration was also given by the United States to a number of more distant places, including Hong Kong and Port Arthur.[175] Finally it was agreed to meet in a demilitarized area in the vicinity of Panmunjom.

Status of negotiators   In spite of international agreements about diplomatic immunity, difficulties can arise about the status of negotiators, although a US authority on negotiation recommends that disputes about status should if possible be avoided.[176] Difficulties about the status of negotiators arose in Indonesia in 1948, after the Netherlands had said that it might be necessary to institute searches of the personal effects of Republican delegates because it had been alleged that they were trafficking in opium. The UN Good Offices Committee (GOC) was sceptical about these charges, and reported to the Security Council that its chairman had asked that the representatives of the parties should be accorded a status 'similar to that of an officer under a flag of truce'. This concept was subsequently elaborated as follows: 'members of both the delegations, while in the territory controlled by the other, would have the status of "a distinguished and honoured guest and of a parliamentary officer under a flag of truce".' At a later stage, the GOC suggested 'a practical minimum of immunities' which the delegations should enjoy, including the right to enter and leave territory

---

[173] Phillipson, pp. 94-5, 114-16.
[174] FRUS, 1947, vol. VI, 1972, pp. 1066; Jessup, p. 48.
[175] Goodman, pp. 39-41.
[176] Fred Charles Iklé, *How Nations Negotiate*, pp. 94-5.

in which the GOC was situated and 'freedom from any molest-
ation of person or interference with personal effects'. Immunity
should be withdrawn only if there were 'convincing evidence'
of subversive or illegal activities.[177]

Agenda[178]   The agenda should be the first item to be discussed,
and this is achieved by having a provisional agenda, if necessary
drafted with third-party assistance, and making the adoption of
the agenda the first item of business. In practice, the agenda
may seem to one or both parties to prejudge matters of substance. When the UN Commission for India and Pakistan
(UNCIP) proposed that India and Pakistan should meet at
ministerial level in 1949, India wished to add to the proposed
agenda the disarming and disbanding of Azad Kashmir forces,
but Pakistan took the view that this did not arise from UNCIP's
resolution of the previous August, which was to be the basis of
the negotiations. UNCIP withdrew its proposal for a meeting
at ministerial level and suggested instead that the parties should
refer the points at issue to arbitration, but that proposal also
was unavailing.[179]

Publicity[180]   Diplomatic negotiations are conducted in private,
though each party is free to interpret its own role to the press
or public.

    When negotiations for a Korean armistice began in July
1951, the Unified Command proposed that twenty journalists
should be attached to its delegation and should have access to
the conference area, but not to the conference room itself. The
Communists did not respond to this proposal immediately, but
on 12 July North Korean or Chinese armed guards prevented
journalists attached to the Unified Command from having
access to the conference area. The Unified Command suspended
negotiations, but the chief Communist negotiator said that this
was a minor problem which must not be allowed to interrupt

---

[177] SCOR, 3rd year, Supplement for December 1948, pp. 36-9, paras. 105-15 of
S/1085.
[178] See Iklé, pp. 95-9, 218-21.
[179] SCOR, 4th year, Special Supplement no. 7, pp. 34-5, 130-41, paras. 185-9 of
and Annexes 27-34 to S/1430.
[180] Phillipson, pp. 125-6.

the negotiations: in future, twenty journalists would be regarded by the Communist side as part of the working personnel of the delegation of the Unified Command.[181]

The presence of the media in the vicinity of sensitive negotiations does not necessarily advance diplomatic progress. Six weeks after the question of allowing journalists into the Kaesong conference area had arisen, North Korea and China alleged that an aircraft of the Unified Command had bombed the conference zone. Colonel Andrew Kinney, a liaison officer of the Unified Command, was sent to examine the evidence, and was questioning a Chinese soldier about whether the aircraft said to have been responsible for the bombing had shown lights. At this point a Communist newspaperman intervened, charging Kinney with tricking the soldier with a 'trap' question. Kinney thereupon demanded that the press be excluded, and the Communist side 'complied after some argument'.[182]

In his book on the Korean negotiations, Admiral Joy wrote that press coverage of armistice negotiations should be 'as unfettered as physical facilities permit'. If you are honest and sincere, he wrote, you need not fear the press.[183] This is true so far as it goes, but it may be that Admiral Joy's views arose from the special circumstances in Korea. Time and again, biased or premature publicity by one or both sides has caused ill will and disrupted negotiations. Much damage was done by the Netherlands army press service in Indonesia, and Israeli press leaks in 1949 and 1950 interfered with the delicate work of the Palestine Conciliation Commission.

Partisan reporting by the media exacerbated all the conflicts covered by this study. In the Kashmir case, Secretary-General Lie's personal representative stressed to the Commission for India and Pakistan (UNCIP) the damage done by 'objectionable propaganda', and both India and Pakistan complained to UNCIP of the activities of the press and radio of the other side. UNCIP addressed identical communications to the two sides asking that influence should be brought to bear 'in the proper quarters' so as to bring about an end to 'propaganda

---

[181] SCOR, 6th year, Supplement for July-September 1951, pp. 23-5, 35, S/2266, S/2277.
[182] Ibid., p. 67, S/2311.
[183] C. Turner Joy, *How Communists Negotiate*, p. 169.

which goes beyond legitimate political activity', but the appeal went unheeded. Both of the truces in Indonesia included provisions for restraint in broadcasting and other forms of propaganda.[184] It must be admitted that this can be a difficult problem where the press is not normally subject to government control.

Recent theoretical studies of bargaining have led to more sophisticated ideas about diplomatic negotiation. Harold Nicolson's approach had been to specify the main traits required in his ideal diplomat: truthfulness, mental tranquillity, patience, modesty, loyalty, and precision—qualities that were traditionally inculcated in prefects at an English public school.[185] Fred Iklé, in a recent and more sophisticated study, does not deal with the personality of the diplomat but with techniques and methods of negotiation. He advises that flagrant lies should be avoided, promises should be kept, explicit threats should not be issued (but warnings are in order), agreements should not be blatantly violated, mutual understanding should not be deliberately misconstrued, the other side's domestic difficulties should not be exploited in public, motives should not be impugned, invective should not be resorted to, and so on. On a more mundane level, Iklé recommends the avoidance of disputes about status ('Never kill a negotiator'), adherence to the agenda, and reciprocation of concessions and favours; and Iklé notes the utility of linkages and package deals.[186]

INQUIRY[187]

I have referred earlier to the distinction between *investigation*, as a means by which the Security Council may acquire information about a matter before it, and *inquiry*, as a means of pacific settlement of disputes (which in the UN system is often allied to or an integral part of mediation or conciliation). The Statute of

[184] SCOR, 3rd year, Special Supplement no. 1, S/649/Rev. 1, p. 73, para. 7 (b) and (c); 4th year, Special Supplement no. 5, S/1373 and Corr. 1, p. 61, para. 4 (a); Special Supplement no. 7, pp. 7-9, 67, 77-8, paras. 18, 22, 24 and Appendix IV of and Annex 2 to S/1430. For secrecy in negotiations and public opinion, see Iklé, pp. 29, 85-6, 132-42, 227.
[185] Harold Nicolson, *Diplomacy*, London, Oxford University Press, 1950 (Home University Library), pp. 109-26.
[186] Iklé, pp. 8-16, 64-5, 69, 77-9, 86-121, 222-4, 255.
[187] See Arthur Lall, *Modern International Negotiation*, pp. 9-12.

the International Court of Justice includes a provision by which the Court may authorize an inquiry conducted by a special agency,[188] and any means of peaceful settlement involving third parties is likely to include an attempt to establish the relevant facts and to elucidate those aspects of the dispute where incomplete or misleading information has been an unnecessary cause of contention.

Professor Nissim Bar-Yaacov, in his definitive work on inquiry in the settlement of disputes, concludes that the technique of bilateral inquiry should be distinguished from conciliation and other means of settlement. When arbitral and judicial tribunals engage in fact-finding, this should not be regarded as an application of the method of inquiry but rather as 'elements of the arbitral or judicial process'.[189]

MEDIATION, GOOD OFFICES, CONCILIATION[190]

Although it is possible to make some distinctions between these three means of settlement, there would be no advantage in dealing with them separately in this study. All involve the introduction of a supposedly disinterested person, state, or agency to help the parties to reach agreement.

In the first year or so, the Security Council itself tried to promote agreement in matters not involving directly the two power blocs, but it was found increasingly necessary to entrust such functions to the President of the Council, a subsidiary organ, or the Secretary-General, since it was usually desirable to have a quieter form of diplomacy than was then customary in the Security Council itself.

In the cases studied, one or a combination of techniques have been used, as shown in Table 5.

It may be doubted whether any general conclusions can be drawn about the comparative utility of the three methods. When one method becomes ossified, another has to be tried.

---

[188] Article 50 of the Statute.

[189] Bar-Yaacov, *The Handling of International Disputes by Means of Inquiry*, London, Oxford University Press (for the RIIA), 1974, pp. 2-4, 9, 17-19, 134-40, 241-4, 323-4, 327-9.

[190] See Phillipson, pp. 76-8; Jean-Pierre Cot, *International Conciliation*, trans. R. Myers, London, Europa, 1972; Lall, pp. 12-15, 18, 84-100; Iklé pp. 145-6, 214.

Table 5

Mediation, good offices, and conciliation

Case	Title	Res. no.	Tasks
Indonesia	Good Offices Committee (GOC)	SC 31 (S/525, II)	'tender its good offices to the parties in order to assist in the pacific settlement of their dispute...'
	Commission for Indonesia	SC 67 (S/1234)	'all of the functions assigned to the Committee of Good Offices... The Commission shall assist the parties in the implementation of this resolution and in the negotiations to be undertaken...'
Kashmir	Commission for India and Pakistan (UNCIP)	SC 39 (S/654)	'The Commission is...to exercise... any mediatory influence likely to smooth away difficulties...'
		SC 47 (S/726)	'place its good offices and mediation at the disposal of the Governments...'
	Representative for India and Pakistan	SC 80(S/1469)	'place himself at the disposal of the Governments of India and Pakistan and to place before those Governments or the Security Council any suggestions which...are likely to contribute to the expeditious and enduring solution of the dispute... [and to] exercise all of the powers and responsibilities devolving upon the United Nations Commission for India and Pakistan by reason of existing resolutions...'

Table 5 (contd)

Case	Title	Res. no.	Tasks
	President of the Security Council (Gunnar Jarring of Sweden)	SC 123 (S/3793)	'to examine with the Governments of India and Pakistan any proposals which...are likely to contribute towards the settlement of the dispute...'
Palestine	Mediator	GA 186 (S-2)	'use his good offices with the local and community authorities in Palestine to... (iii) Promote a peaceful adjustment of the future situation of Palestine...'
	Palestine Conciliation Committee (PCC)	GA 194 (III)	'To assume...the functions given to the United Nations Mediator...to assist the Governments and authorities concerned to achieve a final settlement of all questions...'
	Secretary-General	SC 113 (S/3575)	'to arrange with the parties for the adoption of any measures which... would reduce existing tensions...'
Korea	Good Offices Committee	GA 498 (V)	'to bring about a cessation of hostilities in Korea and the achievement of United Nations objectives...by peaceful means [and] to use their good offices to this end.'
Cyprus	Mediator	SC 186 (S/5575)	'use his best endeavours...for the purpose of promoting a peaceful solution and an agreed settlement...'

In 1949 the UN Commission for India and Pakistan reached the following conclusion:

The Commission doubts whether a five-member body is the most flexible and desirable instrument to continue in the task. The designation of a single person with broad and undivided responsibility offers a more practical means of finding the balance and compromise necessary to advance the settlement of the dispute.[191]

The Security Council took the hint and appointed a single mediator (the UN Representative for India and Pakistan).[192]

Yet at the same time as this advice was proffered and acted on, the Acting Mediator for Palestine was suggesting that it would be helpful if the functions of a single intermediary were transferred to the three-member Palestine Conciliation Commission,[193] and this the Security Council proceeded to do. Within a month, however, it was being suggested that the Palestine Conciliation Commission had served its purpose and that what was now needed was 'a one man mission'.[194] As none of the changes in these two cases resulted in significant progress towards a settlement, it is difficult to draw any useful conclusions from them.

Both the General Assembly and the Security Council have examined the various means of peaceful settlement available. In 1948, following a British initiative, the General Assembly reviewed the League of Nations system of appointing a rapporteur (or conciliator) to help the parties to find a solution to their difficulties, but after debate the matter was allowed to lapse.[195] The following year the General Assembly decided to create a panel of persons who could be called on for inquiry or conciliation, and commended to the Security Council the practice of using a rapporteur or conciliator to assist in resolving situations or disputes.[196] The Panel for Inquiry and Conciliation was duly set up. Although there has been no formal resort to it, the Security Council appointed a member of

[191] SCOR, 4th year, Special Supplement no. 7, p. 62, para. 285 of S/1430.
[192] SC res. 80 (S/1469), 14 March 1950.
[193] SCOR, 4th year, Supplement for August 1949, S/1357, p. 6.
[194] SC res. 73 (S/1376, II), 11 Aug. 1949; Azcárate, pp. 157-8.
[195] GAOR, 3rd session, part I, *Ad Hoc* Political Committee, 28th mtg (9 Dec. 1948), p. 327.
[196] GA res. 268 (III), 28 April 1949.

the Panel as Representative for India and Pakistan in 1951, and the US ambassador said that his government had looked informally at the names on the Panel before reaching a conclusion.[197] In 1950 the Security Council took note of the General Assembly's advice about a rapporteur or conciliator and decided to 'base its action' on 'the principles contained' in the resolution should an appropriate occasion arise[198]—which is about as noncommittal as it is possible to be.

If the Security Council offers third-party assistance, the parties to the matter at issue may not have a clear idea as to what will be involved. Two months after the Security Council had offered good offices in the Indonesian case, the US consul general in Batavia (Djakarta) cabled to Washington three times in August 1947 that the Indonesian Republicans did not know what good offices implied. Washington emphasized in reply that what was contemplated was in conformity with the well-known international understanding of the term, 'an attempt to induce negotiations between disputants'. It was not until the end of October, after the UN Good Offices Committee had arrived on the scene, that the Republicans for the 'first time clearly understood limitations good offices'.[199]

It has never been absolutely clear to what extent an organ with several members represents the body that appointed it or the states that compose it or whether the members serve in their individual and personal capacities. The secretary of the Palestine Conciliation Commission took what can only be described as a heretical line on this. In an organ composed of states, he wrote, the governmental representatives should 'base their conduct ... on the general interests represented in the United Nations'. If, on the other hand, an organ were composed of individuals, 'their conduct ... could not fail to be dictated by the governments they represent'.[200] The reality was different. Although the US member of the Good Offices Committee in Indonesia told the Dutch Governor-General that he was 'an uninstructed representative', it is clear from the documents published in *Foreign Relations of the United States* for 1947-50 that

[197] SCOR, 6th year, 543rd mtg (30 April 1951), para. 30.
[198] SC res. 81 (S/1486), 24 May 1950.
[199] FRUS, 1947, vol. VI, 1972, pp. 1017-19, 1022, 1028-9, 1065.
[200] Azcárate, pp. 134-5.

US members of the Good Offices Committee in Indonesia, the Commission for Indonesia, the Commission for India and Pakistan, and the Palestine Conciliation Commission were in continuous and close touch with Washington and consulted the White House or the State Department before introducing important proposals of procedure or substance. Moreover, the US members of these bodies gave the impression that their colleagues had a similar relationship with their own capitals. The US member of the Good Offices Committee in Indonesia complained that the members from Australia and Belgium were proving 'nearly as uncompromising as parties themselves'.[201]

In the early stage of its work, the Good Offices Committee in Indonesia made proposals privately and published them only if both parties agreed. Later the Committee reached the conclusion that if there were to be a successful outcome, it must exercise greater initiative and exert greater pressure. The Committee told the Security Council after the *Renville* truce agreements that in future it wished to 'make and publish suggestions to the parties...without necessarily waiting for the parties to request it to do so'. When the Committee returned to Indonesia, however, a different technique was used. Instead of the Committee acting formally as a corporate entity, the individual members acted informally on a personal basis, and it was in this way that the US member submitted his own comprehensive plan for a settlement on 10 September 1948.[202]

An honest broker acting under the authority of a UN organ must consider how much he is bound by previous UN decisions. No problem arises if the Security Council or a subsidiary organ merely elaborates a previous resolution. This was how the UN Commission for India and Pakistan (UNCIP) saw its own resolution of 13 August 1948. But as time passed, UNCIP found the 1948 resolutions less and less applicable to a changing situation, so that, instead of being pointers to a settlement, they became a prison.[203]

[201] FRUS, 1947, vol. VI, 1972, p. 1079; 1948, vol. VI, 1974, p. 300.

[202] SCOR, 3rd year, 247th mtg (17 Feb. 1948), pp. 146-7; 259th mtg (28 Feb. 1948), pp. 371-2; FRUS, 1948, vol. VI, 1974, pp. 329, 333-7, 347-50, 391-3, 416-18.

[203] SCOR, 4th year, Special Supplement no. 7, pp. 40, 46, 59-62, paras. 204, 225, 274-5, 279-83 of S/1430.

Is a mediator at liberty to propose changes to a UN plan of peaceful settlement? Count Bernadotte took the line that his task was not to act as an advocate of UN decisions but to help the parties to solve the problem. He could not be bound by the General Assembly's partition resolution, which he described as 'unfortunate', and which in his view had already been 'outrun and irrevocably revised by the actual events of recent Palestine history'. 'I have not considered myself bound by the provisions of the 29 November resolution, since, had I done so, there would have been no meaning to my mediation.' Bernadotte was constantly irritated by the tendency of the Security Council to take decisions that interfered with his efforts. Of one such decision taken as Bernadotte was beginning his work he wrote:

For my part, I could not feel particularly pleased at this measure. It seemed fairly obvious that my task must be made a great deal more difficult by the fact that just before my arrival in Palestine the Council had taken precisely the measures that I myself had been appointed to be responsible for.

Israel expressed 'surprise' that Bernadotte proposed changes in the partition plan, but Bernadotte said he could by no means accept the Israeli statement: his mediation, he repeated, would be meaningless if he could not take account of 'the new situation'.

Whatever may be the precise legal significance and status of the 29 November resolution, it would seem quite clear to me that the situation is not of such a nature as to entitle either party to act on the assumption that such parts of that resolution as may be favourable to it may be regarded as effective, while those parts which may, by reason of changes in circumstances, be regarded as unfavourable, are to be considered as ineffective.

Bernadotte saw his task as one of 'offering suggestions on the basis of which further discussions might take place'.[204]

The same issue arose for the UN Mediator in Cyprus with regard to the treaties and the constitution of 1960. The Mediator reported to the Security Council in 1965 that, as the aim of the Council was to achieve an agreed settlement, and as the treaties

---

[204] GAOR, 3rd session, Supplement no. 11, A/648, pp. 5, 9, 22, 24, 26; Bernadotte, pp. 5, 33, 94, 118, 127, 131, 146, 155-6, 171.

and the constitution had led up to the situation that had required the Council to intervene, it was clear that to return to the situation that had existed at the end of 1963 would provide no solution. 'It is obvious that the Cyprus problem cannot any longer be solved by trying to implement fully the Nicosia Treaties and the Constitution governed by the Treaties.' The Security Council, by the very act of appointing a Mediator, had concluded that 'some new solution' would have to be found to end the crisis.[205]

In the case of Sinai-Suez in 1956-7, Secretary-General Hammarskjold stuck faithfully (some would say rigidly) to the decisions of the Security Council and the General Assembly, but the circumstances were different from those in Palestine in 1948 and Cyprus in 1964. From the time that the Suez crisis erupted in July 1956, Hammarskjold was acting not as a mediator but as the Secretary-General of the United Nations and agent of its organs, and he took the view that his loyalty had to be to the United Nations and the decisions of its policy-making bodies. In his search for peace earlier in 1956, he had similarly taken as his starting point the four armistice agreements and those decisions of the Security Council as were still applicable.

The UN Mediators in Palestine found great difficulty in combining mediation and supervision of the cease-fire in 1948-9. This was not because the amount of work was excessive (although it was) but because the duties were sometimes incompatible. Count Bernadotte reported to the General Assembly that he had been 'inevitably drawn into the settlement of disputes' and that his position and decisions as supervisor of the cease-fire had jeopardized 'the more fundamental task of mediation'. His successor, Ralph Bunche, made much the same point to the Security Council the following year.

Our experience in Palestine...was that the duties of truce supervision and enforcement [*sic*] often conflicted with the functions of mediation; that having held discussions with the parties, and having created a situation in which we thought we could make progress towards settlement, some problem of truce violation would arise at an inopportune moment...

[205] SCOR, 20th year, Supplement for January-March 1965, pp. 237-8, para. 129 of S/6253.

Count Bernadotte had difficult experiences of this nature, and so did I...[206]

John Reedman, who worked closely with Bernadotte and Bunche, has written that Bunche was acutely conscious, 'more so than anyone else I believe', of the conflict between his role as Acting Mediator and that of supervisor of the cease-fire. 'This is something we often discussed together.'[207]

In Cyprus, a separation was made between the peace-making and peace-keeping functions, and this is now standard practice.

The timing of a mediation effort is crucial. Even an *offer* of third-party assistance may increase the intransigence of one or both parties. After the first Dutch 'police action' in Indonesia, the US consul general in Batavia (Djakarta) sent a top secret and urgent cable to Washington warning of the dangers of offering good offices—the only result would be 'burned fingers'. There simply were no people on the Republican side, he reported, capable of implementing any promises they might make. 'I fear good offices now would be great error and do irreparable damage... I still maintain my old thesis that 95% of Indonesians are sick of republic...[State] Department is urged not to offer good offices until better class Indonesians installed...'[208]

Count Bernadotte, on the basis of his experience in Palestine, wrote that 'Mediation cannot be finally successful so long as either party believes that it can, with relative impunity, resort to armed force and thereby achieve for itself a more favourable settlement.'[209] The honest broker has few means of leverage. Paul van Zeeland stressed in the Indonesian context that the Good Offices Committee had only two weapons: first, the moral force and prestige of the Security Council and, behind and above it, the ideal of the United Nations; second, the conviction of the members of the Commission that they simply had to succeed because the conflict was 'more in the nature of a

[206] GAOR, 3rd session, Supplement no. 11, A/648, p. 43, para. 2; SCOR, 4th year, 434th mtg (4 Aug. 1949), p. 28.
[207] Letter to the author, 29 May 1977.
[208] FRUS, 1947, vol. VI, 1972, pp. 1004-6.
[209] GAOR, 3rd session, Supplement no. 11, A/468, p. 3, para. 6.

tragic misunderstanding than of fundamental opposition between irreconcilable aspirations'.[210] He might have added that
sometimes a threat to publish a report and to name the stubborn
party is itself a form of pressure.

GOOD OFFICES OF THE PRESIDENT OF THE SECURITY COUNCIL

The President of the Council for the month, by virtue of his
office, represents the Council in its corporate capacity.[211] If
the Council meets in closed session, it is the President who
gives any necessary report. In March and April 1948 there
were private consultations on Palestine, first of the permanent
members and then of all members of the Council willing to take
part. Following the consultations among the permanent members, the United States reported to the Council, but after the
private meetings of the full Council it was the President for
the month (Colombia) who stated what had been achieved.[212]
If a phase of open debate is to conclude with a statement sum-
marizing the views expressed or giving the consensus of the
Council, it is the President who negotiates the text and presents
it to the Council.[213] This procedure of a presidential statement
may be useful when there is a fair degree of agreement, but
when difficulties would arise if a precise text were put to the
vote, or if it is useful or necessary to place on record more than
one view.[214]

During the crisis in Cyprus in August 1964, there was a
strong sentiment in the Council in favour of an appeal to all the
parties to end military action, but Cyprus itself was opposed to

[210] SCOR, 3rd year, 248th mtg (17 Feb. 1948), pp. 158, 161.
[211] Rule of Procedure 19.
[212] SCOR, 3rd year, 270th mtg (19 March 1948), pp. 141-3; 282nd mtg (15 April 1948), pp. 2-4; FRUS, 1948, vol. V part 2, 1976, pp. 705-23, 725-8, 732-7, 739-41, 803 n. 4, 809-11, 817-21.
[213] For such statements on Kashmir, see SCOR, 3rd year, 382nd mtg (25 Nov. 1948), p. 26; 4th year, 399th mtg (13 Jan. 1949), pp. 4, 8: on Palestine, SCOR, 4th year, 453rd mtg (25 Oct. 1949), pp. 3-4; 9th year, 685th mtg (11 Nov. 1954), para. 15; 10th year, 688th mtg (13 Jan. 1955), paras. 98-101; 698th mtg (19 April 1955), paras. 149-50; 13th year, 844th mtg (15 Dec. 1958), paras. 107-9; on Cyprus, SCOR, 19th year, 1143rd mtg (9/11 Aug. 1964), para. 358.
[214] SCOR, 7th year, 572nd mtg (31 Jan. 1952), paras. 28-35; 19th year, 117th mtg (18 May 1964), paras. 3-6, 16, 19-20.

any decision of the Council that failed to condemn Turkey. In times of crisis, the Council is disinclined to indulge in condemnation, since to do so may make the situation worse. After a night meeting that began on Saturday 8 August, at which no decision was possible, the Council met again on the Sunday morning. The Ivory Coast quickly intervened, ostensibly on a point of order, to ask the President of the Council to appeal to Greece and Turkey to suspend military operations. The President (Norway) immediately responded with an appeal that was so carefully worded as to create the impression that it had been drafted in advance. This was approved by the Council without a vote.[215]

The President has sometimes, on his own initiative, issued an appeal to the parties to exercise restraint or, at the request of the Council, has met the parties in order to search for agreement. An example of the first occurred in January 1948 after India had complained to the Security Council about Kashmir, but before Pakistan had submitted a counter-complaint. The President of the Council (Belgium) sent telegrams to the two foreign ministers asking that they 'refrain from any step incompatible with the Charter and liable to result in an aggravation of the situation'. During the rest of the month, the President kept in touch with the representatives of India and Pakistan, submitted two draft resolutions which were approved by the Council, and twice reported to the Council on the progress of negotiations that had taken place under his auspices. When the end of the month arrived, no agreement on the terms of a settlement had been reached, so a succession of presidents of the Council (Canada, China, Colombia) continued the effort.[216]

If negotiations are prolonged, it may be a serious drawback that a different ambassador has to pick up the threads at the beginning of each month, and it may also happen that the alphabetical rotation of the presidency may bring to office a representative from a state which is not neutral about the matter

[215] Ibid., 1143rd mtg (9/11 Aug. 1964), paras. 6-14.
[216] Ibid., 3rd year, 226th mtg (6 Jan. 1948), pp. 4-5, S/636; 229th mtg (17 Jan. 1948), pp. 121-2, 125-8; 230th mtg (20 Jan. 1948), pp. 129-31; 231st mtg (22 Jan. 1948), pp. 164-5; 236th mtg (28 Jan. 1948), pp. 265-71, 279; SC res. 38 (S/651), 17 Jan. 1948; SC res. 39 (S/654), 20 Jan. 1948; FRUS, 1948, vol. V part 1, 1975, pp. 266-7, 271-94, 300-1, 313-21. 323-8.

at issue. In December 1949, the President of the Council, General A. G. L. McNaughton of Canada, was asked to discuss with India and Pakistan the possibility of finding an acceptable basis for dealing with Kashmir. On 29 December he gave the Council an oral progress report, and the Council asked him to continue his efforts even though, as the Soviet ambassador pointed out, his term as President of the Council and Canada's term as a non-permanent member of the Council would lapse at the end of the month. It was not until the following February that McNaughton issued another report.[217] Eight years later, in a similar procedure, the President of the Council (ambassador Gunnar Jarring of Sweden) was asked to examine with India and Pakistan any proposals that might contribute towards a settlement of the Kashmir dispute.[218]

The President for the month has unique opportunities for making his good offices available, but nobody can ensure that he is impartial and nobody can be compelled to take advantage of good offices if they are not so inclined.

GOOD OFFICES OF THE SECRETARY-GENERAL

It was Dag Hammarskjold who greatly developed the scope of the Secretary-General to exercise good offices. Hammarskjold took the view that Articles 97-9 of the Charter defined certain minimum responsibilities for the Secretary-General: he was chief administrative officer of the United Nations, should perform such functions as the policy-making organs entrusted to him, and had the special duty to draw the Security Council's attention to any matter that in his opinion might threaten peace and security. But that did not exhaust his responsibilities, for other diplomatic or operational tasks 'flowed' from what is stated in the Charter.[219] This meant that a Secretary-General had to perform tasks implicit in his office in the widest sense, as well as the functions in the peace and security field that the General Assembly or the Security Council might entrust to him.

---

[217] SCOR, 4th year, 457th mtg (17 Dec. 1949), pp. 5-8; 458th mtg (29 Dec. 1949), pp. 4-22; 5th year, Supplement for January to May 1950, pp. 3-16, S/1453.

[218] SC res. 123 (S/3793), 21 Feb. 1957.

[219] GAOR, 15th session, 5th Committee, 769th mtg (18 Oct. 1960), paras. 10, 17; SCOR, 16th year, 964th mtg (28 July 1961), para. 86; Lall, pp. 29-31.

It was in this latter capacity that Hammarskjold undertook his mission to the Middle East in the early months of 1956. The armistice agreements between Israel and its Arab neighbours had been in force for seven years but had not brought real peace to the area. Moreover, the armistice régime itself was in danger of collapse. Arab infiltrators crossed the demarcation lines to attack targets in Israel, and Israel retaliated against the Arabs. The flow of arms into the area was reaching alarming proportions, and there were ideologues on both sides who gave voice to grandiose notions for using military power to re-organize the region.

There were informal consultations at UN headquarters in March 1956, and it became apparent that Hammarskjold was prepared to make direct contact with the leaders in the region in an effort to resuscitate the cease-fire obligations that the parties had assumed in 1948 and 1949, but Hammarskjold wished to be formally entrusted with the mission by the Security Council. The Security Council, in a unanimous decision, asked the Secretary-General 'to undertake, as a matter of urgent concern, a survey of the various aspects of enforcement of and compliance with the four General Armistice Agreements and the Council's resolutions'.[220]

Hammarskjold spent a month visiting the five capitals, and he was also able to see something of UN field operations. He succeeded in extracting from all of the parties new cease-fire commitments, but it was his personal contacts with some of the political leaders of the region that were to have the more enduring effect. The Security Council held six meetings at the end of May and the beginning of June to consider his reports. The Council was unanimous in commending 'the Secretary-General and the parties' and in asking Hammarskjold 'to continue his good offices with the parties'.[221]

Two years later, after a new series of critical developments, the General Assembly meeting in emergency special session unanimously asked Hammarskjold 'to make...practical arrangements...to help in upholding the purposes and principles of the

---

[220] Urquhart, pp. 137-40; SC res. 113 (S/3575), 4th April 1956.
[221] Urquhart, pp. 141-52; Hammarskjold, pp. 111-15; SC res. 114 (S/3605), 4 June 1956.

Charter in relation to Lebanon and Jordan'. In pursuance of that decision, and without further authorization from a policy-making organ, Hammarskjold established an office in Amman and appointed a Special Representative to head the office.[222] Later in the year, after further incidents in the area, Hammarskjold informed the Security Council of his intention of visiting the Middle East 'in the hope of breaking the present trend and soliciting [the] full support [of the countries concerned] for our efforts to attack the underlying problems'.[223]

ARBITRATION

Arbitration involves the reference of matters in dispute to a tribunal usually consisting of one or two arbitrators chosen by each party and an additional arbitrator or arbitrators chosen by mutual agreement, who render an award based on respect for law. This award is binding on the parties. Proposals for arbitration were submitted in connection with the Indonesian and Kashmir questions.

Australia suggested arbitration in the Indonesian case, believing that this would be acceptable to the Republicans and hoping that the Netherlands would agree out of gratitude for Australia's role during the Second World War. The first resolution of the Security Council called for a settlement 'by arbitration or by other peaceful means'.[224] The Republicans were willing to accept arbitration or any form of third-party assistance, but the Netherlands was opposed. Also opposed were the Soviet Union and India (a non-voting participant in the proceedings of the Security Council). The United States favoured good offices, and this had the support of China, the two Latin American and three West European members of the Council, and (once arbitration had been rejected) Australia. The Council agreed to establish a committee of good offices, but the Soviet Union, Poland, and Syria abstained.[225]

---

[222] GA res. 1237 (ES-III), 21 Aug. 1958; A/3934/Rev. 1, 29 Sept. 1958 (mimeo), paras. 29-31.
[223] SCOR, 13th year, 844th mtg (15 Dec. 1958), para. 7.
[224] FRUS, 1947, vol. VI, 1972, pp. 997-8; SC res. 27 (S/459), 1 Aug. 1947.
[225] SCOR, 2nd year, 171st mtg (31 July 1947), pp. 1626, 1635-7; 178th mtg (7 Aug. 1947), pp. 1853-4; 184th mtg (14 Aug. 1947), p. 2003; 194th mtg (25 Aug. 1947), p. 2009; SC res. 31 (S/525, II), 25 Aug. 1947.

In the Kashmir case the proposal for arbitration came from the UN Commission for India and Pakistan (UNCIP). It was suggested that Admiral Chester W. Nimitz of the United States, who had already been accepted as Plebiscite Administrator for Kashmir, should in addition be designated as arbitrator, to resolve the differences that had arisen between India and Pakistan over the implementation of that part of the Commission's resolution of 13 August 1948 relating to a truce. The decisions of the arbitrator were to be 'according to equity, and...binding on both parties'. The arbitration proposal was presented to the parties by the Chairman of UNCIP, Oldrich Chyle of Czechoslovakia, who later made it clear that in his opinion the proposal for arbitration was outside UNCIP's terms of reference. Chyle also objected to the fact that UNCIP's 'secret arbitration offer', as he called it, had found its way into British and US hands before being presented to India and Pakistan, and that a senior UN official of US nationality, Andrew Cordier, had 'withheld' a communication from the Chairman of UNCIP (Chyle himself) to the President of the Security Council for the month (Soviet ambassador Tsarapkin). As for arbitration, Pakistan agreed to UNCIP's proposal, but India took the line that 'the creation of public confidence and of a peaceful atmosphere [was] a necessary preliminary to preparation for a plebiscite' and that such a 'fundamental condition' could not be left 'to the decision of an arbitrator'.[226]

Two years later, Britain and the United States submitted to the Security Council a proposal that provided that if, after discussions between the UN mediator and the parties on the demilitarization of Kashmir, any differences remained, outstanding points should be submitted to arbitration by 'an arbitrator, or a panel of arbitrators, to be appointed by the President of the International Court of Justice after consultation with the parties'. This was approved by the Council, but never acted on.[227] In 1957, as part of a renewed effort to settle the dispute, ambassador Gunnar Jarring of Sweden again raised the possibility of arbitration or, as Jarring put it, 'more in the

[226] SCOR, 4th year, Special Supplement no. 7, pp. 17-18, 35-6, 141-52, 195-6, 202, paras. 105-12 and 189-96 of and Annexes 35-40 and Addendum to S/1430; FRUS, 1949, vol. VI, 1977, pp. 1733-4, 1736-8, 1740-2.
[227] SC res. 91 (S/2017/Rev. 1), 30 March 1951.

nature of a determination of certain facts which, in the Indian view, were incontrovertible'. Pakistan, 'after a certain hesitation', agreed, but India again 'felt that the issues in dispute were not suitable for arbitration'.[228]

JUDICIAL SETTLEMENT[229]

The Charter states that legal disputes should 'as a general rule' be referred by the parties to the International Court of Justice, although nothing in the Charter prevents UN Members from solving their differences through other tribunals.[230] The first part of this wording suggests that there are certain disputes that can be classified as 'legal' and settled by the appropriate means: in real life, of couse, legal elements are mixed up with political, psychological, and other factors.

In the course of dealing with the cases covered by this study, the Security Council has received several proposals that aspects of a legal nature should be referred to the International Court of Justice, but these proposals were not proceeded with. The West European members of the Council wished to ask the Court for an advisory opinion on whether the Security Council was competent to deal with the Indonesian question in 1947, but a Belgian proposal to that effect was defeated.[231] In connection with Hyderabad, Pakistan suggested that the question of the Council's competence should be submitted to the Court for an advisory opinion, but no formal proposal to do this was made.[232] In discussing the Kashmir question in 1957, Colombia proposed that 'the problem' should be referred to the Court, but later withdrew the proposal.[233] In the Palestine case, Syria wanted the Court to be asked for an advisory opinion on 'the status of Palestine arising from the termination of the Mandate',

---

[228] SCOR, 12th year, Supplement for April-June 1957, pp. 15-16, paras. 17-19 of S/3821; see also 767th mtg (8 Feb. 1957), para. 23.

[229] See Lall, pp. 7-8, 345-54.

[230] Articles 36 (3) and 95.

[231] SCOR, 2nd year, 173rd mtg (1 Aug. 1947), p. 1678; 194th mtg (25 Aug. 1947), pp. 2193-4, S/517; 195th mtg (26 Aug. 1947), p. 2224.

[232] Ibid., 4th year, 426th mtg (24 May 1949), pp. 28-9.

[233] Ibid., 12th year, 771st mtg (18 Feb. 1957), para. 7; 773rd mtg (20 Feb. 1957), paras. 28-32; Supplement for January-March 1957, pp. 8-9, S/3791/Rev. 1.

but a proposal to this effect was rejected.[234] In the Cyprus case, Greece suggested that, if there were any doubt about the meaning of the Treaty of Guarantee, an advisory opinion from the Court should be requested, but no formal proposal to this effect was submitted.[235]

REGIONAL AGENCIES OR ARRANGEMENTS[236]

The Charter stipulates that 'local disputes' should if possible be settled through regional agencies or arrangements, and the Security Council is supposed to encourage this.[237] The relationship between regional and UN processes of settlement has created difficulties over a number of Latin American issues. It also arose in the cases studied, as follows.

In the Palestine case, the Arabs maintained that their military intervention was in support of a fellow-member of the Arab League, Palestine, whose territory had been attacked by the Jews: the Security Council should be grateful to the Arab League for taking on the task of pacification. The United States pointed out, however, that enforcement action by regional agencies should be undertaken only if the Security Council expressly authorizes it[238]—a remark that was to be thrown back at the United States in subsequent cases.

When troubles occurred in the Lebanon in 1958, the Security Council twice postponed its consideration of the matter at the request of the Arabs in the hope, vain as it turned out, that the Arab League would be able to resolve the question on a regional basis.[239]

---

[234] Ibid., 3rd year, 334th mtg (13 July 1948), pp. 52-3, S/894; 340th mtg (27 July 1948), pp. 33-4.

[235] Ibid., 19th year, 1095th mtg (18 Feb. 1964), para. 241; 1099th mtg (28 Feb. 1964), para. 119.

[236] See Lall, pp. 15-16.

[237] Article 52 (3).

[238] SCOR, 3rd year, 297th mtg (20 May 1948), pp. 12-13; 298th mtg (20 May 1948), p. 20; 299th mtg (21 May 1948), pp. 13-15; 302nd mtg (22 May 1948), pp. 42-3; 307th mtg (28 May 1948), p. 22. See Higgins, *Development of International Law*, p. 169.

[239] SCOR, 13th year, 818th mtg (27 May 1958), paras. 8, 12-14, 41; 822nd mtg (5 June 1958), paras. 1, 5; 823rd mtg (6 June 1958), paras. 2-5, 191; 824th mtg (10 June 1958), para. 2; Supplement for April-June 1958, p. 44, S/4018.

In the Cyprus case, Cyprus itself insisted that if there had been intervention by the three guaranteeing powers, this would not have come within the UN Charter provisions for regional arrangements.[240]

Because organizations may have more than one function, there has sometimes been confusion between the responsibilities under the Charter of regional agencies and the responsibilities of organizations for collective self-defence (military alliances).[241] This confusion was apparent in the Cyprus case where there was an effort to involve NATO in both peace-making and peace-keeping. This aroused strong hostility on the part of the Soviet bloc: the Czechoslovak representative pointedly recalled how the Nazis had attacked Czechoslovakia, ostensibly to protect a minority but in reality to partition and then destroy a small state which had been abandoned by its friends. Was the world to see once again that mediation could lapse into appeasement?[242]

It was natural that NATO should have been concerned about Cyprus as the three guaranteeing powers were NATO members, but it may be doubted whether it was ever realistic to conceive of a collective NATO intervention. NATO's essential role, defined in Article 5 of the Treaty, is to provide for collective self-defence if an armed attack occurs against one or more of its members. NATO as a collectivity was not in a position to intervene in Cyprus, partly because the consent of the Cyprus government was not forthcoming and partly because most NATO members lacked the political will to involve themselves directly in a post-colonial crisis.

The Charter requires that, when regional agencies undertake or contemplate activities for the maintenance of international peace and security, the Security Council shall be kept fully informed 'at all times': measures taken in the exercise of the right of individual or collective self-defence shall be reported to

---

[240] Ibid., 19th year, 1103rd mtg (13 March 1964), paras. 76-9.
[241] Articles 51-4.
[242] Dirk Stikker, *Men of Responsibility: A Memoir*, New York, Harper and Row, 1966, pp. 347-8; Alastair Buchan, *Crisis Management: The New Diplomacy*, Boulogne-sur-Seine, Atlantic Institute, 1966, pp. 27-8; Philip Windsor, 'The Cyprus Dispute 1963-64', London, RIIA, 1966 (mimeo).

the Security Council 'immediately'.[243] During the period 1946-64 seventy-five communications from the Organization of American States or the Inter-American Peace Committee were sent to the Security Council, and communications were subsequently received from the Organization for African Unity. I recall no communication to the Security Council during this period from any other regional agency under Article 54 or from an agency for collective self-defence under Article 51.

'...OR OTHER PEACEFUL MEANS OF THEIR OWN CHOICE'

Sometimes the Security Council, either baffled by the complexity of the situation or afraid that precision about the means of settlement will increase the intransigence of one or other of the parties, simply reminds the parties that the Charter requires that they should refrain from using force and should settle matters peacefully. The Council's first resolution on Indonesia urged the parties to settle their disputes by arbitration 'or by other peaceful means', and a subsequent resolution reminded the parties of the Council's call for a peaceful settlement. In June 1948 the President of the Council (Syria) agreed to send a fairly bland message to the Netherlands and Indonesia encouraging them 'to continue their efforts towards the attainment of a peaceful adjustment', and the following month the Council, noting that negotiations were at a standstill, called for the early and full implementation of the *Renville* agreements.[244] The Council's first resolution on Kashmir asked India and Pakistan to do what they could 'to improve the situation' and to refrain from acts that might make things worse, and later in 1948 the Council again appealed for restraint and the avoidance of any action that might prejudice negotiations.[245] Several of the Council's resolutions on Palestine included a reminder to

[243] Articles 51 and 54.
[244] SC res. 27 (S/459), 1 Aug. 1947; 32 (S/525, III), 26 Aug. 1947; SCOR, 3rd year, 326th mtg (23 June 1948), p. 35; SC res. 55 (S/933), 29 July 1948.
[245] SC res. 38 (S/651), 17 Jan. 1948; SCOR, 3rd year, 382nd mtg (25 Nov. 1948), p. 26.

the parties of their obligations under the Charter and the armistice agreements.[246]

3.5 TERMS OF SETTLEMENT

When a dispute or situation imperils world peace, there are certain things that, under the Charter, the Security Council 'may' do and certain things that under specified circumstances it 'shall' do. The Council *may*, at any stage and on its own initiative, recommend appropriate procedures or methods of adjustment, and if the parties to a dispute so request, the Council *may* make recommendations with a view to a pacific settlement. The Security Council *shall* call upon the parties to settle their dispute by peaceful means when it deems this necessary, and it *shall* decide whether to recommend actual terms of settlement if it considers that the continuation of a dispute is likely to endanger the maintenance of international peace and security.[247] There are thus two aspects to the Council's responsibilities, one concerned with procedures or means of peaceful settlement or adjustment and the other, when peace is endangered, with the actual terms of settlement. The distinction between the two aspects is in practice not always clear.

In connection with several of the early cases (Kashmir, Indonesia) the Council recommended fairly elaborate plans of settlement[248] or, in the Palestine case, accepted the General Assembly's partition plan pending any alternative proposals that the UN Mediator might submit for the peaceful adjustment of the situation.[249] Since 1949, however, the Council has been reluctant to put forward actual terms of settlement except in relation to southern Africa, where anger at the colonial and racist policies of white minorities has meant that notions of peaceful settlement have increasingly given way to a clamour for coercive measures.

In the early months of 1948 there was a feeling in US government circles that the Security Council might have to recommend terms of settlement for Kashmir under Article 37 (2) of the

[246] SC res. 89 (S/1907), 17 Nov. 1950; 92 (S/2130), 8 May 1951; 93 (S/2157), 18 May 1951; 171 (S/5111), 5 April 1962.
[247] Articles 33 (2), 36 (1), 37 (2), and 38.
[248] SC res. 47 (S/726), 21 April 1948; SC res. 67 (S/1234), 28 Jan. 1949.
[249] GA res. 186 (S-2), 14 May 1948.

Charter.[250] Although the Security Council had in January decided to establish a Commission to investigate the facts and exercise mediatory influence, the Council in April approved a detailed plan for military withdrawals and a plebiscite in Kashmir, which was later to prove a straightjacket which limited the freedom of manoeuvre of the UN Commission and its successors. Moreover, the Council in later resolutions added to the details of its 1948 framework.[251] Pakistan from the start regarded the holding of a plebiscite as an obligation under Article 37 (2) of the Charter,[252] but India always maintained that, while the Security Council had the power to *recommend* terms of settlement, it did not have the power to *compel* the parties to accept such terms.[253]

In the difficulties following the nationalization of the Suez Canal Co. in 1956, one member of the Security Council (Peru) consistently took the view that Britain and France were inviting the Security Council under Article 37 to recommend terms of settlement of their dispute with Egypt, and it is certainly possible to regard the six agreed principles for the operation of the Suez Canal in that light.[254]

After 1954, there was a growing disposition in UN policy-making organs to ask the Secretary-General himself to seek solutions of major problems in ways that would accord with the Charter, either directly or through the good offices of persons designated by him, and it is now unusual for the Security Council to specify detailed long-term solutions.

3.6 LET THE PEOPLE DECIDE?

The principle of equal rights and self-determination of peoples is enshrined in the UN Charter, but no principle should be

---

[250] FRUS, 1948, vol. V part 1, 1975, pp. 280-2, 300-1, 304-6, 325-8.

[251] SC res. 39 (S/654), 20 Jan. 1948; 47 (S/726), 21 April 1948; res. 80 (S/1469), 14 March 1950; 91 (S/2017/Rev. 1), 30 March 1951; 98 (S/2883), 23 Dec. 1952; 122 (S/3779), 24 Jan. 1957; 126 (S/3922), 2 Dec. 1957.

[252] SCOR, 12th year, 761st mtg (16 Jan. 1957), para. 109.

[253] Ibid., 767th mtg (8 Feb. 1957), para. 93; 773rd mtg (20 Feb. 1957), para. 111; 774th mtg (21 Feb. 1957), para. 30.

[254] Ibid., 11th year, 734th mtg (26 Sept. 1956), paras. 69-70; 737th mtg (8 Oct. 1956), paras. 7-8; 743rd mtg (13 Oct. 1956), para. 87; SC res. 118 (S/3675), 13 Oct. 1956.

applied without reference to other valid principles. The principle that is most frequently set against self-determination is the concept of the territorial integrity of the nation. Major wars have been fought to prevent minorities from seceding. The question, as it has been presented to UN organs, has been how to respond to claims that particular groups can never be sure that their rights will be respected if they remain as minorities within a larger framework and that their future can be safe-guarded only by creating separate entities under their own control. That, essentially, was the case of the Azad Kashmiris and the Jewish Palestinians in 1947-8 and of the Turkish Cypriots in 1964.

When the Maharajah of Kashmir sought to accede to India, Lord Mountbatten took the line that, once law and order had been restored, the question should be settled by reference to the people. Much of the time of the Security Council and its subsidiary organs in the ensuing years was taken up with deter-mining the conditions under which the people of Kashmir could engage in the exercise of self-determination. In the Palestine case the General Assembly decided that the territory should be partitioned, but during the first cease-fire, Count Bernadotte toyed with the idea of submitting his proposals for a political settlement directly to the people. He realized, however, that the Jews and Arabs would have to vote separately, as Arabs then outnumbered Jews in Palestine by two to one.[255] In the first phase of the Cyprus case, there was virtually no inter-national support for the idea that the Turkish minority should be allowed to secede, but the situation would have been dif-ferent if the Greek majority had proceeded with the plan for union with Greece.[256]

If a UN organ is told that an election or plebiscite is to be held in disputed territory, it is likely to be concerned not only with supervision of the electoral process but with ensuring that the administration is free and fair. It was part of the *Renville* truce agreement in Indonesia in 1948 that free elections would be held so that the people of the different islands could deter-mine their relationship to a United States of Indonesia. On 21

---

[255] Bernadotte, p. 132.
[256] SCOR, 20th year, Supplement for January-March 1965, pp. 239-50, paras. 132-65 of S/6253.

February 1948, the Indonesian Republicans complained to the Security Council that the Netherlands had been conducting separatist activities in some areas before the necessary conditions of freedom had been established. The response of the Security Council was to ask the UN Good Offices Committee (GOC) 'to pay particular attention to ... political developments' in the areas in question 'and to report to the Council thereon at frequent intervals'. The GOC was not able to observe the electoral process while it was taking place, as a month had already elapsed before the GOC was asked to report. In due course the GOC informed the Security Council that the previous January a plebiscite had been held in Madura which 'conformed largely to traditional practice', and that there had been indirect elections to a West Java Conference: the GOC did not feel called on to determine whether the voting had been free, but it transmitted to the Council a factual account of what had occurred as well as complaints of the Indonesian Republicans and the replies of the Dutch authorities.[257]

In the Kashmir case, the Security Council decided that the government of Indian Kashmir should constitute an interim administration but that 'major political groups' should share 'equitably and fully' in the conduct of the administration. The UN Commission for India and Pakistan subsequently provided that areas from which Pakistani forces withdrew would be administered 'by the local authorities under the surveillance of the Commission'.[258]

The intention of the Council was that the future of Kashmir should be decided by a 'free, fair, and unfettered' plebiscite. India maintained, however, that before there could be serious consideration of a plebiscite, steps had to be taken to end the fighting. In any case, the holding of a plebiscite must not be allowed to encroach on the ordinary sovereign powers of the State of Jammu and Kashmir. Pakistan, on the other hand, wanted to see an impartial administration in Kashmir before

---

[257] Ibid., 3rd year, Special Supplement no. 1, p. 76, Appendix XIII to S/649/Rev. 1; 252nd mtg (21 Feb. 1948), pp. 237-8; SC res. 40 (S/689), 28 Feb. 1948; SCOR, 3rd year, Supplement for January-March 1948, p. 41, S/703; Supplement for June 1948, pp. 11-41, 65-6, S/729, S/786, S/787.

[258] SC res. 47 (S/726), 21 April 1948; SCOR, 3rd year, Supplement for November 1948, p. 33, para. 75 of S/1100.

the question of accession was submitted to the people.[259] Sheikh Abdullah, the Kashmiri nationalist leader who at this stage was co-operating with India, said he was as anxious as anyone to ensure a free vote, but how could the neutrality of the administration of Kashmir be guaranteed? While it might be desirable to have a neutral administrator in Kashmir, said Abdullah, anticipating Khrushchev's line twelve years later, where would the Security Council find a neutral individual? 'Frankly speaking, even if the Security Council were to request Almighty God to administer the State of Jammu and Kashmir during this interim period, I do not feel that He could act impartially. After all, one must have sympathy either for this side or for that side.'[260]

When the UN Commission for India and Pakistan (UNCIP) reached the subcontinent, it elaborated a phased plan for a cease-fire followed by a truce in Kashmir, with a commitment that the future status should be determined 'in accordance with the will of the people'. India accepted the plan with reservations, but insisted that Pakistan should play no part in the organization and conduct of a plebiscite. Pakistan also expressed reservations, and these, in UNCIP's view, amounted to a rejection. Pakistan stressed that it would be affected by the result of a plebiscite at least as much as would India, and therefore the two governments should be placed on a position of absolute equality and advantage. UNCIP found the attitudes of the parties so divergent that it 'wished to leave open the possibility...of alternative solutions mutually agreeable to both parties'. UNCIP probably had in mind the possibility of partitioning the State, perhaps with a plebiscite limited to the Vale of Kashmir.[261]

In spite of this hint, UNCIP proceeded to work out detailed arrangements for 'a free and impartial plebiscite', to be held when the truce arrangements had been carried out. A Plebiscite Administrator, to be nominated by the UN Secretary-General,

[259] SCOR, 3rd year, 231st mtg (22 Jan. 1948), p. 165; 236th mtg (28 Jan. 1948), pp. 268, 272, 275-6; 239th mtg (3 Feb. 1948), pp. 314, 318, 327-31; 242nd mtg (6 Feb. 1948), pp. 39-41, 51-3; 244th mtg (11 Feb. 1948), pp. 94-7; 266th mtg (10 March 1948), pp. 68-77; 269th mtg (18 March 1948), pp. 121-6, 129-30; FRUS, 1948, vol. V part 1, 1975, pp. 271-6, 281, 305.

[260] SCOR, 3rd year, 241st mtg (5 Feb. 1948), pp. 23-4.

[261] Ibid., Supplement for November 1948, pp. 31-3, 43, 56-7, paras. 75-6, 97, 153 of S/1100; FRUS, 1948, vol. V part 1, 1975, pp. 417-18, 424-7, 437-44.

would be 'appointed to office' by the government of Kashmir. Once the truce had taken effect and UNCIP had been satisfied that peaceful conditions had been restored, UNCIP and the Plebiscite Administrator would determine, in consultation with India, the final disposal of Indian and State armed forces and, 'in consultation with the local authorities', the final disposal of armed forces in Azad Kashmir. The Plebiscite Administrator would report the result of the plebiscite to UNCIP, which would certify to the Security Council whether the plebiscite had been free and impartial. India and Pakistan accepted this formula, though it later became apparent that their interpretations of it differed in major respects. A cease-fire became effective at 23.59 hours on 1 January 1949, but there was never an agreed truce.[262]

When UNCIP returned to the subcontinent in 1949, it found that India no longer agreed that the future of Azad Kashmir forces should be settled by the Plebiscite Administrator in consultation with local authorities: India was now insisting that there could be no question of withdrawing Indian forces from Kashmir until arrangements had been made for disbanding and disarming Azad Kashmir forces. UNCIP suggested that this and other matters in dispute should be dealt with at a bilateral meeting at ministerial level, but Pakistan rejected any reference in the proposed agenda to the disbanding and disarming of Azad forces. UNCIP then suggested that outstanding issues be referred to arbitration, but this was unacceptable to India.[263]

In submitting its third report in 1949, UNCIP had commented that the holding of a plebiscite depended on the demilitarization of Kashmir but that the plan of demilitarization contained in UNCIP's own resolutions was no longer adequate.[264] What was needed was a comprehensive plan for dealing with the disposal of all armed forces in the State.[265] This

---

[262] SCOR, 4th year, Supplement for January 1949, pp. 22-5, 33-45, paras. 10-16 and Annexes 3-6 of S/1196; FRUS, 1948, vol. V part 1, 1975, pp. 445-85.

[263] SCOR, 4th year, Special Supplement no. 7, pp. 137-40, 143-7, 173-5, 183-5, Annexes 32, 36, 48-51 of S/1430; FRUS, 1949, vol. VI, 1977, pp. 1708, 1717-20, 1726-8, 1732, 1748-9.

[264] SCOR, 4th year, Special Supplement no. 7, pp. 52, 61-2, paras. 249, 283 of S/1430.

[265] Ibid., p. 52, para. 25.

question of demilitarization prior to a plebiscite was to be the focus of UN efforts in the ensuing years, and the Security Council never abandoned its commitment to a plebiscite.[266]

In Indonesia in 1949, after the second 'police action', the Council decided that the Republican government should be restored and should exercise 'appropriate functions', and it recommended that elections should be held for an Indonesian constituent assembly, the elections to be observed by a new UN Commission for Indonesia. The Council later issued a directive to the Commission for Indonesia which, by stressing other elements in its previous resolution, implied that it was no longer essential to proceed with elections to a constituent assembly. In the event, a constitution for Indonesia was negotiated among the parties at a round table conference held in the Hague later in 1949.[267]

UN bodies were asked to observe the electoral process in Korea. In 1947 the General Assembly established the Temporary Commission on Korea (UNTCOK) and asked it to observe elections to be held throughout Korea on the basis of adult suffrage and by secret ballot. UNTCOK was unable to obtain access to North Korea but, having consulted the Interim Committee of the General Assembly, decided to carry out its mandate in such parts of Korea as were accessible to it. The election, which was held on 10 May 1948, was not entirely free, but UNTCOK considered that the result of the ballot represented a valid expression of the will of the electorate of South Korea.[268]

3.7 PARTITION

Minorities, if they are sufficiently numerous, tend to favour partition. A tiny minority has no option but to make the best of things, but a substantial minority with a distinctive ethnic, linguistic, religious, or cultural background may feel that it

---

[266] SC res. 80 (S/1469), 14 March 1950; 91 (S/2017/Rev. 1), 30 March 1951; 96 (S/2392), 10 Nov. 1951; 98 (S/2883), 23 Dec. 1952; 122 (S/3779), 24 Jan. 1957; 126 (S/3922), 2 Dec. 1957.

[267] SC res. 67 (S/1234), 28 Jan. 1949; SCOR, 4th year, 421st mtg (23 March 1949), pp. 5, 25-6; Special Supplement no. 6, pp. 15, 53-91, para. 40 of and Appendix VI to S/1417.

[268] GA res. 112 (II), 14 Nov. 1947; GAOR, 3rd session, Supplement no. 10, A/583, pp. 18-21; Supplement no. 9, A/575, vol. I, pp. 46-7.

can preserve its special identity only under some kind of autonomy or separation. Partition is the remedy of those who are or fear they may become minorities; majorities prefer what they consider to be a straightforward democratic solution in which the minority have their say but the majority have their way. Thus Pakistan, confident that Azad Kashmir would win in a free plebiscite, always opposed partition, while as Indian confidence that its Kashmiri allies had majority support dwindled, so Indian interest in formal or *de facto* partition began to manifest itself.[269] In 1947-8 the Jews accepted partition in Palestine, while the more numerous Arabs denounced it as illegal and immoral; but as the demographic situation changed as a result of the exodus of Palestinian refugees and the influx of Jewish immigrants in substantial numbers, so the attitudes were reversed. Many Palestine Arabs would now accept a settlement based on the UN partition plan of 1947, while many Jewish Israelis believe that there can be no second state in what was formerly Palestine. In Cyprus it was the minority Turkish community that hankered after partition and, indeed, achieved it *de facto* in 1974.

It is interesting how quickly Britain and the United States came to the conclusion that partition would be the most likely outcome in Kashmir. The initial Indian complaint was dated 1 January 1948, and debate in the Security Council began on 6 January. On that day, US Secretary of State George Marshall told ambassador Warren Austin in New York that a dossier of background information was being prepared, but that acocunt should be taken of 'some form of partition'. Four days later, the British suggested to Austin that the final result might well be 'some kind of partition'. It was not until after the Security Council had adopted a resolution calling for a plebiscite in Kashmir that Indians began to dabble with the partition idea. V. P. Menon raised the matter with the US ambassador in India in the second week of May 1948, saying that India could not propose partition but would accept it if it were proposed by the UN Commission for India and Pakistan (UNCIP). By August, most members of UNCIP were 'inclined toward partition'. UNCIP shrank from actually advocating partition,

[269] FRUS, 1948, vol. V part 1, 1975, pp. 343, 352, 356, 418, 427, 442-3.

however, but it did hint to the Security Council that a solution other than a plebiscite might have to be considered, and it later reported to the Council that partition existed *de facto*.[270]

In the Palestine case, the decision to partition was taken by the General Assembly, and implementation was left to the Security Council. The Jewish Agency for Palestine accepted the partition scheme and co-operated with the UN Palestine Commission in carrying it out. The Arabs, having first resisted partition on the diplomatic level, now tried to defeat it by military means. When they sent their armies into Palestine, Secretary-General Trygve Lie was so shocked at this defiance of the United Nations that he considered resigning.[271] The outright opposition of the Arabs to partition had the sympathy of other Islamic countries, and there was a certain understanding of the Arab predicament in UN circles. What caused surprise and consternation was the unhelpful if not obstructive policy of Britain. Having handed over the Palestine problem to the United Nations, Britain did little to help in implementing UN decisions beyond warning with irritating sanctimony that violence would increase as soon as the Mandate ended and Britain withdrew.[272] It was not until the British withdrawal had been effected and a Jewish state established in part of Palestine that Britain discovered a more constructive role in UN affairs, that of supporting Count Bernadotte's mediatory efforts— although Foreign Minister Bevin remained deeply suspicious of Jewish intentions to the end of his life. Bernadotte, while he did not feel he had to accept the General Assembly's partition plan in detail since it had been 'outrun and irrevocably revised by … history', considered that the Arab case for a unitary Palestine was 'unrealistic', for there already existed in Palestine 'a form of partition'.[273] This 'form of partition' continued until the occupation of East Jerusalem, the West Bank, and the Gaza Strip in 1967.

[270] Ibid., pp. 271, 277, 312, 343, 363, 424-6, 438-9; SCOR, 3rd year, Supplement for November 1948, pp. 56-7, para. 153 of S/1100; 4th year, Special Supplement no. 7, para. 227 of S/1430.

[271] Lie, pp. 170-1, 178-9; FRUS, 1948, vol. V part 2, 1976, pp. 999-1001.

[272] SCOR, 3rd year, 253rd mtg (24 Feb. 1948), pp. 271-2; 260th mtg (2 March 1948), pp. 402-3; Special Supplement no. 2, pp. 1-28, S/663, S/676, S/695; GAOR, 2nd special session, Supplement no. 1, para. 3 of A/532.

[273] GAOR, 3rd session, Supplement no. 11, A/648, pp. 5, 6, 16 (paras. 4, 12, 8).

In Cyprus, partition was expressly excluded by the treaty of guarantee of 1960. In one of the early Security Council debates, Czechoslovakia caused a degree of *frisson* by comparing the role of the Western powers in Cyprus with Hitler's carve-up of Czechoslovakia. Hitler continually asked for more and more concessions, including constitutional changes. '[A] similar atmosphere prevailed around Cyprus in the course of the last weeks...' Appeasement at Munich was followed six months later by the Nazi occupation of Prague, and after another six months by world war. 'A sacrifice of millions of human victims had to atone for the sins of those Munich policies.' The United Nations must not provide the umbrella for another Munich.[274]

The Greek community, being the majority, consistently opposed partition. The Greek ambassador in New York became extremely apprehensive on the eve of the second phase of Security Council debate, when a rumour reached him that the State Department now favoured partition. The ambassador at once sought an urgent meeting with Adlai Stevenson, as a result of which the State Department was persuaded to issue a denial.[275] What the more militant Greek Cypriots failed to comprehend was that threats against the Turkish community, however justified they might seem, only added to Turkish insecurity and made the case for partition sound increasingly plausible.

3.8 RECOMMENDATIONS AND PROVISIONAL MEASURES

Chapter VII of the UN Charter is headed 'Action with respect to threats to the peace, breaches of the peace, and acts of aggression'. Article 39 of Chapter VII states that the Security Council 'shall' determine when such dangerous conditions obtain, and Articles 40 to 42 set out a graduated series of steps that the Council 'may' or in one eventuality 'shall' take, as follows.

---

[274] SCOR, 19th year, 1097th mtg (25 Feb. 1964), para. 56.
[275] Dimitri S. Bitsios, *Cyprus: the Vulnerable Republic,* 2nd rev. edn., Salonika, Institute for Balkan Studies, 1975, pp. 141-3.

Purpose	Action	Article(s) of Charter
To prevent an aggravation of the situation	The Security Council may call upon the parties concerned to comply with such provisional measures as the Council deems necessary or desirable, such measures being without prejudice to the rights, claims, or position of the parties.	40
To maintain or restore international peace and security	The Security Council shall make recommendations or decide what measures of enforcement shall be taken under Articles 41 and 42.	39
To give effect to the decisions of the Security Council [and to maintain or restore international peace and security]	The Security Council may decide what measures not involving the use of armed force are to be employed and may call upon UN Members to apply such measures.	39 and 41
To maintain or restore international peace and security	If non-military measures would be or have been inadequate, the Security Council may take such action by air, sea, or land forces as may be necessary.	39 and 42

The graduated steps open to the Council are thus recommendations under Article 39 or provisional measures under Article 40, non-military enforcement under Article 41, and military enforcement under Article 42. In practice the Council has not usually distinguished between provisional measures and recommendations, and it is convenient to consider them together.

The Charter does not specify what provisional measures the Council may use or what recommendations it shall make. From an examination of the decisions taken in the cases studied, it would seem that provisional measures or recommendations have related to a cease-fire or truce and have included actions designed to bring about a cessation of military activity; respect for an existing agreement to suspend military operations; demarcation of lines of separation; withdrawal of military

forces from positions occupied during the fighting; establishment of demilitarized zones; co-operation in the detection of
violations and the prevention of infiltration and incidents;
release of prisoners; respect for life and property; embargoes on
military supplies and personnel.

In two of the cases studied, the Security Council made a
determination under Article 39 or used its language, and then
called for or ordered specified action. The first instance followed the expiry of the first general cease-fire in Palestine in
1948. The Council determined that a threat to peace existed
within the meaning of Article 39 of the Charter and, 'pursuant
to Article 40 of the Charter', ordered the governments and
authorities concerned to desist from further military action.
The Council also declared that failure to comply with the order
would constitute a breach of the peace, requiring 'further
action' under Chapter VII of the Charter. Four months later,
after the renewal of fighting in the Negev, the Council recalled
its earlier decision and, 'as a further provisional measure under
Article 40 of the Charter', called on the parties to negotiate
with a view to the immediate establishment of an armistice in
all sectors of Palestine. After the armistice agreements had
been concluded, the Council reaffirmed the order to desist from
military action 'pursuant to Article 40'.[276]

In the other case, Korea in 1950, the Council, using the
language of Article 39, determined that there had been 'a
breach of the peace', called for the immediate cessation of
hostilities and the withdrawal of North Korean forces, and
asked UN Members to assist in the execution of the resolution.[277]

The question has arisen whether the Council may make
recommendations or decide on provisional or enforcement
measures under Articles 39 to 42 without implicitly or explicitly
making a prior determination under Article 39. Although, in
the Indonesian context, Belgium took the view that action

---

[276] SC res. 54 (S/902), 15 July 1948; SC res. 62 (S/1080), 16 Nov. 1948; SC res. 73
(S/1376, II), 11 Aug. 1949.
[277] SC res. 82 (S/1501), 25 June 1950.

should not be taken under Article 40 without a prior or con-
current finding under Article 39,[278] it has also been held that
no such finding is essential, and that even without a determination under Article 39, UN Members must implement
measures of the Security Council because of the general obligation to accept and carry out decisions of the Council under
Article 25.[279] Indeed, the Council has gone even further and
implicitly taken the view that it may take provisional measures
under Article 40 even if none of the conditions specified under
Article 39 obtain. Before the Council approved a set of six
principles for the operation of the Suez Canal in 1956, Paul-
Henri Spaak of Belgium urged 'the absolute necessity' of
applying Article 40: 'it is clear ... that there is no legal problem
about applying this principle from Chapter VII to the matters
referred to in Chapter VI'.[280]

In the Kashmir case, consideration was given to making a
formal determination under Article 39, followed by an order to
stop fighting, as was done in the Palestine case; but in the end
the Council left it to the UN Commission for India and Pakistan
to pursue a mediatory role.[281] In 1957 a proposal was submitted to the Security Council which would have noted a
Pakistani proposal for the use of a temporary UN force in connection with the demilitarization of Kashmir. India argued
strongly that the Security Council had no authority to send
troops to Kashmir in the absence of Indian consent, except
by acting under Chapter VII, and the Soviet Union pointed
out that the Council had made no formal determination under
Article 39. The proposal to note the possible establishment of a

[278] SCOR, 2nd year, 172nd mtg (1 Aug. 1947), pp. 1653-4; 4th year, 398th mtg
(11 Jan. 1949), pp. 10-11.
[279] Ibid., 2nd year, 193rd mtg (22 Aug. 1947), pp. 2175-6; 195th mtg (26 Aug.
1947), p. 2216; 209th mtg (9 Oct. 1947), p. 2527; 215th mtg (29 Oct. 1947), p. 2661;
3rd year, 389th mtg (22 Dec. 1948), p. 43; 390th mtg (23 Dec. 1948), p. 7; 393rd mtg
(27 Dec. 1948), p. 19; 395th mtg (28 Dec. 1948), p. 62; 4th year, 397th mtg (7 Jan.
1949), p. 27; 398th mtg (11 Jan. 1949), p. 3; 11th year, 749th mtg (30 Oct. 1956),
paras. 115-16; 19th year, 1103rd mtg (13 March 1964), paras. 86-7.
[280] Ibid., 11th year, 743rd mtg (13 Oct. 1956), paras. 63-5.
[281] FRUS, 1948, vol. V part 1, pp. 426-7, 445-8, 467-8.

UN force was, nevertheless, pressed to a vote and vetoed by the Soviet Union.[282]

On a number of occasions the question has arisen whether to include in a resolution of the Council the phrase from Article 40 of the Charter, 'without prejudice to the rights, claims, or position of the parties'. Australia proposed that the words in question should be included in a call to cease hostilities in Indonesia after the first Dutch 'police action' in 1947, but this paragraph was deleted by a US amendment.[283] Later in the year, the Good Offices Committee in Indonesia put forward a provisional truce plan which would have been 'without prejudice to the rights, claims or positions of the parties', but this was rejected by the Netherlands.[284] In May 1948, in connection with Palestine, the United States put forward a resolution calling for a cease-fire, and the 'without prejudice' clause was added on the proposal of China.[285] Later that year, after the third phase of fighting in Palestine, the Security Council called on the parties 'without prejudice to their rights, claims or position' to withdraw from positions occupied after 14 October and to establish 'neutral or demilitarized zones'.[286] The absence from a text of the 'without prejudice' clause does not, of course, prejudice the rights, claims, or position of the parties.

3.9 MILITARY EMBARGOES

There are two kinds of Security Council embargo on sending military supplies or personnel to areas of conflict: those imposed against one party only, and those relating to all the parties.

[282] SCOR, 12th year, 761st mtg (16 Jan. 1957), para. 112; 766th mtg (30 Jan. 1957), para. 86; 767th mtg (8 Feb. 1957), paras. 91-4; 769th mtg (15 Feb. 1957), paras. 152-3; 770th mtg (18 Feb. 1957), paras. 123-8; 773rd mtg (20 Feb. 1957), paras. 20, 79-80, 126; Supplement for January-March 1957, pp. 7-8, S/3787.
[283] SCOR, 2nd year, Supplement no. 16, p. 149, S/449; 171st mtg (31 July 1947), p. 1626, S/454.
[284] SCOR, 3rd year, Special Supplement no. 1, S/649/Rev. 1, p. 10, para. 22: the truce plan had 'positions' in the plural.
[285] SCOR, 3rd year, 302nd mtg (22 May 1948), pp. 58-9; SC res. 49 (S/773), 22 May 1948; see n. 67 above.
[286] SC res. 61 (S/1070), 4 Nov. 1948. The text printed in *Resolutions and Decisions of the Security Council 1948* has 'positions', but the text actually approved had 'position' in the singular, as has Article 40 of the Charter: see SCOR, 3rd year, 377th mtg (4 Nov. 1948), pp. 40-1, and Supplement for November 1948, p. 7, S/1070.

Either kind may take the form of a recommendation or appeal, or may be a mandatory order under Chapter VII of the Charter.

There have been two instances in the cases studied of Security Council appeals for an embargo against one party only. In the Kashmir case, the Council asked Pakistan to use its best endeavours to prevent 'any furnishing of material aid to those [tribesmen and Pakistani nationals] fighting in the State'.[287] Pakistan maintained that it was impossible to implement this appeal because non-official Pakistanis could not be prevented from showing sympathy and support for the Azad Kashmir movement. In any event, three regular Pakistani battalions entered Kashmir within a couple of weeks of the decision of the Security Council.[288] Some countries, including the United States, imposed their own embargoes on the supply of arms to both India and Pakistan in 1948. Britain enforced no embargo but told each country what was being sent to the other.[289]

The other Security Council call for a military embargo against one party only was included in the first resolution adopted after the outbreak of war in Korea. The Council determined that the armed attack from North Korea constituted a breach of the peace (thus bringing the decision within the scope of Chapter VII of the Charter) and called on 'all Member States' to 'refrain from giving assistance to the North Korean authorities'.[290] The resolution was adopted by nine votes to none, Yugoslavia abstaining and the Soviet Union absent. The countries of the Soviet bloc disregarded this call, but other UN Members respected it so long as the fighting continued.

The first case of a general military embargo applying to a region of conflict rather than a named party was in Palestine in 1948, and the Security Council's first call was not to the suppliers of weapons but to the recipients. On 17 April the Council called on 'all persons and organizations' in Palestine to refrain from

---

[287] SC res. 47 (S/726), 21 April 1948.

[288] Akbar Khan, *Raiders in Kashmir*, Karachi, Pak Publishers, 1970, p. 101; Fazlal Muqeem Khan, *The Story of the Pakistan Army*, Karachi, Oxford University Press, 1963, p. 100; Prithivi Nath Kaul Bamzai, *A History of Kashmir...*, Delhi, Metropolitan Book Co., 1962, pp. 691-2; FRUS, 1948, vol. V part 1, 1975, pp. 340, 345, 349, 353.

[289] FRUS, 1948, vol V, part 1, 1975, pp. 436, 496-7, 513-14, 519-20; 1949, vol. VI, 1977, pp. 25, 1689-91, 1696-8, 1727.

[290] SC res. 82 (S/1501), 25 June 1950.

'importing or acquiring or assisting or encouraging the import-
ation or acquisition of weapons and war materials' and to refrain
'from bringing and from assisting and encouraging the entry
into Palestine of armed bands and fighting personnel'; and
governments were asked to assist in the implementation of the
measures in the resolution, 'particularly those referring to the
entry into Palestine of armed bands and fighting personnel...
and weapons and war materials'. Six weeks later the Council
broadened its appeal by calling on all governments and authorities to 'refrain from importing *or exporting* war material' into
Palestine or the Arab countries, and not to introduce fighting
personnel or men of military age into the area 'during the
cease-fire'.[291] The United States had instituted its own arms
embargo the previous November. Britain had imposed a partial
embargo in December, though this was not made public until
4 February 1948: after the Security Council's second appeal,
Britain imposed a total embargo. Both Israel and the Arabs
disregarded the embargo, Israel in a systematic way and on a
large scale. Weapons for the Jews and later Israel were sent
from Czechoslovakia to Corsica or across Hungary to the
Dalmatian coast, and then by sea to the Middle East. An airfield near Žatec, about forty-five miles north-west of Prague,
was placed at the disposal of Jewish organizations. Jews,
wearing Czechoslovak army uniforms, underwent training at a
military base, and some airmen received instruction at Ceske
Budějovice. Israel also obtained arms clandestinely from non-
official sources in France, Italy, and the United States. On the
Arab side, British officers seconded to the Arab Legion were
withdrawn from Palestine after the second appeal of the Security
Council, although Sir Alec Kirkbride (British minister in
Amman at the time) comments that he was 'not sure' that they
all stayed east of the River Jordan for long. Kirkbride was
disconcerted that Britain was so meticulous in observing the
embargo (except for the supply of 'a quantity of barbed wire'),
and Sir John Glubb (Glubb Pasha) was surprised that the

[291] SC res. 46 (S/723), 17 April 1948; res. 50 (S/801), 29 May 1948 (my italics).

Western powers refused to smuggle weapons, 'even to their friends'.[292]

In order to check on the embargo, Count Bernadotte used the military observers, who also had to supervise the cease-fire, and he was able to secure naval vessels and aircraft as follows:

France	1 corvette (*Elan*)
United States	3 destroyers (*Henley, Owens, Putnam*)
	1 cargo ship (*Marquette*)
	1 escort carrier (*Palau*)
	4 C-47s (*Dakotas*)
Britain	4 *Auster* observation aircraft

Bernadotte received only ten specific complaints that the embargo was being violated during the first cease-fire, five from Israel, two from the Arab League, two from the United States, and one from Britain, and one major violation was detected by the UN observers (the *Altalena* incident—see pp. 279-80). Perhaps because of the small number of complaints, Bernadotte reached the unduly optimistic conclusion that the arms embargo was 'substantially implemented and supervised', but this was a tribute to the guile of the violators rather than the efficacy of the supervisors.[293] During the second cease-fire, Bernadotte again had the use of one French corvette, three US destroyers, and four US *Dakotas*, and the United Nations itself ordered fourteen small aircraft.[294] In the case of ships and aircraft placed at Bernadotte's disposal for supervising the embargo, these were fully manned (the crews of the British aircraft were civilians), and UN efforts were supplemented by observation under national auspices by the main Western powers. When

---

[292] FRUS, 1948, vol. V part 2, 1976, pp. 581, 1100-1, 1177, 1179, 1279-85, 1517, 1520-2, 1524, 1530-2, 1537, 1571, 1579, 1585-9, 1682; Lie, p. 181; Bernadotte, pp. 70, 188; Azcárate, p. 101; Ben-Gurion, pp. 118, 268; Dayan, p. 73; Allon, p. 36; Shimon Peres, *David's Sling*, London, Weidenfeld & Nicolson, 1970, pp. 32-4; Arnold Krammer, *Forgotten Friendship: Israel and the Soviet Bloc, 1947-1953*, London and Chicago, University of Illinois Press, 1974, pp. 60-5, 78-106, 110-11; Glubb, pp. 149, 191, 211; Kirkbride, pp. 34-5, 53, 63.

[293] S/1025, 5 Oct. 1948 (mimeo), paras. 2-4, 31-3, 46, and pp. 29-31, paras. 11-3 of Annex A.

[294] GAOR, 3rd year, Supplement no. 11, A/648, p. 37, para. 5.

the United Nations acquired its own aircraft, Bernadotte himself recruited air crews.[295]

Bernadotte also had to verify the ban on introducing military personnel into the region, which was not at all to the liking of the Israelis. 'We cannot agree to a formula', said Israeli Foreign Minister Moshe Shertok, 'whereby, if the Arabs stop shooting, we will halt immigration.' Bernadotte's idea was to place male Jewish immigrants between the ages of eighteen and forty-five in UN-supervised camps for the duration of the cease-fire. Israel acknowledged that the Security Council's cease-fire appeal had sought to prevent the entry of 'fighting personnel', but argued that the resolution allowed the introduction of 'men of military age' so long as they were not mobilized or subjected to military training. When Bernadotte found that Israel was unyielding on this matter, he cabled to the President of the Security Council asking whether the Council's decision meant that all men of military age were to be excluded. It happened that the President for the month was an Arab, Faris El-Khouri of Syria, and El-Khouri told Bernadotte that it was up to him to interpret the resolution but that its basic intent was that no military advantage should accrue to either side as a result of the cease-fire. When this bland reply was conveyed to Bernadotte by the US ambassador in Cairo, he gave a wry smile 'accompanied by an ejaculation'. Bernadotte considered asking the Security Council for an authoritative clarification, but Trygve Lie was opposed to this. '[I]t might lead to unfortunate consequences if the Security Council sat down and gave a definite reply to [Bernadotte's] questions. It might even mean that the whole question of a truce might be torn up afresh.' Bernadotte proceeded to Haifa for discussions with Shertok, whom he found excited and voluble. Bernadotte thought that perhaps the Israelis were not interested in a cease-fire, and he said as much to Shertok. This led to a calmer atmosphere, and they parted the best of friends.[296]

[295] Letter from John Reedman, 25 April 1979.
[296] SCOR, 3rd year, Supplement for June 1948, pp. 77, 82-4, S/823, para. 6 of S/829; 313rd mtg (3 June 1948), pp. 28-9; 314th mtg (7 June 1948), p. 2; Bernadotte, pp. 45, 51-5, 59-60; FRUS, 1948, vol. V part 2, 1976, pp. 1086-7, 1090-1, 1098-9; Ben-Gurion, pp. 135, 138-40.

Bernadotte stationed observers at or near ports and airfields in Palestine and arranged for regular reconnaissance patrols. All incoming aircraft and ships were checked and their log books examined, and observers were sent to Cyprus 'from time to time'. Except for the *Altalena* incident, Bernadotte was satisfied that violations were on a trivial scale. Between 260 and 265 Jews of military age entered Palestine legally and were placed in camps, fewer than Bernadotte had expected.[297]

When Ralph Bunche submitted the four Middle Eastern armistice agreements to the Security Council in 1949, he pointed out that the mandatory cease-fire had been replaced by the armistices and that it was no longer necessary to impose on the parties 'the restrictive conditions' of the cease-fire. It would be 'consistent with the realities' of the new situation and would safeguard UN objectives in Palestine if the Security Council were to declare that the armistice agreements had made it 'unnecessary' to prolong the mandatory cease-fire and were to reaffirm the order to desist from further military action and call for continued observance of an unconditional cease-fire. He suggested that it was not necessary to maintain the arms embargo, but he thought that it would be a good idea if the main suppliers of weapons would impose certain restraints. The Council made a number of changes in Bunche's proposals after two of its members (Canada and France) had consulted him. First, the armistice agreements were said to have superseded the mandatory cease-fire rather than to have made it 'unnecessary'. Second, the reaffirmation of the call to desist from military activity was deleted, and the call for an unconditional cease-fire was said to arise from the Council's binding resolution of the previous July rather than being a new recommendation. These changes significantly strengthened the cease-fire obligation. The three Western powers responded to Bunche's suggestion about arms supplies by indicating in similar but not identical terms that they would limit the flow of arms to the area.[298]

[297] SCOR, 3rd year, Supplement for July 1948, pp. 50-1, paras. 10-1 of S/888; 333rd mtg (13 July 1948), pp. 16-18; S/1025, 5 Oct. 1948 (mimeo), paras. 2, 31-3.
[298] SCOR, 4th year, Supplement for August 1949, pp. 5-7, part III of S/1357; 433rd mtg (4 Aug. 1949), pp. 5-9; 434th mtg (4 Aug. 1949), pp. 21, 27; 435th mtg (8 Aug. 1949), pp. 2-3, S/1367; 437th mtg (11 Aug. 1949), pp. 2, 13-14; SC res. 73 (S/1376, II), 11 Aug. 1949; FRUS, 1949, vol. VI, 1977, pp. 1277-80, 1341-2.

In the Sinai-Suez case, the Security Council was stymied by Anglo-French vetoes, but a US proposal recommending that UN Members should refrain from introducing military goods into the area of hostilities was approved by an overwhelming vote of the General Assembly.[299]

In addition to the General Assembly's recommended embargo in the Sinai-Suez case and the Security Council's embargoes relating to Kashmir, Palestine, and Korea, the Security Council has also appealed for the exercise of restraint and the avoidance of provocation. When tension erupted in Cyprus in 1964, for example, the Council made no express appeal for an arms embargo but twice called on states to refrain from any action that might exacerbate the situation.[300]

3.10 OTHER SANCTIONS

Apart from military embargoes, the Security Council can impose other sanctions short of outright military enforcement. Article 41 of the UN Charter provides a partial list of such measures: interruption of economic relations and of rail, sea, air, postal, telegraphic, radio, and other means of communication, and the severance of diplomatic relations. The Council may propose to the General Assembly the suspension from Membership or expulsion of a Member if the circumstances specified in Articles 5 or 6 of the Charter have been satisfied. Other measures may be taken which are not expressly mentioned in the Charter.

Proposals to apply non-military or military enforcement measures were made in several of the cases studied. When the Netherlands had failed to withdraw its forces in Indonesia in 1947, the Soviet Union submitted a proposal to the effect that, if Dutch non-compliance should continue, a situation would arise that might lead to the necessity of applying enforcement measures. The proposal was, in the event, defeated by four votes (the West) to two (Soviet bloc), with five abstentions.

---

[299] GA res. 997 (ES-I), 2 Nov. 1956.
[300] SC res. 186 (S/5575), 4 March 1964; res. 193 (S/5868), 9 Aug. 1964.

Instead, the Council called for consultations between the parties to give effect to the cease-fire.[301]

After the collapse of the first cease-fire in Palestine in 1948, Count Bernadotte went to New York in person and urged the Security Council to *order* a cease-fire, 'backed by a firmly expressed determination to have prompt recourse to the provisions of Articles 41 and 42 of the Charter' if the order should not be complied with. The Council approved a US proposal which determined that peace was threatened in Palestine, ordered a cease-fire as Bernadotte had suggested, and warned that failure to comply would require immediate consideration of 'further action under Chapter VII of the Charter'.[302]

After the Israeli offensive in the Negev later in the year, Britain and China proposed that the Security Council should appoint a sub-committee to consider measures that might be needed if either Israel or Egypt should fail to comply with the decisions of the Council. The proposal was opposed by the Soviet Union on the ground that not all peaceful remedies had been explored, but, after minor amendment, the draft was approved by eight votes to one (Ukrainian SSR), Colombia and the Soviet Union abstaining (the latter so as to avoid a veto). Ralph Bunche, the Acting UN Mediator, argued in the sub-committee and later in the Council that the authority of the United Nations should be directed towards armistice negotiations rather than the punishment of the party or parties refusing to withdraw, and the Council's next decision was that 'an armistice shall be established', with a call on the parties to negotiate, either directly or through Bunche.[303]

After the Sinai-Suez invasion in 1956, there were several Soviet and Third World proposals for sanctions. Egypt complained that the Israeli attack constituted aggression and called for Israel's expulsion from the United Nations. After British and French forces had landed in Egypt, the Soviet Union pro-

[301] SCOR, 2nd year, 215th mtg (29 Oct. 1947), pp. 2661-2, S/589; 219th mtg (1 Nov. 1947), p. 2751; SC res. 36 (S/597), 1 Nov. 1947.
[302] SCOR, 3rd year, 333rd mtg (13 July 1948), p. 8; SC res. 54 (S/902), 15 July 1948.
[303] SCOR, 3rd year, 374th mtg (28 Oct. 1948), pp. 12-13, 35, S/1059; 375th mtg (29 Oct. 1948), pp. 15-16; SC res. 61 (S/1070), 4 Nov. 1948; SC res. 62 (S/1080), 16 Nov. 1948.

posed that the two super-powers should give military and other assistance to Egypt if the invading countries did not stop their military action within twelve hours, but the Council declined even to consider the Soviet proposal.[304] Later, a group of six Islamic countries submitted to the General Assembly a proposal for denying all military, economic, or financial assistance to Israel while its non-compliance with the resolutions of the General Assembly continued, and this had strong Communist support. It was a threat that continued until Golda Meir had announced that Israel would withdraw from Sharm El-Sheikh and the Gaza Strip and Secretary-General Hammarskjold had reported that precise arrangements for withdrawal had been agreed between Israel and the UN Emergency Force.[305]

Although members of the Security Council have not hesitated to use strong words in criticism of Israel or minority régimes in southern Africa, the Council has been circumspect when it has come to enforcement action, and most proposals for enforcement are exposed to the risk of veto if put to the vote. In the Indonesian case, the United States was prepared to go further than other Western countries in applying pressure against the Netherlands, but on its own initiative rather than in response to UN decisions. The United States suspended arms deliveries as soon as the fighting began and did not permit US ships to carry arms for the Netherlands. Consideration was given to the suspension of US Marshall Plan aid to the Netherlands, and when the United States announced its allocation of funds for 1949, it was made clear that there was no actual commitment of funds to the Netherlands for use in Indonesia.[306]

In the Palestine case in 1948, there was firm opposition to sanctions against the Arabs on the part of Britain and against Israel on the part of the Soviet Union and President Truman, although some of the senior people in the State Department

---

[304] SCOR, 11th year, 748th mtg (30 Oct. 1956), paras. 68-9; 755th mtg (5 Nov. 1956), paras. 27, 42, 67-8; Supplement for October to December 1956, pp. 128-30, S/3736.

[305] GAOR, 11th session, Annexes, Agenda item 66, p. 62, A/3557, 660th plenary mtg (26 Feb. 1957), paras. 108-9; 666th plenary mtg (1 March 1957), paras. 1-24; 667th plenary mtg (4 March 1957), paras. 200-2; 668th plenary mtg (8 March 1957), paras. 138-40.

[306] FRUS, 1947, vol. VI, 1972, pp. 993, 1068; 1948, vol. VI, 1974, pp. 209-10, 299, 483, 517, 550-2.

(George Marshall, Robert Lovett, Warren Austin) concluded in October that sanctions would have to be imposed against the party or parties refusing to comply with the Security Council's call for withdrawal.[307]

In the Sinai-Suez episode, the Anglo-French vetoes in the Security Council were short-circuited when the Council placed the matter in the hands of the General Assembly. While the United States did not hestitate to apply economic and financial pressures against the three delinquents, these were kept firmly within US control and were lifted sooner than would have been the case if the decision had been left to the General Assembly.

3.11 ASSISTANCE FOR THE VICTIM

The obverse of the application of pressure against the offender is the provision of aid for the victim. The only instance of this in the cases studied was in Korea, where the Security Council recommended that UN Members should furnish South Korea with 'such assistance ... as may be necessary to repel the armed attack and to restore international peace and security', and should provide a Unified Command with 'military forces and other assistance'. The Council also requested that assistance should be provided for the 'relief and support of the civilian population of Korea'.[308] The military aid to be provided was not with a view to the immediate ending of the fighting but in order to resist an aggressor and, at a minimum, to restore the situation as it had been before the fighting began. To present a balanced picture, one must add that UN Members that responded positively to the Security Council's appeal did so in spite of their distaste for the oppressive nature of the South Korean régime. It is the essence of the UN system that all states, even the most barbarous, are entitled to have their territorial integrity and political independence respected— though there has been an increasing tendency to regard the use of armed force in liberation struggles against racist or colonialist régimes as not inconsistent with the Charter's general prohibition of the threat or use of force.

[307] FRUS, 1948, vol. V part 2, 1976, pp. 1498, 1504, 1518-20.
[308] SC res. 83 (S/1511), 27 June 1950; res. 84 (S/1588), 7 July 1950; res. 85 (S/1657), 31 July 1950.

3.12 VOTING PROBLEMS

As noted on pp. 45-47, problems have arisen in connection with the right of the five permanent members to veto substantive proposals and the provision in the Charter that substantive decisions on the peaceful settlement of disputes require 'the concurring votes' of the permanent members. Difficulties have also arisen if members of the Security Council are not present when decisions have to be taken, whether the absence is intentional or involuntary.

3.12.1 VETOES

It is sometimes said that, on all important matters, the Security Council is impotent because of the threat or use of the veto or the double-veto. What are the facts regarding the veto and double-veto in the period 1946-64?

There was not a single successful instance of the use of the double-veto in the seven cases. In a matter closely allied to the Korean case—a Chinese complaint in 1950 that the United States had engaged in aggression against Taiwan—Nationalist China tried to exercise a double-veto retroactively on a proposal to invite the People's Republic of China to participate in the debate in the Security Council, but the President of the Council ruled that the main proposal had been adopted. Nationalist China then proposed that an advisory opinion on the matter should be sought from the International Court of Justice, but the President regarded this as a challenge to his ruling and put the challenge to the vote. The matter ended anti-climactically when it was discovered that there were no votes in favour of the challenge, no votes against, and no abstentions![309]

As for simple vetoes, there were 108 in the period 1946-64, of which sixteen were in connection with the seven cases studied or closely related matters. To evaluate the effectiveness of these vetoes, we need to discover precisely what was prevented by the proposals that were not adopted because of negative votes. These sixteen vetoes are numbered consecutively for ease of reference.

[309] SCOR, 5th year, 507th mtg (29 Sept. 1950), pp. 4-8.

Indonesia 1947-8

No. 1 After the first Dutch 'police action', the Security Council called for a cessation of hostilities and a settlement of the dispute by peaceful means. At a later stage, Australia and China submitted a proposal that requested Council members with career consuls in Batavia (Djakarta) to provide the Council with information and guidance. The Soviet Union, rightly suspecting that this was a device to create an organ from which Communist countries would be excluded, submitted an amendment whereby the new organ would be composed of all the members of the Security Council. This amendment was vetoed by France, its second exercise of the veto; whereupon the original proposal was approved, seven members voting in favour, and the Soviet Union and three others (including Britain) abstaining.[310]

Kashmir 1947-9 No vetoes were cast during the period leading up to the agreement on the demarcation of the cease-fire line in 1949, but there were two subsequent Soviet vetoes.

No. 2 A proposal was submitted in February 1957 by which the President of the Security Council for the month, Gunnar Jarring of Sweden, would have been asked to visit the Indian subcontinent in an effort to settle the dispute about Kashmir, having regard to previous resolutions and 'the proposal for the use of a temporary United Nations force'. This was vetoed by the Soviet Union, whereupon a proposal was submitted in almost identical terms but without any reference to a UN force; and this was approved with ten votes in favour, the Soviet Union abstaining.[311]

No. 3 After a lengthy debate on Kashmir in 1962, Ireland introduced a rather anodyne proposal which would have reminded India and Pakistan of earlier resolutions and urged them to negotiate with a view to a peaceful settlement. The Soviet Union objected to this text because the 'central idea'

[310] Ibid., 2nd year, 193rd mtg (22 Aug. 1947), pp. 2173-4, n. 3, S/513; 194th mtg (25 Aug. 1947), pp. 2197-200; SC res. 30 (S/525, I), 25 Aug. 1947. Text of vetoed proposal in Bailey, *Voting in the Security Council*, p. 167.

[311] SCOR, 12th year, Supplement for January-March 1957, pp. 7-8, S/3787; 773rd mtg (20 Feb. 1957), para. 126; SC res. 123 (S/3793), 21 Feb. 1957. Text of vetoed proposal in Bailey, *Voting in the Security Council,* pp. 183-4.

of the earlier resolutions had been to hold a plebiscite in Kashmir. This, in the Soviet view, cast doubt on the fact that Kashmir belonged to India, and it would have represented 'open inter- ference' in India's domestic affairs. The proposal was duly vetoed.[312] Whether a different text acceptable to all concerned would have been approved was never put to the test, for the weary diplomats had had a surfeit of Kashmir. A writer in *The Economist* epitomized the mood at the United Nations after a marathon exercise in listening:

Unless you may happen to be a Kashmiri
The Security Council has lately been dreary.[313]

Palestine 1947-9 Considering the complexity of the issue and the differing interests of the permanent members of the Security Council in 1947-9, it is noteworthy that there was not a single veto during the Palestine war or during the negotiations leading up to the armistice agreements. Beginning in 1954, however, the Soviet veto was used to help the Arabs, and from 1972 the US veto was used to help Israel. Five Soviet vetoes were cast on Palestine and related questions during the period covered by this study.

No. 4 The first Soviet veto on Palestine came after Syria had complained to the Security Council that Israel was changing the course of the Jordan River in and near the Hula demili- tarized zone. After debates in the Security Council extending over two months, Britain, France, and the United States sub- mitted a balanced proposal which, as amended, would have asked the UN Chief of Staff 'to explore possibilities of recon- ciling the Israeli and Syrian interests involved in the dispute'. The Soviet Union gave the impression of favouring an amended text, partly to give greater emphasis to the need for Israeli- Syrian agreement rather than the intermediary role of the UN Chief of Staff, and partly to satisfy the Arab demand for greater stress on the inviolability of the armistice agreements and the status of the demilitarized zone. When the three-power proposal

---

[312] SCOR, 17th year, Supplement for April-June 1962, p. 104, S/5134; 1016th mtg (22 June 1962), paras. 73-81, 92. Text of vetoed proposal in Bailey, *Voting in the Security Council,* pp. 193-4.
[313] *The Economist,* 21 December 1957, p. 1058.

was put to the vote on 22 January 1954, Lebanon joined the Soviet Union in voting against, and Brazil and Nationalist China abstained.[314]

No. 5　No sooner had the Security Council disposed of the Syrian complaint than a request was received from Israel that the Council should consider the Egyptian blockade of the Suez Canal and the Gulf of Aqaba in the light of the Council's earlier finding that the Egyptian policy of blockade was inconsistent with 'the objectives' of the armistice agreement and should be terminated.[315] This was followed at once by an Egyptian counter-complaint that Israel had violated the El Auja demilitarized zone. After debate spread over two months, New Zealand put forward a proposal that would have called on Egypt to comply with the 1951 decision. The Soviet Union complained that the resolution failed to deal with the basic question of Palestine. An attempt was being made to impose a solution, whereas what was needed was encouragement to Egypt and Israel to sit at the same table and negotiate. Moreover, the New Zealand text was not to the liking of the Arabs. The Soviet Union wondered why a more persistent attempt had not been made to find a solution acceptable to the parties: what was the point of reaffirming the 1951 decision, which had manifestly failed to solve the problem?

Instead of dealing seriously with questions which may be settled by means of negotiation, you are putting to the vote the same ancient, two-year-old, moth-eaten resolution, dragged out of the archives, merely in order to show that you are doing something...But life does not call for resolutions: it calls for decisions which can promote the settlement of important international questions...

A negative vote, claimed the Soviet representative, would prevent the Security Council from impairing its own prestige and authority. The Soviet Union was again joined by Lebanon in voting 'no', and Nationalist China again abstained.[316]

---

[314] SCOR, 8th year, Supplement for October-December 1953, pp. 79-80, S/3151/ Rev. 2; 651st mtg (21 Dec. 1953), paras. 22-3, 29-30; 654th mtg (29 Dec. 1953), paras. 22, 25; 9th year, 655th mtg (21 Jan. 1954), paras. 98, 101. Text of vetoed proposal in Bailey, Voting in the Security Council, pp. 178-9.

[315] SC res. 95 (S/2322), 1 Sept. 1951.

[316] SCOR, 9th year, Supplement for January-March 1954, p. 4, S/3188/Corr. 1; 664th mtg (29 March 1954), paras. 37, 42, 46-50, 90, 94-6, 106. Text of vetoed proposal in Bailey, Voting in the Security Council, p. 179.

No. 6 The third Soviet veto on the Middle East during this period was not technically on the Palestine question but arose from the Anglo-French complaint following Egypt's nationalization of the Suez Canal Co. After the two conferences in London, there was debate and discussion of the matter at the United Nations, including seven open and three closed meetings of the Security Council, as well as private negotiations among the powers principally involved under the auspices of Secretary-General Dag Hammarskjold. Following some suggestions of Selwyn Lloyd, the British Foreign Minister, Hammarskjold submitted six principles for the future operation of the Suez Canal, and Britain and France incorporated these principles into a draft resolution. This part of the Anglo-French draft was approved unanimously.[317] The remainder of the draft would have endorsed the proposals of the first London conference. The Soviet Union regarded this part of the Anglo-French proposal as inconsistent with the Constantinople Convention of 1888 and as an infringement of Egyptian sovereignty. Yugoslavia joined the Soviet Union in voting against this part of the draft.[318] Sixteen days later, Israel invaded Sinai, and Britain and France intervened shortly thereafter.

No. 7 The next Soviet veto over Palestine was after an incident at Almagor in Israel in 1963 in which two farmers were killed. Israel claimed that the incident was caused by Arab infiltrators from Syria, whereas Syria maintained that Israel had opened fire from within the demilitarized zone. UN observers suggested that the first violation had come from the Syrian side, and Britain and the United States introduced a proposal that would have condemned 'the wanton murder' at Almagor. The Soviet Union took the line that one incident should not be isolated from the rest of the Arab-Israeli conflict, that the evidence about Almagor was by no means conclusive, and that the draft resolution contained one-sided accusations. The Soviet Union would vote in the interests of justice and to prevent the Security Council from adopting an anti-Arab stand. The Soviet representative added, however, that the discussion

---

[317] SC res. 118 (S/3675), 13 Oct. 1956.
[318] SCOR, 11th year, Supplement for October-December 1956, pp. 19-20, S/3671; 742nd mtg (13 Oct. 1956), paras. 60, 84-6, 90. Text of vetoed proposal in Bailey, *Voting in the Security Council,* p. 181.

had nevertheless been an important step in bringing the difficulties in the Middle East to the attention of world opinion. There were eight votes in favour of the draft resolution, two against (including the Soviet Union), and one abstention.[319]

No. 8 The last Soviet veto on Palestine during this period concerned an incident in 1964 at a place called Tel-el-Qadi in Arabic and Tel Dan in Hebrew, concerning which Syria and Israel again submitted inconsistent complaints. As in the Almagor incident, UN observers concluded tht firing had been started from the Syrian side, but the UN Chief of Staff commented that the situation had been exacerbated by Israel's refusal to recognize any *locus standi* to Syria in the Hula demilitarized zone and by Syria's refusal to end its conflict with Israel. Britain and the United States submitted a draft resolution which, after amendment by Morocco, would have deplored the renewal of fighting and regretted the loss of life. The Soviet Union objected to the fact that the draft resolution put the victim of aggression and the aggressor on the same footing. Czechoslovakia and Morocco joined the Soviet Union in voting against the draft resolution, the other eight members of the Council voting in favour.[320]

This, like veto No. 3, was a case where a more persistent effort might have led to agreement, but the United Nations was under exceptional pressure at the time. The General Assembly was in session but was unable to take decisions because of a dispute about whether the Soviet Union should be deprived of its vote because it was in financial arrears regarding UN peace-keeping. The Security Council met nine times over Palestine and, in a three-week period, no fewer than seventeen times about the Belgian action in sending paratroops to rescue hostages from Stanleyville in the Congo (renamed Zaire in 1971). When the Soviet veto was cast on 21 December, more than one diplomat considered that the health of representatives on the

---

[319] Bull, pp. 52-3; SCOR, 18th year, Supplement for July-September 1963, p. 149, S/5407; 1062nd mtg (30 Aug. 1963), paras. 22, 27-8, 34, 37; 1063rd mtg (3 Sept. 1963), paras. 87-8, 91-2. Text of vetoed proposal in Bailey, *Voting in the Security Council*, pp. 194-5.

[320] SCOR, 19th year, Supplement for October-December 1964, pp. 318-21, S/6113, S/6116; 1167th mtg (3 Dec. 1964), paras. 40, 44-6, 49-53, 58, 62; 1179th mtg (17 Dec. 1964), paras. 24, 26, 45; 1182nd mtg (21 Dec. 1964), para. 14. Text of vetoed proposal in Bailey, *Voting in the Security Council*, pp. 196-7.

Security Council required that a Christmas break should take priority over a possibly fruitless continuance of the search for an agreed text on the Middle East.

Indonesia 1948-9

No. 9 After agreement between the Netherlands and Indonesia had been reached at the round table conference in the Hague in 1949, Canada submitted to the Security Council a draft resolution which would have noted 'with satisfaction' a report from the UN Commission for Indonesia and commended the Commission for its work, congratulated the parties, welcomed the forthcoming establishment of an independent United States of Indonesia, and asked the UN Commission to report on the implementation of the Hague agreements. The Soviet line was that the UN Commission was simply a tool of the United States and other colonial powers, and that the Hague agreements redounded to the exclusive benefit of colonial aggressors. The Soviet Union and the Ukraine voted against all paragraphs of the proposal.[321]

This was an interesting example of a veto that, while regrettable, prevented nothing of significance. It would have been nice had the Security Council been able to congratulate the parties, to welcome the creation of the Indonesian Union, and to commend the UN Commission for Indonesia; but everyone knew that nine of the eleven members of the Council wished to express these sentiments. Even the failure to request the Commission for Indonesia to discharge its responsibilities was without effect; the Commission continued to operate under the previous directives of the Security Council, including observing and assisting in the implementation of the agreements reached at the round table conference. It even issued four more reports on its activities, in spite of the fact that a request that it should do so had been vetoed.

Korea 1950-3 When the Korean War broke out, the Soviet Union was boycotting meetings of the Security Council because of the failure to expel Nationalist China, and the decisions to

[321] SCOR, 4th year, Supplement for September-December 1949, pp. 13-14, S/1431; 456th mtg (13 Dec. 1949), pp. 5-12, 36-7. Text of vetoed proposal in Bailey, *Voting in the Security Council,* p. 173.

support South Korea were taken in the absence of the Soviet Union. The Soviet representative returned to the Council when it was his turn to preside, and for a month there were neither decisions nor vetoes. Thereafter there were five Soviet vetoes on Korea and related matters.

No. 10 When it became known that the Soviet Union would return to the Council on 1 August 1950, the United States proposed that the Security Council should condemn North Korea for its continued defiance of the United Nations. This was an interesting example of a resolution that was introduced precisely in order that it should be vetoed. 'A veto by them [the Russians] of a resolution along these lines would be enormously valuable', cabled the acting US ambassador in New York to Dean Acheson. No action on the US proposal was possible during the Soviet tenure of the presidency, but the proposal was put to the vote in September, Yugoslavia abstaining and the Soviet Union voting against, as the United States had intended.[322]

No. 11 After the People's Republic of China had complained that US military aircraft had dropped bombs on Chinese territory, the United States proposed that the Security Council should establish a commission composed of India and Sweden to investigate China's allegations 'on the spot'. The Soviet Union held that this was an attempt to side-track the Council: in any case, a decision could not be taken in China's absence. There were seven votes in favour of the US proposal, the Soviet Union against, India and Yugoslavia abstaining, and Nationalist China not participating in the vote because it was 'a mistake from the very beginning for the Security Council to put such an item as [the People's Republic of China had proposed] on its agenda'.[323]

No. 12 After China had intervened in the Korean War, a draft resolution was submitted by a group of Western and Latin American states calling for a denial of assistance or encouragement to North Korea, emphasizing the danger of con-

---

[322] FRUS, 1950, vol. VII, 1976, p. 496; SCOR, 5th year, 479th mtg (31 July 1950), pp. 7-8, S/1653. Text of vetoed proposal in Bailey, *Voting in the Security Council*, p. 173.

[323] SCOR, 5th year, 497th mtg (7 Sept. 1950), pp. 18-19, S/1752; 501st mtg (12 Sept. 1950), pp. 4-5 (S/1752), 7-8, 16-17, 27. Text of vetoed proposal in Bailey, *Voting in the Security Council*, pp. 173-4.

tinued Chinese intervention, and affirming the inviolability of
the frontier between Korea and China. The Soviet Union
again argued that no decision should be taken in China's
absence and that the proposal was based on a complete falsifi-
cation of history. The Soviet Union voted against the draft
resolution, Yugoslavia abstained on three paragraphs, and
India did not participate in the vote as its delegation had not
received 'final instructions' from New Delhi.[324]

Nos. 13 and 14 Following allegations that US forces in
Korea had engaged in bacterial warfare, the United States
proposed that the charges should be investigated by the International Committee of the Red Cross. The Soviet Union,
during a sustained attempt at filibustering, objected to any
discussion of the matter in the Security Council without Chinese
and North Korean participation, and complained that the
United States had presented a one-sided version of events. All
the other members of the Security Council voted in favour of
the US proposal, but the negative Soviet vote constituted a
veto (no. 13). The United States then submitted a new text to
condemn the fabrication of false charges. This time Pakistan
abstained on the ground that it was unhelpful for the super-
powers to engage in mutual condemnation, and the Soviet
Union again used the veto (no. 14).[325]

Sinai-Suez 1956-7 Only two proposals to stop fighting were
vetoed during the eighteen-year period covered by this study,
and these followed the Israeli invasion of Sinai in 1956.

Nos. 15 and 16 The first cease-fire proposal was sponsored
by the United States and the second by the Soviet Union and
amended by Nationalist China. Britain and France, whose
representatives in New York were not fully informed about
the policies of their governments, simply said that the draft

[324] SCOR, 5th year, 521st mtg (10 Nov. 1950), pp. 6-9, 16 (S/1894); 528th mtg
(29 Nov. 1950), pp. 18-19, 22, 25, 27-8; 530th mtg (30 Nov. 1950), pp. 12-18. Text of
vetoed proposal in Bailey, *Voting in the Security Council,* pp. 174-5.
[325] SCOR, 7th year, Supplement for April-June 1952, p. 17, S/2671; 580th mtg
(23 June 1952), paras. 5-6, 14, 24-41, 48, 58; 581st mtg (25 June 1952), paras. 8-10,
41-3, 53, 62; 584th mtg (1 July 1952), paras. 70, 77, 80; 585th mtg (1 July 1952),
paras. 11, 60; 587th mtg (3 July 1952), paras. 23 (S/2688), 28; 588th mtg (8 July
1952), paras. 46, 69; 589th mtg (8 July 1952), para. 67. Text of vetoed proposal in
Bailey, *Voting in the Security Council,* pp. 175-6.

resolutions were not the best or most appropriate courses of action for the Security Council in the prevailing circumstances, and they voted against in both cases—although Britain would have preferred to abstain.[326] Yugoslavia then moved that the General Assembly should be convened within twenty-four hours under the Uniting for Peace procedure, and this, being procedural and thus not subject to veto, was approved.[327] Pressure was then exerted in the General Assembly, the fighting stopped, and the three invading states withdrew. It was ironic that Britain and France should have maintained that they had intervened in Egypt because the persistent Soviet abuse of the veto had rendered the Security Council impotent:[328] this may have been sincerely believed, but it soon became clear that the two Anglo-French vetoes, like those of the Soviet Union, had not changed the realities of the power.

Cyprus 1964   There were no vetoes.

EFFECTS OF VETOES

In examining the effect of these vetoes, it is necessary to distinguish seven kinds of proposal submitted to the Security Council. A draft resolution is likely to contain proposals of more than one kind in its operative paragraphs: thus the vetoed proposal on the Suez Canal (No. 5 above) recalled a previous decision, expressed opinions on two aspects of the problem ('*Notes* with grave concern... *Considers* that...'), and made a recommendation ('*Calls upon* Egypt...').

1. *Amendments*   This is illustrated by veto 1, by which France prevented the adoption of a Soviet amendment which, *inter alia*,

---

[326] Macmillan, vol. II, p. 151; Selwyn Lloyd, *Suez, 1956: a personal account*, London, Cape, 1978, p. 199.

[327] SCOR, 11th year, Supplement for October-December 1956, pp. 110, 112, S/3710, S/3713/Rev. 1; 749th mtg (30 Oct. 1956), paras. 125, 144, 188, 191-2; 750th mtg (30 Oct. 1956), paras. 19-22, 84; 751st mtg (31 Oct. 1956), para. 71, S/3719; SC res. 119 (S/3721), 31 Oct. 1956. Text of vetoed proposals in Bailey, *Voting in the Security Council*, pp. 181-2.

[328] GAOR, 1st ESS, 561st plenary mtg (1 Nov. 1956), paras. 75, 89-90, 111; 562nd mtg (1 Nov. 1956), para. 221.

would have had the effect of changing the composition of a subsidiary organ to be set up in Indonesia.

2. *Approval of action already taken* This is illustrated in one paragraph of veto 4:

Endorses this action of the Chief of Staff...

3. *Reaffirmation of previous decisions* There are three instances of this in the vetoed proposals, including the following (veto 4):

Recalls its resolution of 27 October 1953...

4. *Expressions of opinion* Many resolutions contain expressions of opinion (e.g. '*Notes* with grave concern..., *Considers*..., *Deplores*..., *Welcomes*..., *Congratulates*..., *Commends*...'). The following is from veto 10:

Condemns the North Korean authorities...

5. *Recommendations* Virtually every proposal includes at least one recommendation, often starting with the words '*Calls upon*...', although other formulations are possible ('*Invites*..., *Urges*..., *Appeals to*...'). The following wording was vetoed twice (vetoes 15 and 16):

Calls upon Israel and Egypt immediately to cease-fire...

6. *Entrusting tasks to existing organs* These paragraphs begin '*Directs*...' or, more usually, '*Requests*...' The following is from veto 9:

Requests the United Nations Commission for Indonesia to continue to discharge the responsibilities entrusted to it...

7. *Conferring new responsibilities* These paragraphs usually begin '*Decides*...' or '*Requests*...', for example (veto 13):

Requests the International Committee of the Red Cross to...

Let us consider the seven groups in turn.

1. *Amendments* The French veto of a Soviet amendment over

Indonesia (veto 1) did not prevent anything from being done: it simply ensured that the proposal of Australia and China was put to the vote (and approved) in the form in which it was originally submitted.

2. *Approval of action already taken*   The failure to endorse the Chief of Staff's action in veto 4 in no way countermanded the action.

3. *Reaffirmation of previous decisions*   The failure to recall previous decisions in vetoes 3, 4, and 5 did not invalidate those decisions.

4. *Expressions of opinion*   In three cases, vetoes of expressions of opinion did no serious harm. Veto 4 prevented the Security Council from expressing the view that there could be no peace unless Israel and Syria were strict in implementing the armistice agreement. Veto 9 prevented the Council from expressing satisfaction, from congratulating the parties, from commending the UN Commission, and from welcoming the establishment of the United States of Indonesia. Veto 14 prevented the Council from expressing the view that the charges about bacterial warfare were without substance and from condemning the fabrication and dissemination of false charges.

    In the other five cases, the vetoing of expressions of opinion was mildly harmful. Veto 5 prevented the Council from noting with grave concern that Egypt had not lifted the blockade of the Suez Canal and from expressing the view that the matter should be dealt with by the Mixed Armistice Commission. Veto 6 prevented the Council from endorsing the proposals of the first London conference on the Suez Canal and from expressing the opinion that dues should be paid to the Suez Canal Users' Association. In the case of vetoes 7 and 8, the Soviet Union regretted the loss of life but was unwilling to vote for proposals that, by implication, were critical of Syria. Veto 10 prevented the Council from condemning North Korea for defying the United Nations but did not detract from the four earlier resolutions of the Security Council on Korea, adopted in the absence of the Soviet Union. Although the Security Council as a corporate entity was unable to express the vetoed sentiments in these five cases, this did not alter the fact that at least seven of the Council's eleven members identified them-selves with the opinions that were subjected to negative votes. The most one can say is that, if the Council had approved the vetoed texts, this might conceivably have restrained some hot-heads and encouraged some moderates.

5. *Recommendations* In nine cases, the failure to approve a recommendation was without serious effect. In the case of veto 2, a resolution in similar terms, but without any reference to a UN force, was passed the following day; the veto did not prevent the President of the Security Council from undertaking the mission about Kashmir, though it did reduce the scope of his mandate in one respect. In five cases (vetoes 3, 4, 7, 10, 12), an appeal would have been addressed to governments or other authorities, and it is fair to conclude that those willing to heed the appeal would do so, and those unwilling to heed the appeal would decline to do so, whether the appeal was vetoed or ap-proved. Vetoes 6, 15, and 16 were connected with Suez in 1956. Veto 6 would have asked Egypt, Britain, and France to continue to negotiate. In the light of what we now know of the intentions of Britain and France at the time, it may be doubted whether the Soviet veto had a major effect on events, except to indicate Soviet sympathy for the Arabs. The other two vetoes of recom-mendations over Suez were by Britain and France and were the only ones in the period 1946-64 that prevented the adoption of cease-fire resolutions (vetoes 15 and 16); but they did not prevent a cease-fire from coming into force a week later as a result of pressure exerted outside the Security Council. This was a unique case, because two permanent members of the Security Council from Western Europe were confronting an unusual tactical alliance of the two super-powers and the Third World.

There was one other vetoed proposal that contained a recom-mendation. Veto 5 prevented an appeal to Egypt to accept the obligation of the UN Charter and to comply with the decisions of the Security Council over the blockade of the Suez Canal; as already noted, this veto was mildly harmful.

6. *Entrusting talks to existing organs*   The ten cases of failure to entrust tasks to existing organs (vetoes 2, 3, 4, 7, 8, 9, 12, 13, 14, 15) were of little effect as the organs continued to operate under previous directives.

7. *Conferring new responsibilities*   Three proposals were vetoed which would have conferred new responsibilities. One (veto 2) was followed by an agreed resolution containing most of the recommendation that had been vetoed. In the other two cases, the veto prevented investigations (vetoes 11 and 13), and these must be regarded as damaging.

To summarize, of the sixteen vetoes in connection with the seven cases and related matters in the period 1946-64, two seem to have been damaging (vetoes 11 and 13), five to have been mildly irritating or harmful (vetoes 5, 6, 7, 8, 10), and nine to have been without serious effect (vetoes 1, 2, 3, 4, 9, 12, 14, 15, 16). In two of the five mildly irritating or harmful cases (5 and 7), the official records of the Security Council give one the impression that UN diplomats were defeated mainly by exhaustion.

There is one respect, however, in which the above analysis may possibly underestimate the negative effect of the veto power, for it necessarily disregards the deterrent effect of *the existence* of the veto. We shall never know how many proposals were never introduced because it was thought possible or likely that they would run into a veto: all we know for certain are which proposals were actually introduced and which of them were not approved because a permanent member cast a negative vote.

3.12.2 VOLUNTARY ABSTENTIONS

As noted on pages 46-47, voluntary abstentions are cases when permanent members of the Security Council voluntarily abstain from voting, intending this as a concurring vote rather than a veto. During the period 1946-64, there were fifty-nine voluntary abstentions by permanent members in connection with the cases studied and related matters, forty-two of them by the Soviet Union. In addition, nine decisions were approved by the Security Council without any vote being taken on the proposal as a whole,[329] and five decisions were taken in the absence of a permanent member.[330] Since 1949 there has been little disposition to challenge the view that a voluntary abstention by a permanent member is a form of concurrence.[331]

3.12.3 ABSENCE

There are two circumstances in which members of the Security Council may be absent from meetings: if representatives have failed to reach the place where the Council is meeting (which is likely to occur only if the Council is meeting away from head-quarters) or as a result of a deliberate boycott of the proceedings of the Council—as a form of protest, or in order to be able to allege later that the proceedings were illegal. Absences should, in theory, not occur, at any rate not when the Security Council meets at UN headquarters, as the Charter states that the Council 'shall be so organized as to be able to function continuously' and that members of the Council 'shall for this purpose be represented at all times at the seat of the Organization'.[332] Both kinds of absence occurred, however, in connection with the cases dealt with in this study.

The Security Council normally meets 'at the seat of the United Nations', but the Council may meet elsewhere if this will 'facilitate its work'.[333] The Council decided to meet in London in 1946 and in Paris in 1948 and 1951-2, and it has subsequently met also in Addis Ababa and Panama City.

The last few months of 1948 were a time of great international turbulence, and this imposed considerable strains on the UN system. The General Assembly, in session for the second time that year, was dealing with the civil war in Greece, violations of human rights in Bulgaria and Hungary, the Korean question, disposal of the former Italian colonies, attitudes to the Franco

[329] SC res. 27, 56, 59, 60, 62, 67, 72, 80, and decision at 367th mtg (19 Oct. 1948), pp. 37-8, S/1044.
[330] SC res. 82, 83, 84, 85, and decision at 471st mtg (12 April 1950), p. 5.
[331] For a more detailed study of the abstention problem, see the author's 'New Light on Abstentions in the Security Council', *International Affairs,* vol. 50, no. 4 (October 1974), esp. pp. 564-73.
[332] Article 28 (1).
[333] Article 28 (3) and Rule of Procedure 5.

régime in Spain, treatment of people of Indian origin in South Africa, deadlock over the admission of new UN Members, the Security Council veto, disarmament, the international control of atomic energy, and the Universal Declaration of Human Rights. The Security Council was concerned with Palestine, Kashmir, the Berlin blockade, and elections to the International Court of Justice.

International communications could not be relied on. A critical telex conference between the US delegation in Paris and the State Department in Washington was interrupted on 18 October by a circuit failure, and even the record of the uncompleted exchange was not seen by ambassador Warren Austin until 2 November, an unexplained delay of fifteen days. Some urgent cables from Europe were taking forty-eight hours to reach the State Department. One dispatch from India did not reach Washington for sixteen days, and one from Saigon took more than five weeks. On 15 December, Sir Alexander Cadogan had complained in the Security Council that UN staffs were reduced and the equipment inadequate, and two days later the Security Council had operated without simultaneous interpretation.[334]

Moreover, the US delegation at the United Nations was bereft of the top leadership. Warren Austin, the permanent representative, had been taken ill in November and had returned to the United States. George Marshall, the Secretary of State, left Paris for Washington on 21 November, having been away for more than two months. Marshall designated John Foster Dulles, a Republican, as acting chairman of the US delegation to the General Assembly and Professor Philip Jessup (who had been handling Palestine) as acting chief of the US mission and US representative on the Security Council. On 8 December, however, Jessup was taken ill with pneumonia and entered the American Hospital at Neuilly. Eleanor Roosevelt and Benjamin Cohen, the two senior Democrats, were thought to be too committed to Israel to handle Middle Eastern matters while Jessup was ill, so Dean Rusk cabled Robert Lovett in Washington asking for advice. Lovett consulted Truman, who

---

[334] SCOR, 3rd year, 384th mtg (15 Dec. 1948), p. 6; 386th mtg (17 Dec. 1948), p. 1; FRUS, 1948, vol. V part 1, 1975, pp. 427, 433, 479; 1949, vol. VII part 1, 1975, p. 18.

authorized Dulles to speak for the United States. Jessup left hospital on 15 December and appeared in the Security Council in his overcoat. Two days later, he departed for the Riviera to convalesce.[335]

After the Security Council had rejected Israel's application for UN Membership on 17 December, the Soviet Union formally asked for three days' notice if the Council should have to be convened over the holiday period, and the President (Belgium) promised that the Soviet request would be met 'to the fullest possible extent'.[336]

The following night, 18/19 December, the Netherlands launched its second 'police action' in Indonesia. Jessup flew back to Paris, and the United States immediately joined with Australia in calling for an emergency meeting of the Security Council. When the Council assembled the next day, however, the seats of Colombia, the Soviet Union, and the Ukrainian SSR were empty. Soviet Foreign Minister Molotov had cabled to say that a Soviet diplomat could not reach Paris before 22 December, and it was not until 27 December that a Ukrainian representative put in an appearance, apparently because of delays in obtaining a French visa.[337]

A Security Council without the Soviet Union, the Ukrainian SSR, and Colombia was not in a position to take a decision on Indonesia, because Belgium and France were certain to abstain on any text acceptable to the other members. Thus there were only six members willing to vote affirmatively, one short of the number of votes needed to take a decision when the Council had eleven members. Colombia was represented when the Council met on 22 and 23 December, and on Christmas Eve the Council was at last able to call for the cessation of hostilities in Indonesia. The Ukrainian SSR was still absent, but the President ruled that it should be counted as having abstained.[338]

The first case of deliberate boycott of the Security Council had occurred in 1946, when the Soviet Union stayed away

---

[335] FRUS, 1948, vol. I part 1, 1975, pp. 17-20; vol. I part 2, 1975, pp. 482 n. 1, 483; vol. V part 1, 1975, p. 448; Jessup, pp. 69-70.

[336] SCOR, 3rd year, 386th mtg (17 Dec. 1948), p. 37.

[337] Ibid., 387th mtg (20 Dec. 1948), pp. 1-2; 393rd mtg (27 Dec. 1948), p. 3.

[338] SC res. 63 (S/1150), 24 Dec. 1948; SCOR, 3rd year, 392nd mtg (24 Dec. 1950), p. 30.

from debates on the Iranian question. In 1950 the Soviet representative again withdrew, on this occasion because of the Council's failure to expel the representative of the Kuomintang régime based on Taiwan. When it was the turn of the Soviet Union to preside over the Council (August) the Soviet representatives resumed their participation.[339]

During the absence of the Soviet Union, the Security Council adopted four resolutions on Korea, adopted one resolution and took one other decision on Kashmir, took a procedural decision about disarmament, approved in a highly cautious manner a recommendation of the General Assembly on the means that might be used for the peaceful settlement of disputes, and made a change in one of its rules of procedure relating to credentials. The Soviet Union and its friends have always maintained that these decisions were not in accordance with the Charter requirement that substantive decisions need 'the concurring votes' of all the permanent members, and that these had not been secured because the Soviet Union had been absent and China's seat had been unlawfully occupied by the Kuomintang.[340] The other permanent members, however, took the line that deliberate absence was tantamount to a voluntary abstention.[341] Moreover, the British government included in a White Paper on Korea an appendix dealing with the legal aspect of the Soviet absence. The Attorney-General had stressed in the House of Commons that it was 'unthinkable' that permanent members of the Security Council, 'by violating their duty to be present', should 'by a kind of general anticipatory veto' be able to hold up the work of the United Nations. Prime Minister Attlee had emphasized that the practice of the

[339] Ibid., 5th year, 459th mtg (10 Jan. 1950), pp. 1-4; 460th mtg (12 Jan. 1950); 461st mtg (13 Jan. 1950), pp. 1-10; S/1665, 31 July 1950 (mimeo).

[340] SCOR, 5th year, Supplement for June-August 1950, pp. 29-30, 33-4, 47-9, 77, 79-89, S/1517, S/1523, S/1545, S/1596/Rev. 1, S/1598, S/1600, S/1603; 480th mtg (1 Aug. 1950), pp. 15-16, 20; 482nd mtg (3 Aug. 1950), pp. 4, 8, 17; 486th mtg (11 Aug. 1950), p. 22; 519th mtg (8 Nov. 1950), p. 4; 523rd mtg (16 Nov. 1950), pp. 20-1, 22, 24; 528th mtg (29 Nov. 1950), p. 20; 6th year, 531st mtg (31 Jan. 1951), p. 9.

[341] Britain: SCOR, 5th year, 486th mtg (11 Aug. 1950), pp. 6-7; Nationalist China: ibid., 475th mtg (30 June 1950), p. 15; France: 475th mtg (30 June 1950), p. 15; 487th mtg (14 Aug. 1950), pp. 11-12; 494th mtg (1 Sept. 1950), p. 20; United States: 462nd mtg (17 Jan. 1950), p. 10; 526th mtg (28 Nov. 1950), p. 16.

Council, which the Soviet Union had initiated and supported, had been to regard a voluntary abstention by a permanent member as not constituting a veto. If a permanent member should choose to refrain from exercising its right of voting, 'not by failing to vote when present, but by refraining from attending the meeting at all, that member must be regarded as having deliberately abstained from voting'. On the question of Chinese representation, Attlee pointed out that both Britain and the Soviet Union recognized the People's Republic of China, but the Security Council had accepted as valid the credentials of the representative of Nationalist China. 'Therefore, according to the rules and practice of the Security Council, Dr Tsiang [the Kuomintang ambassador] is at present entitled to occupy the Chinese seat and cast the Chinese vote.'[342]

Although the Soviet Union still maintains that decisions that the Security Council has taken in the absence of a permanent member are null and void, this remains very much a minority view.

---

[342] *Summary of Events relating to Korea*, London, HMSO, 1950 (Cmd 8078), pp. 14-16.

CHAPTER 4

Problems in the field

4.1 DEMARCATING THE LINES OF SEPARATION

If a cease-fire is to be respected, the lines separating the forward
military positions of the parties should be frozen at once and
demarcated as soon as possible. In logic, the demarcation
should be done on the ground initially, if necessary with the
help of impartial international personnel, and later should be
marked on large-scale maps. In the case of the Israel-Syria
demarcation line on the Golan Heights in 1974, Henry Kissinger
produced large aerial photographs with 'extraordinarily ac-
curate detail', and these rather than maps were used for demarcating the line.[1] Even so, the lines did not in all cases correspond
to natural features, leading to permanent violations by both
sides.

While it may be logical to demarcate the line on the ground
first, the crisis atmosphere at the end of a war means that it is
not always possible to follow strict logic. For one thing, UN
observers may not be available to help with resolving differences
of opinion at an early stage. Count Bernadotte wrote that a
major difficulty regarding the cease-fire that took effect in Palestine on 11 June 1948 was that UN observers were not deployed
until well after the fighting had stopped. 'The last group of
observers...reached Palestine only three days before *the end* of
the truce.' It proved impossible to establish the lines as they
had existed when the fighting was supposed to have ended, and
this proved to be 'a serious handicap' in dealing with 'allegations
from each side that the other side was engaged in attempts to
improve its lines or position'. Bernadotte instructed the observers that no military advantage was to accrue to either side

---

[1] William B. Quandt, *Decade of Decisions: American Policy Toward the Arab-Israeli Conflict, 1967-1976*, Berkeley, Los Angeles, and London, University of California Press,
1977, p. 242, n. 51. The International Peace Academy suggests that the lines should
first be delineated on a map and later marked on the ground and translated into a
clear-cut, exact, written description: *Peacekeeper's Handbook*, chapter V, para. 21.

during the cessation of fighting, and this meant maintaining
the military *status quo*. He considered that the value of the
observer operation was to be found 'mainly in the moral and
psychological effect', and Ralph Bunche was to note a year
later that any attempt to maintain the military *status quo* for a
long time inevitably perpetuated conditions that became so
intolerable as to induce one side or the other to undertake
'corrective measures', even if this meant open defiance of an
agreed or imposed cease-fire.[2]

When the second cease-fire went into effect on 18 July 1948,
Bernadotte encountered exactly the same problem as in June;
but once the lines had been established and marked on maps,
difficulties were reduced, although the existence of differing
maps of demilitarized areas in Jerusalem was to cause head-
aches for UN officials until 1967. In the two general cease-
fires in Palestine, as in other cases studied, the number of
incidents and allegations was 'particularly heavy' during the
first few days, when the lines had not been demarcated and the
observers were not in place.[3]

Another difficulty encountered when demarcating the lines
of separation is that the military *status quo* at any particular
time is not likely to take full account of topographical conditions,
still less of the normal needs of the civilian population. In its
proposals of 3 December 1947, the UN Good Offices Committee in Indonesia proposed that the forward military positions
of the parties should be separated by demilitarized zones, and
that the factors to be taken into account in demarcating these
should include not only the military positions of the parties
when the fighting had stopped but also the welfare of the local
population, administrative boundaries, and geographical and
topographical features. The Good Offices Committee stressed
that the welfare of the local population referred not simply to
law and order but to living conditions, interpreted in a common-
sense way. In the event, the agreement reached the following
month on board the USS *Renville* provided for the legitimizing

---

[2] S/1025, 5 Oct. 1948 (mimeo), paras. 16-7 and Annex A, para. 6 (my italics);
SCOR, 4th year, Supplement for August 1949, p. 4, part II para. 5 of S/1357.

[3] S/1025, 5 Oct. 1948 (mimeo), paras. 18, 39; GAOR, 3rd session, Supplement
no. 11, A/648, p. 38, para. 9.

of the lines that had been promulgated the previous August by
the Netherlands Governor-General (the van Mook line).[4] In
the Korean case, the initial position of the Unified Command
in the armistice negotiations was to ask for a line based on
'military realities', but General Ridgway defined these as
referring not only to the actual location of the existing military
front lines but also to 'the necessity of retaining defensible
terrain'.[5]

In discussions about the location of the *status quo* line, both
parties are likely to wish to squeeze military advantage from
the decision. In the Kashmir case, India expressly noted that
the lines would have to run 'close to the Pakistani frontier',[6]
and in Korea, the Unified Command first proposed a line
slightly to the north of the battle lines prevailing at the time, a
line that exceeded the Unified Command's real requirements.[7]

The most difficult cases, however, are those in which the
military forces are intermingled or in which the forces of one or
both of the parties are operating behind the enemy's line: I
consider how this problem might be approached on pages 331-7
below. This situation existed in the Negev after the fighting in
October 1948. Count Bernadotte had written the previous
month that much of the Negev was 'wasteland, where there are
no front lines'. Most of the area was under Egyptian control
when the October fighting began, but there were more than
twenty Israeli settlements in the Negev, and these had been
defended by mobile military forces. Abba Eban, in presenting
the Israeli case to the Security Council, stressed that much of
the Negev had been allocated to the Jews under the UN partition
plan. He noted that before the October fighting Egyptian and
Israeli forces had been 'mingled in a chaotic fashion'. This had
created a situation that was 'impossible in practice and inadmissible in principle'. Following recent military operations, in
which Egyptian forces had been summarily ejected from a

[4] SCOR, 3rd year, Special Supplement no. 1, pp. 10-12, 72, paras. 22, 24 of, and para. 1 of Appendix XI to, S/649/Rev. 1.
[5] SCOR, 7th year, Special Supplement no. 3, p. 2, S/2377; GAOR, 7th session, Annexes, Agenda item 16, p. 5, A/2228; Matthew B. Ridgway, *The Korean War*, pp. 202-3; Vatcher, p. 46.
[6] SCOR, 3rd year, Supplement for November 1948, p. 34, para. 77 (iv) of S/1100.
[7] Vatcher, p. 47; Joy, p. 60.

position of political and military advantage, confusion had been replaced by clarity, conflict by stability. For the first time there was complete unity between the legal and the actual position. It would be folly to return to 'the previous tangle and chaos'.[8]

In its resolution of 4 November, the Security Council asked the Acting Mediator to 'establish provisional lines beyond which no movement of troops shall take place', and it was in pursuance of this resolution that Ralph Bunche established a provisional line, which for Israel ran north of Ashkelon and Majdal, leaving much of the Negev either demilitarized or under Egyptian control. Israel interpreted the Bunche letter as not requiring withdrawal of such Israeli forces as had been south of the Bunche line for defensive purposes before the fighting had broken out, but requiring that forces that had entered the Negev on or after 14 October were to be withdrawn north of the Bunche line.[9] The Security Council had, in any event, by now called for the delineation of permanent armistice lines.[10] The rest of the Negev was taken by Israeli forces in later phases of fighting, and was left under Israeli rule under the 1949 armistices.

In the Indonesian case, demarcation lines had to be established after the round table Conference in the Hague in 1949, and here again 'serious difficulties' were encountered because the armed forces of the Netherlands and the Indonesian Republic were 'closely intermingled'.[11]

It is the need to freeze the situation at short notice that makes cease-fire lines so precarious: truce and armistice lines arise from negotiations between the parties and are likely to contain fewer anomalies. It is usual to mark truce or armistice lines on maps attached to the agreement, although in the Egypt-Israel armistice agreement in 1949, the demarcation line in the Bethlehem-Hebron area was left for settlement between Israel and Jordan.[12] Markers on the ground may be erected, as was

[8] GAOR, 3rd session, Supplement no. 11, A/648, p. 38, para. 9; SCOR, 3rd year, 373rd mtg (26 Oct. 1948), pp. 20-1; 374th mtg (28 Oct. 1948), pp. 17-20.
[9] SC res. 61 (S/1070), 4 Nov. 1948; UN press release PAL/381, 13 Nov. 1948; S/1081, 19 Nov. 1948 (mimeo).
[10] SC res. 62 (S/1080), 16 Nov. 1948.
[11] SCOR, 5th year, Special Supplement no. 1, p. 2, para. 12 of S/1449.
[12] SCOR, 4th year, Supplement no. 3, S/1264/Rev. 1, Art. VI.

repeatedly proposed by UN observers in the Middle East[13] and was provided for in the Korean armistice.

A demarcation line is not a permanent boundary and is not intended to prejudice the rights, claims, or position of any party. In the Israel-Jordan armistice agreement, provision was made for possible revisions of the demarcation line by later agreement between the parties.[14] Any crossing of a demarcation line by military personnel is prohibited, and civilians may cross only with consent.

However much care is taken when lines are demarcated, they are almost certain to seem arbitrary to the local civilian population. Secretary-General Hammarskjold commented in 1956 that the armistice demarcation lines in the Middle East had 'no basis in history or in the distribution of population or private property', and General Odd Bull, at one time Chief of Staff of the UN observer mission, noted that the lines had been demarcated in such a way that many Arab farmers were cut off from their land, yet these unfortunate people failed to qualify for international assistance as refugees because they had not lost their homes. General Bull believed that it was these people who were responsible for much of the infiltration.[15]

UN staff have consistently advocated marking truce or armistice lines on the ground, and in 1956 Hammarskjold informed the Security Council that Egypt and Israel had agreed to the placing of 'conspicuous markers' along the demarcation lines in the Gaza area; but when General Burns, then Chief of Staff of the UN observers, visited Israel the following month, he found that Hammarskjold had misunderstood the Israeli stance: 'Mr Ben-Gurion said Israel had never agreed to it.'[16]

Hammarskjold favoured the erection not only of markers but also of barbed wire or other physical obstacles along the demarcation line in the Middle East. Israel wanted to have two barbed wire barriers with a space between them: Egypt objected to

[13] Burns, p. 80; Bull, p. 51.

[14] SCOR, 4th year, Supplement no. 1, S/1302/Rev. 1, Art. VIII.

[15] Ibid., 11th year, Supplement for April-June 1956, p. 33, para. 12 of S/3596; Bull, pp. 48, 50, 61, 88.

[16] SCOR, 11th year, Supplement for April-June 1956, p. 49, para. 81; Burns, pp. 80, 154; Carl von Horn, *Soldiering for peace,* p. 60; Bull, pp. 51, 60, 62, 74, 78, 176, 190.

obstacles along the line itself but was willing to erect barbed wire fences along 'certain positions' inside the Gaza Strip.[17] Agreement on this matter had not been reached when fighting broke out the following October. When General van Horn took over command of the UN observers in 1958, he complained that the 'ill-defined' armistice lines had still not been marked on the ground. Five years later, General Bull succeeded van Horn, but there were *still* no markers. In some cases, noted Bull, the lines were defined as following water courses or valleys, but these were liable to change after heavy rain. Moreover, the marks on maps indicating the lines had been made with a thick wax pencil, and this represented 'anything from 6 to 40 metres on the ground'. General Bull concluded that the hastily drawn-up demarcation lines between Israel and Jordan 'did more to encourage infiltration across the border than to check it'.[18]

4.2 DEMILITARIZATION

Demilitarized areas are those from which all combatants, weapons, military equipment, and military installations are excluded and from which no hostile military acts or activities in support of or related to the conduct of military operations are undertaken. The immunity of non-defended places from attack was recognized in the Brussels Declaration of 1874[19] and in the Regulations attached to the Hague Conventions of 1899 and 1907 on the laws and customs of war on land.[20] To strengthen that protection, the Geneva Conventions of 1949 provided that, by agreement between the parties, neutralized zones may be created close to the fighting front for wounded or sick persons, both combatant and non-combatant, and for civilians performing no work of a military character; and that hospital and safety zones may be created for wounded or sick

[17] SCOR, 11th year, Supplement for April to June 1956, pp. 49, 64, para. 80 and Annex 8 of S/3596.

[18] Horn, p. 60; Burns, pp. 49, 57-8, 61.

[19] *Documents Relating to the Program of the First Hague Peace Conference,* Oxford, Clarendon Press, 1921, p. 35, Articles 15-17.

[20] *Hague Conventions of 1899 (II) and 1907 (IV) respecting the laws and customs of war on land,* pp. 18-19, Articles 25 and 27.

persons, both combatant and non-combatant, and for specified civilian elements, in thinly populated areas that are free from military objectives and large industrial or administrative establishments.[21] The new Additional Protocol I to the Geneva Conventions again leaves the establishment of special status zones of this kind to the parties: an inhabited place in or near the fighting zone, which is open to occupation by the opposing party, may be given the status of a non-defended locality by declaration or agreement, and demilitarized zones may be created by express agreement between the parties.[22]

Since the Second World War demilitarization has been used for four main purposes.

1. It has provided sanctuary during time of armed conflict for persons who are entitled to be immune from direct attack, that is to say, medical and religious personnel, diplomats, persons responsible for cultural property, and other non-combatants.
2. Special areas have been set aside to facilitate the negotiation and/or the supervision of the cessation of hostilities.
3. Interim demilitarization has been used for areas subject to contending claims regarding sovereignty.
4. Demilitarization has often been used to reduce tension along demarcation lines by means of a disengagement of forces.

The immunity from attack of undefended areas in group 1 is a basic rule of international law: in all other cases, non-military areas have come about as a result of the agreement of the parties, even if the precise demarcation of the limits of the area is left for subsequent negotiation. Thus the Netherlands and the Indonesian Republicans negotiated demilitarized zones for Indonesia in 1948; the *de facto* Jewish and Arab authorities in Palestine accepted the proposal for three civilian sanctuaries in Jerusalem in 1948; Israel and Jordan negotiated in 1948 for a No Man's Land in Jerusalem and for the demilitarization of Mount Scopus, and agreed to respect the neutral status of the former Red Cross sanctuary around Government House;

[21] Geneva Conventions, 1949, I, Article 23 and Annex I, and IV, Articles 14, 15, and Annex I.

[22] A/32/144, 15 Aug. 1977 (mimeo), Appendix I, Articles 59 and 60.

Egypt and Israel agreed to the demilitarization of El-Auja in 1949; Israel and Syria agreed to the demilitarization of the Hula area in 1949; India and Pakistan agreed to demilitarization along the cease-fire line in Kashmir in 1949; and the Unified Command negotiated with North Korea and China for a neutral conference zone around Kaesong and Panmunjom in 1951 and, as part of the armistice, for a buffer zone along the military demarcation line in Korea in 1953.

The Security Council has never sought to impose demilitarization by a mandatory resolution. The Council ordered a mandatory cease-fire in Palestine in 1948, but the proposal for the demilitarization of Jerusalem took the form of an instruction to the Mediator 'to continue his efforts' to bring this about,[23] and the later proposal of the Council for demilitarization in the Negev was to come about as a result of 'negotiations ... between the parties'.[24] In the case of Jammu and Kashmir, the Security Council asked its subsidiary organs to help to bring about demilitarization as a necessary condition for a plebiscite, and asked the parties to negotiate for that purpose—although complete demilitarization was never achieved.[25]

Demilitarization can, of course exist *de facto* and without the express agreement of other interested parties. Egypt kept Sinai substantially demilitarized from 1957 to 1967.[26]

SANCTUARIES DURING ARMED CONFLICT

These are usually established at short notice when fighting is imminent or actually taking place. Interesting examples date from 1948, when three such sanctuaries were established in Jerusalem as a result of an initiative of the International Committee of the Red Cross (ICRC), to some extent modelled on the safety zones established in Madrid in 1936 and Shanghai in 1937. The United Nations and the ICRC had initially hoped

[23] SC res. 54 (S/902), 15 July 1948.
[24] SC res. 61 (S/1070), 4 Nov. 1948.
[25] SC res. 80 (S/1469), 4 March 1950; SC res. 91 and 96 (S/2017/Rev. 1 and S/2392), 30 March and 10 Nov. 1951; SCOR, 7th year, 572nd mtg (31 Jan. 1952), paras. 34-5; SC res. 98 (S/2833) 23 Dec. 1952; SC res. 126 (S/3922), 2 Dec. 1957.
[26] Yair Evron, *The Demilitarization of Sinai,* Jerusalem, Leonard Davis Institute of International Relations, 1975, pp. 6-10; Walter Eytan, *The First Ten Years: A Diplomatic History of Israel,* p. 33; Burns, pp. 134, 170.

that the parties would agree that the entire Jerusalem area should be neutralized and demilitarized, under the UN or perhaps the Red Cross flag. With the intensification of hostilities when the British mandate came to an end in the middle of May, and in the absence of agreement on wider demilitarization, the ICRC proposed a more modest arrangement for three separate zones under Red Cross protection:

Zone 1: the King David Hotel, the YMCA hostel, and the Terra Santa convent

Zone 2: Government House, the Arab College, the Jewish Agricultural School, and the married quarters at the Allenby Barracks

Zone 3: the Italian Hospital and School

Agreement about the zones came about as a result of the acceptance of the ICRC proposals by the *de facto* authorities, the Arabs on 9 May and the Israelis on 17 May. The zones were clearly marked with the Red Cross emblem. The only persons admitted were women and children, together with refugees on a temporary basis while fighting was actually taking place. Civil administration was by the *de facto* authorities, but supervision of the status of demilitarization was by the ICRC. Military personnel were excluded from the zones, and combatants were asked to accord to the zones 'absolute respect'.[27]

Dr Dov Joseph, the first Israeli governor of Jerusalem, wrote that the zones were remote from Jewish areas and that no Jewish women or children found refuge in them: this, in Joseph's view, led to a suspicion among the Jews that the International Committee of the Red Cross, 'possibly through failure to realize the political implications of what they were doing, were serving British interests'. As soon as the state of Israel came into being on 15 May, the Italian Hospital and School (zone 3) were occupied by Israeli forces. 'The Italians', as Dov Joseph put it, 'had agreed to entrust the hospital to Jewish guards', and the sanctuary status of the zone was thus terminated. Count Bernadotte, the UN Mediator, wished to use one of the buildings in

---

[27] *Hospital Localities and Safety Zones*, pp. 26-8; Jacques de Reynier, *A Jérusalem un drapeau flottait sur la ligne de feu*, pp. 87-8; Azcárate, p. 124.

zone 1 for UN staff, but the ICRC objected on the rather
questionable ground that this would violate the neutrality of
the zone. Bernadotte reacted vigorously, and the ICRC consulted the parties and on 15 June handed over the King David
Hotel in zone 1 to the United Nations. The nearby YMCA
provided sanctuary for about eighty-five refugees (although
Dov Joseph suspected that it had become 'a centre of Arab
espionage'), and the Terra Santa convent housed about fifty
more. Mattresses and blankets were supplied by the YMCA,
and non-perishable food came from stocks left by British troops.
Part of the staff of the King David Hotel and the YMCA remained in the zone and worked under ICRC supervision,
though they were employed and paid by the owners of the
buildings. When the fighting was resumed in July, UN staff
left the King David Hotel, which was then occupied by Israeli
forces, whereupon the Arabs concluded that the immunity of
the zone had come to an end and began to fire into it. The
ICRC 'demanded' that Israeli forces should be withdrawn, but
with no success. In the circumstances, the ICRC had no option
but to declare that the immunity of zone 1 would cease, and
this took formal effect on 22 July. Later attempts by the UN
Palestine Truce Commission to create a neutral or demilitarized
area from the former Red Cross zone 1, together with the US
and French consulates, were rejected by Israel.[28]

Until the end of August 1948, the Arab College and the
Jewish Agricultural School in zone 2 housed some thirty Arab
women and children, and Arab women from neighbouring
villages entered the zone each day for medical attention. Food
and medicines were brought in with great difficulty by donkey
from the Old City of Jerusalem. The sanctuary status of the
zone was respected until 16 August, when Israeli forces attacked
Arab positions across the zone and occupied part of the Arab
College and the Jewish Agricultural School, whereupon Arab
forces surrounded Government House. The UN Central Truce
Supervision Board decided that Israeli forces had committed

[28] *Hospital Localities and Safety Zones,* pp. 29-30, 34-5; Report on the work of the
International Committee of the Red Cross, 1 July 1947-31 December 1948, Geneva,
1949, pp. 107-8; Bernadotte, pp. 85, 140; Reynier, pp. 93-4; Azcárate, pp. 10-11,
47-8, 101; SCOR, 3rd year, Supplement for October 1948, pp. 49-50, S/1023; Joseph,
pp. 129, 272, 280-2.

'flagrant violations' by attacking Egyptian positions and remaining within the Red Cross zone. It was clear that the close
proximity of the forces of the two sides had placed the status of
the zone in jeopardy, so the UN Truce Supervision Board
decided to create an enlarged neutral area surrounding the
Red Cross zone, to be supervised by UN observers. After
Bernadotte had threatened UN sanctions, Israeli and Arab
troops that had penetrated the zone withdrew. Count Bernadotte
visited the Jewish Agricultural School on the day of his death,
as he had been told by his Chief of Staff that those in charge
were refusing to comply with the agreement on demilitarization.
'Various defence installations ... had not been removed, and
eighteen young Jews were being housed there contrary to
regulations.' The Israelis had asked to be allowed to bring in
more young men 'to be engaged in cleaning up', but Bernadotte
had refused. When Bernadotte reached the building on 17
September, there was some discussion about the precise terms
of the agreement on demilitarization, and the ICRC representative suggested that they should proceed to the YMCA,
where he kept his papers. It was during this journey that
Bernadotte and a French colleague were assassinated. In
October the ICRC handed over the Red Cross zone to the
United Nations, in accordance with a written understanding of
the previous April. Dov Joseph believed that the departure of
the ICRC was in breach of a promise not to leave without
informing him 'in good time beforehand'.[29]

DEMILITARIZED AREAS FOR THE NEGOTIATION AND/
OR SUPERVISION OF THE CESSATION OF HOSTILITIES

Two areas have been demilitarized to provide a convenient
base for the negotiation and/or supervision of agreements to
cease military operations: Government House in Jerusalem

[29] Joseph, p. 282; *Hospital Localities and Safety Zones*, pp. 31-5; Report of the International Committee of the Red Cross, 1 July 1947-31 December 1948, p. 108; UN doc.
S/992, 7 Sept. 1948 (mimeo); GAOR, 3rd session, Supplement no. 11, A/648, p. 40,
para. 15; SCOR, 12th year, Supplement for July-September 1957, pp. 38-9, 50-1,
para. 3 of and Annex D to S/3892; Jacques de Reynier, *A Jérusalem un drapeau flottait sur
la ligne de feu,* p. 94; Bernadotte, pp. 224, 255-6, 258, 267-8; Azcárate, pp. 124-5;
FRUS, 1948, vol. V part 2, 1976, pp. 1319, 1375.

and the Kaesong-Panmunjom-Munsan conference area in Korea.

The core of the Government House area in Jerusalem had been a Red Cross sanctuary until it was handed over to the United Nations in October 1948, and the demilitarized status was continued when Israel and Jordan concluded a cease-fire agreement for the Jerusalem area on 30 November 1948. During the armistice negotiations in 1949, Israel proposed that, as the zone lay between the two front lines, it should be partitioned, but Jordan refused. The armistice agreement of 3 April 1949 defined the demarcation lines as corresponding to those in the earlier local cease-fire agreement, and they were to be subject to such rectifications as might subsequently be agreed upon by the parties. In June 1949, Israeli forces penetrated the Government House neutral zone, but, after the Acting UN Mediator (Ralph Bunche) had invoked US diplomatic help, the troops withdrew. One difficulty about keeping the area tranquil was the existence of maps held by Israel and Jordan showing different limits for the zone, both initialled by the same UN official.[30]

In the Korean case it was necessary to select a convenient place in 1951 so that the Unified Command and the Communist side could meet to discover if Soviet ambassador Malik's radio address and a number of informal diplomatic approaches provided a satisfactory basis for negotiations. The Unified Command at first suggested that representatives of the two military commands should meet on the Danish hospital ship *Jutlandia* in Wonsan harbour. North Korea and China responded by proposing that the meeting should be in Kaesong, near the 38th parallel. This was accepted by the Unified Command, and discussions were duly opened. Although it had been agreed that the Kaesong conference area should contain no armed personnel except for the minimum needed for military police purposes, demilitarization was not properly respected at first. Armed guards of the Communist side 'infested' the conference area, wrote General Matthew Ridgway: 'Red soldiers with

---

[30] Dayan, p. 115; FRUS, 1949, vol. VI, 1977, pp. 1094, 1098 n. 1, 1114, 1127, 1131-3; Azcárate, pp. 128-9; SCOR, 12th year, Supplement for July-September 1957, pp. 38-42, 50-1, 57, paras. 3-8 of and Annexes D and H of S/3892; Supplement for October-December 1957, p. 1, S/3892/Add. 1.

Tommy guns gruffly ordered our envoys about.' At one point a Chinese unit 'complete with machine guns and 60-mm. mortars' marched directly across the path of jeeps of the Unified Command. Ridgway protested, and provocation by armed personnel from the North ceased. After an incident involving the right of journalists to have access to the conference area, the negotiations were suspended by the Unified Command. The Unified Command, having considered a number of more distant places (including Hong Kong and Port Arthur), then proposed that the two sides should meet in a circular neutral zone with a five-mile radius from the centre of Kaesong, and North Korea and China agreed, on the understanding that a minimum number of personnel with small arms would be allowed into the zone for military police purposes. Both sides violated the Kaesong area, however, whether intentionally or unwittingly, and there was a two-month suspension of nego-tiations. Agreement was finally reached on a new conference area with a radius of 1,000 yards in the vicinity of Panmunjom, joined to two demilitarized areas with a radius of three miles each, one for North Korea and China at Kaesong and one for the Unified Command near Munsan. No hostile acts were to be carried out against the area by regular or irregular forces of either side. Armed personnel were to be excluded from the area, except for military police detachments consisting of two officers and fifteen men from each side. There was to be free access to the area and free movement within it.[31]

Panmunjom was used for the ensuing armistice negotiations, although both sides committed violations of the area. In 1953 Panmunjom was incorporated in a demilitarized buffer zone along the military demarcation line, and it provided a base for the Military Armistice Commission, the Neutral Nations Repatriation Commission, the Indian Custodial Force, the Neutral Nations Supervisory Commission, and various sub-sidiary bodies. There is an agreement between the two sides

[31] SCOR, 6th year, Supplement for July-September 1951, pp. 16-17, 21-5, 35, 53-6, 65-72, 79-80, S/2265, S/2266, S/2277, S/2304, S/2311, S/2326, S/2341; Sup-plement for October-December 1951, pp. 12-13, 36-8, 43-4, 49-50, 57, S/2361, S/2408, S/2410, S/2412, S/2432; 7th year, Special Supplement no. 3, pp. 2-3, S/2377; Supplement for January-March 1952, pp. 6-8, S/2469; Ridgway, pp. 198-202; Hermes pp. 16, 18, 28, 40-50; Joy, pp. 31-6; Vatcher, pp. 3, 5, 24-5, 31-7, 55-66, 73-5; Goodman, pp. xiii n. 3, 39-41, 58-9, 118.

about the Panmunjom joint security area, which in 1976 was divided into two parts, one under North Korean and Chinese control and the other under the control of the Unified Command.[32]

INTERIM DEMILITARIZATION BECAUSE OF CONTENDING CLAIMS TO SOVEREIGNTY

This form of demilitarization was proposed for the Jerusalem area in 1948 and for the whole of Kashmir from 1950 onwards, and was implemented for the Mount Scopus area of Jerusalem in 1948 and the El-Auja and Hula areas in 1949.

The UN partition plan for Palestine had provided that Jerusalem and the surrounding area would be demilitarized and neutral.[33] Partition as envisaged by the General Assembly was never achieved, but just before the resumption of fighting in the Middle East in July 1948, Count Bernadotte proposed to the two sides that Jerusalem should be demilitarized. Israel replied that it was prepared to discuss the idea 'under certain assumptions', but the Arabs gave a rather vague refusal. The Security Council persisted with the matter and, in its resolution of 15 July establishing a mandatory cease-fire, the Council instructed Bernadotte to 'continue his efforts' to bring about the demilitarization of Jerusalem, without prejudice to its future political status. Two days later the Arab League sent a cable to Secretary-General Trygve Lie stating that the Arab states had previously accepted Bernadotte's proposal 'in principle'. Although this message was contrary to Bernadotte's understanding of what had happened earlier in the month, he at once submitted to the two sides a working paper which he hoped would serve as a basis for technical discussion. The Arabs responded by again rejecting demilitarization but agreeing to 'a permanent cease-fire' in Jerusalem, while Israel turned

[32] SCOR, 8th year, Supplement for April-June 1953, pp. 10, 18-19, 32, S/2991, S/2999, S/3017; 30th year, Supplement for October-December 1975, p. 24, para. 2 of S/11861; 31st year, Supplement for October-December 1976, pp. 57-8, paras. 2-3 of S/12263; S/12544, 27 Jan. 1978 (mimeo), para. 2 of Annex; testimony of Maj. Gen. John K. Singlaub to the Investigations Sub-committee of the Committee on Armed Services of the US House of Representatives (HASC 95-71), 25 May 1977, p. 49.

[33] GA res. 181 (III), 29 Nov. 1947, Annex, part III, para. 4 (a).

down Bernadotte's plan because he was at that time intending that Jerusalem should ultimately come under Arab rule. As there was now uncertainty as to precisely what Israel's position was, UN officials pursued the matter with Dov Joseph, the Israeli representative in Jerusalem, who said that Israel had never agreed to demilitarization in principle but had simply indicated that its readiness to discuss any plan 'did not exclude' the possibility of discussing demilitarization, including the demilitarization of Jerusalem. Bernadotte considered that Israel's new position was 'especially regrettable', particularly as the Arabs had by now submitted to Bernadotte their own 'far-reaching' proposal for the demilitarization of Jerusalem. In the circumstances, Bernadotte had no option but to inform the Security Council that demilitarization was unlikely to be attained 'in the near future', although he still believed that demilitarization, more than any other action, would ensure the safety of the Holy Places and religious buildings.[34] His final report to the Security Council proposed that Jerusalem and the surrounding area should be placed under UN control, and the demilitarization of Jerusalem remained a UN aspiration. In 1949 the General Assembly restated its intention to place Jerusalem under a special international régime administered by the United Nations, although the Security Council had some weeks previously decided to postpone indefinitely its discussion of demilitarization.[35]

Demilitarization was, however, achieved for the Mount Scopus area of Jerusalem, comprising the Hadassah Hospital, the Hebrew University, and the village of Issawiya (normally inhabited by Arabs but controlled by Israel) and the Augusta Victoria Hospice (controlled by Jordan). This enclave occupied a key position overlooking Jerusalem. 'Whoever controls Mount Scopus', wrote one senior UN official, 'controls the road northwards to Ramallah and Nablus, and eastwards

---

[34] SCOR, 3rd year, Supplement for July 1948, pp. 61, 79, para. 31 of S/888 and S/906; Supplement for August 1948, pp. 154, 162-3, S/961, S/979; SC res. 54 (S/902), 15 July 1948; GAOR, 3rd year, Supplement no. 11, A/648, pp. 12-13; Bernadotte, pp. 145, 148, 160-1, 163, 186, 189, 195, 203-4, 206-7; Joseph, pp. 281, 312-16.

[35] GAOR, 3rd year, Supplement no. 11, A/648, p. 18, para. 4 (g); GA res. 303 (IV), 9 Dec. 1949; SCOR, 4th year, 453rd mtg (25 Oct. 1949), p. 4.

towards Jericho and Amman.'[36] In April 1948, a Jewish convoy
taking supplies to Mount Scopus had been savagely attacked
by the Arabs in revenge for the carnage at Deir Yasin.[37] The
United Nations was able to secure an agreement about Mount
Scopus just before the renewal of fighting in July 1948 as a
result of a direct meeting between the commanders of the Israeli
and Jordanian forces. The text was hastily written on the back
of an envelope and typed the following day. It provided that the
area delineated on 'the attached map' was to be under the UN
flag and under UN protection, the United Nations being responsible for the security of the area. Access was to be through
UN check posts. All military personnel were to withdraw, and
the area was not to be used as a base for military operations;
nor would it be attacked or unlawfully entered. Arab and Jewish
armed civilian police were to be 'placed on duty under the
United Nations Commander'. Except with the agreement of
the parties, the population was to be limited to those persons
needed for the operation of the area 'plus the present population
of the [Arab] village of Issawiya'. The United Nations was to
ensure the supply of food and water, for visits by 'properly
accredited individuals', and for the replacement of 'necessary
personnel in residence on Mount Scopus'.[38]

The trouble about 'the attached map' was that, as with the
Government House area, there were two of them, showing different lines, both initialled by the same UN official, so that
there were areas regarded by Israel as within their enclave and
by Jordan as outside it.[39]

The armistice agreement between Israel and Jordan (3 April
1949) provided for the creation of a special committee of the

[36] GAOR, 3rd session, Supplement no. 11, A/648, p. 35, para. 18; Burns, p. 158;
Horn, p. 3.
[37] Azcárate, p. 19; Reynier, pp. 69-77, 79-81, 213; Joseph, pp. 77-8; Harry Levin,
Jerusalem Embattled: A Diary of the City under Siege, March 25th, 1948 to July 18th, 1948,
London, Gollancz, 1950, pp. 68-9, 71.
[38] S/1025, 5 Oct. 1948 (mimeo), para. 25; Theodor Meron, 'The Demilitarization
of Mount Scopus: A Regime that Was', *Israel Law Review*, vol. II, no. 4 (1968), p. 519
n. 73; SCOR, 3rd year, 333rd mtg (13 July 1948), p. 3; 8th year, Supplement for
April-June 1953, pp. 30-1, Annex to S/3015; Bernadotte, pp. 86, 137-8, 140-3, 182,
192-4, 197-9; Azcárate, pp. 187-8; Burns, p. 157, Joseph, pp. 248-9, 266, 278-9,
289, 315.
[39] SCOR, 13th year, Supplement for April-June 1958, p. 94, para. 80 of S/4030.

two parties to enlarge the scope of and improve the armistice agreement. Among the matters to be dealt with by the special committee was 'resumption of the normal functioning of the cultural and humanitarian institutions on Mount Scopus and free access thereto'.[40] The committee met a few times but was unable to reach further agreement about Mount Scopus. Jordan wished to maintain the *status quo* until the political climate improved, whereas Israel regarded Jordan's unwillingness to make progress as 'standing non-compliance from the side of Jordan'.[41]

The original Mount Scopus agreement was supplemented in November 1949 by an annex providing that, in the first and third weeks of every month, half of the Jewish personnel in the area would be relieved and that supply convoys would have access to the area, both operations to be under UN supervision.

A year later, the UN Chief of Staff issued a directive about convoys to Mount Scopus. No arms, ammunition, military equipment, or documentary material containing military information were to be allowed in the convoys. Each convoy was to be inspected by UN observers in the presence of Israeli and Jordanian officers, and each convoy was to be protected by the Arab Legion while passing through territory under Jordanian control.[42]

There were frequent difficulties about access to and the policing of Mount Scopus, complicated by inconsistent interpretations of the various agreements. A number of incidents in 1952 and 1953 were investigated by UN observers. In 1957-8, a personal representative of Secretary-General Hammarskjold visited the area and reached new understandings with the governments of Israel and Jordan, designed to clarify and to some extent strengthen the original demilitarization agreement. In particular, the United Nations was to check on the implementation of the original agreement, to assume 'the exclusive

[40] Ibid., 4th year, Special Supplement no. 1, S/1302/Rev. 1, Article VIII.
[41] Ibid., 6th year, Supplement for October-December 1951, pp. 21-2, paras. 28-31 of S/2388; 7th year, Supplement for October-December 1952, p. 18, para. 36 of S/2833; 11th year, Supplement for April-June 1956, pp. 54, 61-2, para. 99 of and Annex 6 to S/3596; 12th year, Supplement for October-December 1957, pp. 13-15, para. 2-11 of S/3913.
[42] Theodor Meron, 'The Demilitarization of Mount Scopus: A Regime that Was', *Israel Law Review,* vol. II, no. 4 (1968), p. 509.

responsibility' for ensuring that convoys conformed to the agreed procedures, and to investigate complaints.[43]

Problems continued,however, particularly in areas in which Arabs lived or worked but which were patrolled by Israeli police. There was a serious incident in 1958 when four Israelis lost their lives and a UN observer, Lt-Col. G. A. Flint of Canada, was killed by a bullet that had almost certainly been fired from territory under Jordanian control. Part of the trouble stemmed from the two maps of the enclave, with Arabs sniping at Israeli police patrolling in a provocative way in the disputed areas.[44]

The question of demilitarizing the Negev arose following the renewal of fighting in October 1948. The Negev contained a number of isolated Jewish settlements which had been defended by Israeli forces, but the bulk of the area was under Arab control. The Security Council called for a cease-fire followed by a withdrawal of forces, but the vacated territory was not to be reoccupied by the Arabs. There would thus be created 'such neutral or demilitarized zones as may appear advantageous'.[45]

Israel was determined to retain the territory taken during the October fighting, and there followed some strenuous negotiations between Ralph Bunche and Abba Eban. Finally, on 13 November, Bunche issued a memorandum that was acceptable to Israel, indicating provisional demarcation lines. There was to be 'an orderly observed withdrawal of forces' from positions in the Negev not held before the fighting started in October and the creation of a wide area from which all patrolling and military movement would be excluded. Movement of

[43] Joseph, pp. 248-9; Eytan, p. 40; E. H. Hutchinson, *Violent Truce: A Military Observer Looks at the Arab-Israeli Conflict, 1951-1955,* New York, Devin-Adair, 1956, pp. 20-9, 40-1, 86-9; Burns pp. 153-4, 157-8, 161; Horn, pp. 83-5, 93-4, 250; Bull, pp. 63-7, 88-91; SCOR, 7th year, Supplement for October-December 1952, pp. 17, 19, paras. 27-8 and 37-8 of S/2833; p. 27, S/2833/Add. 1; 8th year, Supplement for April-June 1953, pp. 28-30, S/3015; 13th year, Supplement for April-June 1958, p. 92, para. 76 and n. 12 of S/4030; UN press release SG/653, 18 Jan. 1958.

[44] SCOR, 13th year, Supplement for April-June 1958, pp. 34-7, 74-101, 130-1, S/4011, S/4012, S/4030; Supplement for July-September 1958, pp. 1-3, S/4030/Add. 1; 22nd year, Supplement for April-June 1967, pp. 60-3, 70-8, 89-90, 92-4, 126-8, S/7867, S/7873, S/7876, S/7882, S/7886, S/7922; Horn, pp. 69, 83-5, 93-4, 250; Bull, pp. 63-7, 70, 88-91.

[45] SCOR, 3rd year, 367th mtg (19 Oct. 1948), pp. 37-8; 374th mtg (28 Oct. 1948), p. 33; 378th mtg (9 Nov. 1948), p. 63; Supplement for November 1948, p. 3, para. 5 of S/1064; SC res. 61 (S/1070), 4 Nov. 1948.

armed forces and military supplies would be at the discretion of the UN observers, but there would be no limitations on the movement of normal non-military supplies. Israel would withdraw from Beersheba, which would become a demilitarized Arab town under an Egyptian civil administrator. All this was to be provisional only, and the good offices of UN personnel would be available to help the parties to establish permanent lines and neutral or demilitarized zones.[46]

In the event, Israel completed the occupation of the Negev in the following months. During the armistice negotiations in Rhodes, Egypt took up Bunche's proposal that Beersheba should have an Egyptian military governor and also suggested that the armistice demarcation line should follow the provisional line that Bunche had proposed on 13 November, on the ground that no advantages gained from a breach of the binding cease-fire should be confirmed in the armistice agreement. Israel regarded the Egyptian proposal for Beersheba as 'absurd' and the matter was not pursued, but it was during the discussion of this that there arose the idea of a demilitarized zone in the El-Auja area.[47]

After Israel had rejected the proposal for an Egyptian governor in Beersheba, Egypt made a similar proposal, first for Bir Asluj and then for El-Auja. Israel was quite unwilling that Egyptian forces should return to El-Auja but offered to withdraw the main body of its own troops from the area, leaving only a token force under UN supervision, and to make El-Auja the seat of the Mixed Armistice Commission. Eventually Bunche put forward a proposal to demilitarize the area completely, and after a certain amount of haggling this was accepted by both Egypt and Israel.[48]

The armistice agreement provided that the village of El-Auja and vicinity should be demilitarized, with both Egyptian and Israeli armed forces totally excluded. The entry of armed forces into the area, or any failure to respect demilitarization, if confirmed by UN personnel, would constitute 'a flagrant violation'

---

[46] UN press release PAL/381, 13 Nov. 1948.

[47] Eytan, pp. 33-5; FRUS, 1949, vol. VI, 1977, pp. 689-90, 707, 718, 749, 752, 755, 760, 764.

[48] FRUS, 1949, vol. VI, 1977, pp. 689-90, 701-2, 705-7, 713, 718-19, 731-2, 734-5, 749, 752, 761; Burns, p. 26.

of the armistice. On the Egyptian side, defensive positions would not be allowed nearer to the zone than Abu Aweigila and Kuseima.[49]

There were increasing difficulties in El-Auja and the surrounding area, and in 1955 Israeli forces entered the zone and Egypt established defensive positions in the prohibited area. When Dag Hammarskjold visited the Middle East in the spring of 1956, he concluded that both Israel and Egypt 'are, or must be presumed to be, to a greater or lesser extent,' violating the armistice agreement. A plan for the restoration of full compliance was submitted to the parties and, reported Hammarskjold, 'has not met with any objections'.[50]

In July 1956 Israel began to restrict the movement of UN observers in the zone, and in the first phase of the Sinai campaign in October Israel took full control. After Israel's withdrawal from Sinai in 1957, the demilitarization of El-Auja was not continued, as Israel took the view that the armistice agreement was no longer in effect.[51]

There was also a demilitarized zone in the Hula area east and north of Lake Tiberias, most of which had been allocated to the Jewish state in the UN partition plan but which had been largely occupied by Syrian or other Arab forces in the fighting in 1948. During the armistice negotiations between Israel and Syria, the most difficult question to resolve was what arrangements should be made for this area, since both parties believed they had a valid claim to it. It was Syria that first proposed demilitarization, and at a later stage Ralph Bunche devised an acceptable compromise whereby three sectors with a total area of slightly over 25 square miles would be demilitarized.[52]

[49] SCOR, 4th year, Special Supplement no. 3, S/1264/Rev. 1, Article VIII; Burns, p. 92.

[50] SCOR, 5th year, Supplement for September-December 1950, pp. 56-8, paras. 2-4 of S/1797; 9th year, Supplement for January-March 1954, p. 5, S/3172; 11th year, Supplement for April-June 1956, pp. 46, 50, 61, paras. 67-71, 84 of and Annex 5 to S/3596; Urquhart, p. 136; Burns, pp. 92-8, 101, 104-7, 134-5, 145-6, 160, 181; Bull, pp. 55-6.

[51] SCOR, 11th year, Supplement for July-September 1956, pp. 58-60, Annex to S/3659; 748th mtg (30 Oct. 1948), paras. 17-18; Eytan, p. 33; Burns, pp. 134, 170.

[52] Bar-Yaacov, *The Israel-Syrian Armistice*, pp. 43-63; Eytan, p. 43; Netanel Lorch, *The Edge of the Sword: Israel's War of Independence, 1947-1949*, London and New York, Putnam's, 1961, p. 448; FRUS, 1949, vol. VI, 1977, pp. 1030-2, 1053-5, 1100-1, 1225, 1231, 1233-5.

It was stated in the armistice agreement that the demarcation lines were to be 'midway between the existing truce lines' or 'along the international boundary', and the demilitarized zone was to comprise the areas between those demarcation lines and the international boundary. Most of the zone had formed part of mandated Palestine, but a narrow strip in the central sector lay on the Syrian side of the frontier. The Hula zone was declared to have a two-fold purpose: to minimize the possibility of friction and incident by separating the armed forces of the two parties, and to provide for 'the gradual restoration of normal civilian life' without prejudice to an ultimate settlement. All military and para-military forces were to be excluded from the zone. The chairman of the Mixed Armistice Commission was empowered to authorize the return of civilians and the employment of 'limited numbers of locally recruited civilian police ... for internal security purposes'.[53] Ralph Bunche made clear during the negotiations that administration in the Hula zone was to be 'on a local basis, without raising general questions of administration, jurisdiction, citizenship, and sovereignty'. The chairman of the Mixed Armistice Commission would not 'assume responsibility for direct administration' of the zone, but local administration would 'take shape' under his general supervision.[54]

The Hula demilitarized zone was a constant source of contention. So long as there was hostility between Israel and Syria, there were bound to be suspicions on both sides. Syria, of all Israel's Arab neighbours, was the least willing to accept Israel's right to exist, still less her right to gain military advantage from demilitarization. There were endless disputes about land cultivation and policing and about the competence of the Mixed Armistice Commission and its UN chairman.[55]

[53] SCOR, 4th year, Special Supplement no. 2, S/1353/Rev. 1, Article V and Annex II.

[54] Ibid., 6th year, 542nd mtg (25 April 1951), para. 98.

[55] Ibid., Supplement for April-June 1951, pp. 17-22, 24-34, 40-58, 72-9, 87-8, 94-105, 111-18, 122-3, 139-42, 158-9, 174-7, part IV of S/2049, S/2067, S/2084, S/2088, S/2099, S/2101, S/2111, S/2113, S/2118, S/2120, S/2122, S/2123, S/2424, S/2127, S/2136, S/2138, S/2139, S/2141, S/2148, S/2173, S/2185, S/2213; Supplement for July-September 1951, pp. 2-4, 44-52, S/2234, S/2300; Supplement for October-December 1951, pp. 5-10, 23-32, S/2359, S/2389; 7th year, Supplement for October-December 1952, pp. 10-27, paras. 45-61 of S/2833; 8th year, Supplement for October-December 1953, pp. 23-36, S/3122; 645th mtg (3 Dec. 1953), paras. 15-20; 10th year,

In the case of Kashmir, the cease-fire was never converted into a truce, but Britain persistently advocated the establishment of neutral or demilitarized zones.[56] India and Pakistan agreed in 1949 to establish a demilitarized buffer zone along the cease-fire line.[57] Demilitarization in this zone was a useful step, but it fell far short of the wish of the Security Council to bring about the complete demilitarization of all of Jammu and Kashmir by the withdrawal of non-Kashmiri tribesmen and Pakistani nationals and the progressive withdrawal of Indian forces.[58]

DEMILITARIZATION IN ORDER TO MINIMIZE TENSION ALONG THE DEMARCATION LINES BY A DISENGAGEMENT OF MILITARY FORCES

Demilitarization of this kind was resorted to in Indonesia (1948), the No Man's Land agreement for Jerusalem (1948), Kashmir (1949), and Korea (1953). U Thant proposed in 1964 that demilitarized buffer zones should be established in Cyprus between the opposing armed forces, but this was criticized by the Greek Cypriots as being likely to perpetuate the notion of partition.[59]

Supplement for January-March 1955, pp. 1-25, S/3343; 11th year, Supplement for July-September 1956, pp. 62-4, 68-70, Section III of Annex and Appendix B to S/3659; 12th year, Supplement for April-June 1957, pp. 4-8, S/3815; Supplement for July-September 1957, pp. 2-9, S/3844; 13th year, Supplement for October-December 1958, pp. 23-32, S/4124; 15th year, Supplement for January-March 1960, pp. 11-50, S/4270; 18th year, Supplement for July-September 1963, pp. 84-139, S/5401 and Adds; 21st year, Supplement for October-December 1966, pp. 51-4, 64-8, S/7561/ Rev. 1, S/7573; SC res. 93 (S/2157), 18 May 1951; Bar-Yaacov, pp. 66-113, 182-213, 283-7, 318-38; Burns, pp. 111, 113-18; Horn, pp. 69, 77-80, 115-25; Bull, pp. 49-52, 54, 77, 87-8, 95, 101-3, 110.

[56] FRUS, 1948, vol 5 part 1, 1975, p. 447.

[57] SCOR, 4th year, Special Supplement no. 7, pp. 126-9, Annex 26 of S/1430/ Add. 1; See also map in SCOR, 5th year, Supplement for September-December 1950, p. 52, S/1791, Annex II.

[58] SC res. 80 (S/1469), 4 March 1950; SC res. 91 and 96 (S/2017/Rev. 1 and S/2392), 30 March and 10 Nov. 1951; SCOR, 7th year, 572nd mtg (31 Jan. 1952), paras. 34-5; SC res. 98 (S/2833), 23 Dec. 1952; SC res. 126 (S/3922), 2 Dec. 1957.

[59] SCOR, 19th year, Supplement for July-September 1964, pp. 291, 337, paras. 33 and 232 (b) of S/5950; 1151st mtg (16 Sept. 1964), para. 22.

Indonesia In the negotiations following the Netherlands 'police action' in Indonesia in 1947, the UN Good Offices Committee (GOC) included in its first plan a provision for demilitarized zones, to be established on the basis of proposals submitted by the parties, taking account of geographical and topographical features. If the parties should not be able to agree on the limits of the zones, the matter would be referred to the GOC. All military personnel together with arms and equipment would be withdrawn, but civil police would remain. The zone would be supervised by the military observers. This element of the Good Offices Committee's plan was acceptable to the two sides, but the Netherlands was not satisfied with other aspects.[60]

When the truce was finally agreed on board the USS *Renville*, the demilitarization arrangements proposed by the GOC were repeated, with four additional provisions:

1.   the 'average width' of the zones was to be 'approximately the same' on each side of the *status quo* line;
2.   the zones were to be without prejudice to the rights, claims, or position of the parties;
3.   the term 'civil police' did not exclude the temporary use of military personnel under civil control for police purposes;
4.   the zones were to be expanded as the atmosphere improved.

Demilitarized zones were delineated in most areas without difficulty, but the Netherlands opposed a proposal to extend the depth of the zones on the ground that the Republican side had not put a complete stop to infiltration and espionage. Demilitarization continued until the second Dutch 'police action' in December 1948.[61]

Jerusalem A demilitarized No Man's Land was created in Jerusalem in 1948 as a result of an agreement concluded under UN auspices between the Israeli and Jordanian military commanders. The limits of the area were fixed 'as far apart as possible' and were to be marked on the ground with barbed

[60] Ibid., 3rd year, Special Supplement no. 1, pp. 10-13, paras. 22-4 of S/649/Rev. 1.
[61] Ibid., pp. 72-5, Appendix XI; Supplement for June 1948, pp. 58, 144-5, chapter V of S/787 and chapter V of S/848/Add. 1.

wire. Even civilians were to be excluded from living in the area, but they were to have access to one well between the German Hospital and the Hebrew University, and the Arab Hospital at Beit Safafa was to be 'respected as a medical institution'. One Arab police station was to be allowed in the zone at an agreed location, and limited patrols by the Arab Legion were to take place in part of the zone at the discretion of the UN Mediator. A UN observer was to visit the area 'regularly' to ensure that the agreement was being observed. There were special provisions whereby civilians could enter the zone to recover personal possessions, for the removal of Arab municipal records of a non-military nature, for the recovery of Jewish articles of religious value, and for the return of disabled Arab ambulances. The UN Mediator later reported that the Agreement was 'generally accepted and adhered to', though a small number of incidents had occurred.[62]

Fighting was resumed in July 1948, and when a mandatory UN cease-fire went into effect it was not possible to renew the No Man's Land agreement. There was, however, a *de facto* no man's land between Israeli and Jordanian forces, running from Jerusalem to Latrun and beyond, which was 'considered to be in United Nations hands'. This situation was confirmed in the armistice agreement, but when military officers from the two sides came to demarcate the lines they were attacked by angry villagers, who objected to having their land and houses divided up on the basis of military convenience. There was a show of force by the two armies the next day and the disagreeable task was duly completed.[63]

Kashmir   In the Kashmir case, the cease-fire line was demarcated by the Indian and Pakistani military commanders in 1949. It was agreed that troops on each side would remain at least 500 yards from the line except for one sector along a river. Provision was also made for a demilitarized area running south from Minimarg to the agreed demarcation line, from which troops were to be entirely excluded.[64] The demilitarization of

[62] S/845, 21 June 1948 (mimeo); S/1025, 5 Oct. 1948 (mimeo), para. 23; GAOR, 3rd year, Supplement no. 11, A/648, p. 35, para. 18.
[63] GAOR, 3rd year, Supplement no. 11, A/648, p. 41, para. 24; Dayan, pp. 115-16.
[64] SCOR, 4th year, Special Supplement no. 7, pp. 126-9, Annex 26 of S/1430/Add. 1.

the Minimarg area continued *de facto* after the wars of 1965 and 1971.[65]

Korea Britain repeatedly proposed that, when the fighting in Korea stopped, a demilitarized buffer zone should be established to separate the military forces of the two sides, but General MacArthur considered this to be a cowardly device to protect the North Korean régime, and he said that Britain's policy of appeasing the Communists reminded him of Munich.[66]

Both parties to the armistice negotiations favoured the creation of a buffer zone when the fighting stopped, and the first substantive item of the agenda concerned the fixing of a demarcation line between the two sides 'so as to establish a demilitarized zone'. The Communist side proposed a zone 10 kilometres in depth on each side of the 38th parallel, whereas the Unified Command wanted a zone 20 miles wide following or slightly to the north of the military line of separation. As negotiations proceeded, both sides modified their positions, and in the end agreement was reached on a demilitarized zone 2 kilometres in depth on each side of the line of contact at the time the armistice went into effect. It took only a week when fighting was quiescent for officers of the two sides to draw up the boundaries for the demilitarized zone.[67] Suitable markers were to be erected along the limits of the zone, under the supervision of the Military Armistice Commission. No hostile acts were to take place within, from, or against the zone, and the only persons allowed in the zone would be those concerned with relief or civil administration (not exceeding 1,000 from each side) and persons specifically authorized to enter by the Military Armistice Commission. The number of civil police and the arms to be carried by them should be specified by the

[65] I am grateful to George Sherry of the UN Secretariat for information on this point (letters of 16 Feb. 1979, 21 Feb. 1979, 15 March 1979).
[66] Acheson, p. 465; Courtney Whitney, *MacArthur: His Rendezvous with History,* New York, Knopf, 1956, pp. 411, 417; Shiv Dayal, *India's Role in the Korean Question: A Study in the Settlement of International Disputes under the United Nations,* Delhi, Chand, 1959, p. 118.
[67] SCOR, 7th year, Special Supplement no. 3, pp. 11-12, S/2507; Hermes, pp. 113-19, 484-5; Vatcher, pp. 79-86, 201; Leland M. Goodrich, *Korea: A Study of US Policy in the United Nations,* pp. 187-8; Ridgway, pp. 202-3, 255.

Military Armistice Commission, which was also empowered to authorize other personnel to carry arms.[68]

There have, in the event, been numerous violations of the demilitarized zone, of which the most spectacular were the tunnels constructed by North Korea under the zone.[69]

RESPECT FOR DEMILITARIZATION: THE UN EXPERIENCE

In wartime emergency, a non-defended sanctuary may be created hurriedly without much attention to such matters as the limits of the area, which categories of protected persons shall have access, how it shall be supervised, and the emblems to be used to indicate its non-military status. Sanctuaries may be created in areas enjoying diplomatic immunity or under Red Cross or UN protection, but they are likely to be short-lived: they soon will either lose their non-military status or be converted into more enduring kinds of demilitarized area.

In the two studies by the UN Secretary-General on human rights in armed conflict, considerable attention was devoted to procedures that might be used for establishing civilian sanctuaries. In the first report, the Secretary-General suggested that four 'conditions and requirements' would need to be taken into account: (1) that the designation and recognition of civilian sanctuaries should be possible in time of peace; (2) that the creation of sanctuaries should not confer military advantages on any party to a conflict; (3) that sanctuaries should be identified by special markings and insignia; and (4) that an effective and realistic 'system of control and verification' would be needed. In his second report, the Secretary-General suggested that 'limitation of accommodation and other circumstances' might make it necessary to establish priorities for admission to sanctuaries: first, wounded and sick civilians, the aged, children under fiteen, expectant mothers and mothers of children under seven; then 'as large a part of the civilian population as possible'; and it was noted that all of these categories are already entitled to protection under international law. The Secretary-

---

[68] SCOR, 8th year, Supplement for July-September 1953, pp. 22-3, Article I.

[69] Ibid., 30th year, Supplement for October-December 1975, pp. 24-5, Annex to S/11861; Goodman, pp. 41, 58-9, 118.

General, taking account of the provisions of the Hague Convention for the Protection of Cultural Property, thought that it might be necessary to establish in time of peace an international register of civilian sanctuaries.[70] The work of the UN Secretary-General in 1969 and 1970 was of considerable help when Additional Protocol I to the Geneva Conventions was being drafted.

It would seem that there is almost always a general obligation to respect the status of non-military areas, since one or more of three circumstances will normally obtain.

1. The area is demilitarized and undefended because it contains protected persons, buildings, or installations.
2. The status of demilitarization arises from agreement between the parties. If there is agreement to demilitarize, it must be assumed that the area consists entirely of territory under the sovereignty of one or other of the parties or is the subject of their contending claims. If all claimants have agreed to demilitarization, the status would seem to be valid for others, since the right to make or exclude military deployments on one's own territory cannot normally be challenged.
3. The status of demilitarization arises from a binding resolution of the Security Council under Article 40 of the Charter.

The Kaesong-Panmunjom-Munsan conference area of Korea continues to be demilitarized, and there are still buffer zones in Kashmir and the Middle East. Much of the experience of non-military zones since 1945 comes from the Middle East, which may be *sui generis* because of incompatible territorial claims.

Except when the status arises from the presence of protected persons, demilitarization provides no security in time of war, and Professor N.Bar-Yaacov insists that the object of a demilitarized zone is 'confined to peacetime'.[71] Israel has occupied several demilitarized areas in preparation for or in the

[70] A/7720, 20 Nov. 1969, paras. 145-52, and A/8052, 18 Sept. 1970, paras. 45-87 (both mimeo).

[71] Bar-Yaacov, pp. 157, 318. It is possible to capture and occupy an undefended sanctuary without attacking protected persons.

course of hostilities: two of the Red Cross sanctuaries in Jerusalem in May and July 1948; the El-Auja demilitarized zone in
1955; and the Jerusalem-Latrun No Man's Land and the
Mount Scopus and Hula demilitarized zones in 1967.

Demilitarized areas in my groups 2, 3, and 4 above (p. 231)
have features in common, and similar problems tend to arise.

It hardly needs stressing that the perimeters of such areas
should be clearly delineated both on large-scale maps and by
physical markers on the ground, as has been done for the joint
security area in Korea. It is difficult enough if there is a lack
of congruence between maps and ground-markers, but a pre-
posterous situation arises if (as was the case for the Mount
Scopus and Government House areas of Jerusalem) there exist
inconsistent official maps. A party may be reluctant to have the
perimeters of a non-military area marked on the ground for
fear that a line on the ground in course of time becomes an
international frontier: that was why Israel objected to marking
the limits of the Hula demilitarized zone. It should be affirmed,
however, as Israel has often stressed, and as Ralph Bunche
noted in the Hula context, that demilitarization does not *per se*
affect sovereignty.[72]

Any agreement to create a non-military area should provide
for a prohibition of weapons and military installations other
than those that are expressly permitted, and there should be
agreement about over-flights by military aircraft.

General Odd Bull, with considerable experience of UN
operations, believes that, for the effective supervision of demilitarized areas, it is necessary for international military forces
to be stationed on the ground. 'The experience of UNTSO
showed that observers alone are not enough.'[73] But whatever
system of supervision and monitoring is used, there should be
the possibility of random checks both inside the area and of
persons and materials entering it. The experience with sophisticated sensors and surveillance techniques used by the US-
manned Sinai Field Mission since 1975 could be of great importance for the effective supervision of other non-military

---

[72] Ibid., pp. 57, 64, 84-6, 320; Burns, p. 113; Bull, pp. 50, 51, 103.
[73] Bull, p. 176.

areas.[74] The normal principles regarding freedom of movement of supervisory personnel should apply.

The question of personnel allowed to reside in or visit non-military areas is even more difficult than the question of military hardware. In theory it would seem straightforward to admit civilians, including medical staff and chaplains, and fighters who have been rendered *hors de combat* (sick and wounded) as well as specified categories of personnel for guard and security duties, but this hardly takes account of persons who are farmers by day and irregular fighters by night. Palestinian guerrillas have often operated from primarily civilian refugee camps, and the Israeli *nahal* is a settlement of young people undertaking both agricultural and military functions.

Moreover, in inhabited areas there is police work to be done, and in many parts of the world it is customary for some or all police to bear arms. General Burns of Canada, who headed the UN observer organization in the Middle East and later commanded the UN Emergency Force in Sinai, has noted that Israeli frontier police 'are more than an ordinary police-force … they are all trained soldiers [and] their introduction into the [Hula] demilitarized zone was essentially a violation of the demilitarization principle...' Generals Carl von Horn and Odd Bull, both of whom served as chief of staff of the UN observers, have written of the provocative activities of the Israeli police in the Mount Scopus demilitarized enclave. One of them records how the police 'tricked' the UN observers, who then 'broke faith' with the other party to the demilitarization agreement. One senior UN official always places the word 'police' in inverted commas when writing of the Israeli activities in the Mount Scopus area, and he also mentions more than once that Israeli police in the Hula demilitarized zone used armoured personnel carriers.[75] Agreements for non-military areas usually provide for civilian police for the purpose of maintaining law and order, but after the *Renville* agreement on Indonesia, the parties accepted as a temporary

---

[74] Eight half-yearly reports have been made to the US President and transmitted to Congress. It is understood that a history of the establishment and activities of the mission is in draft.

[75] Burns, pp. 96, 114, 117; Horn, pp. 69, 83-5, 93, 119, 123; Bull, pp. 65-7.

measure that military personnel under civilian control might be used for police purposes.[76] The Mount Scopus agreement specified maximum numbers of police and stated that they would be 'placed on duty under the United Nations Commander'—an unhappily ambiguous phrase.[77] In the Kaesong conference area in Korea, a minimum number of military police were allowed, but General Ridgway considered that the Communists were not respecting the agreement when they introduced personnel with machine-guns and mortars.[78] In an ideal world, policing of non-military areas would be done by UN personnel, but then an ideal world would be one large non-military area and policing would be unnecessary.

It is usual to specify whether limited numbers of military personnel should be allowed in non-military areas for security and guard duties, as well as the arms they may carry. In the agreement on the headquarters area for the Military Armistice Commission in Korea, the number of 'security personnel' from each side is specified, and it is laid down that each man is allowed one rifle or one pistol. Even an agreed limitation of this kind is no guarantee that difficulties will not occur, or that seemingly trivial incidents will not escalate. In 1976, a group of security guards from the Unified Command were trimming a tree in the joint security area near Panmunjom when they were attacked by North Korean guards, and two US officers, one of whom was unarmed, were beaten to death with clubs and axes.[79]

None of the non-military areas since 1949 was expressly created in accordance with the Geneva Conventions, and non-military areas have not yet been established in accordance with Additional Protocol I. The importance of the Geneva texts is not that they should be followed to the letter, but that they constitute guidelines to be adapted to differing circumstances. The disadvantage of the provisions of Additional Protocol I, as became apparent in a conference of government experts con-

[76] SCOR, 3rd year, Special Supplement no. 1, S/649/Rev. 1, p. 73, Appendix XI, Article 5; Supplement for June 1948, p. 145, S/848/Add. 1, Chapter V, section 6.

[77] Ibid., 8th year, Supplement for April-June 1953, p. 31, S/3015, Article 4.

[78] Ridgway, p. 199.

· [79] SCOR, 31st year, Supplement for October-December 1976, p. 59, para. 6 of S/12263.

vened by the International Committee of the Red Cross, is
that they may be thought to have the effect of weakening the
general protection to be extended to civilians.[80] This can hardly
be prevented by clever legal drafting, however: it is a problem
of psychology rather than of law.

4.3 SUPERVISORY PERSONNEL

The most immediate task in the field after the fighting has
stopped is to stabilize the line of separation and to institute a
dependable system for deterring violations, for settling local
incidents, and for reporting substantial and deliberate infractions. While in theory this could be undertaken jointly by
the parties, in practice the amount of suspicion at the end of a
war is almost always such that independent assistance is needed.
Joint patrolling by the adverse parties along all of the cease-
fire lines in Palestine had been proposed by the United States
in 1948, but the idea had caused hilarity in UN circles in the
field. Pablo de Azcárate, the secretary of the UN Palestine
Conciliation Commission, gives one example of short-lived
joint supervision: for a few weeks in 1949, Israel and Jordan
operated joint patrols for the protection of Government House,
the UN base in Jerusalem. Azcárate had been sceptical about
the 'bold experiment' at Government House, but he found that
it 'functioned perfectly efficiently'.[81]

Three other systems of supervision have been used: military
observers seconded from local consular posts, UN observers
forming a single integrated organization, and a commission
consisting of military officers from countries nominated by the
contending parties. Since 1956, peace-keeping forces have also
served an interposition and supervisory role and, in the Middle
East, have been consolidated with UN observer operations.
Even in cases where the parties have negotiated an armistice
agreement and have established a joint commission to deal with
military problems, it is necessary to supplement this with a
supervisory organization not under the control of either of the

---

[80] *Report on the Work of the Conference of Government Experts on the Reaffirmation and
Development of International Humanitarian Law Applicable in Armed Conflicts*, Geneva,
ICRC, 1972, para. 3. 205.

[81] FRUS, 1948, vol. V part 2, 1976, pp. 1251-2, 1264-5; Azcárate, pp. 127-8.

parties (the UN Truce Supervision Organization in the Middle East, the Neutral Nations Supervisory Commission in Korea).

INDONESIA

The first supervision of a UN cessation of fighting was in Indonesia and was by military assistants (as they were called) from the consular offices of the six states that formed the Consular Commission in Batavia (Djakarta) (see page 257).[82] The call to cease hostilities in Indonesia was approved by the Security Council on 1 August 1947. As this was the first occasion on which the Security Council had called for fighting to stop, there were no precedents about the means for supervising the situation on the ground, nor was there a UN organ in the field that could improvise arrangements. Australia proposed that the Security Council should appoint a commission to facilitate negotiations for a just and lasting settlement and to assist in the observance of the cease-fire, and the Netherlands responded with a suggestion that 'all the career consuls stationed in Batavia [Djakarta] should jointly and immediately ... draw up a report on the present situation ...' China then submitted a text in the form of an amendment to the Australian proposal, which would have noted the Dutch intention about consular representatives and have accepted it as a step in the right direction. Australia did not object to the consuls being asked to help but wanted to bring them within the authority of the Security Council. A provision to that effect was then incorporated in a new proposal co-sponsored by Australia and China. A Soviet proposal to replace the Consular Commission by a body composed of all the members of the Security Council was vetoed by France, and the proposal of Australia and China was then approved.[83] On 1 September, twenty-seven military officers attached to the

---

[82] SCOR, 2nd year, Special Supplement no. 4, S/586/Rev. 1, p. 1; 3rd year, Supplement for June 1948, p. 57, S/787; 6th year, Special Supplement no. 2, pp. 33-4, Appendix II to S/2087; Alastair Taylor, *Indonesian Independence and the United Nations*, Ithaca, NY, Cornell University Press, 1960 (under the auspices of the CEIP), p. 424, n. 74; Alastair Taylor, 'The Indonesian Independence Conflict (1945-1950)', London, RIIA, 1966 (mimeo), p. 11.

[83] SCOR, 2nd year, 185th mtg (15 Aug. 1947), p. 2013; 187th mtg (19 Aug. 1947), pp. 2066-7, 2070-1; 193rd mtg (22 Aug. 1947), pp. 2173-4; 194th mtg (25 Aug. 1947), pp. 2196-7; SC res. 30 (S/525, I), 25 Aug. 1947.

Table 6

Military observers in Indonesia

		Oct. 1947	May 1948	Feb. 1950	Sept. 1950
Members of the Good Offices Committee	Australia	4	15	9	3
	Belgium	2	4	9	3
	United States	8	15	9	3
Other members of the Consular Commission	China*	4	5	–	–
	France	3	6	4	2
	United Kingdom	4	10	4	2
		25	55	35	13

* In May 1949 the military observers from Nationalist China were withdrawn.

consular representatives were asked to observe the orders to
cease hostilities and to investigate alleged breaches, but after a
few weeks the number of military observers had dropped to fifteen.[84]

When the Good Offices Committee (GOC) reached Indonesia
at the end of October, the Consular Commission suspended its
work and the military observers from the three members of the
GOC (Australia, Belgium, United States) continued the task of
observation and investigation. Although the GOC would have
liked to have had more observers, it decided not to make use of
the military officers from the three countries forming the Consular Commission but not belonging to the GOC, although
senior representatives from these countries attended certain
meetings in a non-voting role.[85]

After the *Renville* truce agreements on 17 January 1948, the
GOC was able to increase the number of military observers to
fifty-five, but later the number dropped to about fifty. A military
executive board consisting of the senior military assistants from
each country was set up in Batavia, with the United States as
permanent chairman. Often the evidence available to the GOC
was 'inadequate and irreconcilable'. The military executive
board sent weekly reports on the situation to the GOC, but the
GOC did not consider it necessary to report every violation to
the Security Council. The GOC reported in May 1948 that the
cease-fire orders had 'generally been well observed'.[86]

KASHMIR

In the Kashmir case, there was initially an unsupervised cease-
fire. The UN Commission for India and Pakistan was provided
with a Military Advisor in 1949, and it was with his assistance

[84] SCOR, 2nd year, Special Supplement no. 4, S/586/Rev. 1, p. 1; Organization
and Procedure of United Nations Commissions, Memorandum by the Secretary-
General to the Interim Committee of the General Assembly, no. IV, Consular Commission at Batavia, 1949, para. 17.

[85] Ibid., paras. 45-51.

[86] SCOR, 3rd year, Supplement for June 1948, pp. 57, 62, S/787; Organization
and Prodecure of United Nations Commissions, Memorandum by the Secretary-
General to the Interim Committee of the General Assembly, no. V, Good Office
Committee on the Indonesian Question, paras. 77-84.

that the parties were able to demarcate the cease-fire line. The parties agreed that their forces would remain at least 500 yards from the line and that there would be no increase of forces or strengthening of defences. It was subsequently agreed that the following activities would constitute breaches of the cease-fire agreement:

1. approaching closer than 500 yards to the cease-fire line or crossing the line;
2. firing and using explosives within five miles of the cease-fire line without giving advance warning to UN observers;
3. new wiring or mining of positions;
4. reinforcement of forward defended localities or strengthening of defences;
5. forward movement of war-like stores, equipment, and personnel other than reliefs and maintenance;
6. over-flying of the territory of the other side.[87]

Table 7

Military observers in Kashmir

	Sept. 1949*	Sept. 1954*
Australia	-	8
Belgium	8	5
Canada	8	7
Chile	-	2
Denmark	-	2
Mexico	6	-
New Zealand	-	3
Norway	5	-
Sweden	-	2
United States	15	8
Uruguay	-	1
	—	—
* plus 4-8 air crew.	42	38

[87] SCOR, 4th year, Special Supplement no. 7, pp. 126-9, Annex 26 to S/1430; 20th year, Supplement for October-December 1965, p. 344, para. 4 of S/6888.

About forty observers were recruited, as shown in Table 7.[88] US observers were progressively withdrawn after Nehru had criticized the United States for sending arms to Pakistan, and Finland and Italy then provided three observers each. The observers fromed a single and integrated organization, the UN Military Observer Group in India and Pakistan (UNMOGIP).[89]

PALESTINE

When Count Bernadotte set about supervising the cease-fire in Palestine in June 1948, he was improvising in much the same way as the United Nations had done in Indonesia the previous year. There was one important similarity between Indonesia and Palestine, and that was the confusion arising from the existence of two different bodies in each area concerned with supervising the cease-fires: the Good Offices Committee and the Consular Commission in Indonesia, and the truce supervisors recruited by Bernadotte and the Consular Truce Commission in Palestine. The Consular Truce Commission (which had decided in April to call itself the Palestine Truce Commission) asked on 23 May to be provided with non-British military advisors, preferably with experience of the Arab world. The President of the Security Council for the month (France) proposed transmitting the request to the three governments forming the Truce Commission, and the Council seems to have agreed—although the official records of the Council are not absolutely clear on this point.[90]

On the day after the Palestine cease-fire entered into force, Count Bernadotte and the Truce Commission decided that the Commission would supervise the cease-fire and deal with incidents in Jerusalem and that the Mediator would be respon-

[88] Ibid., 4th year, Special Supplement no. 7, S/1430, pp. 27, 31, paras. 147, 164; Sylvain Lourié, 'The United Nations Military Observer Group in India and Pakistan', p. 22; FRUS, 1948, vol. V part 1, 1975, pp. 369-70, 453; 1949, vol. VI, 1977, pp. 1686-8.

[89] Lourié, p. 22; SCOR, 20th year, Supplement for October-December 1965, p. 7, para. 4 of S/6699/Add. 9.

[90] SCOR, 3rd year, 299th mtg (21 May 1948), p. 3, S/762; Supplement for May 1948, pp. 97-8, S/778; 306th mtg (27 May 1948), pp. 13-14, 16-17; GAOR, 3rd session, Supplement no. 11, A/648, pp. 33, 35-6, 41-2, paras. 8, 15-20, 23-30.

sible elsewhere. Bernadotte reported to the Security Council
that the respective spheres of authority were 'somewhat vague
and ... never clearly defined', and just before the second cease-
fire took effect the Truce Commission asked the Security
Council to 'specify its exact functions ... in particular with
regard to its collaboration with the Mediator'. It had originally
been intended that the International Committee of the Red
Cross (ICRC) would handle relief supplies for both sides in
Jerusalem, but when it was discovered that this would be contrary to ICRC 'internal policy', responsibility was transferred
to the Truce Commission.[91]

After the first cease-fire had entered into force, Count Bernadotte recruited 5 Swedish officers, 31 officers each from Belgium,
France, and the United States, and 70 US technical personnel,
and Secretary-General Trygve Lie arranged for 51 guards from
the UN Secretariat to be transferred to the Middle East, giving
the observation mission a total paper strength of 219.[92] After
the second cease-fire had entered into force, Bernadotte asked
for 50 officers and 50 enlisted men from Belgium, and 125
officers and 125 enlisted men each from France and the United
States, together with 10 Swedish officers, 78 technical personnel
from the United States, and 4 from France. While this gave a
paper strength of over 700, actual strength probably never
went much beyond 500 (table 8). As in Kashmir, these observers formed a single integrated entity, the UN Truce Supervision Organization (UNTSO). Observers were later recruited
from Sweden, Denmark, Canada, New Zealand, and other
Western countries.[93]

UNTSO supervision was buttressed after 1949 by four Mixed
Armistice Commissions (MACs) composed equally of Arab
and Israeli military officers under UNTSO chairmanship,

[91] SCOR, 3rd year, Supplement for May 1948, p. 38, S/732; Supplement for June
1948, pp. 83-4, para. 5 (8) of S/829; Supplement for July 1948, pp. 53-4, 89, paras.
14-15 of S/888 and part VII of S/915; Supplement for August 1948, pp. 84-5, S/938;
GAOR, 3rd session, Supplement no. 11, A/648, pp. 33, 35, paras. 5, 7; Joseph,
pp. 227-33.

[92] S/1025, 5 Oct. 1948 (mimeo), para. 3. Bernadotte's final report refers to 'some
10 auxiliary technical personnel' from the United States, but the actual number was
about 70 (GAOR, 3rd session, Supplement no. 11, A/648, pp. 32-3, para. 2).

[93] GAOR, 3rd session, Supplement no. 11, A/648, p. 37, para. 4; Hutchinson,
p. 6; Higgins *United Nations Peacekeeping, 1946-1967*, vol. 1, p. 71.

although these bodies very quickly fell into disuse. On crucial, issues, the members of the MACs from the parties were ranged against each other, so the vote of the UNTSO chairman was decisive. General Vagn Bennike, who served as UN Chief of Staff in 1953-4, reported that 'one delegate acted as the prosecuting attorney, the other [as] defence [attorney], and I had to sit as a judge, without the benefit of a jury.'[94] When it became

Table 8

Military observers in Palestine

	First cease-fire	Second cease-fire
Sweden: military officers	5	10
Belgium: military officers and enlisted men	31	100
France: military officers and enlisted men	31	250
France: technical personnel	-	4
United States: military officers and enlisted men	31	250
United States: technical personnel	70	78
UN guards	51	51
	—	—
	219	743

impossible to hold formal MAC meetings, it was often possible for UNTSO to arrange sub-committee meetings or other informal contacts between the parties.[95]

The first heads of UNTSO, originally known as Chief of Military Staff and later as Chief of Staff, were appointed by the UN Mediator, but later appointments were by the Secretary-General. The head of UNMOGIP, known as Chief Military Observer, has always been appointed by the Secretary-General. The heads of observer missions have themselves recruited military observers from countries not involved in the immediate

---

[94] SCOR, 8th year, 635th mtg (9 Nov. 1953), p. 21.
[95] Ibid., 7th year, Supplement for October-December 1952, pp. 19-20, paras. 39-41 of S/2833; 10th year, Supplement for October-December 1955, pp. 30-1, para. 28 of S/3516.

situation, and civilian staff have been assigned from the UN Secretariat.[96]

In the case of the military observers in Indonesia, there was perplexity about how military personnel could reconcile a national oath of allegiance with loyalty to the United Nations. Because of this difficulty, orders and directives to the military observers were transmitted through the senior national military assistant, subject to the approval of his own consul general.[97] No problems in this regard were encountered in the integrated organizations in Kashmir and Palestine.

UN personnel cannot operate without the consent of the host country, except when undertaking enforcement measures under Chapter VII of the Charter. Naturally, there are cases of uncertain or disputed sovereignty, but UN practice has been to deal with the *de facto* authorities. Host governments have sometimes sought the right of veto about the nationalities from which supervisory personnel shall be drawn. UN Secretaries-General have recognized that this is a matter of genuine concern to the host country, but they have insisted that the final decision has to be taken by an organ of the United Nations.

The functions of supervisory personnel were defined by Count Bernadotte in 1948 in his first instructions to observers. The main task was to apply the cease-fire 'in such a manner as to ensure that no military advantage will accrue to either side'. The observer should report immediately any war-like act or failure to follow the conditions of the cease-fire. Breaches by one side did not release the other side from its obligations. The observer had no executive authority to prevent violations, but he was to ensure that any violating party was fully acquainted with 'the conditions and interpretations' of the cease-fire. The observer should investigate all complaints of alleged violations, referring 'matters of serious concern' to his superior officer.[98]

Supervisory personnel must be fully mobile and have their own communications and transport equipment, including aircraft. During the cease-fires in the Middle East in 1948, UN

---

[96] For General von Horn's difficulties with civilian staff, see Horn, pp. 68, 71-4, 235-8.

[97] SCOR, 3rd year, Supplement for June 1948, p. 57, S/787.

[98] S/928, 28 July 1948 (mimeo); S/1025, 5 Oct. 1948 (mimeo), Annex A.

observers had the use of naval vessels to help in verifying the arms embargo, but it was never possible to secure the agreement of the parties for a naval patrol on Lake Tiberias.[99] After the Sinai-Suez War in 1956, Israel proposed that the United Nations should institute a naval patrol in the Strait of Tiran, but Hammarskjold took the position that this would 'go beyond the prevention of belligerent acts' and was not possible within the resolutions of the General Assembly.[100]

The observer is entitled to the right of access to all military positions and to buildings or places not under military control if he has reason to suspect that they are being used in connection with a violation. UN aircraft should enjoy 'certain rights of over-flight over the territory of the host country'. In the Palestine case, the Security Council expressly called on governments and authorities to allow UN observers 'ready access to all places where their duties require them to go including airfields, ports, truce lines and strategic points and areas', to facilitate freedom of movement and transport of UN personnel, and to ensure their safety and safe-conduct.[101] Restrictions on the freedom of movement of supervisory personnel have varied from petty interference with day-to-day operations, such as delays in authorizing travel, to the complete suspension of UN observation by the authorities of the host country prior to and during military operations.[102]

---

[99] SCOR, 3rd year, Supplement for July 1948, p. 124, S/929; S/1025, 5 Oct. 1948 (mimeo), para. 4; GAOR, 3rd year, Supplement no. 11, A/648, p. 37; Burns, pp. 215, 219-20.

[100] Lourié, p. 25; GAOR, 11th session, Annexes, Agenda item 66, p. 71, A/3563; Urquhart, p. 209.

[101] SC res. 30 (S/525, I), 25 Aug. 1947; S/1025, 5 Oct. 1948 (mimeo), Annex A, paras. 6-8; SC res. 59 (S/1045), 19 Oct. 1948; See also SC res. 66 (S/1169), 29 Dec. 1948; S/1308, 16 April 1949 (mimeo); SC res. 93 (S/2157), 18 May 1951; SCOR, 8th year, Supplement for July-September 1953, p. 25, S/3079, para. 13 (j); SC res. 108 (S/3435), 8 Sept. 1955; SC res. 113 (S/3575), 4 April 1956; SCOR, 11th year, Supplement for April-June 1956, pp. 37, 52, paras. 27, 91 of S/3596; SC res. 114 (S/3605), 4 June 1956.

[102] For obstruction of UN observers in the Middle East, see SCOR, 3rd year, Supplement for October 1948, pp. 46-8, S/1022; 365th mtg (14 Oct. 1948), pp. 18-20; 373rd mtg (26 Oct. 1948), pp. 4, 5, para. 3 of part I and para. 9 of part II of S/1055; Supplement for December 1948, pp. 300-5, S/1152, S/1153 and Corr. 1; 11th year, 748th mtg (30 Oct. 1956), para. 17; GAOR, 1st ESS, Annexes, Agenda item 5, p. 10, A/3284; Hutchinson, pp. 79-80; Burns, pp. 52-7, 90, 95-7, 106, 139, 159-60, 167, 170, 172, 179-81, 184, 186, 188, 195, 277; Horn, pp. 69-70.

Host governments have not always been happy with the idea of foreign military observers having freedom of movement on their territory, and some have tried to pre-empt UN surveillance by inviting observation by personnel more amenable to guidance or control. When pressure began to mount for the participation of the Security Council in a plebiscite in Hyderabad, Prime Minister Nehru sought to forestall UN involvement by inviting the diplomatic corps in New Delhi to see for themselves what was happening.[103] In January 1949, at a time when UN observation was suspended, the Netherlands authorities in Indonesia arranged for military and naval liaison officers attached to 'some of the consular officials in Batavia' (Djakarta) to go on a conducted tour of military areas, but the UN Good Offices Committee informed the Security Council that these were not military observers of the United Nations and that their reports were 'not available' to the Committee of Good Offices, 'even if their tour was the type of field investigation and observation required by the functions of the Committee'.[104]

Difficulties arose in both Indonesia and Palestine because supervisory personnel had been entrusted with responsibilities by more than one subsidiary organ of the Security Council (the Consular Commission and Good Offices Committee in Indonesia,[105] the Truce Commission and the Mediator in Palestine[106]). In the Middle East there were difficulties after 1949 because UNTSO personnel had responsibilities under resolutions of the Security Council and different responsibilities under the armistice agreements.[107]

Count Bernadotte and his staff came to the conclusion that the mediating and supervisory functions should not be entrusted to the same person or organ. When UN observers in Palestine had to take strong positions on infractions of the cease-fire, this inevitably endangered Bernadotte's mediatory role. In Kashmir and Cyprus, the diplomatic and peace-keeping functions were

[103] FRUS, 1948, vol. V part I, 1975, pp. 411, 421 no. 1.
[104] SCOR, 4th year, Supplement for January 1949, p. 16, para. 15 of S/1189.
[105] Ibid., pp. 16-18, para. 16 of S/1189, S/1190; SC res. 67 (S/1234), 28 Jan. 1949.
[106] Azcárate, pp. 80-93.
[107] David Brook, *Preface to Peace: the United Nations and the Arab-Israel Armistice System,* pp. 100-1.

separated, and it is not now the practice to place supervisory and mediating responsibilities on the same person.[108]

Most UN observers would like to have the most efficient equipment to which the parties will agree: light reconnaissance aircraft, helicopters, armoured vehicles, naval vessels. Where infiltration is a problem, UN observers should be provided with tracker dogs and sophisticated detection devices of the kind that have proved so successful with the US-manned Sinai Field Mission. It would be desirable for inspections of non-military areas or zones of limited armaments to be conducted without advance warning, but the parties are understandably reluctant to agree to this. Agreement should if possible be reached for a limited area of demilitarization around each observation post so as to avoid a situation in which UN observers are used as a shield for military operations. UN observation requires men of high calibre, impartiality, independence of judgement, 'capable of putting up with isolation, a hostile environment, climatic extremes, and unjustified criticism'.

National governments have not scrupled to seek to undermine the loyalty of UN personnel: human failure is unavoidable, but the record of those who have served with the United Nations in this role is on the whole a distinguished one.[109]

KOREA

In Korea, the system of supervision was quite different from the seconded military officers in Indonesia and the integrated observer organizations in Kashmir and Palestine. The form of supervision in Korea resulted from negotiations between the parties before the armistice entered into force. We know something of these negotiations from the twice-monthly reports of the Unified Command to the Security Council, and from a number of books by persons who had access to US records.[110]

[108] Lourié, p. 24.

[109] Horn, pp. 57-9, 62, 87-9, 98-114, 237; Bull, pp. 54, 92, 133, 135, 147, 152, 154-5, 162-9, 177; Lourié, p. 28.

[110] SCOR, 7th year, Supplement for January-March 1952, pp. 22-3, S/2514; Special Supplement no. 3, pp. 16-17, 26, 32-4, 54-5, 82-3, 92-3, 100, S/2541, S/2550, S/2593, S/2605, S/2619, S/2629, S/2662; Supplement for July-September 1952, pp. 2, 14-18, S/2700, S/2715; Hermes, pp. 121-9, 152-6, 160-3, 166-7; Vatcher, pp. 40, 63-6, 75-87, 90-103, 109-13; Joy, p. 124.

The agenda for armistice negotiations in Korea contained an item that was neither simple nor elegant: 'Concrete arrangements for the realization of a cease-fire and an armistice in Korea, including the composition, authority and functions of a supervising organization for carrying out the terms of a cease-fire and armistice'. The previous item of the agenda had concerned the military demarcation line and the establishment of a demilitarized zone. It was known that negotiation on supervision would be difficult, since North Korea and China would hardly welcome the kind of strict and unfettered supervision that the Unified Command believed to be necessary to detect, and therefore to deter, violations. The main issues to be negotiated on supervision were the level of military capabilities of the two sides, the limits on troop rotations, the composition of the supervisory organ, and the system of inspection to be used.

It was agreed without difficulty that there should be an armistice commission formed on an equal basis from the two sides. The Unified Command proposed a military freeze, to which North Korea and China countered with a proposal for the total withdrawal of foreign troops, which effectively would have led to the disappearance of forces from both China and the Unified Command. In the end, the position of the Unified Command prevailed, subject to limits on the rotation of forces.

The Unified Command began by proposing a limit on the rotation of troops at 75,000 a month, to which the Communists responded with a proposal for 5,000 a month: agreement was eventually reached on a maximum of 35,000 a month.

It was soon agreed that inspection teams should be drawn from neutral nations, but negotiations on who exactly had been neutral over Korea lasted for many months. It was not until the final phase of negotiation that it was agreed that a Neutral Nations Supervisory Commission should consist of military officers from Czechoslovakia, Poland, Sweden, and Switzerland.

It was agreed that inspection teams should be based on ports of entry and centres of communication, with 'convenience of movement', whatever that may mean. General Ridgway wanted to propose that there should be forty inspection teams, but Washington insisted that this should be scaled down. In the negotiations, the Unified Command initially proposed inspection from twelve ports of entry in each part of Korea, the Communists suggested three each side, and agreement was eventually reached on five each side. The Unified Command proposed that ground inspection should be reinforced by aerial reconnaissance, but this was not seriously intended and was soon abandoned. A proposal of the Unified Command for a ban on the rehabilitation of military airfields proved very troublesome, and the Unified Command eventually withdrew its proposal on this.

There was disagreement as to whether the inspection teams should simply report to the armistice commission (proposed by North Korea and China) or be responsible to and subject to the directions of the commission (proposed by the Unified Command). Agreement was eventually reached on all three: 'shall be responsible to, shall report to, and shall be subject to the direction of...'

Following the Sinai-Suez war, a peace-keeping force (the UN Emergency Force, UNEF) was interposed between the forces of Egypt and those of the invaders, and UNEF was supplemented by the residue of UNTSO operating in the Egypt-Israel sector. In Cyprus, supervision was undertaken by the UN Force (UNFICYP), which included a police contingent.

4.4 PEACE-KEEPING FORCES

SINAI-SUEZ

The form and functions of the first UN peace-keeping force were determined by the particular circumstances confronting the United Nations following the invasion of Sinai-Suez in 1956. Ostensibly, Britain and France had intervened to separate the belligerents and protect the Suez Canal. Although few people took such pretensions at face value, Lester Pearson of Canada quickly saw that the most effective way of inducing the European invaders to withdraw was to build on the claim of Britain and France to have intervened only until the United Nations was itself able to interpose an international force between the Egyptian and Israeli armies.

The concept of an international force deployed along the armistice demarcation lines had been under consideration in a rather desultory way for a year or more. General Burns, head of the UN observer mission in the Middle East, had discussed the possibility with Anthony Eden in London, and later with Selwyn Lloyd when the latter visited Israel. The need in November 1956 was to create a force that could effectively separate the Egyptians and the invaders without the operation being considered by Egypt as an instrument of coercion. That is why there was so much stress on Egyptian consent as a *sine qua non.*[111]

If credit for the idea of an interposition force was largely due to Lester Pearson, it was Dag Hammarskjold and his closest colleagues in the UN Secretariat, and General Burns in the Middle East, who added flesh to Pearson's skeleton. The first resolution of the General Assembly had defined the purpose of the force as being 'to secure and supervise the cessation of hostilities'. Supervision was already a responsibility of the UN Truce Supervision Organization: the new element was how to 'secure' the cease-fire, a conveniently imprecise expression. Although the force was to be composed of military units and was therefore 'more than an observers' corps', it was not entering Egyptian territory to fight anyone, and it was not an army of occupation or an arm of the host government. Its tasks in the initial stage were defined by Hammarskjold as being 'to help maintain quiet during and after the withdrawal of non-Egyptian troops, and to secure compliance with the other terms established in the resolution [997] of 2 November 1956'. In the first phase, the force would physically replace the Anglo-French forces in the Suez Canal area, though it would have different functions. In the second phase, Israeli forces would withdraw eastwards from Sinai and then from the Gaza Strip, and the international force would follow, continuing to separate Israeli and Egyptian armed forces. In a third phase, of uncertain duration, the force would help to maintain quiet along the

---

[111] GAOR, 1st ESS, 561st plenary mtg (1 Nov. 1956), paras. 79, 111; 563rd plenary mtg (3/4 Nov. 1956), paras. 281, 292, 303; Pearson, vol. 2, pp. 244-7; Urquhart, pp. 176-8; Burns, pp. 98-9, 136-7, 217.

border, ideally deployed on both sides of the armistice demarcation line, but if necessary on the Egyptian side only. Hammarskjold later suggested that the force should be deployed in
the Sharm El-Sheikh area as well 'in support of mutual restraint',
and this was approved by the General Assembly and accepted
by the parties.[112]

The creation of an international force, in the UN view, did
not affect the validity of the armistice agreement or the legal
status of the territory on which the force was deployed, although
Israel had taken the position that the armistice agreement was
no longer in effect. Egypt co-operated with the UN Emergency
Force (UNEF) in preventing infiltration into Israel, and infiltrators apprehended by UNEF were handed over to the
Egyptian authorities. When incidents occurred, the parties
used different procedures: Egypt continued to submit complaints to the Mixed Armistice Commission, which Israel was

Table 9

Composition of the UN Emergency Force

	15 Sept. 1957	31 July 1964
Brazil	545	629
Canada	1,172	971
Colombia	522	-
Denmark	424	428
Finland	255	-
India	957	1,265
Indonesia	582	-
Norway	498	495
Sweden	349	538
Yugoslavia	673	607
	5,977	4,933

[112] GAOR, 1st ESS, Annexes, Agenda item 5, pp. 14, 19-22, A/3289, A/3302;
11th session, Annexes, Agenda item 66, pp. 9-10, 42-4, 47-50, 57-9, 72-3, A/3375,
A/3500 and Add. 1, A/3512, A/3527, A/3568; 12th session, Annexes, Agenda item 6,
pp. 5-7 paras. 30-47 of A/3665; 13th session, Annexes, Agenda item 65, pp. 9-12,
15-17, 27-32, paras. 5-23, 51-71, 148-93 of A/3943; GA res. 998 (ES-1), 4 Nov. 1956;
1000 (ES-1), 5 Nov. 1956; 1001 (ES-1), 7 Nov. 1956; 1125 (XI), 2 Feb. 1957;
Urquhart, pp. 177-81, 209-10; Burns, pp. 188-92, 247; Pearson, vol. 2, pp. 253-4,
256-7, 272.

boycotting, while Israel submitted complaints to UNEF. The same person, General Burns, acted in the dual role of Commander of UNEF and Chief of Staff of the UN Truce Supervision Organization for the Egypt-Israel sector.[113]

CYPRUS

While the Suez Canal and Gaza areas are densely populated, much of the work of the UN Emergency Force was in the rough terrain of the Sinai desert with only a nomadic population. Conditions were very different in Cyprus, which was well provided with an administrative infrastructure and means of communication, but where Greek-speaking and Turkish-speaking Cypriots often lived cheek by jowl. When the request came to establish an international force for Cyprus in 1964, the United Nations had been engaged in peace-keeping in the Gaza-Sinai area for seven years, and was on the point of completing a difficult peace-keeping operation within the Congo (Zaire). There were thus two precedents to guide Secretary-General Thant, and an attempt was made to learn from the past. In particular, a distinction was made between military, political, and mediatory tasks, and these responsibilities were allocated to three different persons.

The mandate of the Cyprus Force (UNFICYP) was 'to use its best efforts to prevent a recurrence of fighting and ... to contribute to the maintenance and restoration of law and order and a return to normal conditions'. UNFICYP was to be stationed on the territory of Cyprus and, as in the case of UNEF, it was not to fight anyone or to serve as an army of occupation or as an arm of the government. Except in Nicosia and Lanarca, there were no front lines along which UNFICYP could be deployed, only a series of places where tension might at any time erupt into violence.[114]

The agreement between the United Nations and the government of Cyprus provided that UNFICYP should enjoy 'freedom

[113] GA res. 1125 (XI), 2 Feb. 1957; GAOR, 13th session, Annexes, Agenda item 65, pp. 16-17, paras. 60, 66-74 of A/3943.
[114] SC res. 186 (S/5575), 4 March 1964; SCOR, 19th year, Supplement for April-June 1964, pp. 12-16, 87-93, 105-10, 211-43, S/5653, S/5671, S/5679, S/5764; Supplement for July-September 1964, pp. 280-337, S/5950.

of movement throughout Cyprus', but UNFICYP encountered many attempts to obstruct its work, mainly by the Cyprus government and the Greek community.[115] UNFICYP sought to disarm trouble-makers and to eliminate provocative fortifications, and in some cases UNFICYP itself dismantled fortifications when negotiations with the parties failed to produce positive results. To the extent possible, freedom of communication for all communities was restored. While UNFICYP was not able to prevent a major build-up of arms, it 'kept a careful watch' on the situation and ensured that Secretary-General Thant was fully informed.

There were endless difficulties over such matters as armed soldiers wearing police uniform, freelance irregular fighters, and the provocative activities of extremist elements not under the control of the communal authorities; and for a time a pirate radio station was able to disrupt air traffic control at Nicosia. All incidents were investigated, but proposals for buffer zones in areas of special tension and for joint patrols by the two communities were rejected. Much of UNFICYP's time was spent in caring for and protecting those civilians who had been displaced by the fighting and in trying to recover persons taken hostage in acts of retaliation. UNFICYP had its own police contingent, but it was not possible to persuade Turkish-speaking police or officials to return to an integrated service. Every effort was made to restore the judiciary, public utilities, and social services, and to resume normal economic life.

UNFICYP was often fired on by both sides, and U Thant considered that UNFICYP was 'in the most delicate position that any United Nations mission has ever experienced... A civil war is the worst possible situation in which a United Nations peace-keeping force can find itself'.[116] While it is true that a cease-fire after a civil war is precarious, Thant's judgement about the delicacy of the situation in Cyprus was perhaps

[115] SCOR, 19th year, Supplement for January-March 1964, p. 178, S/5634; Supplement for July-September, 1964, pp. 128-30, 152-3, 285-7, S/5843, S/5869, paras. 13-19 of S/5950.

[116] Ibid., Supplement for April-June 1964, pp. 91-3, 107-9, 213-36, 238-40, Annex I to S/5671, paras. 4, 10-13 of S/5679, paras. 7-55, 61-99, 103, 107, 113-14, 117, 120 of S/5764; Supplement for July-September 1964, pp. 285, 290-7, 303-25, 333, 335-6, paras. 11, 32-61, 94-100, 103-95, 221, 229.

over-dramatic. But at least UNFICYP was in place when the crisis came in August 1964, and the fighting was contained with only minimal external intervention.[117]

Table 10

Composition of the UN Force in Cyprus, 4 December 1964

	Military	Civilian police
Australia	-	40
Austria	48	34
Canada	1,146	-
Denmark	996	40
Finland	962	-
Ireland	1,060	-
New Zealand	-	20
Sweden	844	40
United Kingdom	1,049	-
	6,105	174

Personnel with UN peace-keeping forces serve in national contingents. Secretary-General Hammarskjold recognized that UN military personnel cannot be under the same formal obligations as staff members of the Secretariat, but he expected 'full loyalty to the aims of the [United Nations] Organization' and abstention from acts that might deprive UN peace-keeping of its international character. The Regulations for UN forces in Gaza-Sinai and Cyprus provided that members, 'although remaining in their national service', are, during their assignment to the United Nations, 'international personnel under the authority of the United Nations' and 'subject to the instructions of the Commander', through the chain of command.[118]

UN peace-keeping forces have to take care that their activities do not impinge excessively on internal or local problems and do

[117] SCOR, 19th year, Supplement for April-June 1964, pp. 220-1, paras. 41-2 of S/5764; Supplement for July-September, pp. 297-304, 326-9, 337-40, 350-1; 396-9, paras. 62-92, 96, 196-206 of S/5950, S/5950/Add. 2, S/5954, S/5992.

[118] ST/SGB/UNEF/1, attached to A/3552, 21 Feb. 1957; GAOR, 13th session, Annexes, Agenda item 65, pp. 24, 29-30, paras. 127-9, 168 of A/3943; ST/SGB/UNFICYP/1, 25 April 1964.

not have the effect of promoting or obstructing any particular political solution. UN personnel should act with restraint and impartiality. They are supposed never to take the initiative in the use of armed force, which may be used only in self-defence or to prevent the UN operation itself from being jeopardized. Force should be used only when all peaceful means of persuasion have failed. Should it be necessary to resort to arms, advance warning should be given whenever possible, the principle of minimum force should always be applied, and firing should continue only as long as is necessary to achieve its immediate aim.[119]

UN military forces should, of course, operate in accordance with the relevant norms of international law, and the question has arisen whether or not the United Nations should become a party to the appropriate international instruments. The International Red Cross movement has taken the view that the best course would be for the United Nations to adopt a solemn declaration accepting that the Geneva Conventions apply to its peace-keeping forces, and that those responsible for national contingents should ensure that their forces comply with the Conventions and help to prevent infringements. In 1969, the President of the International Committee of the Red Cross went further and proposed to Secretary-General Thant that the United Nations should, by regular accession, 'formally undertake to have applied the Geneva Conventions ... each time the forces of the United Nations are engaged'. Thant's line was that humanitarian principles would be best protected if states providing military contingents would apply the humanitarian conventions rather than by having the United Nations 'undertake obligations whose discharge would involve the exercise of an authority it has not yet been granted'.[120]

[119] GAOR, 13th session, Annexes, Agenda item 65, pp. 17, 27, 29-31, paras. 70, 149, 166-7, 178-9 of A/3943; SCOR, 19th year, Supplement for April-June 1964, pp. 14-15, paras. 16-19 of S/5653; Supplement for July-September 1964, p. 283-4, paras. 7 (b) and (c) of S/5950.

[120] Report on the work of the International Committee of the Red Cross for 1963, Geneva, 1964, pp. 49-50; A/7720, 20 Nov. 1969 (mimeo), para. 114 and p. 102; A/8781, 20 Sept. 1972 (mimeo), paras. 216-19; A/9669, 12 Sept. 1974 (mimeo), p. 32, n. 52; A/10195, 5 Sept. 1975 (mimeo), p. 28, n. 42; A/31/163, 18 Aug. 1976 (mimeo), p. 26, n. 19; Allan Rosas, *The Legal Status of Prisoners of War: A Study in International Humanitarian Law Applicable in Armed Conflicts,* pp. 108-9, 236-9; D. W. Bowett and others, *United Nations Forces,* London, Stevens, 1964 (under the auspices of the David Davies Memorial Institute), pp. 484-516.

4.5 VIOLATIONS

The primary purpose of a supervisory or peace-keeping system is not to detect violations: it is to deter them. A subsidiary purpose is to settle incidents as promptly as possible on a local basis and to report any substantial and deliberate infringements to an appropriate agency.

The most effective form of supervision is when the parties freely co-operate to do the job jointly, but usually the conflict that led to the fighting results in such a degree of suspicion that the parties have no alternative but to call on third-party assistance. Local commanders' agreements had an important role in the Palestine case, mainly in the Israel-Jordan sector. That was how the demilitarized areas in Jerusalem were brought into existence, and there were several subsequent local agreements of fixed or unlimited duration. The UN Truce Supervision staff played a crucial role in initiating and facilitating the necessary contacts between the parties. The local commanders' agreements provided for regular meetings between the parties and in several cases for a direct telephone link. In 1953 there were weekly meetings at eleven different points along the Israel-Jordan demarcation line. Matters covered by the agreements included the exchange of information needed to maintain tranquility along the armistice line, the prevention of sniping, the apprehension of infiltrators, and the never-ending problem of straying cattle. Incidents were if possible resolved without resorting to the formal machinery of the Mixed Armistice Commission or UNTSO. The Chief of Staff of UNTSO told the Security Council that Jordan had attributed more importance to local commanders' agreements and regular meetings of the parties than had Israel. Abba Eban confirmed that this was so, but he added that Israel would not be discouraged by disappointment.[121]

As noted above, four other systems of supervision were used in the cases studied: by military officers seconded from local

---

[121] SCOR, 6th year, Supplement for October-December 1951, p. 19, para. 21 of S/2388; 7th year, Supplement for October-December 1952, pp. 12-13, para. 14 of S/2833; 8th year, Supplement for April-June 1953, pp. 38-9, para. 2 of S/3030; 630th mtg (27 Oct. 1953), paras. 29-42; 635th mtg (9 Nov. 1953), para. 55 and pp. 17-19, 25, 36-9; 637th mtg (12 Nov. 1953), paras. 83-4; 10th year, Supplement for April-June 1955, pp. 25-6, S/3394; Hutchinson, pp. 18-19, 42, 100-2; Burns pp. 71-3, 80-1; Brook, pp. 114-21.

consular offices (Indonesia); by observers recruited from countries not involved in the conflict, integrated into a single organization (Kashmir, Palestine); peace-keeping by forces composed
of national contingents drawn from countries not involved in the
conflict, under a single command (Sinai-Suez, Cyprus); and supervision by a commission drawn from 'neutral nations' (Korea).

INDONESIA

Military observers were provided by consular offices in Batavia.
The observers visited the main operational areas and hoped, by
their presence, to have a calming effect. When incidents occurred, an attempt was made to establish the facts by questioning military and civilian leaders as well as members of the
public on both sides. The Consular Commission considered
that no useful purpose would be served by reporting in detail to
the Security Council on all of its investigations.[122]

After the Good Offices Committee (GOC) had reached
Indonesia, it worked out a new set of procedures for investigating complaints. The GOC and the observers were to be free
to move in the territories of both parties. Investigations could
be conducted at the request of either side or on the initiative of
the GOC itself. Both parties were asked to co-operate in providing facts, but members of the GOC should not be given
confidential information 'under conditions which bind them to
silence'. Advance warning should be given of major military
movements.[123]

Teams of two to four observers were deployed along the status
quo lines and made daily observation trips on both sides of the
line. Incidents inside the demilitarized zones were investigated
by the observers, and reports of the investigations went to the
GOC: incidents outside the demilitarized zones were in practice
not investigated unless there were prima facie evidence that
they had been instigated by the official authorities of one of
the parties. Observers investigated incidents, advised the

---

[122] SCOR, 2nd year, Special Supplement no. 4, S/586/Rev. 1, pp. 10-14; Organization and Procedure of United Nations Commissions, Memorandum by the
Secretary-General to the Interim Committee of the General Assembly, no. IV,
Consular Commission at Batavia, 1949, paras. 41-3.
[123] SCOR, 3rd year, Special Supplement no. 1, p. 14, para. 29 of S/649/Rev. 1.

parties on the maintenance of law and order, and assisted in demarcating the *status quo* lines and demilitarized zones.[124]

KASHMIR

The observers formed an integrated organization and were divided into small teams and stationed along the cease-fire line. In addition to the investigation of complaints, the observers sought to prevent civilians from entering the buffer zone along the cease-fire line and confirmed the agreed military deployments. Investigation of incidents was undertaken on the initiative of the observers or at the request of one or both parties. Reports on incidents, including recommendations for action to be taken by the parties or the Chief Military Observer, were sent to the headquarters of the observation mission. In the occasional cases of actual fighting, the observers merely reminded the local military commanders of their cease-fire obligations, and this was enough to end the fighting. Both parties at one time or another erected new military installations or encroached on the demilitarized buffer zone, and there were the usual problems of civilian infiltrators and straying cattle. The Chief Military Observer made a routine monthly report to the UN Secretary-General, and reported more frequently at times of special tension.[125]

PALESTINE

Great difficulties were encountered in supervising the two general cease-fires in Palestine, partly because both sides had no confidence that the cease-fires would hold and therefore planned to resume military operations at an advantageous

[124] Ibid., pp. 72-5, Appendix XI; Supplement for June 1948, pp. 58, 62-3, 145-6, S/787, S/848/Add. 1; Organization and Procedure of United Nations Commissions, Memorandum by the Secretary-General to the Interim Committee of the General Assembly, no. V, Good Office Committee on the Indonesian Question, paras. 80-6. After the second Dutch 'police action', a similar system of supervision was put into effect: see SCOR, 5th year, Special Supplement no. 1, pp. 5-8, paras. 24-34 of S/1449; FRUS, 1949, vol. VII part 1, 1975, pp. 478-82, 519-21.

[125] SCOR, 20th year, Supplement for October-December 1965, p. 344, para. 5 of S/6888; Lourié, pp. 23-4, 28-30.

juncture, and partly because of the provocative activities of private armies and other fighters not under the control of the recognized parties to the conflict. The opposing forces in Jerusalem were very close to each other and tension was high. During the month of the first cease-fire, there were 131 complaints by Israel of violations in the Jerusalem area and 39 complaints by the Arabs, and the observers investigated 27 incidents on their own initiative. Most cases involved sporadic sniping where it was impossible to identify the party that had committed the first breach, but there were also cases of erecting new fortifications and barricades as well as of looting. In spite of the many incidents, there was no major outbreak of fighting in Jerusalem during this period. The situation during the second cease-fire was more tense, and both the Truce Commission and the UN Mediators made a number of special reports to the Security Council.[126]

In other parts of Palestine, there was a certain amount of sniping, and in some cases lengthy exchanges of fire; and there were many complaints of harvesting of crops across the midpoint between the cease-fire lines or of firing on those engaged in harvesting. Bernadotte reported that the Arabs 'did not seem to understand' that the rules of land warfare did not entitle them to harvest their crops if it meant crossing into Israeli-held territory.[127] Both sides tried to improve their military positions by erecting fortifications or road blocks, digging trenches, laying mines, emplacing guns, occupying hills or strategic junctions, or moving troops or military supplies. An Arab airliner over Arab territory was shot down by an Israeli fighter and there were Arab complaints of over-flights by Israeli aircraft; these flights were probably for reconnaissance purposes or to drop supplies. Surprisingly, there were very few specific complaints that the arms embargo was being violated.

[126] SCOR, 3rd year, 299th mtg (21 May 1948), p. 3, S/762; Supplement for August 1948, pp. 151-4, S/961; 354th mtg (19 Aug. 1948), pp. 40-1, S/977; S/1025, 5 Oct. 1948 (mimeo), paras. 26, 40; GAOR, 3rd session, Supplement no. 11, A/648, pp. 33, 35-6, 41-2, paras. 8, 15-20, 23-30.

[127] S/1025, 5 Oct. 1948 (mimeo), para. 41; Burns, pp. 49-50, 70; Bull, pp. 48, 50, 61, 88.

The United States twice warned that aircraft from the United States might be proceeding to Israel in contravention of official US policy, and Britain reported that two tanks from Haifa had disappeared. There was constant Arab interference with Israeli convoys, and both the Arabs and Israel obstructed the work of UN observers. Complaints were investigated by UN observers and, if possible, settled locally. Where an incident could not be resolved locally, the report of the observers was sent to UN headquarters at Haifa for settlement by the UN Chief of Staff or, in the most serious cases in 1948, by a Central Truce Supervision Board. These decisions were then reviewed by the Mediator and, if approved, were forwarded to the parties concerned. Only major breaches that could not be rectified by these procedures were reported to the Security Council. There were fewer complaints during the second cease-fire, but the incidents were 'on the whole, more serious than during the first period', and the parties (and especially the Israelis) were less co-operative.[128]

The problems of policing a cease-fire or truce can be illustrated by examining the major violations in Palestine in 1948 after the first cease-fire entered into force on 11 June.

1. The *Altalena* was a former US tank landing ship, purchased by American supporters of the Irgun Zvai Leumi (Natural Military Organization) but operating under the Panamanian flag. It had left Port de Bouc (near Marseilles) on 11 June, the day the first cease-fire and arms embargo took effect, carrying several hundred immigrants and a large cargo of weapons, a considerable proportion of the arms being of French origin. The operation was being master-minded by the Irgun, and it was in breach of the UN arms embargo and the agreement that Bernadotte had reached with Israel that male Jewish immigrants of military age would be placed in UN-supervised camps for the duration of the cease-fire. Menachem Begin, the Irgun leader in the Middle East, was reluctant to break the arms embargo without official sanction and he twice cabled to France asking that the ship should not leave; but the Irgun people on the spot took the view that once the *Altalena*

---

[128] S/1025, 5 Oct. 1948 (mimeo), paras. 39-46 and pp. 32-8; GAOR, 3rd session, Supplement no. 11, A/648, pp. 38-9, 41, paras. 9-12, 18-22; SCOR, 3rd year, 320th mtg (15 June 1948), p. 2, S/837; Kirkbride, pp. 34-5, 53, 63; Glubb, pp. 149, 211.

had reached Israel 'the Israel Government would give its blessing to an accomplished fact'. This was far from being the case, however, and Moshe Shertok (Foreign Minister) told the Israeli Cabinet on 20 June: 'We may now be facing a blatant public violation of the truce by Jews, without our being personally responsible for it.' Irgun's intention was to evade UN surveillance by unloading the ship at night and moving away from the coast during the hours of daylight. The Irgun leaders claimed that they had been told on 15 June that the government was not opposed to this plan. There was, however, disagreement as to the disposition of the arms: the government wanted all the arms for the official Israeli forces (the Haganah), while the Irgun insisted that 20 per cent should go to their own contingent in the Jerusalem area. This dispute had not been resolved when the *Altalena* was sighted offshore. On the evening of 20 June, Begin went on board and the passengers began to disembark at Kfar Vitkin, north of Netanya. It was then noticed that two Israeli corvettes had taken up position near the *Altalena*, and the Haganah demanded that the ship and its cargo be handed over. As this demand was disregarded, the Haganah attacked from the land side and the corvettes fired warning shots. The *Altalena* then put to sea and, during the night of 21/22 June, was beached at Tel Aviv. The Irgun still insisted that they should have 20 per cent of the arms, and when it was apparent that deadlock was complete, the Haganah opened fire, the *Altalena* received a direct hit, and the cargo blew up. Sixteen members of the Irgun and two Haganah soldiers were killed during this incident. For the Israeli government, the defiance of its authority by a private Jewish army was as serious as the violation of the UN embargo. 'It is tragic that we should have to use force against fellow-Jews', David Ben-Gurion told the State Council: 'But it is a far greater tragedy that they should have forced us to....' The official Israeli communications to Bernadotte seemed to him evasive, and Bernadotte told the Israeli government that its explanation was 'not satisfactory'.[129]

---

[129] S/1025, 5 Oct. 1948 (mimeo), paras. 2, 31-3, 36; SCOR, 3rd year, Supplement for July 1948, pp. 1, 13-18, S/854, S/861 and Add. 1; Bernadotte, pp. 115-17, 123-4, 148; Ben-Gurion, pp. 132-3, 135, 165-73; Begin, pp. 154-8, 166-75; Samuel Katz, *Days of Fire,* New York, Doubleday, 1968, pp. 206, 228, 232-50.

2. One of the major difficulties for Israel was to supply the isolated Jewish settlements in the Negev. Bernadotte took the position that no party should suffer a military disadvantage as a result of the cease-fire and that Israeli convoys should be allowed to take food and other essential supplies to the be-leaguered settlements in convoys under UN control and escort. On 25 June, Egyptian forces turned back a convoy near Negba and two Egyptian Spitfires fired on a UN observer in an *Auster* plane that had landed in Israeli territory. Bernadotte at once protested, but as soon as Egypt agreed to allow Israeli convoys to resume, Bernadotte decided to let the matter drop. A few days later, Arab irregulars again interfered with an Israeli convoy, but an Egyptian officer intervened 'whose behaviour was co-operative and correct'. Just before the expiry of the first cease-fire, the Egyptian commander in Gaza notified the UN observers that he had been instructed to stop future Israeli convoys, and the matter was unresolved when the first cease-fire lapsed.[130] On 28 August, after the second cease-fire had entered into force, there was another incident in the Gaza area, leading to the death of two unarmed UN observers of French nationality. A UN *Auster* plane was fired at by Egyptian anti-aircraft guns and forced to land. Saudi irregulars under Egyptian command then killed and robbed the UN observers, although regular Egyptian forces intervened and several Egyptians were wounded in hand-to-hand fighting with the Saudis. The Arabs said they had at first thought that the plane was an Israeli one, and Bernadotte agreed that there was an element of UN responsibility because of a misunderstanding at the UN radio transmitters in Tel Aviv and Haifa, so that the pilot had not approached along the prescribed flight path and the Egyptian authorities had not received advance warning that a UN aircraft was due. Nevertheless, wrote Bernadotte, the Arab conduct was 'indefensible'.[131]

---

[130] S/1025, 5 Oct. 1948 (mimeo), para. 37; SCOR, 3rd year, Supplement for July 1948, pp. 7-11, 18, S/856 and Adds. 1 and 2, S/862; Bernadotte, pp. 120-3; Azcárate, pp. 101-2.

[131] GAOR, 3rd session, Supplement no. 11, A/648, p. 40, para. 16; Bernadotte, pp. 225-6.

3. The main source of water for Jerusalem at Ras el Ein was in Iraqi hands and the pumping station at Latrun was in the agreed No Man's Land but surrounded by Jordanian troops of the Arab Legion. Despite repeated representations to the Arabs by UN staff, no water flowed through the pipeline during the first cease-fire. Bernadotte told the Prime Minister of Jordan that the Arabs had acted 'quite wrongly' in the matter.[132] On the night of 11/12 August, during the second cease-fire, the pumping station at Latrun was blown up. Bernadotte considered this to be 'a flagrant violation' perpetrated by the Arabs, 'possibly irregulars'. This breach did not harm Israel as much as the Arabs had expected, as the Israelis had secretly laid a reserve pipeline to Jerusalem along the so-called Burma Road.[133]

4. Between 18 and 25 of July, there was a heavy Israeli attack on three Arab villages about a dozen miles south of Haifa: Jaba, Ijzim, and Ein Ghazal. Israel claimed that Arab snipers from the villages were raiding the coastal road between Haifa and Tel Aviv, and that the Israeli attack was only a police action: the Arabs alleged that there had been 'massacres'. UN observers had difficulty in establishing the facts because, as Bernadotte put it, the level of intelligence of Arab witnesses was low; but the observers concluded that, after the inhabitants of two of the villages had been driven out, the villages were systematically destroyed by Israeli forces. Bernadotte considered that the destruction caused by Israel was excessive and a violation of 'both the spirit and letter' of the cease-fire.[134]

5. Government House in Jerusalem was in a Red Cross zone established before the first cease-fire. On the night of 16/17 August, Israeli forces attacked Arab positions on the other side of the Red Cross zone and occupied some buildings within the zone, and Arab forces responded by establishing defensive positions around Government House, although

---

[132] S/1025, 5 Oct. 1948 (mimeo), paras. 22, 38; SCOR, 3rd year, Supplement for July 1948, pp. 26-7, S/869; Bernadotte, pp. 140-1, 145; Azcárate, pp. 58-9, 89; Joseph, pp. 226-7.

[133] SCOR, 3rd year, Supplement for August 1948, pp. 155-6, S/963; 349th mtg (13 Aug. 1948), p. 45, S/970; GAOR, 3rd session, Supplement no. 11, A/648, pp. 39-40, para. 14; Bernadotte, pp. 193-4, 215-17, 225; Joseph, pp. 264-5.

[134] GAOR, 3rd session, Supplement no. 11, A/648, pp. 40-1, para. 17; Bernadotte, pp. 226-7; Azcárate, pp. 102-3.

Government House itself was respected and continued to fly the Red Cross flag. The Central Truce Supervision Board ruled that Israel had committed 'flagrant violations' of the cease-fire, and decided to establish an enlarged neutral area with the Red Cross zone as the nucleus. Israel at first refused to withdraw from the buildings in the Red Cross zone, but after Bernadotte had threatened to recommend to the Security Council that sanctions should be imposed, Israeli troops withdrew from the buildings and the Arabs agreed to dismantle the military positions that they had established in the Red Cross zone.[135]

6. The murder of Count Bernadotte and a French colleague by dissident members of the Stern Gang was not simply an accident of war. It took place during the second cease-fire while the Mediator was engaged in a mission of peace. Nahum Goldmann has stressed how this act weakened the moral standing of Israel before world opinion.

The attitude of the majority [of Jews] was that another enemy of the Jews had fallen by the wayside. Few genuine tears were shed. There was not much moral indignation. There was no real public co-operation in the hunt for the assassins.... [W]hat seemed to me the most sorrowful aspect was the absence of any public conscience about this foul deed.[136]

7. The outbreak of fighting in the Negev in the middle of October, known in Israel as Operation Ten Plagues, has been described on pages 135-57 above in connection with the question of whether withdrawal of forces was to precede or follow negotiations between the parties. Israel did not complete the capture of the whole of the Negev in this operation, and a new offensive was launched on the night of 22/23 December. It was strong US pressure rather than action by the now demoralized Security Council that induced the Israelis to call a halt.[137]

---

[135] GAOR, 3rd session, Supplement no. 11, A/648, p. 40, para. 15; S/992, 7 Sept. 1948 (mimeo); Bernadotte, pp. 224, 254-6; Azcárate, p. 126; Joseph, pp. 280-2; FRUS, 1948, vol. V part 2, 1976, pp. 1319, 1375.

[136] Nahum Goldmann, *Memories, the Autobiography of Nahum Goldmann: the Story of a Lifelong Battle by World Jewry's Ambassador at Large,* trans. Helen Sebba, London, Weidenfeld & Nicolson, 1970, p. 246.

[137] SCOR, 3rd year, Supplement for December 1948, pp. 300-5, S/1152, S/1153 and Corr. 1; FRUS, 1948, vol. V part 2, 1976, pp. 1689, 1705-6; 1949, vol. VI, 1977, pp. 594-6, 601-2, 605-7; Azcárate, pp. 105-10.

All of the specific violations described above were serious, but those mentioned in the paragraphs 1-6 were caused by dissident elements or irregular soldiers or were due to local military euphoria. Any of these six incidents had the potentiality for bringing about a total collapse of the cease-fires, but none of them in fact did so. The lesson is that impartial supervision can contain and settle incidents of this kind, but it cannot do more. Once a party has committed itself to a substantial military operation in breach of its obligations, as was the case with both Egypt and Israel in October 1948 and with Israel two months later, the presence of UN observers or even a peace-keeping force is no deterrent, only a minor annoyance, to be ignored or sent packing.

When the four Middle East armistice agreements were concluded in 1949, an attempt was made to improve the procedures for dealing with violations. The UN Truce Supervision Organization (UNTSO) was to continue, and indeed it still exists; but in addition, there were to be four Mixed Armistice Commissions (MACs) composed equally of Arab and Israeli officers with an independent chairman, either the Chief of Staff of UNTSO or a UN observer designated by him. Each MAC was to adopt its own procedure and, to the extent possible, operate on the basis of unanimity. Each MAC would use observers, either from the military organizations of the parties or from UNTSO. Members of the MACs were to have such freedom of movement and freedom of acces as might be necessary. Reports were to go to the parties, with copies to the UN Secretary-General. At its peak in 1948, UNTSO had disposed of several hundred observers, but General Burns, who took over as Chief of Staff in 1954, reported that the number had by then dropped to 'between forty and fifty'.[138] Although it had been hoped that most incidents could be settled locally, the Security Council had to meet on average ten times a year to consider complaints from the parties that had not been settled through UNTSO or the MACs. At first the resolutions of the Council were carefully phrased so as to blame neither party,

[138] Hutchinson, pp. 11-12; Burns, p. 27; Horn, p. 61; Bull, pp. 41, 143-4; Brook, pp. 101-9.

but in 1951 Egypt was told bluntly that there was no justification for its interference with Israeli cargoes, and from 1953 onwards the Security Council was increasingly critical of the scale of Israeli retaliation.[139]

The difficulties after 1949 were not primarily due to obvious defects in the supervisory machinery but to major political factors. Israel was an energetic new state with a massive rate of immigration. The state had no accepted frontiers, only armistice demarcation lines, and these corresponded not with the lines of the UN partition plan but with the *de facto* lines of separation following a series of military actions. UN staff found Israelis increasingly touchy, even hubristic.

That was difficult enough, but the confusion was confounded by the Arab denial of Israel's legitimacy. This meant that any Arab attacking a Jewish target in Israel was thought to be serving the cause of Arab nationalism, whether he was a regular soldier, a guerrilla fighter, a terrorist, or a common criminal. When Arab infiltration became excessive, Israel resorted to massive retaliation, culminating in the heavy raid against the Gaza area in February 1955.[140]

Indiscriminate Arab provocation led to disproportionate Israeli retaliation. Most Israelis wanted nothing more than to be allowed to live and work in peace within the armistice lines, joined each year by increasing numbers of Jewish immigrants; but the Palestinian Arabs were not reconciled to the Zionist idyll, believing that the Arabs had been robbed of a country that was rightfully their own. Extremists on both sides fanned the flames of resentment, vying with each other in intemperance of language and recklessness of action. External powers pursued their own interests in the region with little regard for local susceptibilities. Those Israelis and Arabs who hoped that time would bring healing were overwhelmed by the hot-heads, and the armistice régime seemed increasingly irrelevant. Because the parties had no diplomatic relations and the MACs gradually fell into disuse, UN representatives played an important intermediary role. No Chief of Staff of UNTSO could keep the

---

[139] SC res. 95 (S/2322), 1 Sept. 1951; res. 101 (S/3139/Rev. 2), 24 Nov. 1953; res. 106 (S/3378), 29 March 1955; res. 111 (S/3538), 19 Jan. 1956.

[140] Burns, pp. 21, 38, 58-9, 62, 139, 153; Bull, pp. 94, 101, 146, 153-4, 157-8, 166.

confidence of both sides for long, but the system of supervision continued on the whole to be impartial.[141]

SINAI-SUEZ

After the Sinai-Suez campaign in 1956, a UN Emergency Force (UNEF) was deployed in the Suez area, and then in Sinai and the Gaza Strip as well as in the Sharm El-Sheikh area; UNTSO continued, and in the Egypt-Israel sector was consolidated with UNEF. The military personnel of UNEF totalled 4,933 in 1964, whereas only seven UNTSO observers were assigned to the Egypt-Israel sector. UNEF was deployed on the Egyptian side of the armistice demarcation line, a length of 170 miles, and a small UNEF detachment was stationed at Sharm El-Sheikh and Ras Nasrani to observe naval movements through the Strait of Tiran. Throughout the period, and since, Israel refused to have a UN Force on its own territory, and this was to foreclose one option in 1967 when Nasser withdrew consent for the deployment of UNEF on Egyptian soil. UNEF conducted ground patrols and reconnaissance as well as some reconnaissance flights by light aircraft, but no naval patrols. In the Gaza Strip, the most populous area, there was good cooperation with the local police. The inhabitants were forbidden to approach within 50-100 metres of the demarcation line by day and 500 metres by night. UNEF apprehended infiltrators or people approaching the demarcation line in suspicious circumstances, and handed them over to the local authorities. There was a spate of ground incidents in December 1959 and the early months of 1960: leaving aside this period, there were just over 200 minor ground and naval incidents a year. There was a considerable amount of over-flying, mainly by Israeli or unidentified aircraft. During the period covered by this study, there was not a single serious incident between Egypt and Israel after 1956, although the Mixed Armistice Commission did on one occasion condemn Israel for penetrating

[141] Burns, p. 5.

Egyptian airspace,[142] and the Suez Canal remained closed to cargoes destined for Israel.[143] The Israel-Lebanon sector was quiet,[144] but incidents continued along the Israel-Jordan and Israel-Syria demarcation lines.

CYPRUS

In Cyprus there was no equivalent of the UN Truce Supervision Organization or the Mixed Armistice Commissions, so all aspects of supervision fell to the UN Force (UNFICYP). The functions of UNFICYP included the demarcation of cease-fire lines where these were uncertain or challenged, supervision of the cease-fire at fixed posts or by interposition between the two sides and frequent patrols, intervention to prevent local incidents from escalating, help with maintaining law and order, the manning of a check-point on the road between Nicosia and Kyrenia and other assistance in guaranteeing freedom of movement, aid to displaced persons and refugees, co-operation with the International Committee of the Red Cross in searching for abducted or missing persons, and general help in restoring administrative and economic normality.[145]

The UN Emergency Force in Sinai had broken new ground, as it was the first instance of non-enforcing UN action by military units, undertaken with the consent of the host country. UNEF was deployed along the armistice demarcation line and

---

[142] Bar-Yaacov, p. 308 n. 36; GAOR, 12th session, Annexes, Agenda item 65, pp. 6-7, paras. 41-5 of A/3694; 13th session, Annexes, Agenda item 65, pp. 4, 6, 16-17, paras. 2, 17-18 of A/3899 and paras. 66-74 of A/3943; 14th session, Annexes, Agenda item 28, pp. 22, 25-6, paras. 3, 35-8 of A/4210; 15th session, Annexes, Agenda item 27, pp. 14, 16-17, paras. 5, 22-5 of A/4486; 16th session, Annexes, Agenda item 26, pp. 21, 23-4, paras. 1, 15 of A/4857; 17th session, Annexes, Agenda items 32 and 63, pp. 2, 4, 7-9, paras. 1-2, 14-15 of and Annexes I to V to A/5172; 18th session, Annexes, Agenda item 19, pp. 2, 4, 7-9, paras. 1-3, 16-18 of and Annexes to A/5494; 19th session, Annex no. 6, pp. 1-2, 4, 6-7, paras. 1-2, 17-19 of and Annexes I to V to A/5736; 20th session, Annexes, Agenda item 21, pp. 2, 4, 8-10, paras. 1-3, 19-21 of and Annexes I to V to A/5919; Burns, p. 280; Bull, p. 56; SCOR, 18th year, Supplement for July-September 1963, pp. 145-6, S/5405.

[143] For Israeli complaints, see SCOR, 12th year, Supplement for July-September 1957, pp. 12-13, 21-2, S/3854, S/3870; 14th year, Supplement for January-June 1959, pp. 24-5, S/4173; Supplement for July-September 1959, pp. 5-7, S/4211.

[144] Bull, p. 84.

[145] SCOR, 19th year, Supplement for October-December 1964, pp. 227-31, 256-7, paras. 22-33, 119-21 of S/6102.

in addition exerted a tranquillizing influence in the Gaza Strip and Sharm El-Sheikh areas. The problems were different in Cyprus in 1964, since in most areas there was no front line separating two antagonistic armies along which a UN force could be interposed. The conflict was between two communities within a single country, but with threatened or actual interference by external patrons. Moreover, there was less cooperation on the part of the host government in Cyprus than UNEF had received from Egypt.

KOREA

The Neutral Nations Supervisory Commission (NNSC) in Korea was set up under the armistice agreement of 27 July 1953 to investigate alleged violations of the armistice agreement and to inspect and supervise the rotation of military units and personnel and the replacement of military aircraft, vehicles, weapons, and ammunition by means of inspection teams stationed at five agreed ports of entry on each side. There had been lengthy negotiations on the meaning of 'Neutral Nations'. In February 1952, the Unified Command had suggested Norway, Sweden, and Switzerland, and the Communist side had countered with Czechoslovakia, Poland, and the Soviet Union. There was a short-lived disposition by the Unified Command to suggest the United States, but this could not have been a very serious ploy, and it was decided to drop Norway if the Communists would drop the Soviet Union. There the matter rested until Arpil-May 1953, when agreement was reached on officers from Czechoslovskia and Poland (designated by the Communist side) and Sweden and Switzerland (designated by the Unified Command).

The Swedish and Swiss members of the NNSC were no doubt ideologically sympathetic to the West but felt no particular identification with the South Korean régime and no obligation to protect the interests of the Unified Command. Sweden had contributed about 150 medical personnel to work with the Unified Command during the war, but no combat troops.[146]

---

[146] For Sweden's response to the first two resolutions of the Security Council, see SCOR, 5th year, Supplement for June-August 1950, pp. 61-2, S/1564.

Switzerland had made no contribution of any kind to the Unified Command, was not (and is not) a Member of the United Nations, and had initially been most reluctant to accept a supervisory role for fear that this would compromise Swiss neutrality. Czechoslovakia and Poland, on the other hand, had fraternal feelings for North Korea and China and considered that China had engaged in a defensive war. The Swedish and Swiss members of the NNSC were entirely free of control by or instructions from their governments, but their counterparts from Eastern Europe received binding instructions from their own authorities: if an unexpected proposal were made, the East Europeans would ask for a recess 'in order to get instructions'. A Swiss army officer who served with the NNSC claimed that the members from Eastern Europe obstructed the NNSC when there was any question of investigating an alleged breach by the Communist side; if the allegation concerned the South, on the other hand, the East Europeans 'magnified' the incident and argued that even small technical oversights should be condemned as major and deliberate violations.[147]

The Unified Command was worried from the start that the NNSC was unable to detect even the most blatant evasion of the armistice obligations by the Communist side. During the first year of the armistice, the Unified Command reported 650,000 arrivals and departures of military personnel, whereas the comparable figure reported by the Communist side was 44,000. It was reasonable to expect a higher rate of rotation from the Unified Command, but the figure from the Communist side was barely plausible. The Unified Command reported 16,141 movements of combat aircraft in the first twenty-two months of the armistice: the figure from the Communist side was zero, which seemed ludicrous to those in the Unified Command who had access to intelligence data. Because of the composition of the NNSC, it repeatedly found itself split two-two, which meant paralysis. No doubt the Eastern European members of the NNSC found this as frustrating as did the Swedish and Swiss members.[148]

It had originally been thought that the task of the NNSC would be completed by about the end of 1954, and even before

---

[147] Lecture by Paul Wacker to the Swiss Institute for Foreign Affairs, March 1955.
[148] A/3167, 16 Aug. 1956 (mimeo), pp. 18, 23.

that date Sweden and Switzerland proposed that the NNSC should be disbanded because its work had become farcical. The United States would have agreed to disabandment, but China dissented as long as foreign troops remained in Korea. In 1955, the NNSC itself proposed a reduction in the size of the inspection teams and the number of ports of entry, and this was accepted by the two sides. The following year the Unified Command unilaterally suspended the work of the inspection teams, and in 1957 it announced that, because the Communist side had persistently violated the armistice provisions about the non-introduction of weapons, the Unified Command no longer considered itself bound by those obligations. Thereafter the work of the NNSC did not extend beyond the demilitarized zone and was confined to the statistical processing of reports.[149]

It would probably have been impossible in 1951-3 to have devised a form of supervision for Korea that would have been effective and that both sides would have trusted. Almost all of the published material to which I have had access stresses the grievances of the Unified Command, but I expect that the Communist side soon lost whatever confidence it may originally have had that the supervisory system could be relied on to detect violations.

THE DETERRENCE OF CHEATING

If, as will almost always be the case, joint supervision by a co-operative effort between the parties is not immediately attainable, it would seem that the methods of supervision are, in descending order of reliability and effectiveness:

1.   international peace-keeping forces under a single command, with contingents drawn from countries not directly involved;

2.   an integrated organization of observers recruited from countries not directly involved;

---

[149] GAOR, 9th session, First Committee, 738th mtg (2 Dec. 1954), para. 4; 10th session, Supplement no. 13, A/2947, para. 14; A/3167, 16 Aug. 1956 (mimeo), pp. 13-17; 12th session, Annexes, Agenda item 23, p. 3, Appendix to A/3631; SCOR, 31st year, Supplement for October-December 1976, p. 58, para. 4 (c) and (d) of S/12263.

3. observers seconded from local diplomatic or consular posts, under the control of a subsidiary organ of the Security Council;

4. a commission constituted on the basis of parity to represent the parties to the conflict.

Whatever form the organization may take, it is obvious that there will be no confidence in the supervisory system unless it is clear that personnel are impartial and independent; that there will be no formal or *de facto* veto on the right to investigate incidents, make reports, or take other decisions; and that supervisory personnel will be assured of full freedom of movement on the territory of all parties. More weight should not be placed. on the supervisory machinery than it can bear. An international presence symbolizes an implicit bargain between the parties to keep their behaviour within agreed limits: if the bargain ceases to suit one of the parties, or both, a symbolic international presence has lost its *raison d'être*.

4.6 REPRISALS

Acts of retaliation or retribution are an inevitable part of armed conflict, though subject to political, legal, or moral restraints. A belligerent reprisal is something different: it is a particular form of retaliation that would ordinarily be a violation of the laws and customs of war but is justified by the party committing it on the ground that there has been a prior commission of an illegal act by the other side. The purpose of a reprisal is not to punish the enemy but to induce him to discontinue illegal acts. Reprisals are thus one remedy open to belligerents to secure compliance with the law of armed conflict; but the concept of reprisal is peculiarly open to abuse, especially in the heat of battle. Who can be sure who committed the first violation, and who can be sure when a violator has decided to stop violating?

There are substantial legal restraints on the exercise of reprisals and, as I have suggested on pages 41-3 above, it is probably now the case that the only legitimate belligerent reprisal is to use otherwise unlawful weapons or methods of warfare against enemy combatants or military targets. Both the Security

Council and the General Assembly have sought to reinforce the restriction of acts of belligerent reprisal, and UN Secretary-General Thant suggested that reprisals should be strictly circumscribed if not completely forbidden.[150]

In theory there should never be any doubt as to whether a particular military action is a reprisal or simply an act of revenge or retribution, since a reprisal should be accompanied by a complaint about the illegalities being committed by the other side and an explicit commitment to stop reprisals as soon as the other side's illegalities have ceased. In practice, of course, when a battle for vital interests is raging, the explanation of reprisals may be offered *ex post facto* after it has been realized that a particular military action has seemed to the outside world to have been excessive or illegal.

In Indonesia there was persistent confusion about the distinction between reprisals and retaliation. The Good Offices Committee protested when the Netherlands Army Information Service sought to justify the crossing of the *status quo* line by Dutch troops in response to incidents caused by 'gangs coming from Republican territory'.[151] The truce agreement in August 1949 prohibited 'all acts of reprisal and retaliation', and such an act was defined as

an act committed by a person or persons against another or others to satisfy a grievance, or to get even, for an act previously performed or alleged to have been performed against their interests, or for any opinion held or alleged to be or to have been held contrary to their opinions or interests. The term shall therefore include any act taken by the supporters of one party against people because of their political affiliation to the other party, such as:

(a)   Physical violence;
(b)   Arrest;
(c)   Expulsion from dwelling places;
(d)   Discharge from jobs;
(e)   Seizure, confiscation or destruction of property.[152]

---

[150] A/7720, 20 Nov. 1969 (mimeo), para. 203.

[151] SCOR, 3rd year, Supplement for December 1948, pp. 97-101, S/1085.

[152] SCOR, 4th year, Special Supplement no. 5, pp. 61 (para. 4 (d)), 65, Appendix VIII to S/1373 and Corr. 1.

Count Bernadotte found in Palestine that every violation of the cease-fire was justified as a response to an illegality by the other party. In a cable to the Security Council, he urged that 'reprisals and retaliations' should be declared to be impermissible. Four Western members of the Council incorporated this proposal in a draft resolution which read in part: 'No party is permitted to violate the truce on the ground that it is undertaking reprisals or retaliations against the other party.' This was approved by the Council, though Colombia, Syria, the Soviet Union, and the Ukrainian SSR abstained.[153]

Dov Joseph, the Israeli governor of Jerusalem, took great exception to the prohibition of reprisals, which he thought could have been favoured only by those who were unfamiliar with 'the Arab mentality': to ban reprisals, in Joseph's view, only encouraged aggression.[154] Indeed, it was the general view of Israeli Jews that the only way to stop Arab infiltration was to punish the states that harboured infiltrators.[155] UN observers naturally deplored this policy, which they regarded as both illegal and ineffective.[156]

Secretary-General Hammarskjold always took a strict view of the cease-fire obligations in the Middle East. In his report on compliance with the armistice agreements in May 1956, he devoted considerable attention to this problem. A party to an armistice agreement naturally considered its compliance conditional on compliance by the other party, but he reported that from no side had it been said that a breach of the agreement, to whatever clause it might refer, 'gives the other party a free hand concerning the agreement as a whole'. The cease-fire obligation was 'unconditional', and any reservation by a party regarding the right of self-defence did not alter the fact that self-defence 'is under the sole jurisdiction of the Security Council'. It was Hammarskjold's understanding that a reservation regarding self-defence 'does not permit acts of retaliation, which repeatedly have been condemned by the Security Council'.[157]

[153] S/928, 28 July 1948 (mimeo); SCOR, 3rd year, 354th mtg (19 Aug. 1948), pp. 40-1 (S/977), 50-1; SC res. 56 (S/983), 19 Aug. 1948.
[154] Joseph, p. 261.
[155] Brook, pp. 34-6
[156] Hutchinson, pp. 17, 43, 61, 103-4, 115-16; Burns, pp. 21, 38, 43, 58, 62-3, 90, 119, 133, 139-41, 153, 160, 167, 173-4.
[157] SCOR, 11th year, Supplement for April-June 1956, pp. 34-5, 39-41, paras. 16-19, 40, 44-6 of S/3596.

CHAPTER 5

Humanitarian questions

5.1 THE HAGUE AND GENEVA CONVENTIONS

Attached to the Hague Conventions of 1899 and 1907 on the laws and customs of war on land are 'regulations' that are 'intended to serve as a general rule of conduct for...belligerents'. These regulations, sometimes known also as the Hague Rules, govern the conduct of military operations and seek to place military necessity and humanitarian concern in balance. The Geneva Conventions, by contrast, were inspired by the Red Cross movement and are concerned only indirectly with the conduct of military operations. The primary purpose of the Geneva Conventions is to provide humanitarian protection and relief to those not taking part in the fighting: wounded, sick, and shipwrecked members of the armed forces, prisoners of war, medical and relief workers, ministers of religion, and civilians under occupation. Although the Hague and Geneva streams of law had different origins and purposes, they can no longer be kept entirely separate, as was apparent during the discussions that preceded the adoption of the Hague Convention of 1954 on the protection of cultural property and the Additional Protocols of 1977 to the four Geneva Conventions.

The first Geneva Convention dates from 1864 and was concerned with wounded combatants. This was replaced in 1906 by a revised Convention that covered sick as well as wounded combatants, and this was in its turn superseded in 1929 by a more detailed Convention, and a separate Convention was then adopted to protect prisoners of war. The 1929 Conventions were replaced in 1949 by four new Conventions, of which the fourth gave explicit protection, albeit limited, to civilians under occupation.

The Geneva Conventions of 1929 on sick and wounded combatants and prisoners of war were in force while the fighting was taking place in my first four cases (Indonesia I and II, Kashmir, Palestine), but the Conventions of 1949 had been completed before the outbreak of war in Korea (my case 5).

It is widely held that the obligations of the Geneva Conventions are absolute and do not depend on reciprocity:[1] the
parties have undertaken 'to respect and ensure respect' for the
Conventions 'in all circumstances'.[2] The Hague Conventions
assert some important principles that are still relevant, but in
many respects they have been overtaken by advances in military
technology. The aeroplane has made it possible to attack targets
behind the enemy's lines without defeating an intervening
army. Missiles of ever greater range and accuracy have been
developed, with nuclear warheads of enormous destructive
power, and these can cross oceans and continents to reach an
enemy's homeland. It is now technically possible to destroy
virtually the whole urban population and the economic and
social fabric of an advanced major power in a surprise first-
strike, with indirect harm to those not involved in the conflict,
including cancers and genetic harm affecting future generations.
Neither the laws of war nor the human conscience has yet come
to terms with this awesome capacity to kill, maim, and destroy
on such a massive scale.

The Netherlands government is the depositary for the Hague
Conventions but has played no special part in recent years in
any effort to up-date the Hague law. The situation is different
in the case of the Geneva law, for the International Committee
of the Red Cross (ICRC) regards itself as the custodian of the
Geneva Conventions and of humanitarian principles 'derived
from the usages established among civilized peoples, from the
laws of humanity, and from the dictates of the public conscience'.[3] The ICRC, which is sometimes said to be 'impartial
on the side of the victim', is constantly developing and refining
its ideas, so that legal instruments may keep pace with technical
and other changes.

When hostilities break out, it is the practice of the ICRC to
address a communication to the parties, offering its services
and setting out the basic humanitarian principles and rules that
should be applied irrespective of the nature of the armed conflict

---

[1] A/7720, 20 Nov. 1969 (mimeo), para. 82; *International Review of the Red Cross*,
13th year, no. 153 (Dec. 1973), p. 641; Rosas, pp. 111-12.
[2] Geneva Conventions, Article 1.
[3] Preamble to the Hague Conventions, 1899 and 1907, and Article 63/62/142/158
of the Geneva Conventions, 1949.

and of whether the belligerents are parties to the Geneva Conventions.[4] There may sometimes be uncertainty as to who are the parties to a particular conflict (see pages 69-78 above), but the ICRC deals with the *de facto* authorities. Thus in Kashmir, for example, the ICRC was able to secure declarations to respect the principles and spirit of the Geneva Conventions from India, in respect of Indian Kashmir, and from Azad Kashmir. No approach was made to Pakistan, as Pakistan had confirmed its adherence to the Geneva Conventions on 2 February 1948, three months before Pakistani regular forces entered Kashmir.[5]

The main work of the ICRC in time of armed conflict is concerned with the persons protected by the Geneva Conventions, but it is often necessary to make special representations to ensure that all those entitled to protected status are so recognized. After Indian troops had entered Hyderabad in September 1948, for example, the ICRC had to make representations to the Indian authorities before certain detained persons were granted POW status.[6] Problems not expressly covered by the Conventions are also likely to arise. In Palestine, for example, the ICRC tried (though without success) to arrange a cease-fire or truce for Jerusalem,[7] was able to negotiate the setting up of three civilian sanctuaries in Jerusalem (see pages 232-5 above),[8] provided medical aid and relief after the massacre at Deir Yasin,[9] supervised the surrender of the Old City of Jerusalem and took custody of the seriously wounded,[10] co-operated with UN officials in preparing a plan for the release of beleaguered Arabs in the Faluja area (see pages 332-3 below),[11] provided

[4] See my case 5, Korea, p. 444, 519-522 of vol. II; also *International Committee of the Red Cross in Palestine,* pp. 1-4; Report of the International Committee of the Red Cross for 1956, Geneva, 1957, pp. 23-5.

[5] Report of the International Committee of the Red Cross for 1 July 1947-31 December 1948, Geneva, 1949, p. 96; letter from Miss Lix Simonius of the ICRC, 21 October 1977.

[6] Report of the International Committee of the Red Cross for 1 July 1947-31 December 1948, Geneva, 1949, p. 97.

[7] *Hospital Localities and Safety Zones,* pp. 24-6; Azcárate, p. 83.

[8] See my case, Palestine, p. 175-77, 280-286 of Vol II.

[9] Reynier, pp. 69-77, 213.

[10] Ibid., pp. 143-4; *International Committee of the Red Cross in Palestine*, pp. 10-11, 23; Report of the International Committee of the Red Cross for 1 July 1947-31 December 1948, Geneva, 1949, p. 106.

[11] Report of the International Committee of the Red Cross for 1949, Geneva, 1950, p. 73; SCOR, 4th year, Supplement for March 1949, pp. 7-8, S/1269.

emergency accommodation for Palestine refugees at the Quaker school in Ramallah,[12] and shared with the League of Red Cross Societies and the American Friends Service Committee the responsibility for Palestine refugees until a UN agency could be organized (see pages 318-9).[13] In Indonesia, the ICRC handled a delicate relief operation for the South Moluccas in 1950.[14]

In Korea, there were many difficulties because the Communist side thought that the ICRC was too closely identified with the attitudes and policies of the Unified Command. In 1952 the ICRC sent a communication to North Korea and China explaining its long tradition of impartiality and independence.[15] The ICRC would have been willing, had the parties agreed, to take responsibility for POWs refusing repatriation (see pages 310-6) and to establish an independent commission of experts to investigate allegations that the United States had used bacteriological weapons.[16] It was an initiative taken at an International Red Cross Conference in 1952 that led to the resumption of negotiations to end the fighting and the eventual conclusion of an armistice agreement.[17] Twenty years later, the national Red Cross societies in Korea provided a convenient framework for contacts between the two parts of Korea.[18]

In Cyprus the ICRC organized a joint co-ordinating committee to provide relief for displaced persons and beleaguered members of the Turkish community in 1964, and also used its best endeavours to trace and secure the release of abducted and missing persons (see page 320 below). The ICRC has always considered the taking of hostages to be illegal, but it is under certain conditions prepared to use its good offices for their benefit.[19]

[12] Bernadotte, p. 200; Reynier, p. 84.   [13] GA res. 302 (IV), 8 Dec. 1949.
[14] Report of the International Committee of the Red Cross for 1950, Geneva, 1951, pp. 78-80.
[15] *Comité international de la Croix-Rouge et le Conflit de Corée*, vol. II, pp. 13-14.
[16] See my case 5, Korea, pp. 452 and 523-525 of vol II; Report of the International Committee of the Red Cross for 1952, Geneva, 1953, pp. 107-10.
[17] Report of the International Committee of the Red Cross for 1952, Geneva, 1953, pp. 54, 120; Report of the International Committee of the Red Cross for 1953, Geneva, 1954, p. 51.
[18] GAOR, 28th year, Supplement no. 27, A/9027, paras. 32-40.
[19] Report of the International Committee of the Red Cross for 1964, Geneva, 1965, pp. 15-18; SCOR, 19th year, Supplement for January-March 1964, p. 160, S/5622; Supplement for April-June 1964, pp. 110, 224-5, 233, para. 16 of S/5679,

While the ICRC is reticent about engaging in public condemnation, it sometimes has no option but to speak out, but usually in the form of an appeal to humanitarian conscience in the future rather than an indictment of infractions in the past. When the Jews of Palestine sent to the Hadassah Hospital on Mount Scopus in Jerusalem a convoy in which medical and military vehicles were mixed (13 April 1948), the ICRC delegate pointed out that this was asking for trouble. Jewish civilians understood this perfectly well, he wrote, but the military had refused to listen. The Jews, he wrote sentenciously, had to choose whether they wanted the protection of weapons or of the Geneva Conventions.[20] The same delegate later served in Korea, and when he witnessed some especially horrific examples of South Korea's abuse of political prisoners, the ICRC issued an urgent appeal to President Syngman Rhee to respect humanitarian principles. The ICRC had no access to North Korea during the fighting: in South Korea it encountered occasional problems about freedom of action, and for eight weeks in 1952 'the responsible authorities' in South Korea suspended ICRC visits to POW camps.[21]

Many people find it paradoxical that efforts should be made to subject war to legal and ethical restraints, and yet there seems to be a deep-seated and widespread moral sense that acts of needless cruelty are inadmissible even in the most righteous cause. Lewis Coser, in his important study of the functions of social conflict, shows that the very fact of engaging in conflict brings about rules governing the conduct of hostilities.[22] It is occasionally asserted that, because the cause is just, those who are fighting are free of moral and legal inhibitions; but this rarely carries conviction. The predicament of modern war is

paras. 63-4, 92 of S/5764; Supplement for July-September 1964, p. 327, para. 199 of S/5950; David P. Forsythe, *Humanitarian Politics: The International Committee of the Red Cross,* pp. 97-9; David P. Forsythe, *Present Role of the Red Cross in Protection,* Geneva, Henry Durant Institute, 1975 (Joint Committee for the Reappraisal of the Role of the Red Cross, Background Paper no. 1), pp. 41-4.

[20] Reynier, pp. 80-1.

[21] *Comité international de la Croix-Rouge et le Conflit de Corée,* vol. I, pp. 165-8; Report of the International Committee of the Red Cross for 1951, Geneva, 1952, p. 67; Report of the International Committee of the Red Cross for 1952, Geneva, 1953, pp. 55, 73; Forsythe, *Humanitarian Politics,* p. 135; Hermes, pp. 406-7.

[22] Coser, pp. 121-8.

how to achieve justice without at the same time eroding the
very principles for which the struggle is being conducted.

5.2 PROHIBITED WEAPONS AND METHODS OF FIGHTING

Two general principles in ethics and law govern the conduct of
military operations: that civilians should be immune from
deliberate and direct attack (discrimination), and that combatants should not be attacked in such a way as to cause
unnecessary injury or suffering (proportion).[23] The implementation of these principles raises many questions. In an era of
total war, in which a great part of the adult population is to
some extent involved in the war effort, where should the line
be drawn between combatants and civilians? Is it permissible
to harm civilians as an indirect effect of a strike against a
legitimate military target? How is it possible to measure another
person's suffering? How much weight should be given in the
heat of battle to military necessity? And, the most difficult
question of all, is it possible to enforce the rules of war without
holding in reserve the threat of reprisals, which by definition
is a violation of those rules but is permitted under certain conditions if the sole purpose is to compel the other side to resume
compliance with the rules?

In addition to the general principles of discrimination and
proportion, there are specific prohibitions and restrictions in
international legal instruments. The main instruments in the
period 1946-64 were the Geneva (Red Cross) Conventions of
1929 and 1949 on the protection of war victims, the Hague
Conventions of 1899 and 1907 on the laws and customs of war
(which, *inter alia*, banned the use of poisons), the Hague Decl-
laration of 1899 prohibiting 'bullets which expand or flatten
easily in the human body' (dum-dum bullets), Hague Convention VIII of 1907 prohibiting unanchored automatic contact
mines, the Geneva Protocol of 1925 prohibiting chemical and
bacteriological (biological) methods of warfare, and the Hague
Convention of 1954 on the protection of cultural property.

The Geneva Protocol of 1925 was drafted in revulsion against
the use of poison gas during the First World War. The peace

---

[23] Rosenblad, pp. 12, 53-75, 139-42, 146-8, 153-4.

treaties had declared that the use of asphyxiating, poisonous, or other gases and analogous liquids, materials, or devices was forbidden. This wording was used in the Geneva Protocol, and the prohibition was extended to cover 'bacteriological methods of warfare'. The Geneva Protocol thus bans the use in war of what the ordinary person thinks of as poisons and germs: as it is possible to infect people with biological agents that are not bacteria, it is usual nowadays to speak of biological rather than bacteriological methods of warfare.

It would be tedious to record all the instances in the cases studied of allegations by one party that the other side had violated the laws and customs of war by resorting to prohibited weapons or methods of fighting. If there has been naval or aerial bombardment of well defended areas in conditions of poor visibility, for example, it is likely that damage will have been done to objectives with no military significance such as medical, educational, or cultural institutions.[24] Another common complaint in areas without a piped water supply is of the poisoning of wells. In May 1948, Egypt complained to Count Bernadotte that the Jews had contaminated the water supply of the Egyptian army with dysentery and cholera germs. As 'absolute proof' of this, the Egyptian Prime Minister told Bernadotte that two Jews had been captured with phials of germs who claimed to have been ordered by their superior officers 'to commit this dastardly act'. As it was impossible to buy germs in retail shops, he said, the attempt must necessarily have involved the co-operation of scientists and high officials.[25] Turkey made a similar allegation about the poisoning of wells during the Cyprus crisis of 1964.[26]

The most sustained campaign about illegal methods of fighting took place in 1951-2. On 8 May 1951, the North Korean Foreign Minister sent a cable to the Security Council alleging that the United States and South Korea had used bacteriological weapons in Korea. He claimed that in December 1950 and

---

[24] Of the many examples of allegations of this kind, I select at random a complaint of the Pakistan Red Cross in October 1948 that Indian or Indian Kashmiri forces had bombed hospitals in Azad Kashmir; see Report of the International Committee of the Red Cross for 1 July 1947-31 December 1948, Geneva, 1949, p. 97.

[25] Bernadotte, pp. 24-5.

[26] SCOR, 19th year, Supplement for July-September 1964, p. 122, S/5838.

January 1951, smallpox had appeared in North Korea about a week after US forces had withdrawn, and that shortly after this smallpox had appeared also in Japan, 'the infection having been brought in by American army men, who had taken part in the battles in North Korea and had been infected ... as a result of the use of bacteriological weapons'. Later in the year, North Korea alleged that US forces had used 'bombs containing poison gas'. The charges were renewed the following year: US aircraft had dropped insects carrying plague, cholera, and other infectious diseases. This time, China associated itself with the North Korean charges. Bodies under Communist influence, such as the World Peace Council, took up the campaign in a major way.[27]

At the relevant time, fifteen of the states supplying forces to the Unified Command were parties to the Geneva Protocol of 1925 banning the use of poisons and germs in war, but the United States was one of the non-parties and did not ratify the Protocol until 1975. Neither South Korea nor North Korea were parties, and it was not until July 1952 that China announced that it considered itself bound by the Protocol on condition of reciprocity.

The Soviet Union brought the complaint about germ warfare before the Security Council in 1952, and fourteen meetings were devoted to the matter. The Soviet Union was careful to confine its attack to a demand that the United States should ratify the Geneva Protocol and, when a proposal to that effect had been defeated, to a motion that China and North Korea should take part in the debate on a US proposal for an investigation of Communist charges by the International Committee of the Red Cross (ICRC). Soviet ambassador Malik was careful not to claim that the North Korean and Chinese charges were true, but he repeatedly pointed out that the allegations had been made—although he did on one occasion refer to 'the facts' contained in the communications from North Korea and China.[28]

[27] Ibid., 6th year, Supplement for April-June 1951, pp. 118-20, S/2142/Rev. 1; Supplement for July-September 1951, pp. 42-4, S/2296; 7th year, Supplement for April-June 1952, pp. 21-69, S/2684.
[28] Ibid., 580th mtg (23 June 1952), para. 43; 582nd mtg (25 June 1952), paras. 88-9; 585th mtg (1 July 1952), paras. 66-7; 588th mtg (8 July 1952), paras. 49-54.

The Communist campaign to publicize the charge that the United States had resorted to germ warfare undoubtedly made an impact on public opinion, especially as some US prisoners of war in Communist hands 'confessed' to having used chemical or biological weapons. When the Soviet Union raised the matter in the Security Council, the US government decided to counter-attack. The Soviet appeal to the United States to ratify the Geneva Protocol, not in itself an unreasonable idea, received only the Soviet vote, all the other members of the Council abstaining. When the Soviet Union vetoed the US proposal for an impartial investigation, which the ICRC would have been willing to conduct if all the parties had agreed,[29] the United States at once proposed that the Security Council should condemn the fabrication and dissemination of false charges; but this also ran into a Soviet veto.[30] The United States then took the issue to the General Assembly, which decided to set up a commission (Brazil, Egypt, Pakistan, Sweden, Uruguay) to investigate the Communist allegations, and asked the President of the General Assembly to report when the governments and authorities concerned had agreed to the investigation.[31] As the necessary agreement was never forthcoming, the commission never met.

5.3 IRREGULAR FIGHTERS

I have referred earlier (pages 22-6) to the evolution of conditions under which irregular fighters qualify for protection as combatants under the Hague and Geneva Conventions. During the period 1949-64, these conditions were:

1. that the fighters are members of 'organized resistance movements, belonging to a Party to the conflict';
2. that they are commanded by a person responsible for his subordinates;
3. that they have a fixed distinctive emblem recognizable at a distance;

---

[29] *Le Comité internationale de la Croix-Rouge et le Conflit de Corée,* vol. II, pp. 90-1, 107; Forsythe, *Humanitarian Politics,* p. 43.
[30] Text of the vetoed proposals in Bailey, *Voting in the Security Council,* pp. 175-6.
[31] GA res. 706 (VII), 23 April 1953.

4.   that they carry their arms openly;
5.   that they conduct their operations in accordance with the laws and customs of war.

From the time of the Bandung Conference, there was increasing Communist and Third World pressure to relax these requirements so as to afford protection to all those fighting in national liberation struggles. The first Additional Protocol (1977) to the Geneva Conventions, which was not in effect during the period covered by the cases in volume II, varied the requirement that a fixed distinctive emblem recognizable at a distance should be carried: instead combatants have to distinguish themselves from civilians 'while they are engaged in an attack or in a military operation preparatory to an attack'. When, owing to 'the nature of the hostilities', an armed combatant cannot so distinguish himself, he shall retain his combatant status so long as he carries arms openly 'during each military engagement' and during such time as a combatant is 'visible to the adversary while he is engaged in a military deployment preceding the launching of an attack'.[32]

In most of the cases studied, irregular fighters formed an important element on one or both sides, and some of the worst atrocities were committed by elements not under the effective control of the authorities for which they claimed to be fighting. In the Arab-Israel struggle, both sides have complained that the other was using fighters wearing civilian clothes, and there were endless problems of men who were farmers by day and guerrilla fighters by night.[33] In Korea, there were many difficulties during the armistice negotiations when the Kaesong-Panmunjom-Munsan conference area was violated by South Korean irregulars not under the control of the Unified Command, and the only plausible response of the Unified Command to the complaints of North Korea and China was an admission and an apology.[34] In Cyprus the worst provocations were committed by irregulars attached to EOKA or TMT, the Greek and Turkish guerrilla organizations.[35]

[32] A/32/144, 15 Aug. 1977, Annex I, Article 29 (3). See Rosenblad, pp. 75-102, 148-50.
[33] Burns, p. 68; Bull, p. 61.
[34] Hermes, pp. 42, 44; Ridgway, p. 199; Goodmann, p. 31.
[35] Harbottle, pp. 11-12; SCOR, 19th year, Supplement for April-June 1964, pp. 225-6, para. 67 of S/5764.

UN observers have not always investigated incidents that on the face of it were caused by irregular elements. When the truce went into effect in Indonesia in 1948, there was a good deal of concern that so many violations were committed by Indonesian irregulars. In an attempt to calm the situation, the Good Offices Committee secured the agreement of both parties that incidents would be investigated only if there were prima facie evidence that they had been instigated by a government.[36]

The UN Mediator in Palestine took the view that the governments of Israel and the Arab states should take full responsibility for all activities in areas that they occupied. The difficulty was that Israel was never able to control the activities of some Jewish partisans, and the Arab governments, other than Lebanon after 4 July 1948, disclaimed responsibility for the activities of Arab irregulars. On 18 August 1948 Bernadotte reported to the Security Council on the difficulties he was encountering and suggested that the Council should warn that each party was responsible for violations of the cease-fire, whether caused by opposing armies or by dissident elements or irregulars, and that each party had a responsibility to bring to justice its own dissident elements or irregulars if they breached the cease-fire. Bernadotte's advice was incorporated in a draft resolution and approved.[37] The four armistice agreements the following year prohibited all war-like or hostile acts, whether committed by military or para-military forces, 'including non-regular forces'.

The only case in which the parties expressly agreed about the status of irregular fighters was in Indonesia following the truce that took effect on 1 August 1949. An agreed manual was prepared, and this defined 'armed forces' as comprising the persons covered by the Regulations attached to the Hague Convention of 1907 on the laws and customs of war on land.[38] But this agreement did not end the difficulties. A month after the truce had entered into force, a harassed US consular official cabled to Washington:

[36] SCOR, 3rd year, Supplement for June 1948, p. 62, S/787.

[37] S/1025, 5 Oct. 1948 (mimeo), para. 30; GAOR, 3rd session, Supplement no. 11, A/648, p. 34 (para. 13); SCOR, 3rd year, 354th mtg (19 Aug. 1948), pp. 40-1, S/977; Bernadotte, pp. 124-5; SC res. 56 (S/983), 19 Aug. 1948.

[38] SCOR, 4th year, Special Supplement no. 5, p. 64, Appendix VIII to S/1373 and Corr. 1. The Hague Convention is misdated in the printed records of the Security Council.

What constitutes a military post in case of Republic forces? If small TNI force [Indonesian national army] lived in a kampong [compound] where there were no Dutch troops and based their guerrilla war from there but did not openly wear uniform prior to cease fire, then after cease fire wear uniform and claim kampong as TNI post, is this permissible?[39]

In order to avoid difficulties of this kind, the parties later agreed that all combatants should carry an identity card signed by a senior officer.[40]

5.4 PRISONERS OF WAR

Until modern times, captured soldiers could expect no mercy. Many were killed, on the battlefield or later; those who survived were often held to ransom or enslaved, although slavery as between Christian adversaries was forbidden in 1179 by the Third Lateran Council. Five things were needed to ensure the humanitarian protection of fighters who wished to withdraw from military activity: that those willing to lay down their arms should be able to surrender to the opposing party without fear of being killed or injured; that prisoners should not be punished simply for having fought; that prisoners should be treated humanely while in the custody of the opposing party; that prisoners should not be compelled by the detaining power to take part in military operations against their own side; and that prisoners should recover their freedom at the end of the war.

The first codification of international law regarding prisoners of war was in the Declaration of Brussels, 1874.[41] The law was further developed in the Regulations attached to the Hague Conventions of 1899 and 1907 on the laws and customs of war on land.[42] The first international convention concerned exclusively with the treatment of POWs was completed in Geneva in 1929, and this was superseded by a revised instrument which

---

[39] FRUS, 1949, vol. VII, 1975, p. 481; SCOR, 5th year, Special Supplement no. 1, p. 5, para. 23 of S/1449.

[40] SCOR, 5th year, Special Supplement no. 1, p. 5, para. 23 (c) of S/1449.

[41] *Documents Relating to the Program of the First Hague Peace Conference,* Oxford, Clarendon Press, 1921, pp. 36-7, Articles 23-34.

[42] *Hague Conventions of 1899 (II) and 1907 (IV) Respecting the Laws and Customs of War on Land,* pp. 9-17, Articles 4-20 and 23 (c).

was one of the four Geneva Conventions of 1949.[43] Additional Protocol I to the Geneva Conventions also deals with prisoners of war.[44] It hardly needs saying that captured fighters who do not qualify for POW *status* are entitled to humane *treatment*.

National attitudes towards capture and prisoner status vary. General Burns, who was head of the UN observer mission in the Middle East and later commanded the UN Emergency Force, reports that he encountered 'extraordinary sensitivity' in Israel about Jews falling into Arab hands and that Jewish opinion in Israel was easily inflamed about POWs. He speculates that this was because of Jewish memories of Nazi concentration camps.[45] Some Jewish Israelis have found it difficult to believe that Arabs care about their prisoners in Israeli hands, and have believed that reports of Israeli mistreatment of Arab prisoners were fabricated. In the Korean War, it was taken for granted by the Unified Command that the Communists were in no way restrained by humanitarian considerations in their treatment of captured personnel and that the Communist side regarded the activities of prisoners held by the Unified Command and the treatment of the Unified Command prisoners in their own hands as a continuation of the war by other means. Naturally, I am not asserting that such fears are baseless, but simply that it is often difficult to understand that the opposing party has similar fears.

The main problems likely to arise in connection with POWs are dealt with in the Hague and Geneva Conventions. It is widely held that the detaining power's obligations do not depend on reciprocity, as the parties to the Geneva Conventions have agreed to respect them 'in all circumstances'.[46] Moreover, the Nürnberg Tribunal declared that the rules of land warfare laid down in the Hague Convention of 1907 were declaratory of the laws and customs of war and were recognized by civilized nations. In practice, truce and armistice agreements have often included provisions confirming that international law will be

---

[43] *Geneva Convention, 1929,* (LNTS, vol. 118, no. 343); Geneva Convention III, 1949.

[44] A/32/144, 15 Aug. 1977 (mimeo), Annex I, Aticles 43-7.

[45] Burns, p. 36; Bull, p. 47.

[46] Geneva Conventions, 1949, Article 1; Rosas, pp. 111-12.

carried out.[47] All POWs should be released when the fighting stops, even if the opposing party is in breach of international law; but when one side holds substantially more POWs than the other, it is tempting to propose a man-for-man exchange rather than all-for-all. After the first Dutch 'police action', the Netherlands submitted to the UN Good Offices Committee the names of '197 missing personnel'. The Indonesian Republicans responded with the names of 12 POWs whom they had held, two of whom had died, four of whom had already been exchanged, and only six of whom were still being detained. The Netherlands at once expressed 'deep regret' and stated that there was no basis for an exchange of POWs. A month later, however, agreement was reached by which some 1,500 Indonesians were released by the Netherlands and 6 prisoners by the Indonesian Republicans. More than 1,000 more Indonesians were subsequently released to the Republicans. A later offer by the Good Offices Committee to visit POW camps was accepted by the Republicans but rejected by the Netherlands on the ground that 'the Netherlands authorities were solely responsible for the custody of these prisoners and could not permit interference'. The Netherlands informed the Good Offices Committee that 'in some cases, prisoners had expressed a desire not to return to their homes'. After the second 'police action', the Republicans were also to claim that some prisoners did not wish to return to their former places of residence.[48] This problem was to be very troublesome in Korea.

After the second 'police action' in Indonesia, there were complications about the release of POWs because of separatist activities in parts of the archipelago. In particular, several

[47] In the case of Indonesia I, see SCOR, 3rd year, Special Supplement no. 1, pp. 73-4, para. 7 (f) of Appendix XI to S/649/Rev. 1. For the unimplemented Kashmir truce agreement, see SCOR, 4th year, Special Supplement no. 7, pp. 171-2, para. 5 of Annex 47 to S/1430. In the Palestine case, see SCOR, 4th year, Special Supplement no. 1 (Jordan), S/1302/Rev. 1, Article X; Special Supplement no. 2 (Syria), S/1353/Rev. 1, Article VI; Special Supplement no. 3 (Egypt), S/1264/Rev. 1, Article IX; Special Supplement no. 4 (Lebanon), S/1296/Rev. 1, Article VI. In the case of Indonesia II, see SCOR, 4th year, Special Supplement no. 5, p. 60, para. 2 of Joint Proclamation in Appendix VIII. II to S/1373. In the Korean case, see SCOR, 8th year, Supplement for July to September 1953, pp. 30-4, 43-5, paras. 51-9 of S/3079, S/3084.

[48] SCOR, 3rd year, Supplement for June 1948, pp. 60-1, 143, S/787, S/848/Add. 1; 5th year, Special Supplement no. 1, p. 15, para. 62 of S/1449.

thousand South Moluccan servicemen and their dependents rejected repatriation or settlement in any part of Indonesia, and were eventually transferred to the Netherlands, where their unsatisfied political aspirations have continued to cause difficulties.[49]

The draft truce for Kashmir, which was negotiated but never confirmed, provided for a man-for-man exchange of Indian and Indian Kashmiri prisoners for Pakistani and Azad Kashmiri prisoners, followed by an all-for-all release of the remaining Indian and Indian Kashmiri prisoners as well as 'raiders and Pathans'. The two truce plans of the UN Commission for India and Pakistan, which were not accepted by the/parties, simply provided for the release of all POWs 'within one month'. Although agreement was never reached on a truce in Kashmir, there was an initial exchange of wounded POWs, followed in April 1949 by a general exchange under the auspices of the International Committee of the Red Cross.[50]

During the Palestine war, officials of the United Nations and the International Committee of the Red Cross did what they could to ensure correct treatment for POWs—for example, during the surrender of the Old City of Jerusalem. In talks at the end of 1948 between Moshe Dayan and his Jordanian opposite number, Abdullah El-Tell, it was agreed that there should be an all-for-all exchange: 'about a dozen' members of the Arab Legion for 670 Israelis, mainly from the Old City of Jerusalem or the group of settlements at Kefar Etsyon. Dayan offered to pay El-Tell 'any sum that was asked' by way of expenses, and El-Tell later submitted an invoice for a trivial amount, being the bus fares from the Jordanian camp at Mafrak to Jerusalem. On the other fronts (Egypt, Lebanon, Syria), the POW problem was dealt with in the armistice agreements, and questions not covered in the agreements were to be settled in accordance with the principles of the 1929 Convention. Each

---

[49] Ibid., 4th year, Special Supplement no. 6, p. 21, para. 62 of S/1373; 5th year, Special Supplement no. 1, pp. 13-16, paras. 57-67 of S/1449; 6th year, Special Supplement no. 1, pp. 5-8, 25-9, 47-57, paras. 19-28, 109-32 of and Appendices XI to XVII to S/2087.

[50] Ibid., 3rd year, Supplement for June 1948, pp. 105, 112, 171-2, Annexes 17, 21, 47 to S/1430; Report on the activities of the International Committee of the Red Cross for 1949, Geneva, 1950, p. 87.

Mixed Armistice Commission was to try and locate missing personnel, whether military or civilian. All POWs were to be exchanged, whether regulars or irregulars, including those against whom penal prosecutions were pending or who had already been sentenced. When the beleaguered Egyptian and Sudanese forces in the Faluja area were released in 1949, they 'spontaneously handed over their Israeli prisoners' before proceeding to Egypt.[51]

The heads of the UN Truce Supervision Organization were to give a good deal of attention to POW matters in the years that followed. On one occasion, Syria objected to prisoners being asked if they wished to be exchanged, for fear that Arab POWs in Israeli hands might, under pressure, opt for Israel.[52] After the Sinai-Suez episode, the UN Emergency Force was able to arrange an exchange of Egyptian servicemen in British and French hands for British civilians who had been interned in Egypt. Later an exchange was organized of about 5,600 Egyptians for 4 Israelis.[53]

The most difficult POW case was, of course, in Korea. As noted above, this was not the first occasion on which POWs had been reluctant or unwilling to return home, but the scale and complexity of the problem were without precedent.

The Hague and Geneva Conventions had long provided that sick and wounded prisoners of war should be repatriated as soon as they are fit to travel and that healthy POWs should be released and repatriated without delay once hostilities had ceased.[54] When war broke out in Korea, the International Committee of the Red Cross (ICRC) appealed to North and South Korea and the states supplying armed forces to the Unified Command to apply the humanitarian principles of the Geneva Conventions. South Korea agreed to examine with the ICRC how the principles of the Conventions could be applied.

[51] Azcárate, pp. 70-1, 73; Reynier, p. 143; Dayan, pp. 102-3; Rosenne, p. 64; Report on the activities of the International Committee of the Red Cross for 1949, Geneva, 1950, pp. 73-4.

[52] SC res. 111 (SL/3538), 19 Jan. 1956; Burns pp. 34-5, 38-9, 108-10, 119-20; Bull, pp. 46-9.

[53] Burns, pp. 232, 245-6; Supplement to the *London Gazette,* 12 September 1957, p. 5337.

[54] Geneva Convention III, 1949, Articles 109-10, 118. See Christine Shields Delessert, *Release and Repatriation of Prisoners of War,* pp. 70-1; Rosas, pp. 478-86.

North Korea said that it would apply the principles of the POW Convention but disregarded all requests from the ICRC to allow a representative to visit Pyongyang.[55] Britain sent a guarded reply to the effect that, to the extent that the Geneva Conventions are declaratory of the accepted principles of international law, Britain 'should, of course, regard them as applicable'.[56]

Shortly after the outbreak of war, the State Department had produced a major policy document about the course of action best calculated to advance the US national interest. This included a proposal that treatment of North Korean POWs should be directed towards 'their exploitation, training and use for psychological warfare purposes'. This was approved by President Truman and sent as a directive to General MacArthur, and a copy was issued to US ambassador Warren Austin at the United Nations. Determination to exploit the POW issue was not confined to the Unified Command: the Communists did not regard a prisoner of war as 'a passive human being in need of care and protection until he could be returned to his home, but as still an active soldier determined to fight on'. The United States eventually came to a rather similar position and began to teach its military personnel 'that they had a duty to continue the struggle after capture'.[57]

The question of the disposition of POWs was the fourth item on the agenda of the armistice negotiations. Discussion began on 11 December 1951 and continued, with interruptions, until July 1953. On the face of its, the Unified Command was unwilling to apply the obligation in the Third Geneva Convention of 1949 to repatriate all POWs at the end of the war, at any rate not in the generally accepted sense, and its negotiating position was shaky because it was never possible to be sure precisely

[55] When China and North Korea accepted the Geneva POW Convention in 1956 and 1957 respectively, they made declarations regarding Articles 10 (Protecting Powers) and 12 (transfer of POWs), and reservations regarding Article 85 (prosecution of war criminals), as did other Communist states, although Britain did not consider these declarations or reservations as valid. See Claude Pilloud, *Reservations to the Geneva Conventions of 1949*, Geneva, ICRC, 1976, and Rosas, pp. 118-19.

[56] *Comité international de la Croix-Rouge et le Conflit de Corée*, vol. I, pp. 3-31, 37-8.

[57] FRUS, 1950, vol. VII, 1976, pp. 678, 712 n. 1, 718, 782, 793 n. 2; Joy, p. 152; SCOR, 8th year, Supplement for January-March 1953, pp. 48-9, S/2970; Ridgway, p. 207; Forsythe, *Humanitarian Politics*, p. 136.

how many North Korean and Chinese POWs would refuse
repatriation: on one occasion, the Unified Command was
mortified to discover that more than 2,000 POWs had been
counted twice. At the conference at which the Geneva Convention had been adopted, an amendment had been proposed
by Austria which would have permitted a POW to ask for
transfer to a country other than his own, but this had been
defeated by a large majority.[58] The 1949 Convention provides
that no sick or injured prisoner may be repatriated during
hostilities 'against his will',[59] but there is no qualification of
this kind in the provision for repatriation after the cessation of
active hostilities.[60] All the same, the Geneva Convention did
not envisage that force should be used to compel an unwilling
prisoner to accept repatriation. If objection to repatriation were
genuine, it was argued, then the right of asylum could be held
to prevail over the normal obligation to repatriate. Thus the
Unified Command was basing itself on humanitarian principles
rather than on the letter of the Geneva Convention, and when
this position was criticized, it was little consolation to reply that
the Communist side was in breach of other provisions of the
Geneva Conventions.

   The solution that eventually emerged for Korea was to
entrust POWs refusing repatriation to a supposedly neutral
body, though there were acrimonious negotiations about which
nations had been really neutral during the Korean War and
could therefore be trusted to be fair. During the sixth regular
session of the UN General Assembly in 1952, India submitted
a proposal that was to provide a solution to the POW question.
This stated:

1.   that prisoners of war should be released and repatriated
     in accordance with the Third Geneva Convention of 1949,
     'the well-established principles and practice of inter-
     national law', and the relevant provisions of the armistice
     agreement;

---

[58] Delessert, pp. 160-1, 169-70; Rosas, pp. 477, 480-3; Greenspan, pp. 146-7.
[59] Geneva Convention III, 1949, Article 109.
[60] Geneva Convention III, 1949, Article 118.

2.   that POWs should be free to return to their homelands, but force should not be used 'to prevent or effect their return', and they should at all times be treated humanely;

3.   that POWs unwilling to accept repatriation should be released into the custody of a repatriation commission composed of representatives of Czechoslovakia, Poland, Sweden, and Switzerland, which should make recommendations about their disposition.

On 7 May 1953, the Communists accepted this framework, with the addition of India to the proposed repatriation commission.[61]

Over 7,000 sick and wounded prisoners were exchanged on an all-for-all basis in April and May 1953, and over 88,000 POWs were exchanged in the normal way after the armistice. Some 23,000 prisoners refused repatriation and were placed in the custody of the Neutral Nations Repatriation Commission (NNRC) and an Indian Custodial Force in the demilitarized zone: these comprised 7,900 Koreans and 14,704 Chinese held by the Unified Command, and 335 Koreans, 23 from the United States, and 1 from Britain, held by the Communists.

The NNRC, not unexpectedly, was an unharmonious body. When a contentious issue arose, the Czech and Polish members were always ranged against the Swedish and Swiss members, so the view of the Indian chairman was decisive. It was the NNRC's responsibility to supervise the 'explanations' to be given to the prisoners by representatives of the parties, but when a POW had already made up his mind, it was difficult to induce him to listen to an unpalatable 'explanation'. The NNRC distributed a leaflet to every prisoner stressing the neutrality of the supervisory system and assuring the prisoners of their absolute right to a free choice. Most of the prisoners were more interested in political demonstrations than in having the situation explained to them, and there was a good deal of brutal intimidation. The NNRC found both the Unified Command and the Communist side unhelpful.

---

[61] Acheson, pp. 696-7, 699-705, 765-7; Henry Cabot Lodge, *As It was: An Inside View of Politics and Power in the '50s and '60s,* New York, Norton, 1976, pp. 33-4; GA Res 610. (VI), 3 Dec. 1952; SCOR, 8th year, Supplement for July-September 1953, pp. 66, S/3091.

The armistice agreement had provided that no force or threat of force was to be used to prevent or compel repatriation, but it was unclear how much force could properly be used for other purposes, such as to keep order, segregate prisoners, or bring unwilling prisoners to hear 'explanations'. The Swedish and Swiss members of the NNRC believed that any use of force was contrary to the letter and spirit of the Geneva Convention. The Czechoslovak and Polish members considered that some use of force was permissible, while the Indian chairman took the view that to use force would almost certainly cause an unacceptably large number of casualties. In the end, some force had to be used and three prisoners were killed.

The East European and Indian members of the NNRC concluded in the end that intimidation by South Korean agents was such that a prisoner desiring repatriation had to express his view clandestinely and in fear of his life. The Swedish and Swiss members thought that this was an exaggerated view. All the members of the NNRC agreed, however, that the explanations had been neither complete nor free of improper pressure. After hearing 'explanations', 628 POWs formerly held by the Unified Command opted for China or North Korea, 7,604 for South Korea, 14, 235 for Taiwan, 51 died or escaped or disappeared, and 86 asked to go to a neutral country. Of the POWs formerly held by the Communists, 347 returned to Communist control after hearing 'explanations', 10 went to the Unified Command, and 2 chose a neutral country. The 88 prisoners from the two sides wishing to go to a neutral country were moved to Madras in February 1954. More than 60 of these expressed a desire to settle in the United States, but the chairman of the NNRC had to explain that the United States had not been a neutral nation. Of the prisoners initially refusing repatriation, 8 eventually opted for North Korea or China, 5 for India, and 69 for a Latin American country, leaving 5 who in 1959 had still not been accepted by the country of their choice and one who was mentally disturbed.[62]

---

[62] GAOR, 8th session, Supplement no. 18, A/2641; 9th session, Annexes, Agenda item 17, A/2809; 10th session, Annexes, Agenda item 19, A/2941 and Add. 1; 11th session, Annexes, Agenda item 21, A/3203; 14th session, First Committee, 1064th mtg (26 Nov. 1959), para. 43.

In his analysis of the major problems in obtaining implementation of the Geneva POW Convention, David Forsythe concludes that the main difficulty in Korea was the refusal of North Korea and China to accept the principle that combatants who had surrendered or been captured should 'benefit from a benevolent quarantine'. While South Korea and the Unified Command had accepted the principles of the Geneva Convention, there were some serious problems over implementation.[63] Allan Rosas, on the other hand, considers that the Korean experience should not be considered as a precedent. Most of the states with armed forces in Korea had not formally accepted the obligations of the 1949 Convention, the conflict had both internal and external elements, and the classification of prisoners between those accepting and those refusing repatriation created 'a situation which the drafters of the Convention wanted to avoid'.[64]

In the highly ideological climate in which wars are now fought, one would expect continuing problems over prisoners of war. As in the past, detaining states are likely to try to brainwash POWs in their custody so as to undermine their loyalty, using morally abhorrent means of pressure and intimidation, and to refuse to repatriate some or all prisoners except in exchange for a concession from the other side. POWs risk becoming hostages, although the taking of hostages is a violation of international law.

While one can only deplore the blatant exploitation of POWs for political purposes, the Korean experience did at least suggest the principles that can be applied in cases not expressly covered by international instruments. However mixed its motives may have been, the Unified Command was surely right in insisting that force should not be used to effect or prevent repatriation. POWs who refuse to return home should be released into custody of an impartial agency, either an existing one or an agency created *ad hoc*; but it should be recognized that to be a citizen of a neutral state is not necessarily to be an impartial person. It would have been better, in the Korean case, if POWs refusing repatriation had been released to an independent body

---

[63] Forsythe, *Humanitarian Politics,* pp. 134-6.
[64] Rosas, pp. 481, 483.

like the International Committee of the Red Cross: such a course was not feasible in Korea in the absence of agreement from the Communist side.[65] It should be added that the International Committee of the Red Cross was not happy about some aspects of the way the problem was handled in Korea, believing that repatriation should continue to be the norm.[66]

5.5 REFUGEES AND DISPLACED PERSONS

In UN jargon, refugees are persons who, owing to well-founded fear of persecution for reasons of race, religion, nationality, or political opinion, are outside their country of origin and cannot or, owing to such fear, do not wish to avail themselves of the protection of that country. Persons covered by this definition are entitled to the protection of the UN High Commissioner for Refugees.[67] Most refugees are thus persons who are in a foreign country and cannot or will not return home. Some of the Palestinian refugees are still in what was formerly Palestine: their predicament is not that they are unable or unwilling to go back home, for home is where they say they want to go. Moreover, they cannot avail themselves of the protection of their country of origin, as the Palestine that they or their parents or grandparents left no longer exists. What was formerly Mandated Palestine now comprises Israel within the armistice borders; the West Bank and East Jerusalem, which formed part of Jordan from 1948 until the Israeli occupation of the West Bank and the annexation of East Jerusalem in 1967; and the Gaza Strip, administered by Egypt from 1948 until its occupation by Israel in 1967.

Although Palestine refugees are not encompassed by the standard UN definition, many of them still qualify for international assistance from a special UN agency: the UN Relief and Works Agency for Palestine refugees in the Near East. The resolution of the General Assembly establishing the agency for

---

[65] *Comité international de la Croix-Rouge et le Conflit de Corée,* Geneva, 1952, vol. II, pp. 51-2.

[66] Rosas, p. 481, 485-6.

[67] GA res.428 (V), 14 Dec. 1950.

Palestine refugees contained no definition of persons within the scope of the agency.[68]

Those persons who have been uprooted from their homes by war but who do not qualify as refugees are usually known as displaced persons.

Except when hostilities take place in uninhabited territory, such as the Sinai desert or the mountains of Kashmir, civilians are likely to be driven from their homes by the fighting. If they have been forced out of their own country but wish to return home when peace returns, they are displaced persons; but if for one of the reasons referred to in the UN definition they are unable or unwilling to be repatriated, they are regarded as refugees and are often thought of as a moral responsibility of the international community until they decide or are allowed to return home or are formally settled in the country where they have taken refuge or in some third country. There are often uncertainties or ambiguities about the status of these uprooted people; and agreements between the parties about their protection and right to move are likely to be formulated in such a way as not to foreclose by an arbitrary definition their eventual freedom of choice. Thus a resolution of the Security Council of 21 April 1948 recommended that citizens who had left Kashmir on account of the disturbances should be invited and be free to return to their homes and to exercise all their rights as citizens. The UN Commission for India and Pakistan later suggested that repatriation commissions should be set up in India and Pakistan to 'operate under the direction of the Plebiscite Administrator' in putting the provision into effect. In the event, India decided that a repatriation commission 'would serve no useful purpose' and Pakistan expressed a preference for a joint commission.[69] The Korean armistice provided that

---

[68] GA res. 302 (IV), 8 Dec. 1949.

[69] SC res. 47 (S/726), 21 April 1948; SCOR, 4th year, Supplement for January 1949, p. 24, para. 15 of S/1196; Special Supplement no. 7, pp. 8, 65-6, para. 23 and paras. 11-28 of Appendix III to S/1430; Report on the work of the International Committee of the Red Cross for 1 July 1947-31 December 1948, Geneva, 1949, pp. 96-7; Report on the work of the International Committee of the Red Cross for 1949, Geneva, 1950, p. 87; Report on the work of the International Committee of the Red Cross for 1950, Geneva, 1951, p. 73.

civilians who had resided in North or South Korea before the war but found themselves in territory controlled by the other side should, if they desired to return home, 'be permitted and assisted' to do so; and a joint Committee for Assisting the Return of Displaced Civilians was established to co-ordinate the plans of the two sides.[70] In the Cyprus case, there were in the summer of 1964 about 10,000 displaced Turkish Cypriots in the Nicosia and Kyrenia areas and another 7,000 in predominantly Turkish villages elsewhere in Cyprus. In the reports of the UN Secretary-General, the relevant sections are headed 'displaced persons', but in the text they are usually referred to as 'refugees'.[71]

The Palestine refugees constitute a special case, and it is not easy to describe accurately and simply the circumstances in which they left their homes. The first wave of Arab Palestinians to leave was composed of the more prosperous and cosmopolitan families who began to move to the predominantly Arab parts of Palestine or to neighbouring Arab countries after the UN General Assembly had decided on partition. The second wave was of more authentic war victims who left their homes as the fighting approached, or were driven from their homes as a result of the fighting, or who fled because they did not want to live under Jewish-Israeli occupation. The third wave were mainly victims of terror, those who had witnessed or heard accounts of Jewish excesses, sometimes exaggerated or fabricated. There were smaller waves of refugees after the renewed outbreaks of fighting in October and December 1948 and March 1949. To a greater or lesser extent, almost all the refugees were deceived by Arab propaganda and believed that Zionism was on the point of collapse, but there seems to be no truth in the allegation that they were encouraged to leave by Arab radio broadcasts.[72]

The Palestine refugees were soon to become a bargaining counter in the larger power struggle between Israel and the

[70] SCOR, 8th year, Supplement for July-September 1953, pp. 33-4, S/3079 (Article 59).

[71] SCOR, 19th year, Supplement for April-June 1964, pp. 92, 226, 232-4, Annex I to S/5671, paras. 70, 91-3 of S/5764; Supplement for July-September 1964, pp. 321-2, paras. 177-83 of S/5950.

[72] Erskine B. Childers, 'The Other Exodus', *The Spectator*, 12 May 1961, p. 672.

Arab world. Israel took the line that there could be no substantial repatriation of Arabs in advance of a comprehensive
settlement. The Arabs based their position on part of the resolution of the General Assembly of 11 December 1948 to the
effect that refugees wishing to return home and live at peace
with their neighbours should be allowed to do so and that
compensation should be paid to those not opting for repatriation
—a resolution that the Arabs staunchly opposed at the time.[73]
The refugees themselves, many in miserable camps to this day
after more than three decades, dream of the time when history
will be reversed and they return to the Palestine of their parents
and grandparents. It is not surprising that extravagant political
ideas flourish in such an environment and that there is a steady
flow of recruits for the terrorist organizations and suicide
squads. Here is fruitful breeding ground for future wars.

5.6 ABDUCTED PERSONS AND HOSTAGES

Although hostage-taking was formerly regarded as a legitimate
form of reprisal action, the taking of hostages is now contrary
to the Geneva Conventions, and the taking of civilians as
hostages is regarded as a grave breach.[74] The legal and ethical
basis is that it is wrong to harm innocent people directly, even
if harm to the innocent is sometimes unavoidable as an indirect
consequence of legitimate action.

During the fighting in Kashmir, some 50,000-60,000 women
were abducted by Muslim tribesmen or Azad Kashmiri troops.
When the Commanders-in-Chief of India and Pakistan met in
January 1949, India raised the question of the return of these
people. Pakistan agreed to do what was possible 'but pointed
out the difficulty of obtaining the return of women who had
been abducted by tribesmen'. The International Committee of
the Red Cross later reported one small exchange (140 women
and children by Pakistan against 254 women by India), but it

---

[73] GA res. 194 (III), 11 Dec. 1948.
[74] Geneva Conventions, 1949, Common Article 3 (1) (b) and Geneva Convention
IV, Articles 34 and 147; see also Additional Protocols, A/32/144, 15 Aug. 1977
(mimeo), Annex I, Article 75.2 (c) and Annex II, Article 4.2 (c).

is likely that the majority of abducted women were never re-leased.[75]

By the time the Cyprus crisis erupted at the end of 1963, there had begun a world-wide spate of kidnapping and hostage-taking for political purposes. The first instance of hostage-taking in Cyprus occurred in the early days of the crisis. Omorphita was attacked by Greek Cypriot irregulars under Nicos Sampson and, according to Turkish sources, some 700 Turkish Cypriots were taken hostage, mainly women and children. Duncan Sandys, the British Minister for Common-wealth Affairs, was visiting Cyprus and was able to arrange an exchange of 545 Turks for 26 Greeks. There were further out-breaks of hostage-taking by both communities, and a parti-cularly gruesome incident in Famagusta in May 1964 in which 32 Turkish Cypriots were taken hostage at random after the murder of 3 Greeks who had entered the Turkish sector. This instance of hostage-taking was condemned by President Maka-rios, who appealed for their release, but they were very probably dead by then. Negotiations for the release of all hostages were conducted by the International Committee of the Red Cross, which was eventually able to secure the release of 100 members of the Turkish community and 24 members of the Greek com-munity, leaving 232 Turks and 38 Greeks unaccounted for.[76]

5.7 POLITICAL PRISONERS

A few years ago, an organization with which I am associated wrote to the president of a foreign country suggesting that, as a humanitarian gesture and to improve the regional climate of opinion, some of the less dangerous political prisoners might be conditionally paroled or amnestied. In due course the reply came back that there were no political prisoners in that country,

[75] Report of the International Committee of the Red Cross for 1 July 1947-31 December 1948, Geneva, 1949, p. 96; Report on the work of the International Committee of the Red Cross for 1949, Geneva, 1950, p. 87; SCOR, 4th year, Special Supplement no. 7, pp. 10, 72, para. 33 and section 6 of Annex 47 to S/1430.

[76] H. D. Purcell, *Cyprus,* New York, Praeger, 1969, pp. 325-8, 333, 341; Report on the work of the International Committee of the Red Cross for 1964, Geneva, 1965, p. 16; SCOR, 19th year, Supplement for April-June 1964, pp. 216, 224, 239, paras. 18, 62-4, 117 of S/5764; Supplement for July-September 1964, p. 314, paras. 142-4 of S/550.

only murderers, terrorists, saboteurs, and other persons who had broken the criminal law.

A government that is determined to silence political dissidents can usually find a plausible reason for doing so. If political opponents have not actually broken the law, then the law can be changed: to belong to or associate with a particular political movement can be made an offence. If political dissidents have not broken the law, and if the law cannot be changed in such a way as to bring the opposition within the category of law-breakers, a determined government can invent spurious charges, such as that they have broken some obscure tax or currency regulation. The fact is that no country likes to admit to itself or the outside world that persons are arrested or punished simply for holding dissenting political beliefs.

So although it is rare for a state to admit to holding political prisoners, we all know that such people exist, in foreign countries even if not at home, concealed behind bland bureaucratic jargon: civilian detainees or internees, say, or security prisoners, or persons undergoing moral re-education.

If armed conflict results in territorial occupation, and if the territory is inhabited, then a struggle for the minds of those under occupation is likely to ensue. In that event, those opponents of the occupying power who do not go into exile are likely to find themselves in trouble with the authorities. The Netherlands, after its first 'police action' in Indonesia in 1947, arrested 200 prominent Indonesians in Batavia (Djakarta), and the continued detention of these people was one of the problems that had to be surmounted before the fighting could be effectively halted. The *Renville* truce agreement provided for the release of all prisoners without regard to the numbers held by either side. The Republicans then proposed that, as an act of goodwill and to relieve social tension, there should be an amnesty of those political prisoners whose 'capacities were valuable to the work of reconstruction'. The initial response of the Dutch was that 'no one was detained by the Netherlands authorities or deprived of his freedom exclusively on the grounds of his political convictions'. Some people were detained because, having previously committed 'acts of terrorism', it was feared that they might repeat the offence; and others who had commited no offence were held 'because they were thought likely to create unrest and disorder'. The UN Good Offices Committee took the line that what was needed was 'a general political amnesty', and after six weeks of negotiation agreement was reached on the release of all persons who had been 'entirely or partly, legally and/or actually deprived of their liberty in connection with the extraordinary conditions prevailing in [Java, Madura, and Sumatra] relating to the political dispute existing between the two parties and who are not prisoners of war or criminals'.[77]

After the second 'police action' the problem was much more acute, as the Dutch authorities had arrested almost the entire Republican leadership. Australia proposed in the Security Council that a cease-fire resolution should include a call for the immediate release of President Sukarno and his colleagues, and this was approved by seven votes to none, Belgium and France abstaining because of legal reservations and the Soviet Union because it favoured a stronger text. The Ukrainian SSR was absent but later said that it wish to be counted as having abstained. The wording of the resolution was somewhat odd. The original proposal had been to call on 'the parties' to cease hostilities. The Australian amendment added a second call to 'the parties': to release Republican prisoners. This was, of course, something that only one of the parties could do.[78] Four days later, China proposed that the Council should again call for the immediate release of political prisoners, and this was approved.[79]

The Netherlands certainly handled the question of political prisoners in a clumsy way. On the day the Security Council adopted the second resolution, the Netherlands authorities in Indonesia had told the UN Good Offices Committee (GOC) that fifteen Republicans had been released and that it had been provisionally decided to 'assign residence' to a number of others 'in mountain resorts outside Java'.[80] Ten days later, the

---

[77] SCOR, 2nd year, 184th mtg (14 Aug. 1947), p. 2001; 3rd year, Special Supplement no. 1, pp. 69, 73-4, para. 4 of Appendix IX and para. 7 (f) of Appendix XI to S/649/Rev. 1; Supplement for June 1948, pp. 55-7, S/787.

[78] Ibid., 3rd year, 389th mtg (22 Dec. 1948), p. 39; 390th mtg (23 Dec. 1948), p. 15, S/1145; 392nd mtg (24 Dec. 1948), p.33; SC res. 63 (S/1150), 24 Dec. 1948; FRUS, 1948, vol. VI, 1974, p. 587.

[79] SCOR, 3rd year, 395th mtg (28 Dec. 1948), pp. 49-51; SC res. 64 (S/1164), 28 Dec. 1948.

[80] SCOR, 3rd year, Supplement for December 1948, p. 323, para. 3 of S/1166.

GOC reported that Republican prisoners had not been released, but the same day the Dutch ambassador told the Security Council that the senior Republicans were on the island of Bangka and were 'at complete liberty throughout the entire island'. On 14 January 1949, the GOC was given permission to send a delegation to Bangka, and the visit took place the following day. The GOC found the Republican ministers in 'one doorless bedroom, six metres by six metres, in which are six beds'. Windows were covered with wire netting. The Republicans had been asked to renounce all political activities but had refused. When this report reached the Security Council, the Netherlands expressed 'deep regret': the decisions taken by the Dutch authorities in Indonesia were 'in direct opposition' to the instructions of the Hague government. The Security Council agreed that the imprisoned Republicans should be allowed to use GOC facilities for communicating with the Security Council. On 25 January, the GOC was able to report an improvement in the living conditions of Sukarno and the other Republican prisoners. On 28 January, in a comprehensive resolution, the Council reaffirmed its call for the immediate and unconditional release of political prisoners and the restoration of the Republican government in Jogjakarta.[81]

As negotiations proceeded, it became apparent that the release of the Republican leaders and the restoration of the Jogjakarta government could be achieved only as part of a package deal, and it was Merle H. Cochran, the US member of the Commission for Indonesia, who played the vital intermediary role. Cochran arranged for Mohammed Hatta, the Indonesian Vice-President, to travel from Bangka to Batavia (Djakarta) in the UN aircraft and for J. H. van Roijen, the head of the Dutch delegation in Indonesia, to pay a courtesy visit to Bangka. Cochran believed that the restoration of the Republican government was in the interests of both parties: with the Republicans interned, there were no Indonesians with

---

[81] Ibid., 4th year, 397th mtg (7 Jan. 1949), p. 8; 401st mtg (17 Jan. 1949), pp. 5, 9, 13-15; Supplement for January 1949, pp. 15, 46-52, 62-4, S/1189, S/1199, S/1211, S/1213, part B of S/1224; SC res. 67 (S/1234), 28 Jan. 1949; FRUS, 1949, vol. VII part I, 1975, pp. 132, 134, 136, 142-3, 145, 147, 152-4, 164, 172, 175, 178, 191-3; J. Leimena, *The Dtuch-Indonesian Conflict*, Djakarta, 1949, p. 19.

authority to stop the fighting. Cochran advised van Roijen to work for an informal understanding rather than a formal agreement with Hatta, and he advised Hatta to give primary attention to the restoration of Republican authority, leaving other matters for later consideration.[82]

On 7 May, both parties agreed to negotiate on the basis of the Security Council's decision: a mutual cease-fire was to be accompanied by the immediate and unconditional release of political prisoners. The Republican government would resume its functions in Jogjakarta and would take part in a round table conference in the Hague.[83] A month later, those Indonesians who wished to leave Jogjakarta before the return of the Republicans were evacuated under UN supervision. Dutch forces then withdrew, and on 30 June the Sultan of Jogjakarta assumed responsibility for law and order in Jogjakarta 'on behalf of the Republican Government'. UN observers were deployed between the military forces of the two sides and there were no serious incidents. A week later, Sukarno and Hatta travelled from Bangka to Jogjakarta in a UN aircraft and were 'greeted with noticeable enthusiasm' by the people. A joint Dutch-Indonesian proclamation was issued on 1 August which included a provision for the early release of all those who had been 'deprived of their freedom because of political convictions or functions'.[84]

It was in practice impossible to make a strict distinction between political prisoners and prisoners of war. Lists of prisoners were exchanged and, on the proposal of the Republicans, the two sides proclaimed an amnesty in November 1949, which led to the release of about 4,500 prisoners. Those released were not simply set free at the place of detention but were 'returned to society in an orderly way and transferred to those places which they designated as their place of residence or origin'. By the end of 1949, when sovereignty was transferred

[82] FRUS, 1949, vol. VII part 1, 1975, pp. 208-9, 228, 239-42, 355, 360-1, 363, 375, 379, 380, 386, 389, 423, 425.

[83] SCOR, 4th year, Special Supplement no. 5, pp. 11-12, 19, 40, paras. 18, 56 of and para. 3 of Appendix VI to S/1373; FRUS, 1949, vol. VII part 1, 1975, pp. 350, 383-5, 391-3.

[84] SCOR, 4th year, Special Supplement no. 5, pp. 12-13, 21, 23, 38-9, 58-71, paras. 21-7, 62, 70 of and Appendices V and VIII to S/1373; FRUS, 1949, vol. VII part 1, 1975, pp. 415-16, 422-8, 434-443, 446-55, 458-62, 464-8.

to Indonesia, only 215 political prisoners were still being held. There was for a time some dissatisfaction on the Dutch side about the slow progress on implementing the agreed decisions, and each side suspected that the other was reclassifying political prisoners as ordinary criminals. The Republicans asked for facilities to visit prisons and POW camps, and the Netherlands agreed so long as they were granted reciprocal facilities.[85]

The other instance where political prisoners became an issue, albeit a minor one, was the dispute between India and Pakistan. In April 1948 the Security Council's resolution about a cessation of hostilities and a plebiscite in Kashmir asked India to ensure that the government of Indian Kashmir released 'all political prisoners': no equivalent appeal to Azad Kashmir or Pakistan was deemed necessary. In December the UN Commission for India and Pakistan (UNCIP) devised a set of principles for submission to the parties which included a provision for the release of all political prisoners.[86] The following March Pakistan raised with UNCIP a number of questions about political prisoners in Indian Kashmir, but India maintained that UNCIP's proposals about political prisoners 'cannot be put into force until the truce has been signed and the Plebiscite Administrator appointed'. On 15 April UNCIP submitted truce proposals to India and Pakistan, and these included a provision for the repeal of emergency legislation and for the release within a month of all political prisoners, including those who had already been tried and sentenced. Pakistan made no objection to this provision, but in the Indian view the proposal 'cannot be regarded ... as legitimately connected with the truce'. When UNCIP issued revised proposals on 28 April, the reference to political prisoners was dropped and instead there was a clause suggesting that it should be made publicly known throughout Kashmir 'that peace, law and order will be safeguarded and that all human and political rights will be

[85] SCOR, 5th year, Special Supplement no. 1, pp. 13-16, 60-2, paras. 57-67 of and Appendix VI to S/1449; George McTurnan Kahin, *Nationalism and Revolution in Indonesia,* Ithaca, NY, Cornell University Press London, Oxford University Press, 1952 (under the auspices of the International Secretariat of the Institute of Pacific Relations and the Southeast Asia Program, Cornell University), p. 424.

[86] SC res. 47 (S/726), 21 April 1948; SCOR, 4th year, Supplement for January 1949, pp. 25, 34, para. 15.7 (c) and para. 7 (c) of Annex 3 to S/1196.

guaranteed'. India objected to other provisions in the truce plan and did not consider it necessary to comment on the proposal on human and political rights. Pakistan, on the other hand, was gratified that UNCIP was 'fully alive to the importance of taking concrete steps, such as the release of political prisoners and the abrogation of emergency laws'. Pakistan relied on UNCIP to do 'everything possible' for the restoration of civil rights, otherwise the psychological effect on the people of Kashmir would be 'highly undesirable'.[87]

In the Hyderabad case, Pakistan urged the Security Council to appeal to India to issue a general amnesty, but the Council took no substantive decisions on the Hyderabad question.[88]

5.8 CIVIL RIGHTS

I am primarily concerned in this section with those civil and political rights contained in the Universal Declaration of Human Rights of 1948,[89] the International Covenant on Civil and Political Rights which was approved by the General Assembly in 1966,[90] the Fourth Geneva Convention of 12 August 1949 relating to the protection of civilians and Common Article 3 of the Geneva Conventions relating to internal wars.[91] The two Additional Protocols to the Geneva Conventions also contain fundamental guarantees of humane treatment.[92] It would have been appropriate to head this section 'Human rights' had not the term 'Human Rights in Armed Conflict' acquired a special meaning in UN circles since 1968.

The question of civil rights in the cases studied arose mainly in two contexts: freedom for civilians to engage in political activity, especially during periods of transition from one form of administration to another or prior to a referendum or election, and the rights of civilians under alien occupation. The first comprehensive resolution of the Security Council on Kashmir,

---

[87] SCOR, 4th year, Special Supplement no. 7, pp. 64-5, 105, 110-11, 113, 175, 182, paras. 5-9 of Appendix to S/1430, para. E4 of Appendix to Annex 17, para. 10 of Annex 20, para. IIIF of Annex 21, para. 4 of Annex 48, para. 16 of Annex 49.

[88] Ibid., 4th year, 426th mtg (24 May 1949), p. 29.

[89] GA res. 217A (III), 10 Dec. 1948.

[90] GA res. 2200A (XXI), 16 Dec. 1966.

[91] Geneva Conventions, 1949.

[92] A/32/144, 15 Aug. 1977 (mimeo), Annex I, Article 75, and Annex II, Article 4.

for example, called on India to ensure the release of political prisoners, adequate protection of minorities, and freedom for those citizens who had left the state on account of the disturbances to return and exercise civil rights without fear of victimization. India was also asked to declare that all Kashmiris, 'regardless of creed, caste or party', would be 'safe and free' in expressing their views and in voting on the question of accession, and that there would be 'freedom of the press, speech and assembly and freedom of travel ... including freedom of lawful entry and exit'. The subsequent resolution of the UN Commission for India and Pakistan (UNCIP) of 13 August 1948 looked towards a truce and asked India to ensure that peace, law, and order would be safeguarded and human and political rights guaranteed. A later resolution of UNCIP stipulated that there should be no restrictions on 'legitimate political activity' and 'no threat, coercion, or intimidation, bribery, or other undue influence on the voters'.[93]

Both India and Pakistan complained to UNCIP that the other was engaging in objectionable propaganda, and UNCIP appealed to the two sides to cease 'propaganda which goes beyond legitimate political activity'.[94] Pakistan also complained to UNCIP that civilian prisoners in Kashmir 'were to be executed',[95] and the Indonesians made a similar charge against the Netherlands in 1949.[96] In the Indonesian case, the Security Council called for the safeguarding of life and property. At a later stage, the Council recommended the holding of elections for a constituent assembly under UN supervision and asked that the elections should be 'free and democratic' and for 'freedom of assembly, speech and publication' provided such freedom was not construed as including 'advocacy of violence or reprisals'.[97]

---

[93] SC. res. 47 (S/726), 21 April 1948, SCOR, 3rd year, Supplement for November 1948, p. 33, para. 75 of S/1100 (UNCIP res., part II. B3); 4th year, Supplement for January 1949, pp. 24-5, para. 15 (6) and (7) of S/1196; Special Supplement no. 7, p. 113, part III para. F of Annex 21 to S/1430.

[94] SCOR, 4th year, Special Supplement no. 7, pp. 7-9, 67, 77-8, paras. 18, 22, 24 of and Appendix IV and Annex 2 to S/1430.

[95] Ibid., p. 11, para. 48 of S/1430.

[96] Ibid., 5th year, Special Supplement no. 1, pp. 13-14, para. 58 of S/1449.

[97] SC res. 36 (S/597), 1 Nov. 1947; res. 67 (S/1234), 28 Jan. 1949.

In the Palestine case, two crucial issues were access to and protection of the Holy Places, and rights of Arabs under Israeli rule. In April and May 1948 the Security Council had appealed to the parties not to endanger the Holy Places and not to interfere with access to shrines and sanctuaries. When the second cease-fire entered into force, Bernadotte was asked to ensure protection of and access to the Holy Places and other religious buildings and sites. Because access to the Holy Places involved 'the crossing and recrossing of front lines', Bernadotte believed that Jerusalem and other sensitive areas should be demilitarized, but it was never possible to persuade both parties simultaneously that this was a prudent course.[98]

In addition to the Arab refugees who had left Israel as a consequence of the fighting, there was concern for the civil rights of Arabs who remained and found themselves under Israeli rule. Israel faced an acute dilemma over reconciling the dream of a Zionist state based on democratic principles with the reality of an Arab minority that never fell below 10 per cent of the population. If Zionist principles were to be implemented, there had to be an element of discrimination in favour of Jews in both legislation and administration—for example, the Law of the Return, which makes it possible for foreign-born Jews to acquire Israeli citizenship almost automatically. Israeli Arabs believed not simply that they were a minority: they felt that they were excluded for ever and could never aspire to political or cultural eminence. The contradiction between Zionist ideals and Israeli practice was to become even more acute after the occupation of Arab territory in 1967.

From time to time the Chief of Staff of the UN Truce Supervision Organization (UNTSO) had to take up complaints about expulsions of Arabs from border areas. On one occasion the Security Council asked the Chief of Staff of UNTSO to suggest how the movement of nomadic Arabs should be handled, and asked the relevant Mixed Armistice Commission to arrange for the repatriation of those Arabs who had been expelled from

---

[98] SC res. 46 (S/723), 17 April 1948; res. 50 (S/801), 29 May 1948; res. 54 (S/902), 15 July 1948; GAOR, 3rd session, Supplement no. 11, A/648, pp. 16 (paras. 2-4), 18 (para. 4 (g)), 36 (para. 19); Bernadotte, pp. 205-6.

Israel.[99]

Among the innovations contained in the Geneva Conventions of 1949, two are especially noteworthy in this context. First, all four Conventions contain provisions relating to armed conflicts 'not of an international character'. These provisions establish certain norms 'as a minimum', including humane treatment without discrimination for all who are taking no active part in hostilities, and the prohibition of hostage-taking, violence to life and person, outrages upon personal dignity, and executions without trial before a regularly constituted court.[100]

The second innovation in 1949 was the preparation of a Convention for the protection of civilians under occupation (the Fourth Geneva Convention).[101] The Convention specifies a number of 'grave breaches', including wilful killing, torture or inhuman treatment, wilfully causing great suffering or serious injury, unlawful deportation or transfer, wilfully depriving a protected person of the rights of fair and regular trial, the taking of hostages, and extensive destruction or appropriation of property not justified by military necessity.[102] Also prohibitied are reprisals,[103] collective penalties or the punishment of protected persons for offences they had not personally committed,[104] the exercise of physical or moral coercion,[105] corporal or capital punishment,[106] inhuman conditions of imprisonment or detention,[107] and failure to respect the honour, family rights, and religious beliefs and practices of protected persons.[108]

The only example of the application of the Fourth Convention in the cases studied was during and after the Sinai-Suez conflict of 1956: Egypt, France, and Israel were already parties to the Convention, and Britain agreed to apply the Convention should

---

[99] See, for example, SCOR, 5th year, Supplement for September-December 1950, pp. 56-8, S/1789; 511th mtg (16 Oct. 1950), pp. 3-6, S/1789; 7th year, Supplement for October-December 1952, pp. 14-15, paras. 1-3 of S/2388; 8th year, 635th mtg (9 Nov. 1953), pp. 27-9; 9th year, Supplement for January-March 1954, p. 5, S/3172; FRUS, 1950, vol. V, 1978, pp. 993-1001, 1010-11, 1013-14, 1020-3, 1027-9, 1035-6, 1043-4; Burns, p. 93; Horn, pp. 112-13; Bull, pp. 55-6; SC res. 89 (S/1907), 17 Nov. 1950.

[100] Geneva Conventions, 1949, Common Article 3.

[101] Geneva Convetion IV, 1949.

[102] Articles 5, 32, 34, 49, 53, 68, 71, 72, 147.

[103] Article 33.   [104] Article 33.

[105] Article 31.   [106] Articles 32 and 75.

[107] Articles 37, 69, 76, and 79-126.   [108] Article 27

the occasion arise.[109] It is nevertheless difficult in practice to ensure the full application of the Convention. States may simply refuse to apply it because of some legal technicality. Moreover, it has been the experience of humanitarian organizations that the military are often readier to understand why they should respect the first three Geneva Conventions, which protect combatants, than the fourth, which protects civilians. 'Among even enemy soldiers,' writes David Forsythe, 'there is sometimes a certain mutual respect ... This is lacking in some cultures between soldier and civilian. The result is that the civilian receives less protection and assistance.'

But perhaps the greatest-difficulty of application arises from the fact that there is often no clear distinction between combatants and civilians. Humanitarian organizations like the International Committee of the Red Cross (ICRC) always want the maximum protection of war victims and, in uncertain cases, would hope that states would give doubtful civilians the benefit of the doubt; but states that are or have recently been engaged in armed conflict do not always find it easy to be magnanimous.[110]

The ICRC has for many years wished to give firmer legal protection to civilians in time of war. A set of draft rules to limit the dangers to civilians was circulated in 1956,[111] and the subject has come up regularly at International Red Cross Conferences[112] and formed part of the studies of the UN Secretary-General on respect for human rights in armed conflict.[113] Some but by no means all of the aspirations of the ICRC were achieved in the two Additional Protocols to the Geneva Conventions of 1977.[114] In 1970 the General Assembly approved a set of basic principles for the protection of civilians in armed conflict, which included the principles that fundamental human rights continue to apply fully in situations of

---

[109] Report of the International Committee of the Red Cross for 1956, Geneva, 1957, p. 23; Forsythe, *Humanitarian Politics,* p. 169.

[110] Forsythe, *Humanitarian Politics*, pp. 170-4.

[111] Text in Bailey, *Prohibitions and Restraints in War,* pp. 171-9.

[112] *International Red Cross Handbook,* 11th edn, Geneva, 1971, pp. 451-5.

[113] A/7720, 20 Nov. 1969 (mimeo); A/8052, 18 Sept. 1970 (mimeo), paras. 30-87; A/8370, 2 Sept. 1971 (mimeo), paras. 30-92; A/9215, 7 Nov. 1973 (mimeo), esp. pp. 94-101, 165-7, 169-70, 172-3, 176-7.

[114] A/32/144, 15 Aug. 1977 (mimeo), Annexes I and II.

armed conflict and that civilians should not be the object of 'reprisals, forcible transfers or other assaults on their integrity'.[115] It remains 'an irony of the times' that so much protection should be given to combatants and so little to civilians.[116]

5.9 BELEAGUERED FIGHTERS

When the Netherlands undertook its first 'police action' in Indonesia in 1947, its forces advanced along important lines of communication so that they could dominate an area without actually occupying the whole of it. After the cease-fire had entered into effect, the forward Netherlands positions were linked to form a notional front line. The Indonesian Republic, as the militarily weaker party, had in any event resorted to guerrilla methods of fighting, and the spearhead tactics of the Netherlands left bands of Indonesian fighters behind the Netherlands front lines.

Moreover, the Indonesian fighters were not then a monolithic force. Some were trained soldiers, under proper command and wearing uniforms or distinguishing marks. Others were freelance fighters, perhaps acting patriotically, but not under the control of the Republican authorities. A few were common criminals, taking advantage of the general chaos for their own ends. No doubt some were Dutch agents, deliberately fomenting trouble. This confused kind of situation is not uncommon during and after guerrilla warfare.

What should by-passed fighters do if the Security Council calls for a cease-fire (if, indeed, the fighters know that such a call has been issued)? In the Indonesian case, the Netherlands took the line that the very existence of by-passed Republican soldiers was a breach of the cease-fire, and that their own forces were free to eliminate these by-passed military units in mopping-up operations.[117]

---

[115] GA res. 2675 (XXV), 9 Dec. 1970.

[116] David P. Forsythe, *Present Role of the Red Cross in Protection,* Geneva, Henry Durant Institute, 1975 (Joint Committee for the Reappraisal of the Role of the Red Cross, Background Paper no. 1), p. 29.

[117] SCOR, 2nd year, 207th mtg (3 Oct. 1947), pp. 2493-4; 211th mtg (14 Oct. 1947), p. 2570, para. 3 of S/581; Special Supplement no. 4, S/586/Rev. 1, pp. 7-8, 94-6.

332 Humanitarian questions

The Indonesians, for their part, insisted that penetration was not occupation and that the territory between the Netherlands lines of advance was not occupied territory. They believed that a cease-fire should include a stand-fast, and that it was the patrols and sweeps by Netherlands forces that constituted a breach of the Security Council's call to cease hostilities.[118]

The Netherlands rejected the first plan of the UN Good Offices Committee (GOC) because there was no provision in it for the evacuation of Republican fighters in areas that the Netherlands claimed to have occupied. The GOC proposed that demilitarized zones should be established between the front lines and that all military forces on the other party's side of a demilitarized zone should move peacefully into such zones under UN supervision. The truce agreement signed on board the USS *Renville* the following month approved the procedures for by-passed fighters already agreed, with the addition of a provision that Indonesians behind the Dutch lines would proceed to the demilitarized zones 'as quickly as practicable, and in any case within twenty-one days' after the cease-fire had taken effect. The GOC asked the Netherlands to allow Republican representatives to assist in UN investigations in Netherlands-held territory.[119] In the event, it was necessary to extend the deadline by ten days, and some 35,000 Republican fighters were duly evacuated.[120]

In the Palestine war, there was an encircled Arab group in the Faluja area consisting of Egyptian and Sudanese soldiers and Palestinian civilians who were surrounded by Yigal Allon's forces during the fighting from October 1948 to January 1949.[121] Ralph Bunche, the Acting UN Mediator, urged Israel to allow food convoys to enter the Faluja pocket, but Ben-Gurion was determined to maintain pressure on the Arabs in Faluja until an armistice was concluded. In any case, Ben-Gurion believed

---

[118] Ibid., pp. 71-3, 101, 134-5; 207th mtg (3 Oct. 1947), p. 2494, S/568.

[119] Ibid., 3rd year, Special Supplement no. 1, pp. 9, 11, 13, 53, 74, 77, paras. 19, 22 (9), 25-7 of and Appendices V (Annex I, paras. 8-9), XI (paras. 8-9), XIV to S/649 Rev. 1.

[120] Ibid., Supplement for June 1948, pp. 58-9, 124, S/787, S/848/Add. 1.

[121] Gamal Abdul Nasser fought bravely in these actions; see Ben-Gurion, pp. 314, 316; Allon, p. 41; Gamal Abdul Nasser, *Egypt's Liberation: the Philosophy of the Revolution*, Washington, DC, Public Affairs Press, 1955, p. 23.

that military supplies had been smuggled in at an earlier stage in boxes supposedly containing nothing but food. UN staff in the area believed that magnanimity by Israel would have paid handsome dividends, but the Israeli leadership was adamant. 'The Egyptians are here as enemies, in a country that does not belong to them,' Ben-Gurion told Bunche, 'and as long as there are no peace negotiations, we will not allow them to remove their troops from Faluja.'[122] It was not until after armistice negotiations between Egypt and Israel had opened in Rhodes, and after new cease-fire commitments had been made by the parties, that Israel agreed to allow food and medical supplies to be sent to Faluja under UN supervision.[123]

The Egypt-Israel armistice provided that the Arabs in the Faluja area, described in the agreement as 'the Egyptian Military Forces', were to be evacuated within five days of signing. Sick and wounded were to leave first, then infantry, and finally forces with heavy equipment. Israeli authorities and officers were to extend their full co-operation and Israeli troops were to be kept away from the evacuation route. The whole operation was to be under 'effective United Nations supervision'. Bunche reported in due course that the operation had been successfully undertaken. Egyptian forces totalling 2,900 men had been evacuated, and 1,050 out of some 3,500 civilians in the area had left for Gaza: a further group of civilians subsequently went to Hebron. The Egyptians, according to the International Committee of the Red Cross, 'spontaneously handed over their Israeli prisoners before crossing back into Egypt'.[124]

In Cyprus in 1964, groups of Turkish Cypriot fighters were cut off in the Kokkina and Limnitis areas when the UN cease-fire went into effect, and Greek Cypriot forces maintained a strict blockade of these and other Turkish enclaves. It would have been technically possible for the beleaguered fighters to have left Kokkina and Limnitis by sea, but neither Turkey nor

---

[122] Azcárate, p. 109; Kirkbride, p. 61; SCOR, 3rd year, Supplement for December 1948, pp. 302-3, S/1152; FRUS, 1949, vol. VI, 1977, pp. 597-8, 691 n. 1, 694-5.

[123] S/1227, 25 Jan. 1949 (mimeo); FRUS, 1949, vol. VI, 1977, pp. 700-2, 708-9.

[124] SCOR, 4th year, Special Supplement no. 3, S/1264/Rev. 1, Article III and Annex I; Supplement for March 1949, pp. 7-8, S/1269; Report on the work of the International Committee of the Red Cross for 1949, Geneva, 1950, p. 73.

the Turkish community in Cyprus was prepared to take an action that would have savoured of defeat.

It was assumed by humanitarian organizations that, once the fighting had stopped, essential supplies could be sent to the Turkish Cypriot enclaves, but the Greek Cypriot leaders were initially unwilling to allow any supplies to reach 'Turkish terrorists' who rejected the authority of the Cyprus government. President Makarios said he would not lift the blockade so long as Turkish Cypriots were interfering with the free movement of traffic, especially on the road running north from Nicosia to Kyrenia. When the shortage of food and other essentials became 'particularly critical', the UN Force and the International Committee of the Red Cross made representations to the Cyprus government to allow relief supplies to enter the blockaded areas, and this led to a relaxation of the restrictions on the movement of non-strategic supplies to all the Turkish Cypriot enclaves other than Kokkina. While the continued blockade of Kokkina was a matter of concern to Secretary-General Thant, he reported to the Security Council that the over-all situation regarding supplies 'was not found to be one of great hardship', and that the population was not facing starvation.[125]

But UN staff in Cyprus had probably underestimated the gravity of the situation, for on the day on which Thant's report was issued, Turkey announced that, because of the acute shortage of essential supplies in Kokkina, it would make emergency deliveries in spite of the blockade. If Greek Cypriots should interfere, Turkey would take 'appropriate action' to defend its rights. The United Nations would be informed of the days on which deliveries would be made, and the UN Force would be allowed to check that no military supplies were being sent.[126]

Thant's reaction was that, while he would do all in his power to have the blockade lifted, any plans to send in supplies 'must have the consent' of the Cyprus government. Attempts to send in supplies on any other basis could have dangerous consequences. The Commander of the UN Force and a senior

---

[125] Harbottle, p. 54; SCOR, 19th year, Supplement for July-September 1954, pp. 183-5, 239-40, 325-7, 329, S/5897, S/5916, paras. 193-200, 206 of S/5950.

[126] SCOR, 19th year, Supplement for July-September 1954, pp. 350-1, S/5954.

representative of the International Committee of the Red Cross visited the Kokkina area and, having satisfied themselves that relief supplies were genuinely needed, arranged for food to be sent in by UN helicopters and clothing by UN land vehicles escorted by Greek Cypriot police. This humanitarian intervention ended the utility of the blockade from the Greek Cypriot point of view, and Makarios soon agreed to lift the restrictions.[127]

It is evident that fighters who are stranded behind the enemy's lines when a cease-fire enters into effect face difficulties which they usually cannot overcome without external help. If an attempt is made to effect a land link between beleaguered fighters and their own front lines, this is likely to be resisted by the other party, quickly leading to violations or even a complete breakdown of the cease-fire. If, on the other hand, the beleaguered fighters remain in place, they may soon be starved into submission.

In the medium term, the problem of beleaguered combatants can often be solved by withdrawals of opposing forces or, more usually, by the evacuation of the encircled troops. It is in the short term that acute problems arise. This is because the period between a cease-fire and a truce or armistice is a twilight zone which is not dealt with in international conventions of general applicability, and it is a problem that has arisen only since the creation of the United Nations. Cease-fires almost always enter into force as a result of an appeal by a UN organ and not from direct contact between the parties.

If the adverse party agrees, beleaguered fighters can withdraw to their own lines, but any attempt to withdraw in the face of military opposition is likely to lead to a breakdown of the cease-fire and possibly a major resumption of fighting. Moreover, combatants may be reluctant to withdraw if they are on what they consider to be their own territory.

If beleaguered fighters are to remain in place when a cease-fire takes effect, various arrangements for the supply of basic necessities of life are theoretically conceivable: aid from the opposing party, whether under military or civilian auspices;

---

[127] Ibid., pp. 337-40, 367-70, S/5950/Add. 2, S/5961; 1147th mtg (11 Sept. 1964), paras. 35-6; Report on the Work of the International Committee of the Red Cross for 1964, Geneva, 1965, p. 17.

aid from their own side, military or civilian, with or without the consent of the opposing party; intervention by outside powers; assistance from the United Nations, a regional agency, the International Committee of the Red Cross, or other humanitarian organization.

It may be that appropriate arrangements can be agreed as a result of direct contacts between the opposing parties or their Red Cross societies. Usually, however, some kind of third-party assistance is likely to be needed. In that event, the other party will expect assurances that impartial assistance will not be used to strengthen the military capability of the beleaguered forces.

Beleaguered fighters may be regarded as, in a sense, hostages of the surrounding forces. We could then ask to what extent principles that have been evolved for humanitarian assistance for hostages in other situations might be applicable in the case of surrounded combatants wishing to observe a cease-fire.

Intervention for humanitarian purposes should be separated from the military or political interests of the parties. It should have only two purposes: to avoid unnecessary suffering of the surrounded fighters by meeting their basic needs, and to forestall measures of military self-help which would endanger the cease-fire and world peace. The following principles are based on those that have guided the International Committee of the Red Cross when, as an exceptional measure, it has come to the aid of hostages in time of peace. These principles would accord with the resolution adopted at the International Red Cross Conference in Istanbul in 1969, which envisaged the Red Cross movement acting both to resolve humanitarian problems and in the cause of peace:[128]

(a)   That the cause of peace and the interest of the victims call for the intervention of a humanitarian organization;
(b)   That no other solution is in sight;
(c)   That the party to which the surrounded combatants belong makes the request for help, and that the opposing party agrees;
(d)   That all the parties confirm their intention of respecting the cease-fire and agree not to threaten or use force during the relief operation and not to obstruct the freedom of action and freedom of movement of the humanitarian organization;

[128] Resolution XXI, September 1969.

(e) That the parties undertake to respect in all circumstances the emblem of the humanitarian organization and its vehicles and personnel, which shall be unarmed;

(f) That the humanitarian organization has the exclusive responsibility to choose and supervise personnel for the operation, taking fully into account the views of the parties.

While such principles would have to be applied pragmatically, it would be useful if the International Committee of the Red Cross or an organ of the United Nations were to draft some model rules to provide guidance for cases of this kind in the future. These model rules would have to provide for the dispatch of the basic necessities of life (water, food, medicines) by aircraft (helicopters or parachute drop), ships, or land vehicles, under the auspices of an impartial humanitarian organization, for an interim period.

There would be many difficulties in drafting model rules and adapting them to particular situations. Which are the 'basic necessities of life'? Is any guidance on this question to be found in Article 54 of Additional Protocol I to the Geneva Conventions, relating to objects indispensable to survival? Will the party whose forces are surrounded be willing to reveal how many combatants are beleaguered, so that essential needs can be quantified? Should the opposing party have the right to inspect cargoes? If fighting should subsequently be resumed, will the humanitarian organization be accused of improving the fighting capability of one of the parties? Can an impartial agency call on sufficient supplies and means of transport at short notice?

The legal and practical difficulties are considerable, but without the guidance of model rules, it is possible that a future cease-fire will collapse when combatants attempt to break through the forces encircling them. This can be avoided only if appropriate procedures are known in advance, are seen to be fair, and would be applied if it were the other party whose forces were surrounded.

CHAPTER 6

Mnemonics for peace-builders

What is there that is worth remembering from the attempts by the United Nations to stop armed conflict in the period 1946-64? Can history make men wise?

While wars may in the past have evoked laudable qualities like loyalty and valour, it must be said that modern war, even if fought from the most noble motives, is destructive of justice and morality. To prevent war is an overriding task: to stop a war that has already started is as important.

Wars are more dangerous than they were. Military technology threatens to out-strip the human capacity to control events. Small wars easily become big wars, and it is no longer an exaggeration to assert that a major war using modern weapons would destroy not simply people and animals and crops but the very fabric of our civilization and culture. Moreover, there would be few bystanders. The concept of neutrality would have little meaning in all-out nuclear conflict since radiation does not distinguish between innocent and guilty, and the genetic harm would affect future generations to an extent that cannot be precisely known in advance.

Ordinary rivalries based on perceptions of interest are exacerbated by the intensely ideological character of the age. Modern war, because it affects beliefs as well as interests, brings into play the passions, both selfish and altruistic, that were evoked by the Crusades. To a greater or lesser extent we are all affected by these passions about ideology, since none can be indifferent to political systems that oppress the human spirit. In that sense it is true, as the UNESCO constitution states, that wars begin in the minds of men.

In order to influence events it is necessary to understand them, but this becomes increasingly difficult. The international system grows more complex each year. Since 1946 the number of sovereign units has more than tripled, and the greater ease and speed of communication has meant that more things happen more quickly than formerly.

Building the institutions of peace requires a multiple strategy. Weapons and defence policies often cause anxiety and fear, quite apart from the political causes of which they are symptoms, so attempts at arms control and disarmament have to be un-remitting. Non-military means of showing disapproval, exerting pressure, or resisting aggression will be increasingly relevant, even for the most powerful countries. Peace and conflict re-search may lead to a better understanding of the diplomatic process and point to new institutions for peaceful change as we come to rely less on traditional methods.

The prevention of war is no longer the fad of a fringe of cranks or visionaries, but it still absorbs only a fraction of the resources devoted to military security. Few countries can afford the burden of modern defence, but even the most peace-loving seem to act on the simplistic assumption that to be prepared for war is the most effectual means of preserving peace. Military deterrence is never enough.

It was assumed at San Francisco that the main task of the United Nations would be to deter or punish aggression by collective action of UN Members, co-ordinated by the Security Council; and it was accepted, albeit reluctantly, that there was no possibility of using this form of coercion against any of the permanent members of the Security Council; hence the veto. For two years a half-hearted attempt was made to give sub-stance to the framework for collective security envisaged in Articles 43-50 of the Charter. The effort failed, but this did not mean that the Security Council was impotent. Other methods for maintaining peace were eventually devised, and these were used with partial success in the growing number of conflicts and disputes arising in the Third World.

Peace can be threatened not only by the actions of states, as when a powerful nation strikes against a weak neighbour, but also by actions within recognized frontiers, such as grave colonialist or racist oppression. If intimidation or despotism leads to armed conflict, the Security Council will almost cer-tainly be involved. In such situations, the Council may be torn between the temptation to issue impressive pronouncements and the concern to assist in harmonizing the actions of nations. Nothing is gained if the Council purports to adopt a binding resolution and then finds itself powerless to secure compliance.

The decision to stop fighting rests with the parties, but the Security Council or its organs can facilitate contact, suggest procedures for removing difficulties or reducing tension, and assist in the implementation of agreements. This is a useful role, even if it is a limited one.

Armed conflict in the modern world increasingly involves entities other than states. This was barely foreseen at San Francisco, and the United Nations has not yet adapted its procedures so as to be able to relate effectively to non-state actors.

I have suggested earlier that allegations about human rights have played an important part in armed conflicts in recent decades, and I would expect that trend to continue. Moreover, secessionist claims are likely to increase as social and economic alienation spreads. Nations that led the struggle for liberation from colonial rule may find their own territorial integrity at risk when minorities advance claims for autonomy or even partition. Decolonization in the conventional sense is almost complete, but a different form of decolonization can be expected so long as there are unsatisfied local or regional claims for self-rule. The Security Council has the capacity to help in ensuring that the process is peaceful and that instability is contained.

I am not, of course, asserting that claims and counter-claims about human rights are present in every war. During the period studied, and even more since, there have been wars of a traditional geopolitical kind. Israel has fought more than once to save itself from economic strangulation. Britain and Iceland have engaged in limited conflict about fishing rights. The oil weapon has been used for political purposes, and the United States had made it clear that it would not hesitate to use military force to ensure the free flow of oil. Economic factors played a peripheral role in a number of cases of conflict: oil in the Algerian War of Independence and the Nigerian Civil War, off-shore oil in the Aegean and the China Seas, copper in Katanga, phosphates in Western Sahara, uranium in Namibia. The war in Central America in 1969, though ostensibly arising from a football match, was largely caused by demographic pressures in the densely populated El Salvador. There have been several cases of military intervention, especially by the major powers, in which strategic considerations undoubtedly played a role. There are, however, sufficient cases in which the denial of basic rights has led to armed conflict to affirm that any realistic strategy for the prevention of war must include efforts to protect and promote human rights.

It is a truism that the NATO-Warsaw Pact area has been relatively stable and secure for three decades; yet it is the area where, if war did occur, the consequences could be catastrophic. Elsewhere the proliferation of states has brought to the surface contradictions and conflicts that were previously submerged, and I would expect that the main attention of the Security Council in the years ahead will continue to be directed to Third World issues.

The composition of the Council was established in 1945 so as to give pride of place to the victorious allies. If the Council were being created anew today, it would no doubt be differently composed. It would not be surprising if pressures were to continue to enlarge the Council still further, but the truth is that excessive enlargement will diminish rather than enhance the Council's capacity to act decisively in a crisis, and it would be regrettable if there were any increase in the number of veto-wielding permanent members.

This book has a modest aim, though I hope a practical one. I take it for granted that war is a human disaster, that justice can never be satisfied while the fighting continues, and that it is the task of the international community to end the use of arms as soon as possible.

The belligerents will protest that to adopt an even-handed attitude is to ignore the rights and wrongs of the case, that wars are fought for just causes, and that there can be no cessation of the fighting until the main war aim has been achieved.

There are always rights and wrongs on both sides. War is a consequence of lost opportunities and previous mistakes. But war inevitably harms the innocent, and modern war easily escalates, both vertically and horizontally—even internal war. In the Korean case thirty years ago, the majority of UN Members saw the main task as being to help the victim; but Korea was exceptional, as I have tried to show in volume II. Nowadays the response of most UN Members when war breaks out is to ask how it shall be brought to an end without delay.

Experience since 1946 points to no sovereign remedies. Each war is unique. The cases of successful UN intervention to stop the fighting were diverse in origins and outcome, and future conflicts may develop differently. The lessons of the past do not point to any simple answers but only to some questions that confront foreign offices, diplomats, and international officials.

The questions that follow have been deliberately posed from the point of view of the practitioner. The problem of war termination can be approached from a variety of standpoints, but the primary purpose of this study has been to help those in national capitals and the United Nations who have to take decisions when war breaks out.

6.1 PRELIMINARIES IN THE SECURITY COUNCIL

As soon as armed conflict occurs, the idea of convening the Security Council is sure to be considered both at UN headquarters and in the national capitals. It may be that one of the parties will ask that the Council should meet; in a perfidious world, this will not necessarily be the victim. The members of the Council or other UN Members, particularly the allies or adversaries of the parties, will also weigh the possibility of taking the initiative. If a meeting is not requested by one of the parties or a UN Member, it is open to the Secretary-General to ask that the Council shall meet, either by drawing the Council's attention to the threatening situation[1] or simply by addressing a request to the President.

The President of the Council for the month plays a crucial role at every stage. Even before a formal request for a meeting reaches him, he is likely to be in touch with the Secretary-General or, in his absence, with a senior member of the Secretariat, and he will receive messages or himself make informal contact with the parties and the members of the Council. No firm guidance can be laid down on the sequence of these consultations since this will be partly determined by the nature of the issue and the relationship of the parties to Council members. Consultation beyond the parties and Council members may have to be deferred until later, but the President will often seek an early opportunity for informal discussions with the current

[1] Article 99 of the Charter.

group chairman of the region in which the fighting is taking place.

It is often useful and sometimes essential to hold an informal and private meeting of all Council members before the Council itself is formally convened (see question 4 below).

Many governments are reluctant to take an issue to the United Nations unless they have some idea of the likely outcome;[2] but at such an early stage, the outcome is necessarily speculative. Even in the case of an organ of limited membership such as the Security Council, there are too many imponderables to predict the final result with certainty. The Council includes five members who can prevent action by the use of the veto, and the main currents of world opinion are represented among the non-permanent members. Although the Council has been in existence for more than thirty years and has met more than 2,000 times, there has been little study of the social and political dynamics of its proceedings. In any case, the effectiveness of the Council consists not only in its decisions: debate and diplomacy are often useful regardless of the formal outcome.

The questions that arise in the preliminary proceedings of the Council may all be matters of genuine concern. If armed conflict occurs, it is desirable that the Security Council should be convened expeditiously, that relevant documents should be available, that the agenda should be formulated in an objective way, that the parties should be correctly identified and their views taken into account, that representatives should submit credentials in the correct form, and that the Council should not exceed its competence when approving the agenda. These are all important matters; but they can also provide pretexts for impeding the work of the Council. Is the Council impotent, then, in the face of filibustering?

It is to obviate deliberate obstruction that the Council needs presiding officers who know its rules and customs, who are able to act impartially in private and in public, and who are politically and socially sagacious. The fact that the presidency rotates on a monthly basis means that ambassadors have only limited opportunities to gain experience of the potentialities and pitfalls

---

[2] See, for example, FRUS, 1951, vol. II, 1979, p. 850, record of a meeting of the US delegation to the General Assembly, 12 Dec. 1951.

of the office. Representatives of non-permanent members had only two one-month terms as president during a two-year stint when the Council had eleven members, and it was unusual for the ambassadors of permanent members to have more than four terms as president before being posted away from New York. The UN Secretary-General and his colleagues are able to offer advice and guidance to each incumbent, but not all ambassadors are good at listening or taking advice.

All members of the Council must therefore be alert to detect at once if the President is being misled or is using his position for partisan purposes. In my study of the procedure of the Security Council, I have noted a few matters on which the Council acquiesced in a departure from normal procedure. The Council does not, for example, meet at least once every fourteen days as stipulated in Rule 1, nor does the President sign the official record as required by Rule 53. For the circumstances in which certain provisions of the Charter and Provisional Rules of Procedure have never been applied or have fallen into disuse, I refer readers to the official *Repertoire* of Security Council practice[3] and to my own books on the procedure of the Council.[4] The questions that follow are based on the Council's accepted practice.

There were, to be sure, cases of filibustering during the period covered by this study. If, as is often the case, filibustering takes the form of putting bogus points of order to the President, the President should rule promptly and decisively. If the ruling is challenged, the President should at once submit the challenge to a vote of the Council, being careful to cite no. 30 of the Provisional Rules of Procedure in either the French, Spanish, or Chinese version: if the English version is cited, then it is the ruling and not the challenge that is put to the vote, which is absurd.[5]

If it should happen that it is the President himself who is doing the filibustering (as was the case in August 1950),[6] then the other members have no option but to cajole the President

---

[3] Seven volumes have been issued covering the years 1946-71.
[4] Bailey, *The Procedure of the UN Security Council* and *Voting in the Security Council*.
[5] I discuss this anomaly in *The Procedure of the UN Security Council*, pp. 178-9, 300-1.
[6] Lie, p. 341.

into giving rulings, challenge the rulings, and then insist on the issue being put to the vote.

CONVENING THE SECURITY COUNCIL

1.   Has the Security Council been properly convened?

The Council should be convened in the following circumstances:
(a)   at the request of a member of the Council;[7]
(b)   because the General Assembly has made a recommen-dation to the Council or referred a question to it;[8]
(c)   because the Secretary-General has drawn the attention of the Council to a matter that in his opinion may threaten the maintenance of international peace and security[9] or has asked for a meeting;
(d)   because a dispute or situation has been drawn to the Council's attention.[10]

The Charter requires that the Council 'shall be so organized as to be able to function continuously', for which purpose the members of the Council shall be 'represented at all times' at the seat of the Organization.[11] The Council normally meets at UN headquarters, but it may decide to meet elsewhere.[12]

The Council should be convened with a minimum of delay and with due regard to the degree of urgency implied in the request.

DOCUMENTS

2.   Was proper notice of the meeting given,[13] and was the provisional agenda circulated at least three days before the meeting or, in urgent circumstances, with the notice of the meeting?[14]

Documents should be published in the five languages of the Security Council or in any other language as the Council may

---

[7] Rule 2.
[8] Article 11 (2) and (3) of the Charter, Rule 3.
[9] Article 99, Rule 3.
[10] Articles 11 (3) and 35 (1) and (2), Rule 3.
[11] Article 28 (1).
[12] Article 28 (3), Rule 5.
[13] Rule 25.
[14] Rule 8.

have decided[15] and, except in urgent circumstances, should be circulated at least forty-eight hours in advance of the meeting.[16]

PRESIDENCY

3.   Are the circumstances such as to warrant the cession of the presidency?

If the President deems that for the proper fulfilment of the presidency he should not preside over the Council during the consideration of a question with which he is 'directly connected', the presidency devolves on the member next in English alphabetical order.[17]

PUBLIC OR PRIVATE MEETING?

4.   Is it desirable that the Security Council should decide to meet in private?[18]

The Council meets in private when considering its recommendation regarding the appointment of the Secretary-General, and occasionally when delicate negotiations are taking place. It would be unusual to hold a formal meeting in private at this preliminary stage; if a meeting in private is desirable, it is now the practice to meet informally. When the Council holds a formal meeting in private, it may decide that the verbatim record 'shall be made in a single copy'.[19] At the close of a private meeting, the Council issues a communiqué through the Secretary-General.[20]

CREDENTIALS

5.   Have the reports of the Secretary-General on credentials been circulated in writing and, in the absence of objection, considered as approved?[21]

[15] Rules 46 and 47.
[16] Rule 26.
[17] Rule 20.
[18] Rule 48.
[19] Rule 51.
[20] Rule 55.
[21] Rules 13 and 15.

If there are representatives whose credentials have been objected to or not yet approved, they shall sit 'with the same rights as other representatives' until the matter has been resolved.[22]

AGENDA

6.   Does the agenda refer to all appropriate communications from states, UN organs, or the Secretary-General?[23]

The title of each item and other parts of the agenda should be formulated in a non-contentious and objective way. The agenda should be sufficiently broad to encompass all matters that may reasonably be raised.

COMPETENCE TO ADOPT AGENDA

7.   Is the Security Council competent to approve the provisional agenda and discuss the matter?

PARTICIPATION OF NON-MEMBERS

8.   Are there any non-members of the Security Council whose participation in the discussion is desirable or necessary?

A non-member is invited to participate in the following circumstances:
(a)   if it has brought a dispute or situation to the attention of the Council;[24]
(b)   because it is a party to a dispute under consideration by Council;[25]
(c)   because the Council considers that its interests are specially affected.[26]

A state that is not a Member of the United Nations may participate only if it accepts in advance the Charter obligations of pacific settlement:[27] the Council shall 'lay down such conditions' for the participation of a non-UN Member 'as it deems just'.[28]

---

[22] Rules 16 and 17.
[23] Rules 6 and 7.
[24] Article 35 (1), Rule 37.
[25] Article 32.
[26] Article 31, Rule 37.
[27] Article 35 (2).
[28] Article 32.

It has been the practice since 1964 for the Secretary-General to report on the credentials of representatives of non-members only in case of doubt or difficulty.[29]

9. Are there embryonic governments, entities other than states, members of the Secretariat, or other persons who should be asked to supply the Council with information or give other assistance?[30]

In deciding on invitations to participate, the Council has to ensure that this does not prejudice the subsequent freedom of itself or a subsidiary organ about the persons or organizations with which it will establish formal relations. If the Council defers or rejects an application to participate in the discussion, the applicant can be invited to submit views or comments in writing.

10. Has the Security Council decided to employ the armed forces of a non-member so that the non-member is entitled to 'participate in the decisions' of the Council?[31]

6.2 THE DIPLOMACY OF THE SECURITY COUNCIL

With the preliminaries out of the way, the Council can get down to its main task of considering how to maintain world peace and security. It is not necessary that the Council should make an explicit and formal determination as to the nature of the question before it, but if armed conflict has occurred, members are bound to ask themselves whether the matter comes within the scope of Chapter VII of the Charter, thus opening up the possibility of mandatory action. Certainly the Council will need to consider without delay whether it should call for or order a cessation of hostilities and withdrawal of forces; what form of observation or peace-keeping will be needed in order to deter violations and prevent a recurrence of fighting; and possibly whether means of pressure or coercion will be needed to secure compliance.

At a later stage the Council will need to consider whether the parties would welcome or accept third-party assistance in resolving the issues that led to the fighting.

[29] Letter from Gustav Ortner, UN Secretariat, 5 March 1980.
[30] Rules 22 and 39. [31] Article 44.

COMPETENCE OF THE SECURITY COUNCIL
TO TAKE A DECISION

11.   If a proposal is submitted, is the Council competent to approve it?

WITHOUT PREJUDICE

12.   Will any decision carry greater weight if it is expressly stated that it is without prejudice to the rights, claims, or position of the parties?

IS THERE A DISPUTE?

13.   Has it been claimed that a dispute exists?

Whether there is a dispute is determined by the Security Council. If the Council finds that there is a dispute, three consequences follow. A party to the dispute, if not a member of the Council, 'shall be invited to participate, without vote, in the discussion relating to the dispute'[32] and, if a member of the Council, 'shall abstain from voting' on proposals for peaceful settlement.[33] If the parties fail to settle a dispute by peaceful means, they 'shall refer it to the Security Council'.[34]

WILL THE SITUATION OR DISPUTE DETERIORATE?

14.   Is it likely that the situation or dispute will deteriorate, thus increasing the danger to international peace and security?

If the Security Council considers that a deterioration is likely, the Council 'may investigate' the matter (see question 15)[35] and 'may' also recommend 'procedures or methods of adjustment' (see question 32);[36] and the Council 'shall' decide whether to recommend 'terms of settlement' (see question 33).[37]

[32] Article 32.
[33] Article 27 (3).
[34] Article 37 (1).
[35] Article 34.
[36] Article 36 (1).
[37] Article 37 (2).

INVESTIGATION

15.   Does the Council need to conduct an investigation so as to determine whether the continuance of a dispute or situation is likely to endanger international peace and security?[38]

The Council has used a variety of means of investigation, including direct hearings, entrusting the task to a subsidiary organ, and requests to the Secretary-General. In 1950 the General Assembly created a Peace Observation Commission to observe and report on the situation in any area where there is international tension.[39]

IS THE MATTER WITHIN THE SCOPE OF CHAPTER VII OF THE CHARTER?

16.   Does there exist a 'threat to the peace, breach of the peace, or act of aggression'?

If the Security Council determines that one of these conditions exists, it shall 'make recommendations' or 'decide' what non-military or military measures of enforcement 'shall be taken',[40] and UN Members 'shall join in affording mutual assistance in carrying out' those measures.[41] Decisions which cite Chapter VII of the Charter or use its language are crucial because of the expectation that they may be but a prelude to the taking of binding decisions.

CLAIMS TO BE ACTING IN SELF-DEFENCE

17.   Has one party claimed that it is the victim of an armed attack and that it is therefore acting in self-defence?[42]

Measures taken by UN Members in exercise of the right of self-defence 'shall be immediately reported to the Security Council and shall not in any way affect [its] authority and responsibility'.[43]

[38] Article 34.
[39] GA res. 377B (V), 3 Nov. 1950.
[40] Article 39.
[41] Article 49.
[42] Article 51.
[43] Ibid.

SECURITY COUNCIL'S RESPONSIBILITY TO BRING ABOUT
A CESSATION OF HOSTILITIES

18. If armed conflict is still taking place, how should the Security Council seek to bring about a cessation of hostilities?

The Council may reach a decision on the cessation of hostilities by approving a presidential appeal, adopting an agreed statement of consensus, or voting for a resolution in express terms.

19. Should the decision be a call or appeal, or should it be an order under Chapter VII?

TIMING

20. Should the Council issue a cease-fire call or order at once, or would a delay in taking a decision be more likely to lead to positive responses from all the parties?

The inclination of the Council is to issue an immediate call for the fighting to stop. If, however, one party is more responsible than the other for the outbreak of hostilities, an immediate cease-fire might place it in an unduly advantageous situation.

TO TAKE EFFECT WHEN?

21. When should a call or order to cease hostilities take effect?

The day and time when hostilities are to cease may be specified in the Council's decision, or the Council may leave this to be determined by a subsidiary organ in the field or by the Secretary-General. A short delay might be appropriate if the parties are likely to encounter difficulties in communicating a cease-fire order down their chains of military command (see question 55).

TO WHOM ADDRESSED?

22. Should an appeal or order be directed to named governments and other entities, or should a more general formulation be used?

The Security Council has in the past addressed appeals or orders to named parties, to un-named parties, and to 'Governments and authorities concerned'; and it would not be difficult to devise even more general formulations.

WHICH ACTIVITIES TO CEASE?

23.   Should the appeal or order be for a cease-fire only, or are there other hostile activities that should also stop?

Past resolutions of the Security Council have called for or ordered a cease-fire or have called on the parties to:
—cease acts of violence;
—cease all activities of a military or paramilitary nature, as well as acts of violence, terrorism, and sabotage;
—desist from further military action;
—cease all fighting;
—abstain from any hostile military action;
—cease all acts of armed force;
—immediately discontinue all military operations [and] cease guerrilla warfare;
—immediately cease hostilities.
    It would also be open to the Council to call for or order the cessation of hostile acts of a non-military character such as provocative propaganda or the incitement of subversive activities.

WITHDRAWAL OF FORCES

24.   If armed conflict has led to the occupation of territory, should the Council include in its decision a call or order for a withdrawal of forces to positions occupied before the fighting began?

Withdrawal of forces can be asked for unconditionally or the Council may call for a phased withdrawal. In the latter event, detailed arrangements would have to be worked out in the field, probably with the assistance of a subsidiary organ.
    In considering whether to call for withdrawal, the Council has to take account not only of the situation on the ground but also of the means to be used to enforce a decision if a party should refuse to comply.

COMMUNICATING THE TEXT

25. Is it necessary to give guidance or assistance to the Secretary-General about the means of communicating the text to the parties and others directly affected?

NEED FOR RESTRAINT

26. Should the Council include in its decision an appeal for restraint or a reminder to the parties of their obligations under the UN Charter and other legal instruments?

APPEAL OR ORDER TO NON-PARTIES

27. Should governments and entities other than the parties be asked or ordered to cease supplying arms or giving other assistance to the parties or to cease encouraging the parties to continue military action in defiance of the Security Council?

SUBSIDIARY ORGAN

28. If the Security Council decides to establish a subsidiary organ, what would be an appropriate composition and terms of reference?

Two factors have to be taken into account in deciding on the composition of a subsidiary organ: the need for the organ to operate effectively, and also the importance of being sufficiently representative to command confidence. Difficulties have arisen in the past when subsidiary organs have had overlapping functions.

The normal practice is for subsidiary organs to decide their own procedure.

29. Are special directives needed about the frequency or form of the reports that the subsidiary organ shall make?

SYSTEM OF VERIFICATION

30. Are there available satisfactory means for verifying a cessation of hostilities?

See questions 63 and 65 relating to supervision (observation) and peace-keeping.

REPORTS ON COMPLIANCE

31. How should the Security Council be informed regarding compliance?

The Council has in the past asked for reports on compliance from the parties, the Secretary-General, or a subsidiary organ. At a pinch, the Council could ask for reports from a regional agency under Chapter VIII or even an appropriate non-governmental organization with consultative status under Article 71.

MEANS OF SETTLEMENT

32. Should the Security Council recommend procedures or methods of pacific settlement?[44]

The Charter provides a partial list of means of peaceful settlement of disputes: negotiation, inquiry, mediation, conciliation, arbitration, judicial settlement, resort to regional agencies or arrangements, other peaceful means of their own choice.[45] In addition, good offices is a recognized means of peaceful settlement, whether exercised by the Secretary-General, the President of the Security Council, or some other person or agency. Legal disputes should 'as a general rule be referred by the parties to the International Court of Justice':[46] it is open to the International Court to make use of the method of inquiry or to solicit 'an expert opinion'.[47] The Security Council is to encourage the settlement of 'local disputes' through regional agencies or arrangements.[48]

From time to time the General Assembly has decided to establish new machinery to assist with pacific settlement. In 1949 the Assembly asked the Secretary-General to compile a list of persons fitted to serve as members of commissions of

[44] Article 36 (1).
[45] Article 33 (1).
[46] Article 36 (3).
[47] Article 50 of the Statute.
[48] Article 52 (3) of the Charter.

inquiry or conciliation.[49] The following year the Security Council, on the advice of the General Assembly, decided that it would appoint a rapporteur or conciliator 'should an appropriate occasion arise',[50] and it is always open to the Council to appoint the Secretary-General or a subsidiary organ as rapporteur for a specified question.[51] In 1967 the General Assembly asked the Secretary-General to prepare a register of experts in legal and other fields whose services might be used for fact-finding.[52]

During the Hammarskjold era, the practice developed by which policy-making organs would confer general mandates on the Secretary-General, leaving the details of implementation to him. This was possible because a Secretary-General with a strongly independent outlook coincided with a political environment in which it was plausible to seek to insulate conflicts in the Third World from bloc politics.

If for any reason the Secretary-General is not the most suitable person to fill the role of honest broker, the task may be entrusted to the President of the Security Council. It may be necessary to ask the President to continue this role even if his or her month as president has come to an end, and possibly even if the representative's term on the Council has been concluded.

It is doubtful whether general assertions can usefully be made about the utility of different means of settlement beyond what is explicit in the Charter. The parties themselves often favour negotiation, as it obviates the intervention of those who may be unsympathetic or objective. Inquiry by third parties, arbitration, or judicial settlement tend to be favoured by those who are confident that right is on their side or who would prefer even an unfavourable settlement to a continuation of conflict. Mediation or conciliation have often been resorted to, but some form of good offices has the merit of flexibility and informality. The Security Council itself may appoint a person or establish an organ for mediation, good offices, or conciliation; or the appointment may be delegated to the Secretary-General or the President of the Council. Settlement by regional

---

[49] GA res. 268D (III), 28 April 1949.
[50] SC res. 81 (S/1486), 24 May 1950.
[51] Rules 23 and 28.
[52] GA res. 2329 (XXII), 18 Dec. 1967.

agencies or arrangements is likely to be useful only in the case of cohesive regions of like-minded states.

In the absence of a directive to the contrary, an intermediary is likely to assume that it is more important to settle the dispute with the agreement of all the parties concerned than to conform exactly to previous obligations or agreements while leaving the problem unresolved.

TERMS OF SETTLEMENT

33. Has the time come for the Security Council to recommend terms of settlement?[53]

If all the parties to a dispute so request, the Council 'may ... make recommendations ... with a view to a pacific settlement';[54] but in practice the Council has been reluctant since 1949 to recommend detailed terms of settlement.

RECOMMENDATIONS OR PROVISIONAL MEASURES

34. If Chapter VII is involved, should the Security Council seek to prevent an aggravation of the situation by making recommendations or deciding on provisional measures?[55]

Recommendations and provisional measures under Article 40 are 'without prejudice to the rights, claims, or position of the parties'. They have in the past included calls to stop fighting as well as matters usually dealt with in a truce, such as respect for a previous cease-fire, withdrawal of forces, demarcation of lines of separation, establishment of demilitarized areas, means to deter violations, supervisory arrangements or peace-keeping, release of prisoners, and protection of life and property. UN Members have an obligation to 'join in affording mutual assistance in carrying out the measures decided upon by the Security Council'.[56]

[53] Article 37 (2).
[54] Article 38.
[55] Article 40.
[56] Article 49.

ELECTION, PLEBISCITE, OR REFERENDUM

35.   Is it possible to resolve part or all of a contentious question by reference to the will of the people?

If an election, plebiscite, or referendum is to be held under the authority of the Security Council, the Council will need to determine who will be eligible to vote, to ensure that local administration is fair and that civil rights are respected, and probably to designate a person or agency to supervise the arrangements.

Four processes require impartial supervision: the registration of voters (if a voters' roll is feasible), the registration of candidates (in the case of elections), actual balloting, and the subsequent examination of petitions and complaints. Regulations should be issued regarding the qualifications of candidates and voters. Intimidation, personation, and other offences should be specified, and publicity given to the procedure for making complaints. In cases where not all the voters are literate, it will be necessary for the parties to become identified with simple symbols.

It is impossible for observers to be present at every place and at every stage of the democratic process, but they should be mobile and have the right to conduct spot-checks at their own discretion. In no country in the world is it possible to avoid electoral abuses entirely, but the presence of international observers usually ensures that the result is broadly in accordance with the will of the people.

PARTITION

36.   Is it possible to resolve part or all of a contentious question by the partition of territory?

Partition tends to be resented by the majority and may thus create new problems, but sometimes there is no peaceful alternative.

NON-MILITARY ENFORCEMENT

37.   Is the matter sufficiently grave that the Security Council should decide to employ non-military measures in order to assist

the victim, punish the aggressor, or in other ways give effect to its decisions?

The Charter states that among such non-military measures are 'complete or partial interruption of economic relations and of rail, sea, air, postal, telegraphic, radio, and other means of communication, and the severence of diplomatic relations'.[57]

MILITARY EMBARGO

38. Should the Council decide to impose a military embargo?

The Council will need to consider whether the embargo should apply to all of the parties to the conflict or only to some of them; whether it should cover personnel as well as weapons and military equipment; and whether the Council's call or order should be directed to the suppliers, to the recipients, or to both.

39. What means should be used for supervising or enforcing a military embargo?

The Council may appeal for or order an arms embargo mainly as a gesture of disapproval, realizing that the embargoed parties will do their best to evade its provisions. If the Council is determined that an embargo shall be effective, rigorous means of supervision and enforcement will be needed (see question 74).

MILITARY ENFORCEMENT

40. Have non-military measures proved inadequate, so that the Security Council should consider military action?[58]

The Charter was based on the assumption that UN Members would have concluded special agreements for making armed forces, assistance, and facilities available to the Security Council, as well as the other arrangements dealt with in Articles 43-8 of the Charter. The military measures envisaged in the Charter would have comprised action by air, sea, or land, including demonstrations and blockades. If the Council is itself unable or unwilling to take military action, it may delegate the

[57] Article 41.
[58] Article 42.

task to one or more Members, as in the case of the Unified Command in Korea and the Beira Patrol for supervision of the embargo on oil and petroleum for Rhodesia. If the Council decides to employ the armed forces of a non-member, the Council 'shall' invite the non-member 'to participate in the decisions' of the Council.[59]

CONSEQUENCES OF PREVENTIVE OR
ENFORCEMENT MEASURES

41. Has a state found itself confronted with special economic problems arising from carrying out preventive or enforcement measures?

In that event, the state has the right 'to consult the Security Council' regarding the solution of those economic problems.[60]

42. Has it become necessary to suspend from the rights and privileges of UN Membership a state against whom preventive or enforcement action has been taken?[61]

Suspension from UN Membership (and also expulsion—see question 43) is 'by the General Assembly upon the recommendation of the Security Council'. Restoration of the rights and privileges of Membership is 'by the Security Council'.

PERSISTENT VIOLATIONS OF THE CHARTER

43. Has a UN Member violated the principles of the Charter so persistently that it should be expelled from the Organization?[62]

See comment on question 42.

REINFORCING THE DECISIONS
OF THE SECURITY COUNCIL

44. What diplomatic or other action may be taken by states to increase the moral and political weight of decisions of the Security Council?

[59] Article 44.   [60] Article 50.
[61] Article 5.   [62] Article 6.

The Council does not operate in a vacuum. All UN Members can exert *some* diplomatic or other pressure to help ensure that the decisions of the Council are carried out. Even the most obdurate state is not as indifferent to world opinion as it likes to pretend.

THE PRIMACY OF THE COUNCIL

45. Are there other UN organs that should be informed of action taken by the Security Council?

UN Members have agreed that the Security Council has the 'primary responsibility' for maintaining international peace and security and that it 'acts on their behalf',[63] but it may be necessary to inform other UN organs of the Council's deliberations or decisions. The General Assembly is convoked if the Security Council so requests.[64]

DOMESTIC JURISDICTION

46. Does the action that it is proposed that the Council should take represent intervention in matters that are essentially within a state's domestic jurisdiction?[65]

The Council is not authorized to intervene in essentially domestic matters, but this principle is not to prejudice the application of enforcement measures under Chapter VII.

ADVISORY LEGAL OPINION

47. Is there any legal question on which the Security Council would benefit from an advisory opinion by the International Court of Justice?[66]

This may be intrinsically important, but the process is also useful when it is important to gain time.

---

[63] Article 24 (1).
[64] Article 20.
[65] Article 2 (7); see also GA res. 2131 (XX), 21 Dec. 1965.
[66] Article 96.

CLARIFICATION OF PREVIOUS DECISION OF THE COUNCIL

48.   Is it necessary to clarify a previous decision?

It is sometimes necessary for the Council to interpret or elaborate a previous decision. There is no way of 'amending' a validly approved previous resolution; but if circumstances have changed so that part of a previous decision is no longer relevant, the Council may either adopt a new decision or issue a new directive to the agent that was responsible for implementing the part of the previous decision that has been overtaken by events.

VOTING (INCLUDING THE VETO)

49.   Has the voting been conducted in accordance with the relevant Articles of the Charter?[67]

The Charter states that each member of the Security Council shall have one vote; that decisions require nine affirmative votes; that if the matter is substantive and not procedural, the nine votes should include the concurring votes of the five permanent members; and that the parties to a dispute shall abstain from voting on proposals for peaceful settlement.[68] The practice of the Council is to regard a voluntary abstention by a permanent member as a concurring vote. Voting is by show of hands, recording consecutively those in favour, those against, and those abstaining; sometimes a member asks to be recorded as not participating in the vote. The votes are counted by a member of the Secretariat and announced by the President.

   If there is a disagreement whether a proposal is procedural (not subject to veto) or substantive (subject to veto), the preliminary question should be submitted to a vote of the Council before the main question is voted on, as envisaged in the San Francisco statement of 8 June 1945.[69]

   If, because of a lack of unanimity of the permanent members (the veto), the Council fails to exercise its primary responsibility for the maintenance of international peace and security in any case where there appears to be a threat to the peace, breach of the peace, or act of aggression, the Security Council may by a

----

[67] Rule 40.   [68] Article 27.
[69] UNCIO, 1945, vol. XI, pp. 710-14.

procedural vote convene the General Assembly within twenty-four hours so that the Assembly may recommend appropriate collective measures.[70] Alternatively, the Council may by procedural vote simply delete the matter from the list of items of which it is seized, thus enabling the General Assembly to make recommendations (see question 51).

ABSENCE

50.   Were all the members of the Security Council present when the vote was taken?

If a member of the Council deliberately absents itself when a vote is taken, the Council regards this as tantamount to a voluntary abstention or non-participation in the vote. If a member of the Council is prevented from being present when a vote is taken by *force majeure*, the member may be permitted to indicate subsequently how it would have voted had it been present.

The UN Legal Counsel has advised that the Council may continue to function and take valid decisions notwithstanding the fact that it is not legally constituted.[71]

DELETION OF ITEM

51.   Should the Security Council delete the item from the list of matters of which it is seized in order to facilitate action by the General Assembly?[72]

6.3   PROBLEMS IN THE FIELD

The remaining questions concern problems in the field—though some of them have to be dealt with, at least in part, by diplomatic means at UN headquarters (e.g. questions 63-72, 74, 86, 89-91). At this stage the parties will have little confidence in the good faith of the other side, so that it is urgent to deploy impartial observers or peace-keeping personnel along or near

[70] GA res. 377 (V), 3 Nov. 1950
[71] A/34/PV.118, 31 Dec. 1979 (mimeo), p. 36.
[72] Rule 11.

the front lines, approaching from both sides if necessary. This will involve a certain amount of improvisation, but the one corner that cannot be cut is the consent of the host country.

Every supervisory or peace-keeping mission is different, but the United Nations Secretariat and a number of UN Members have accumulated considerable experience and expertise, and UN personnel in the field will find it useful to consult the *Peacekeeper's Handbook* (International Peace Academy, 1978).

Eventually it may be possible to move from a simple cease-fire to a truce, armistice, or treaty of peace.

MINIMIZING THE RISKS IN AN UNSUPERVISED CEASE-FIRE

52. Can action be taken to minimize the danger that a temporarily unsupervised cease-fire will be violated, leading, perhaps by accident, to retaliation and a resumption of active hostilities?

Impartial observers or peace-keeping personnel should be introduced at key points near or along the *de facto* lines of separation as soon as possible, but this is bound to take two or three days. It is during this time that there is likely to be uncertainty or disagreement about the positions held at the time the cease-fire went into effect. While disputes of this nature are often unavoidable, it should be stressed to the parties that violations are not easily concealed. Sometimes it is possible to introduce into front-line areas non-combatant personnel independent of the parties (international officials, medical and relief workers, ministers of religion, journalists) though it is inevitable that the parties, even if their own intentions are honourable, will be reluctant to have foreigners in sensitive military zones on a substantial scale at this early stage.

If violations are suspected, the parties should be encouraged to report them to UN personnel or the Security Council rather than to engage in military reprisals (see comment on question 84).

DIFFERENT KINDS OF THIRD-PARTY ASSISTANCE

53. Has a clear distinction been made between the various kinds of UN assistance?

It is now generally accepted that various aspects of UN help should be kept distinct and normally entrusted to different persons or organs. The main functions are usually supervision of the cessation of hostilities or peace-keeping; political liaison with the host government and the other parties to the conflict regarding the UN effort to contain the situation; assistance to the parties in resolving the long-term issues that gave rise to the fighting; and humanitarian aid. If humanitarian problems have arisen or are anticipated on a large scale, the UN Secretary-General may appoint a special representative to help with co-ordinating relief efforts (see question 89).

PROTECTED PERSONS

54. If fighting is still taking place or there is a risk that it will be resumed, are any special precautions needed to ensure the safety of medical and religious personnel, diplomats, other civilians, combatants who are *hors de combat*, and other persons entitled to protection?

Protected persons are supposedly immune from direct attack, but are sometimes harmed as an unintended effect of a legitimate military operation. The safety of protected persons can some-times be reinforced if sanctuaries are established for those who are especially vulnerable (the sick, wounded, and disabled, the aged, children, pregnant women, and mothers of young children). The perimeters of sanctuaries should be clearly marked, and they should display red crosses, UN emblems, or similar insignia. Ideally, an independent and impartial agency should take responsibility for ensuring their non-military status, conducting whatever verification is necessary, but this is not always possible at short notice in an emergency. Protected persons are immune from direct attack even if supervision is inadequate.

FORMULATING AN AGREED ORDER
TO CEASE HOSTILITIES

55. Can representatives of the parties meet quickly so as to draft an order to cease hostilities, to be issued simultaneously by the military commands of all the parties to the conflict?

It is difficult to prevent subordinate officers from taking military initiatives in violation of the cease-fire if they believe that these will be undetected but will lead to significant military advantage; but straightforward misunderstanding can be minimized if the same cease-fire order is issued by the military commands of the two sides.

DEMARCATING THE LINES OF SEPARATION

56. What help do the parties need in demarcating the lines of separation on the ground?

UN personnel usually play a vital role in this process. Large-scale aerial photographs and maps are helpful, but there is no substitute for information obtained visually on-the-spot. The needs of civilians should be taken into account, as well as topographical features and military considerations. One or both parties may fear that the passage of time may confer a certain legitimacy on the lines of separation, but it should be stressed that the demarcation of such lines is without prejudice to the rights, claims, or position of the parties.

57. Have the positions on the ground been accurately marked on large-scale maps, signed or initialled by the parties and if necessary witnessed by an independent person or persons?

58. Have the agreed lines of separation been clearly shown on the ground by conspicuous physical markers and/or obstacles?

BUFFER ZONES

59. Should the parties be encouraged to withdraw their forces by short distances from the lines of separation so as to leave demilitarized buffer areas between the front lines?

BELEAGUERED FIGHTERS

60. Is any special directive or guidance needed regarding combatants who are behind the enemy's lines when the cessation of hostilities comes into effect?

See question 88.

DEMILITARIZATION

61. Would tension be reduced or difficulties removed by the creation of demilitarized areas?

Demilitarization in time of peace has been used for three purposes: to provide a base for negotiating or supervising a cessation of hostilities; because of contending claims as to sovereignty; and to reduce tension by a disengagement of military forces along the lines of separation. It is necessary to secure the agreement of the parties regarding such matters as location, how the perimeters shall be marked, the emblem or insignia to be displayed, the persons to be prohibited from living in or entering, the installations and activities to be permitted or banned (including agreement on over-flying), arrangements for policing and guarding sensitive installations, the arms that police and guards may carry, means of verification or supervision (including guarantees of freedom of movement and communication for supervisory personnel),[73] and the duration of the agreement.

It should be stressed that agreement to demilitarize does not affect sovereignty: if there are anxieties on this score, the agreement can be expressly declared to be without prejudice to the rights, claims, or position of the parties.

ZONES OF LIMITED ARMAMENTS

62. If total demilitarization cannot be attained, is it possible to create zones of limited armaments which could later be progressively widened or completely demilitarized?

Continuous verification or spot-checks, either by the opposing party or more probably by impartial observers, will be needed to ensure that such an agreement is being respected.[74] Aerial reconnaissance may provide an additional safeguard.

SUPERVISION

63. What form of supervision (observation) of the cessation of hostilities will be necessary?

[73] *Peacekeeper's Handbook*, Chapter V, paras. 27-32 and p. 69.
[74] Ibid., paras. 33-6 and p. 69.

Joint supervision by the parties will probably not be possible in the early stages. Military observers have in the past been seconded by local consular posts or specially recruited and formed into integrated organizations. Supervisory personnel have also been designated by 'neutral nations', but this form of supervision has not been very satisfactory.

Independent and impartial observers, by their very presence, usually have a calming effect: in addition, they should seek to settle local incidents by persuasion and should report substantial and deliberate violations to a subsidiary organ of the Security Council or to the Council itself. Their aims should be to prevent a renewal of fighting and to ensure that the cessation of hostilities does not result in military advantage or disadvantage to either side. It may be necessary to conduct peaceful but conspicuous patrols, especially in areas where there are dangers of clashes, and occasional spot-checks may also be needed. Supervisory personnel usually operate from fixed posts.

Supervision by UN personnel cannot take place without the agreement of the host country. Supervisory personnel should have their own means of transport and communication, and they should be assured of freedom of movement and reasonable rights of access. They may need helicopters and light reconnaissance aircraft (with specified rights of over-flying), adaptable land vehicles, and (in appropriate cases) small and fast naval vessels. If infiltration is a problem, tracker dogs are useful.

The head of each supervisory mission is appointed by the Secretary-General, and the Secretary-General co-operates with the head of mission in recruiting military observers from countries not directly involved in the conflict. A typical observer mission has numbered several hundred persons, with supporting staff. The cost is normally met from the regular UN budget.

64. Will supervision be facilitated by the use of unmanned sensors?

The Sinai Field Mission (US) has gained considerable experience in the use of sophisticated detection systems.

PEACE-KEEPING

65. If supervision by military observers based at fixed posts is unlikely to prove sufficient, would a peace-keeping force be an appropriate form of supervision?

Although peace-keeping requires the presence of military contingents, its essence is not to coerce. Peace-keeping implies a bargain between the parties that hostilities will not be resumed and that provocative activities will be avoided; and the presence of the Force demonstrates the concern of the international community that minor or unauthorized violations do not escalate.

The international force is not there to impose a solution or even to enforce the cessation of hostilities: its function is partly symbolic, and the safety of UN peace-keeping personnel lies in the brassards or blue berets of its members and not in the weapons they carry.

POLICE IN INTERNATIONAL PEACE-KEEPING

66. Will civilian police also be needed?

If peace-keeping is in an inhabited area, it may be necessary to use internationally recruited civilian police.

PEACE-KEEPING MANDATE

67. How should the purpose and mandate of any peace-keeping operation be defined?

It is usual to formulate the function in rather general terms: to secure and supervise the cessation of hostilities, to help maintain quiet, to prevent a recurrence of fighting, to secure compliance with relevant resolutions, to reinforce mutual restraint, to contribute to the maintenance of law and order, to verify the implementation of agreements, to restore peace and security. The mandate is incorporated in a resolution of the Security Council, and periodic reports on its interpretation and implementation are submitted to the Council by the Secretary-General.

Members of peace-keeping forces should act with restraint and impartiality so that their activities do not promote or prevent any particular political outcome. They should not initiate the use of armed force but they may respond with force in self-defence when all peaceful means of persuasion have failed or to maintain the viability of the operation. Advance warning should if possible be given before force is used, the principle of minimum force should be applied, and armed force should cease as soon as it has achieved its object.

States supplying military contingents should ensure that their personnel are familiar with the main principles of international humanitarian law.

DEPLOYED ON ONE OR BOTH SIDES OF LINE?

68. Is the Force to be deployed on the territory of both parties or of one only?

From every point of view it is desirable to have the Force on the territory of both parties, but this has not always been possible.

COMMANDER AND STAFF

69. Have the Force Commander and civilian staff been appointed?

The Secretary-General appoints the Commander of the Force and informs the Security Council, and the Council then approves the report of the Secretary-General. The Secretary-General assigns civilian staff from the UN Secretariat or recruits special staff by the normal procedures. It may be necessary to recruit indigenous staff to help with interpretation and other tasks where local knowledge is needed.

COMPOSITION

70. From which countries should contingents be recruited?

It is not always possible to know what should be the size of a UN Force before it takes the field, but it will probably number several thousand persons. The Secretary-General reports from time to time on the recruitment of contingents and on changes in composition. He consults the host country and the other parties about the countries from which contingents will be drawn and takes their views fully into account, but the final decision rests with him and the Force Commander. Their aim is to secure a balanced composition from countries not directly involved in the conflict. Originally it was the practice not to recruit contingents from the five permanent members of the Security Council, but it was convenient in 1964 to include a British contingent in the Force in Cyprus, and a French contingent subsequently served in UN peace-keeping in Lebanon.

APPORTIONING THE COSTS

71. How should peace-keeping expenses be met?

There are still differences of view about the allocation of those peace-keeping expenses that are not met by countries contributing contingents and the host country or countries. The states of the Soviet bloc have stressed the primary responsibility of the Security Council for the maintenance of international peace and security,[75] whereas most Western states believe that the Charter entrusts to the General Assembly the apportioning of UN expenses among the Members.[76]

There are, in practice, three main ways of meeting UN peace-keeping expenses; contributions by the parties on an equal or other agreed basis, voluntary contributions by those governments willing to pay, and compulsory assessments on all UN Members. The normal procedure when there are compulsory assessments is for the Secretary-General to submit estimates of cost to the General Assembly and for the Advisory Committee on Administrative and Budgetary Questions (ACABQ) to comment in writing. These two documents then go to the General Assembly's Fifth Committee (consisting of all UN Members) and, if necessary, the Secretary-General or his representative and the chairman of the ACABQ elucidate and comment on the documents. The Fifth Committee then approves a recommendation to apportion the expenses in

[75] Article 24 (1).
[76] Article 17 (2).

accordance with the current scale of assessments, usually reducing the assessments of the poorer Members. This recommendation then goes to the plenary General Assembly, where a two-thirds majority of the Members present and voting is needed for a decision.[77] The Secretary-General reports periodically on the collection of the assessed contributions.

It is nearly always suggested by someone that the aggressor should pay the whole cost, but this is a debating point rather than a serious proposal.

DURATION

72.   How long will the peace-keeping operation last?

The usual procedure is for the Secretary-General to recommend to the Security Council that a peace-keeping operation be launched for an initial period of three, six, or twelve months, and this is incorporated in the authorizing resolution. It is almost always an emergency situation when the operation is launched, and it is hoped that the operation can be terminated after an interim or transitional period, but the Security Council has learned from experience that initial hopes are disappointed.

Before the expiry of the agreed term, the Secretary-General consults the countries directly involved (host country and other parties to the conflict, states supplying contingents) and if they agree he proposes to the Security Council an extension for a further period. This is approved, sometimes by a resolution of the Council, sometimes by a presidential statement of consensus.

PREVENTIVE ACTION BY PEACE-KEEPING PERSONNEL

73.   Do the parties agree that, in order to prevent a recurrence of fighting, the UN Force should have the right to apprehend and disarm infiltrators or trouble-makers and to dismantle provocative fortifications and installations?

This situation is most likely to arise when provocative activities originate with unofficial or dissident persons or groups. If the

[77] Article 18 (2).

parties themselves are unable or unwilling to deal with those who endanger what is probably a precarious peace, they may be glad to entrust this responsibility to the UN Force.

MONITORING A MILITARY EMBARGO

74.   Are international personnel needed to ensure that arms and military personnel are not imported into the region in contravention of a decision of the Security Council?

If an arms embargo is to be effective, the Council probably has to take a mandatory decision under Chapter VII of the UN Charter and to consider carefully who would benefit from violating the decision, for it can be taken for granted that the embargoed parties will try to find loopholes in any supervisory system instituted by the Council. Such a supervisory system would need to have two elements, one designed to monitor the activities of the suppliers of weapons, and this would include a detailed examination of legislative or administrative provisions and export statistics. But such a system of monitoring would not be sufficient on its own because of the existence of an extensive and largely uncontrolled market in second-hand conventional weapons. For this reason, it would be necessary to monitor the recipients by a system of international inspection at key transit points and along the frontiers of the embargoed country or countries, conducted with a vigour comparable to that shown by both sides during the two world wars. This would necessitate aerial surveillance and spot-checks of cargoes at sea or land in the vicinity of the embargoed parties; but even such supervision might be evaded if the embargoed country could mount an airlift on a sufficient scale. The challenge for the Security Council would not be an impossible one technically, given the political will, but it would be far beyond activities normally undertaken under UN auspices.

LOCAL AGREEMENTS

75.   Can the local military commanders be induced to agree to further measures designed to reduce tension?

76.   Will the parties agree to establish direct telephone or

radio links between the two military commands or to arrange for regular meetings of local commanders?

Arrangements of this kind have to be relatively informal and strictly confined to military matters.

DETERRENCE OF VIOLATIONS

77. Are international personnel able to deter violations by their presence and by reminding the parties of their obligations?

The primary purpose of supervision or peace-keeping is not to detect infractions: it is to deter them.

78. Are alleged violations and complaints reported promptly to the supervisory organization or peace-keeping Force?

International personnel should investigate any incident that might lead to a resumption of hostilities,[78] even if no formal complaint is submitted. Incidents that are likely to give rise to complaints include unauthorized crossings of the lines of separation or entries into demilitarized areas, intrusion of military personnel or weapons into zones of limited armaments in excess of the agreed restrictions, military deployments or installations contrary to agreement, firing or other hostile military action across the lines of separation, over-flying, interference with objects or activities needed for the survival of the civilian population, taking of hostages, theft of animals, and (in coastal areas) unauthorized naval intrusions.

International personnel should make it clear to the parties that they do not wish to be given information that would bind them to silence.

FREEDOM OF MOVEMENT

79. Do the parties allow freedom of movement and co-operate with international personnel in investigating incidents?

A party wishing to prevent freedom of movement by international personnel does not necessarily have to resort to blatant interference, since it is usually as effective to use formal devices

---

[78] *Peacekeeper's Handbook*, Chapter V, paras. 101-9 and pp. 45-61.

such as delaying permission to travel. UN personnel should report all such difficulties to the head of mission or Force Commander[79] and through him to the Secretary-General.

COMPLAINTS

80. In the event of a complaint, what is the version of events of the non-complaining party?

81. Is there first-hand evidence from independent witnesses, material evidence, or circumstantial evidence to corroborate the complaint or the reply?

82. If the complaint is confirmed, is it of sufficient gravity for a special report to be transmitted to the Security Council?

Complaints, whether verified or not, may be setbacks; but sometimes they provide opportunities for persuading the parties that it is in their interests to strengthen the system of supervision or peace-keeping.

OTHER INCIDENTS

83. Have there been events that while not strictly breaches of the agreement to cease hostilities, may aggravate the situation and should therefore be reported to the Secretary-General or the Security Council?

MILITARY REPRISALS

84. Do the parties understand that, if a violation is committed by the other side, it is probably safer to seek the protection of the Security Council than to engage unilaterally in those limited military reprisals that are permitted under international law?

Many of the worst atrocities in war-time purport to be retaliation for prior illegalities by the opposing party, but reprisals are not a dependable deterrent of future breaches and almost always spark off counter-retaliation. In any case, probably the only

---

[79] Ibid., p. 67.

licit belligerent reprisal now is to use otherwise illegal weapons or methods of fighting against combatants or military targets.[80] Frits Kalshoven, the outstanding authority on military reprisals, has concluded that reprisals as sanctions of the laws of war are no longer even moderately effective, but rather 'a complete anachronism'.[81] The International Committee of the Red Cross (ICRC), while favouring a total and unconditional prohibition of military reprisals, suggests four limits which the ICRC believes are found in 'the texts of qualified writers or in the publications of specialized institutions'.[82]

(a)   Reprisals cannot be exercised unless the party alleging violation has offered the possibility of an inquiry and impartial observation of the facts.
(b)   The scale of reprisals must not be out of proportion to that of the violation they aim at stopping.
(c)   They must be carried out, so far as possible, only in the same field as that of the violation.
(d)   They should in any case not be contrary to the laws of humanity.

TRANSITION TO TRUCE, ARMISTICE, OR PEACE TREATY

85.   What further conditions need to be satisfied before it will be possible to move from a simple cease-fire to a truce, armistice, or peace treaty?

THIRD-PARTY ASSISTANCE WITH THE
NEGOTIATING PROCESS

86.   Would the parties welcome the help of the Secretary-General, the President of the Security Council, or a subsidiary organ in order to engage in negotiations for resolving the underlying issues or to reach agreement on a truce, armistice, or peace treaty?

---

[80] Rosenblad, p. 148; G. I. A. D. Draper, 'Wars of National Liberation and War Criminality', in Michael Howard, *Restraints on War: Studies in the Limitation of Armed Conflict*, Oxford, Unniversity Press, 1979, p. 152.
[81] Kalshoven, *Belligerent Reprisals*, p. 377.
[82] *Reaffirmation and Development of the Laws and Customs applicable in Armed Conflict*, Geneva, ICRC, 1969, pp. 83-7.

If the parties wish to meet at UN headquarters, the Secretary-General (or, if appropriate, the President of the Security Council) may act as a go-between. If, as is often the case, the parties prefer to meet in the region of conflict, then the intermediary role is likely to fall on a subsidiary organ.

The preliminary matters to be settled before the opening of direct negotiations include the place of meeting (a neutral site, alternately on the territory of the parties, or conceivably an aircraft or on board ship), the agenda, the status of those negotiators who do not enjoy diplomatic immunity, and the degree of confidentiality.

6.4 HUMANITARIAN QUESTIONS

It is sometimes claimed that military intervention is being undertaken for reasons of humanity. For this reason, if for no other, it is necessary to be on guard that military operations are, to the fullest extent possible, conducted in accordance with the humanitarian principles expressed in the Martens clause: the usages established among civilized peoples, the laws of humanity, and the dictates of the public conscience.

Military operations are governed by two general principles of law and ethics, and by a number of specific agreements concerning particular weapons, immunity from direct attack, and the protection of war victims. The general principles are, first, that military force should not be used excessively (the principle of proportion)[83] and, second, that there shall be no direct attacks on non-combatants (the principle of discrimination).[84] In addition, there are treaties banning the use in war of poisons, dum-dum bullets, unanchored automatic contact mines, chemical and bacteriological weapons, and biological weapons; and there are also treaties or declarations governing the deployment and certain uses of nuclear weapons. The Geneva Conventions (1949) and Additional Protocols (1977) provide protection for civilians and those combatants who have surrendered or been captured or who are no longer able to fight (sick, wounded, shipwrecked).

In all matters relating to armed conflict, there is tension

[83] Rosenblad, pp. 53-75, 146-8.
[84] Ibid., pp. 12, 139-42, 153-4.

between the claims of military necessity and humanitarian considerations. The tension is likely to be especially acute in cases where a major role has been played by clandestine fighters, resistance groups, underground units, insurgents, partisans, guerrillas, and other irregular combatants.

Combatants should operate in accordance with the laws and customs of war, and yet it is not always realistic to expect irregular fighters who have no access to manuals of military law or standard legal texts to know what is permitted and what is forbidden. Perhaps it was partly with this in mind that the Red Cross movement recently drafted the following general rules of humanitarian law applicable in armed conflict:

1. Persons *hors de combat* and those who do not take a direct part in hostilities are entitled to respect for their lives and physical and moral integrity. They shall in all circumstances be protected and treated humanely without any adverse distinction.
2. It is forbidden to kill or injure an enemy who surrenders or who is *hors de combat.*
3. The wounded and sick shall be collected and cared for by the party to the conflict which has them in its power. Protection also covers medical personnel, establishments, transport, and *matériel.* The emblem of the red cross (red crescent, red lion and sun) is the sign of such protection and must be respected.
4. Captured combatants and civilians under the authority of an adverse party are entitled to respect for their lives, dignity, personal rights, and convictions. They shall be protected against all acts of violence and reprisals. They shall have the right to correspond with their families and to receive relief.
5. Everyone shall be entitled to benefit from fundamental judicial guarantees. No one shall be held responsible for an act he has not committed. No one shall be subjected to physical or mental torture, corporal punishment, or cruel or degrading treatment.
6. Parties to a conflict and members of their armed forces do not have an unlimited choice of methods and means of warfare. It is prohibited to employ weapons or methods of warfare of a nature to cause unnecessary losses or excessive suffering.
7. Parties to a conflict shall at all times distinguish between the civilian population and combatants in order to spare civilian population and property. Neither the civilian population as such nor civilian persons shall be the object of attack. Attacks shall be directed solely against military objectives.[85]

[85] *International Review of the Red Cross*, 18th year, no. 206 (Sept.-Oct. 1978), pp. 247-9.

ALLEGED BREACHES OF INTERNATIONAL LAW

87. If it has been alleged that there have been war crimes, atrocities, or other breaches of the international law governing armed conflict and the protection of war victims, do the parties agree to an impartial inquiry?

The Geneva Conventions provide for a procedure of inquiry in the event of alleged infractions,[86] and Additional Protocol I provides for international fact-finding when breaches are alleged.[87] The International Law Commission has drafted a set of principles on war crimes, based on the proceedings at Nürnberg,[88] but unfortunately there is no international criminal court in which such cases can be heard.

HELP FOR STRANDED COMBATANTS

88. Is it necessary to provide stranded combatants with humanitarian assistance in the form of food and other non-military essentials or means of transport so that they may return to territory under the control of their own side?

The purpose of such humanitarian assistance should be two-fold: to prevent unnecessary suffering, and to forestall military self-help which would endanger the cessation of hostilities (see question 60).

RELIEF NEEDS

89. Can relief needs be met by the host authorities and local voluntary bodies, or is there also a role for the United Nations or other external agencies?

Sometimes the distinctive UN role will be to establish a focal point for the co-ordination of external help, including that provided by UN agencies (e.g., High Commissioner for Refugees, UNICEF, Disaster Relief Co-ordinator, World Food Council). This liaison function would normally be paid for by the regular UN budget. If the need for relief is sufficiently

[86] Articles 49-54/50-3/129-32/146-9.
[87] Articles 85-91.
[88] GAOR, 5th session, Supplement no. 12, A/1316, paras. 98-126.

acute and likely to be long-term, it may be necessary to create an *ad hoc* humanitarian agency, financed from outside the regular UN budget, but this takes time. There is a precedent for the United Nations entrusting the relief task to designated voluntary agencies (Palestine refugees, 1948-50).

90.   Can the mandate for UN supervisory or peace-keeping personnel reasonably be interpreted as extending to humanitarian tasks, or is additional authority for this required?

The rationale for any UN help is partly humanitarian, but it also has a pragmatic basis because supervisory or peace-keeping personnel cannot do their job properly if the normal life of the local population is severely dislocated by man-made or natural disaster. It is essential that the Secretariat in New York be kept informed as relief needs become apparent, even if there seem to be adequate local means for dealing with such needs. The international community takes time to become aware of humanitarian needs, and the Secretary-General often performs a vital function of information and education.

     Emergency humanitarian tasks for UN personnel are likely to include transport of food and other relief supplies, distribution of rations, provision of tents or other emergency shelter, medical aid, tracing of missing persons, help to war victims wishing to return to their homes, and dealing with complaints about theft, damage, or destruction of crops, animals, and property.

     At a later stage UN personnel may help with the restoration of a normal economic and administrative infrastructure.

RELIEF SUPPLIES

91.   Will it be necessary to import additional supplies of food, medicines, clothing, and shelter?

Once relief needs are specified, it is usually not too difficult to persuade governments and/or voluntary agencies to provide essential supplies at short notice. Sometimes goodwill exceeds discretion, with offers of inappropriate supplies. This is usually worse than useless: traditional rice-eaters may reject wheat, even if they are desperately hungry, and there is not much point in sending greatcoats to tropical areas. In any case, the greatest bottleneck is nearly always the system of distribution in the immediate post-war period.

The allocation of food rations and other aid when there is not enough to go round is always difficult: the humanitarian impulse is to give priority to the most vulnerable (young children and the elderly), but it may be more compassionate in the long run to build up the strength of those who will grow next year's crop or bear the next generation of children.

HARASSMENT AND PERSECUTION

92. Should UN personnel seek to provide sanctuary to those who allege that they are being harassed or persecuted because of their national or racial origins, religious beliefs, or political activities?

This can only be an emergency measure. At the earliest possible moment, the co-operation of the host authorities should be sought regarding both the protection of harassed or persecuted people and official action which might be taken to put a stop to intimidation.

PRISONERS OF WAR

93. Were seriously sick and wounded prisoners of war repatriated as soon as they were fit to travel, without regard to numbers held?[89]

94. If active hostilities have ceased, are other prisoners of war being released and repatriated, without regard to numbers held?[90]

The Geneva POW Convention is to be respected in all circumstances.[91]

Medical and religious personnel are not considered as prisoners of war but they may be detained in order to exercise medical and spiritual functions for the benefit of prisoners of war.[92]

[89] Third Geneva Convention, 1949, Articles 109-10 and Annex I.
[90] Ibid., Article 118.
[91] Ibid., Article 1.
[92] Ibid., Articles 33 and 35.

No sick or injured prisoner of war may be repatriated against his will during hostilities.[93] If prisoners of war object to repatriation when hostilities have ceased, it would accord with the Korean precedent for them to be released into the custody of a neutral agency.

A particular problem concerns prisoners of war captured by irregular combatants. Clearly, irregulars do not always have the means to implement all the provisions of the Third Geneva Convention (1949) and the first Additional Protocol (1977). Perhaps procedures could be worked out in particular cases whereby prisoners taken by irregular groups could be handed over to the International Committee of the Red Cross or a similar humanitarian agency and kept out of the conflict until hostilities have ended.

POLITICAL PRISONERS

95. Have arrangements been agreed for the release of political prisoners, civilian internees, and those detained under emergency or security regulations, without regard to the numbers similarly detained by the opposing party?

This raises difficulties when political prisoners are accused of breaking the ordinary criminal law (e.g. homicide, bank robbery, extortion).[94] Humanitarian agencies like the International Committee of the Red Cross, the International Commission of Jurists, and Amnesty International have some experience of these matters, and assistance could be sought in appropriate cases.

ALLEGATIONS OF BRUTALITY OR TORTURE

96. Has it been alleged that prisoners of war or political prisoners have been brutally treated or tortured?

There has always been a temptation to use brutality or torture against captured enemies, either to extract information or for primitive reasons of sadism or revenge, but techniques of intimi-

---

[93] Ibid., Article 109.
[94] Forsythe, *Humanitarian Politics*, pp. 259-66.

dation have become increasingly sophisticated. The UN General Assembly has adopted a declaration against torture and other forms of mistreatment,[95] and an enforceable convention is being drafted.

REFUGEES AND DISPLACED PERSONS

97. Have arrangements been made for the protection and care of those who have been uprooted from their homes as a result of the fighting?

Protection of refugees is the responsibility of the UN High Commissioner for Refugees. If care of refugees and displaced persons cannot be satisfactorily met by the host authorities, Red Cross or other humanitarian agencies may help. In one case in the past (Palestine refugees) a special UN agency was eventually established.

HOSTAGES AND ABDUCTED PERSONS

98. Have efforts been set in hand by UN or Red Cross agencies for tracing and returning to their homes any persons who have been taken hostage, held to ransom, kidnapped, or abducted?

Under the Geneva Conventions, the taking of hostages is prohibited,[96] and to kill hostages was declared at Nürnberg to be a war crime.[97]

CIVIL RIGHTS

99. Is there respect for basic human rights, especially in areas where armed conflict has taken place or which are subject to contending territorial claims?

Respect for human rights is not simply a matter of natural justice and equity, for denial of human rights often leads to armed conflict in the future. Basic rights are set out in the Universal

[95] GA res. 3452 (XXX), 9 Dec. 1975.
[96] Common Article 3 (1) (b) and Fourth Geneva Convention, Article 34.
[97] Nürnberg Principle VIb; see GAOR, 5th session, Supplement no. 12, A/1316, para. 119.

Declaration of Human Rights (1948)[98] and the two International Covenants (1966);[99] regarding internal wars, in Common Article 3 of the Geneva Conventions (1949) and Additional Protocol II (1977); and regarding civilians under occupation, in the Fourth Geneva Convention (1949).

The Fourth Geneva Convention concerning military occupation prohibits wilful killing of protected civilians, torture or inhuman treatment, the wilful causing of injury or suffering, unlawful deportation or transfer, wilfully depriving a person of the right of a fair trial, the taking of hostages, extensive destruction or appropriation of property not justified by military necessity, reprisals, collective penalties, all forms of physical or moral coercion, corporal or capital punishment, inhuman conditions of imprisonment or detention, and disrespect for honour, family rights, and religious beliefs and practices. These prohibitions have been reinforced by a resolution of the General Assembly urging that civilians should not be the object of reprisals, forcible transfers, or other assaults on their integrity.[100]

These, then, are questions that are likely to arise when the international community tries to stop the fighting. The effort must be pursued with patience and persistence, for the problems are usually more intractable than the above questions and comments have implied. A society at war devotes so much effort to the conduct of military operations that little energy is left for considering how the armed conflict shall be terminated. It cannot be stressed too much that the decision to fight is almost always easier than the decision to stop fighting, and usually third-party assistance is needed. The United Nations has many defects, but the evidence of the case studies in volume II suggests that UN help is always useful and occasionally decisive.

It should nevertheless be stressed that, unless the case studies in volume II are extravagantly untypical, war is not now an effective means of securing justice. Nor are the righteous always victorious. Medieval theologians insisted that a Christian ruler should never go to war unless he was certain of victory, for it

---

[98] GA res. 217A (III), 10 Dec. 1948.
[99] GA res. 2200A (XXI), 16 Dec. 1966.
[100] GA res. 2675 (XXV), 9 Dec. 1970.

was morally intolerable to take up arms and then fail to secure the good ends that alone would extenuate the evil that resort to war necessarily brings in its train. In the contemporary world there can be no certainty of victory, for the race is not always to the swift, nor the battle to the strong.

Incompatabilities of interest are no doubt inevitable in an imperfect world, but the time has now come to terminate *armed* conflict. The alternative is not supine capitulation, but *disarmed* conflict.

Select bibliography

Acheson, Dean, *Present at the Creation*. New York, Norton, 1969.

Additional Protocols to the Geneva Conventions, 1977. Issued in provisional form at the Diplomatic Conference on the Reaffirmation and Development of International Humanitarian Law applicable in Armed Conflicts on 10 June 1977, and in corrected form in July 1977; published in the *International Review of the Red Cross*, 17th year, no. 197-8 (August-September 1977), pp. 1-101, and as Annexes to UN doc. A/32/144, 15 Aug. 1977 (mimeo).

Allon, Yigal, *The Making of Israel's Army*, London, Valentine, Mitchell, in association with Weidenfeld & Nicolson, 1970.

Azcárate, Pablo de, *Mission in Palestine, 1948-52*, pp. 1-205 trans. Teener Hall, Washington DC, Middle East Institute, 1966.

Bailey, Sydney D., *Voting in the Security Council*, Bloomington, Indiana, and London, Indiana University Press, 1969.

Bailey, Sydney D., *Peaceful Settlement of International Disputes*, 3rd ed, New York, UN Institute for Training and Research, 1970.

Bailey, Sydney D., *Prohibitions and Restraints in War*, London, Oxford University Press, 1972 (under the auspices of the RIIA).

Bailey, Sydney D., *Procedure of the UN Security Council*, Oxford, Clarendon Press, 1975.

Bar-Yaacov, N., *The Israel-Syrian Armistice: Problems of Implementation, 1949-1966*, Jerusalem, Magnes Press/London, Oxford University Press, 1967.

Baxter, R. R., 'Armistices and Other Forms of Suspension of Hostilities', *Recueil des cours de l'Académie de Droit International de la Haye*, vol. 149 (1976), pp. 353-99.

Begin, Menachem, *The Revolt: Story of Irgun*, trans. Shmuel Katz, ed. and condensed by Ivan M. Greenberg, New York, Schuman, 1951.

Ben-Gurion, David, *Israel: A Personal History*, trans. Nechemia Meyers and Uzy Nystar, Tel Aviv, Sabra Books/New York, Funk & Wagnalls, 1971.

Bernadotte, Folke, *To Jerusalem*, trans. Joan Bulman London, Hodder & Stoughton, 1951.

Bernard, Rachel, *L'Armistice dans les guerres internationales*, Geneva, Imprimerie Genevoise, 1947.

Brook, David, *Preface to Peace: the United Nations and the Arab-Israel Armistice System*, Washington, DC, Public Affairs Press, 1964.

388 *Select bibliography*

Brownlie, Ian, *International Law and the Use of Force by States,* Oxford, Clarendon Press, 1963.

Bull, Odd, *War and Peace in the Middle East: The Experiences and Views of a U.N. Observer,* London, Cooper, 1976.

Burns, E. L. M., *Between Arab and Israeli,* London, Harrap/Toronto, Clarke, Irwin, 1962.

Calahan, H. A., *What Makes a War End?* New York, Vanguard, 1944.

Carroll, Berenice A., 'How Wars End: An Analysis of Some Current Hypotheses', *Journal of Peace Research* (Oslo), vol. 6, no. 4 (1969), pp. 295-321.

Cessez-le-feu: The Cease-Fire; Recueils de la Société Internationale de Droit militaire et de Droit de la guerre (proceedings of the sixth international congress held in the Hague, 22-5 May 1973), Brussels, 1973.

Comité international de la Croix-Rouge et le Conflit de Corée, Geneva, ICRC, 1952.

Coser, Lewis, *The Functions of Social Conflict,* New York, Free Press/London, Collier-Macmillan, 1964.

Dayan, Moshe, *Story of my Life,* London, Weidenfeld & Nicolson, 1976.

Dedijer, Vladimir, *On Military Conventions: An Essay on the Evolution of International Law,* Lund, Sweden, Gleerup, 1961.

Delessert, Christiane Shields, *Release and Repatriation of Prisoners of War at the End of Hostilities...* Zurich, Schulthess Polygraphischer, 1977.

Eytan, Walter, *The First Ten Years: A Diplomatic History of Israel,* London, Weidenfeld & Nicolson, 1958.

Forsythe, David P., *United Nations Peacemaking: the Conciliation Commission for Palestine.* Baltimore and London, Johns Hopkins University Press, in co-operation with the Middle East Institute, 1972.

Forsythe, David P., *Humanitarian Politics: The International Committee of the Red Cross,* Baltimore and London, Johns Hopkins University Press, 1977.

Fox, William T. R., (special ed.) 'How Wars End', *Annals of the American Academy of Political and Social Science,* vol. 392 (November 1970), pp. 1-172.

Freymond, Jacques, *Guerres, Révolutions, Croix-Rouge: Réflexions sur la rôle du Comité Internationale de la Croix-Rouge,* Geneva, Institut Universitaire de Hautes Études Internationales, 1976.

Geneva Conventions, 12 August 1949. Published in Geneva by the ICRC, 2nd rev. edn, 1950; also in the *Handbook of the International Red Cross,* 10th ed, Geneva, 1953, pp. 100-295, and the *International Red Cross Handbook,* 11th ed, Geneva, 1971, pp. 28-255; UNTS, vol. 75 (1950), nos. 970-3.

Glubb, [Sir] John Bagot, *A Soldier with the Arabs,* London, Hodder & Stoughton, 1957.

Goodman, Allan E., (ed.), *Negotiating while Fighting: The Diary of Admiral C. Turner Joy at the Korean Armistice Conference,* Stanford, Calif., Hoover Institution, 1978.

Goodrich, Leland M., *Korea: A Study of US Policy in the United Nations,* New York, Council on Foreign Relations, 1956.

Greenspan, Morris, *The Modern Law of Land Warfare,* Berkeley and Los Angeles, University of California Press, 1959.

Hague Convention for the Protection of Cultural Property in the Event of Armed Conflict, 14 May 1954, UNTS, vol. 249 (1956), no. 3511.

Hague Conventions of 1899 (II) and 1907 (IV) respecting the Laws and Customs of War on Land, Washington, DC, CEIP, 1915.

Hammarskjold, Dag, *Markings,* trans. W. H. Auden and Leif Sjöberg, London, Faber, 1964.

Handel, Michael I., *War Termination—A Critical Survey,* Jerusalem, Leonard Davis Institute for International Relations, Hebrew University, 1978 (Jerusalem Papers on Peace Problems no. 24).

Harbottle, Michael, *The Impartial Soldier,* London, Oxford University Press, 1970 (under the auspices of the RIIA).

Hermes, Walter G., *United States Army in the Korean War,* vol. 2, *Truce Tent and Fighting Front,* Washington, DC, US Government Printing Office, 1966.

Higgins, Rosalyn, *The Development of International Law through the Political Organs of the United Nations,* London, Oxford University Press, 1963 (under the auspices of the RIIA).

Higgins, Rosalyn (ed.), *United Nations Peacekeeping, 1946-1967: Documents and Commentary,* vol. 1, *the Middle East*; vol. II, *Asia,* London, Oxford University Press, 1969-70 (under the auspices of the RIIA).

Horn, Carl von, *Soldiering for Peace,* London, Cassell, 1966.

Hospital localities and Safety Zones, Geneva, ICRC, 1952.

Hutchinson, E. H., *Violent Truce: A Military Observer Looks at the Arab-Israeli Conflict, 1951-1955,* New York, Devin-Adair, 1956.

Iklé, Fred Charles, *How Nations Negotiate,* New York and London, Harper & Row, 1964.

Iklé, Fred Charles, *Every War Must End,* New York and London, Columbia University Press, 1971.

International Committee of the Red Cross in Palestine, Geneva, ICRC, 1948.

Jessup, Philip C., *The Birth of Nations,* New York and London, Columbia University Press, 1974.

Joseph, Dov, *The Faithful City: the Siege of Jerusalem, 1948,* London, Hogarth Press, 1962.

Joy, C. Turner, *How Communists Negotiate,* New York, Macmillan, 1955.

Kalshoven, Frits, *The Law of Warfare*, Leiden, Sijthoff, 1973.

Kalshoven, Frits, *Belligerent Reprisals*, Leiden, Sijthoff, 1971.

Kirkbride, [Sir] Alec, *From the Wings: Amman Memoirs 1947-1951*, London, Cass, 1976.

Klafkowski, Alfons, 'Les Formes de cessation de l'état de guerre en droit international', *Recueil des cours se l'Académie de Droit International de la Haye*, vol. 149 (1976), pp. 217-86.

Lachs, Manfred, 'La Nouvelle Fonction des Armistices Contemporains', in *Hommage d'une génération de juristes au Président Basdevant*, Paris, Pedone, 1960, pp. 315-27.

Lall, Arthur, *Modern International Negotiation*, New York and London, Columbia University Press, 1966.

Law of Armed Conflict (FM 27-10), Washington, DC, US Government Printing Office, 1956.

Law of War on Land, being part III of the *Manual of Military Law*, London, HMSO, 1958, and subsequent amendments.

Levie, Howard S., 'The Nature and Scope of the Armistice Agreement', *American Journal of International Law*, vol. 50 (1956), pp. 880-906.

Lie, Trygve, *In the Cause of Peace: Seven Years with the United Nations*, New York, Macmillan, 1954.

Lourié, Sylvain, 'The United Nations Military Observer Group in India and Pakistan', *International Organization*, vol. 9, no. 1 (1955), pp. 19-31.

Mohn, Paul, 'Problems of Truce Supervision', *International Conciliation*, no. 478 (1952).

Montluc, Bertrand de, 'Le Cessez-le-feu', doctoral thesis presented in 1971 to the Université de Droit et d'Economie et des Sciences Sociales, Paris. (There is a photocopy in the British Library, Lending Division, ref. fF6.8526.)

Organization and Procedure of United Nations Commissions: memoranda by the Secretary-General to the Interim Committee of the General Assembly, 1949 and 1950.

Pannikar, K. M., *In Two Chinas: Memoirs of a Diplomat*, London, Allen & Unwin, 1955.

Peacekeeper's Handbook, New York, International Peace Academy, 1978. (Issued in loose-leaf form: Chapter 12, 'The Law and International Peacekeeping', is not available yet.)

Pearson, Lester, *Memoirs*, vol. II, *1948-1957: The International Years*, ed. John A. Munro and Alex I. Inglis, London, Gollancz, 1974.

Phillipson, Coleman, *Termination of War and Treaties of Peace*, London, Fisher Unwin, 1916.

Pictet, Jean, *The Principles of International Humanitarian Law*, Geneva, ICRC, n.d.

Respect for Human Rights in Armed Conflict, Reports of the UN Secretary-General, 20 Nov. 1969 (A/7720), 18 Sept. 1970 (A/8052), 2 Sept. 1971 (A/8370), 7 Nov. 1973 (A/9215) (all mimeo).

Reynier, Jacques de, *A Jérusalem un drapeau flottait sur la ligne de feu,* Neuchâtel, Switzerland, Histoire et Société d'Aujourd'hui, 1950.

Ridgway, Matthew B., *The Korean War,* Garden City, NY, Doubleday, 1967.

Rosas, Allan, *The Legal Status of Prisoners of War: A Study in International Humanitarian Law applicable in Armed Conflicts,* Helsinki, Suomalainen Tiedeakatemia, 1976.

Rosenblad, Esbjörn, *International Humanitarian Law of Armed Conflict: Aspects of the Principle of Distinction and Related Problems,* Geneva, Henry Dunant Institute, 1979.

Rosenne, Shabtai, *Israel's Armistice Agreements with the Arab States: A Judicial Interpretation,* Tel Aviv, Blumstein's, 1951 (for the Israel Branch of the International Law Association).

Sibert, Marcel, 'L'Armistice dans le droit des gens', *Revue Generale de Droit International Public,* vol. 40, no. 6 (1933), pp. 657-715.

Stone, Julius, *Legal Controls of International Conflicts: A Treatise on the Dynamics of Disputes- and War-law,* 2nd edn, London, Stevens, 1959.

Tamkoz, Metin, *Political and Legal Aspects of Armistice Status,* Ankara, Middle East Technical University, 1963.

Thant, U [Maung], *View from the UN,* Newton Abbot, David & Charles, 1978.

Truman, Harry S., *Memoirs,* vol. II, *Years of Trial and Hope,* New York, Doubleday/London, Hodder & Stoughton, 1956.

Urquhart, Brian, *Hammarskjold,* London, Bodley Head, 1972.

Vatcher, William H., Jr., *Panmunjom: The Story of the Korean Military Armistice Negotiations,* London, Stevens/New York, Praeger, 1958.

Waldheim, Kurt, *The Challenge of Peace,* London, Weidenfeld & Nicolson, 1980.

Wright, Quincy, *A Study of War,* Chicago, Ill., University of Chicago Press, 1942 (2 vols).

Index

Index 403

Institute (SIPRI) 9-10
Stone, Julius 40
substantive proposals/decisions 45-6
Suez (1956) *see* Sinai-Suez
Suez Canal: closed, 8; Anglo-French claims to separate belligerents, 85; principles for operation of, 93, 183, 194, 209; Egypt blocks access to Israel, 106-8, 121, 208, 215, 217, 287; Britain seeks control of, 120; vetoes, 208, 214, 217
Suez Canal Company 68, 183, 209
Suez Canal Users' Association 216
Sukarno, President A. 322, 324
Sweden 288-90
Switzerland 289-90
Syria 82-3, 92-3, 107, 109, 209-10, 225, 244

Taiwan 74, 92, 116, 118, 134, 205
Tel-el-Qadi (Tel Dan) 210
Ten Plagues, Operation 136, 283
terrorism 25, 321
Thant, U Maung 246, 271-2, 274, 292, 334
Tiberias, Lake 92, 264
Tiran, Strait of 8, 120-21, 264, 286
TMT (Turkish Defence Organization) 304
torture 382-3
truce: defined, 29-33, 36-8; flag of, 30; UN and, 32, 37
Truce Commission in Palestine *see* Consular Truce Commission
Truman, Harris S.: and Palestine, 76, 137-8, 143, 146-9, 154, 156, 203; authorizes Dulles as representative, 220; and Korean prisoners of war, 311
Trusteeship Council (UN) 49, 54
Tsarapkin, S. K. 177
Tsiang, T. F. 223
Tuomioja, Sakari S. 60
Turkey: bombing in Cyprus, 5, 20; as participant in UN debates, 74-5, 77; Cypriot complaints of aggression by, 93; and kith and kin argument, 107; rejects Makarios's proposals, 112; threatens invasion of Cyprus, 122; and conduct of Cyprus negotiations, 173; and Cyprus partition, 191; complains of poisoned wells in Cyprus, 301; and beleaguered fighters in Cyprus, 333-4

Ukraine 77
Unified Command (Korea): forces, 4-5; armistice agreements, 39, 110-11; relief assistance, 54, 204; US commander, 56, 59; as UN agency, 59, 60; Chinese participation in UN debate or report, 74; fact-finding, 101; political settlement, 116, 159-61, 237; call for withdrawal, 134; accused of bombing conference zone, 161; demarcation lines, 227; neutral conference area, 232, 236-8, 249; reports, 266; prisoners of war, 310-12, 315
uniforms 23
Union of Soviet Socialist Republics (USSR): and Suez, 20; Indonesian cease-fire, 33; membership of UN subsidiary organs, 56; seeks Korean solution, 76, 85, 119; relations with China, 76-7, 80, 91, 94; and determination of nature of Korean question, 94; use of veto, 111, 206-13, 216; boycotts Security Council, 211, 221-2; voluntary abstentions, 218-19; alleges use of bacteriological warfare, 302-3
United Nations: Charter, 1-2, 18-20, 44, 46, 49, 53-4, 69, 83-5, 108-9, 157, 181-2, 351, 360; and use of force, 18-20; and ending hostilities, 32; and reprisals, 43; payment for peacekeeping, 55-6; subsidiary organs and commissions, 56-63; means of settlement, 157-8; role of mediators, 169-70; suspension of Members, 360; relief needs, 379-80; *see also* subsidiary organs and agencies
United Nations Central Truce Supervision Board 135, 141, 234-5, 279
United Nations Commission for India and Pakistan (UNCIP): and cease-fire/truce in Kashmir, 37, 39, 124, 186; composition, 56-7; participation in Security Council proceedings, 63; and parties to dispute, 71; and Azad Kashmir, 75, 102; activities, 90, 95, 98, 102; political settlement, 115; and compliance with cease-fire, 131; withdrawal of forces from Kashmir, 133; and conduct of negotiations, 160-61, 164, 167; recommends single mediator, 166; recommends arbitration, 177; settlement terms, 183; self-determination in Kashmir, 186-7;